ultimate venus

Takako Shigematsu

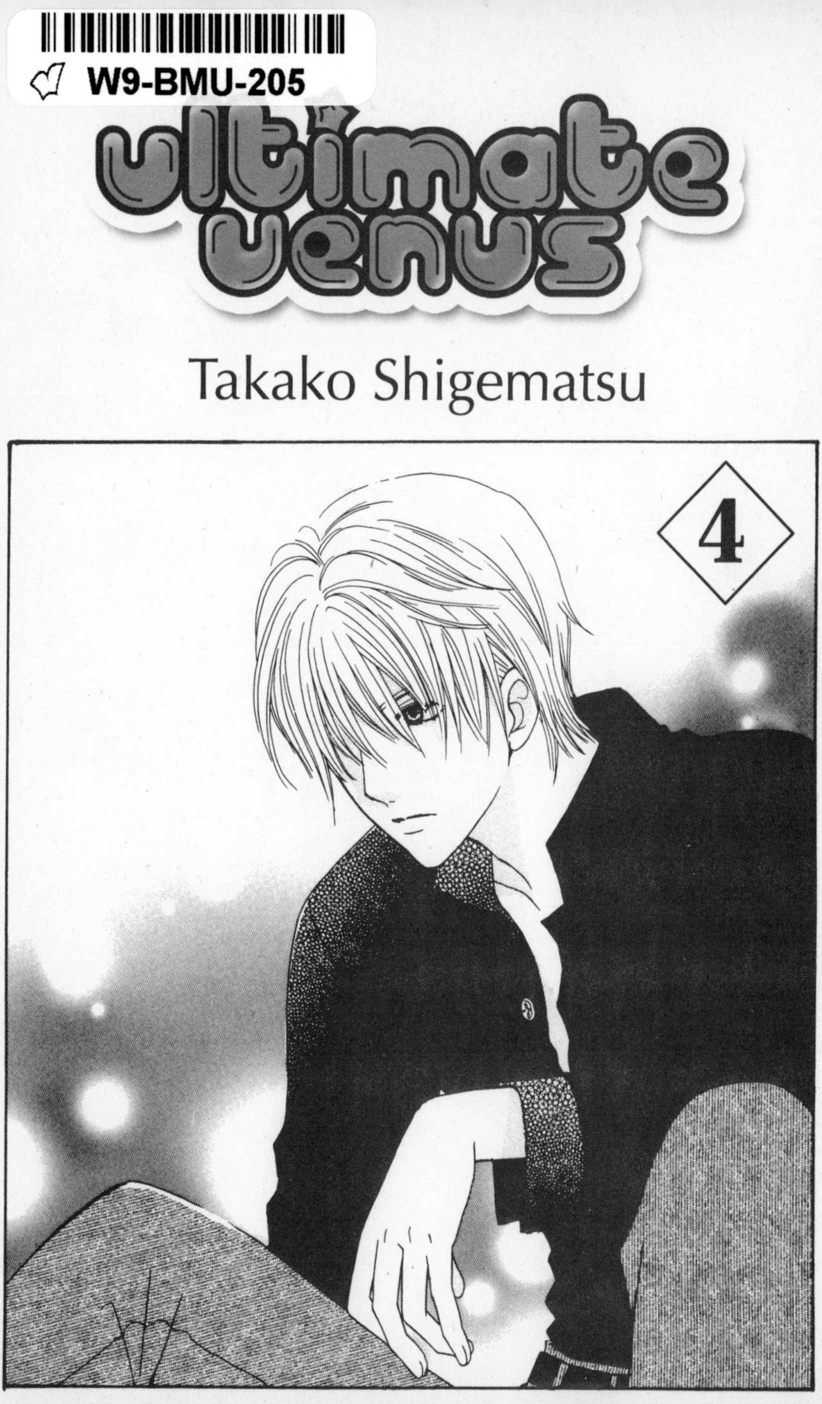
4

Translation –Christine Schilling
Adaptation – Brynne Chandler
Lettering & Retouch – Erika Terriquez
Production Assistant – Suzy Wells
Production Manager – James Dashiell
Editor – Audry Taylor

A Go! Comi manga

Published by Go! Media Entertainment, LLC

Kyukyoku Venus Volume 4
© TAKAKO SHIGEMATSU 2008
Originally published in Japan in 2008 by Akita Publishing Co., Ltd., Tokyo.
English translation rights arranged with Akita Publishing Co., Ltd.
through TOHAN CORPORATION, Tokyo.

Visit us online at www.gocomi.com
e-mail: info@gocomi.com

ISBN 978-1-60510-023-4

First printed in March 2009

1   2   3   4   5   6   7   8   9

Manufactured in the United States of America

by

Takako Shigematsu

Volume 4

go!comi

VOLUME:4
CONTENTS

* Story so far *

Yuzu Yamashita lost her mother and thought she was left all alone in the world until she met Hassaku Kagami and found out she had a grandmother. Her grandmother is President of the Shirayuki Group and is the rich inhabitant of a castle. Once Yuzu becomes her heir, her life becomes filled with such dangers as attempted kidnapping and more. Then she decides to go out with Iyo Hayashibara, a fellow classmate in the Elite A class she joined at Getsuei High. However, she soon realizes that she's fallen for Hassaku instead!

Left with the task of producing a promotional video for a new wedding hall, Yuzu wins the eye of the video's director, Masaya. To her dismay, her grandmother soon announces that Masaya is her fiancé!!

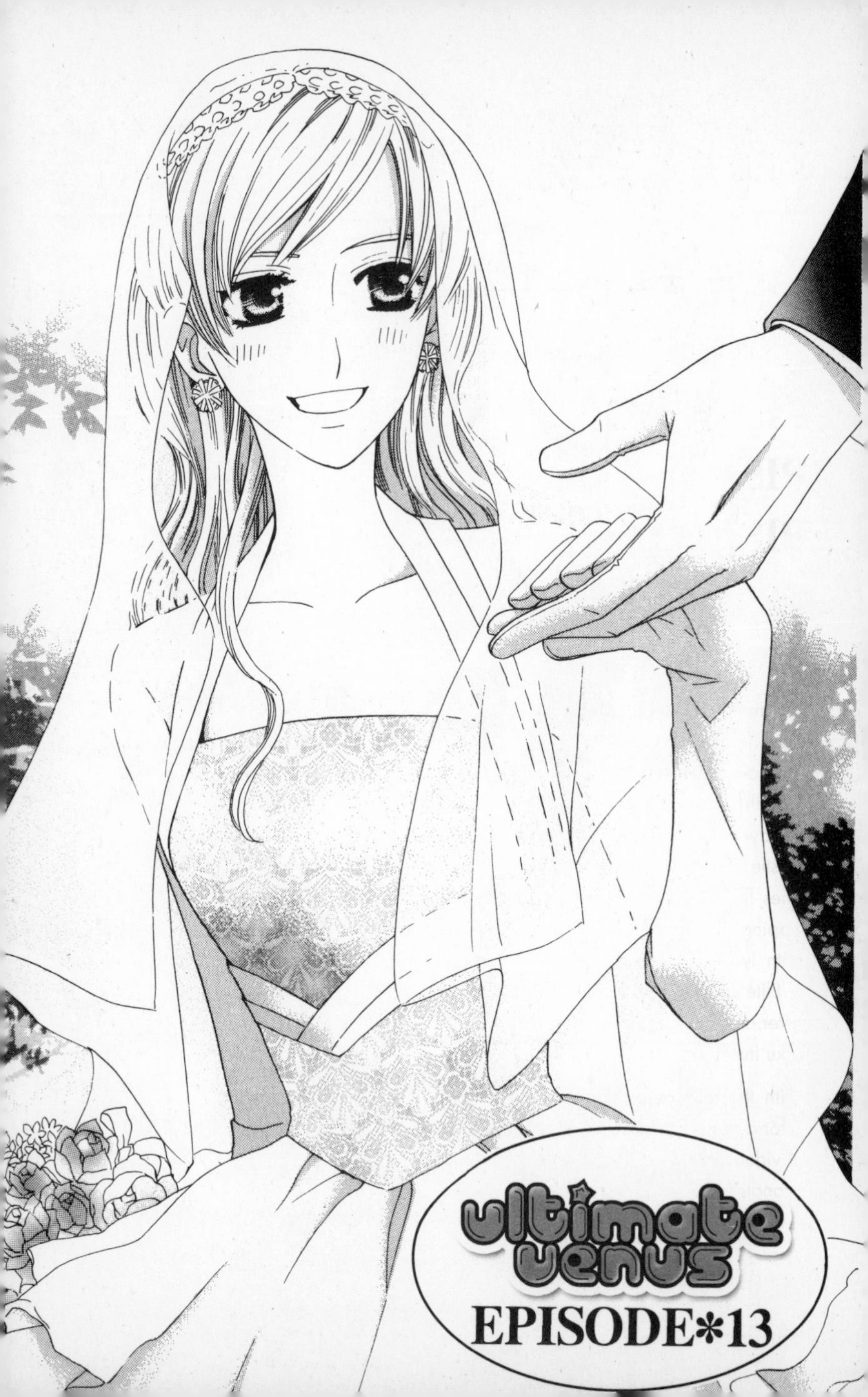
ultimate venus
EPISODE*13

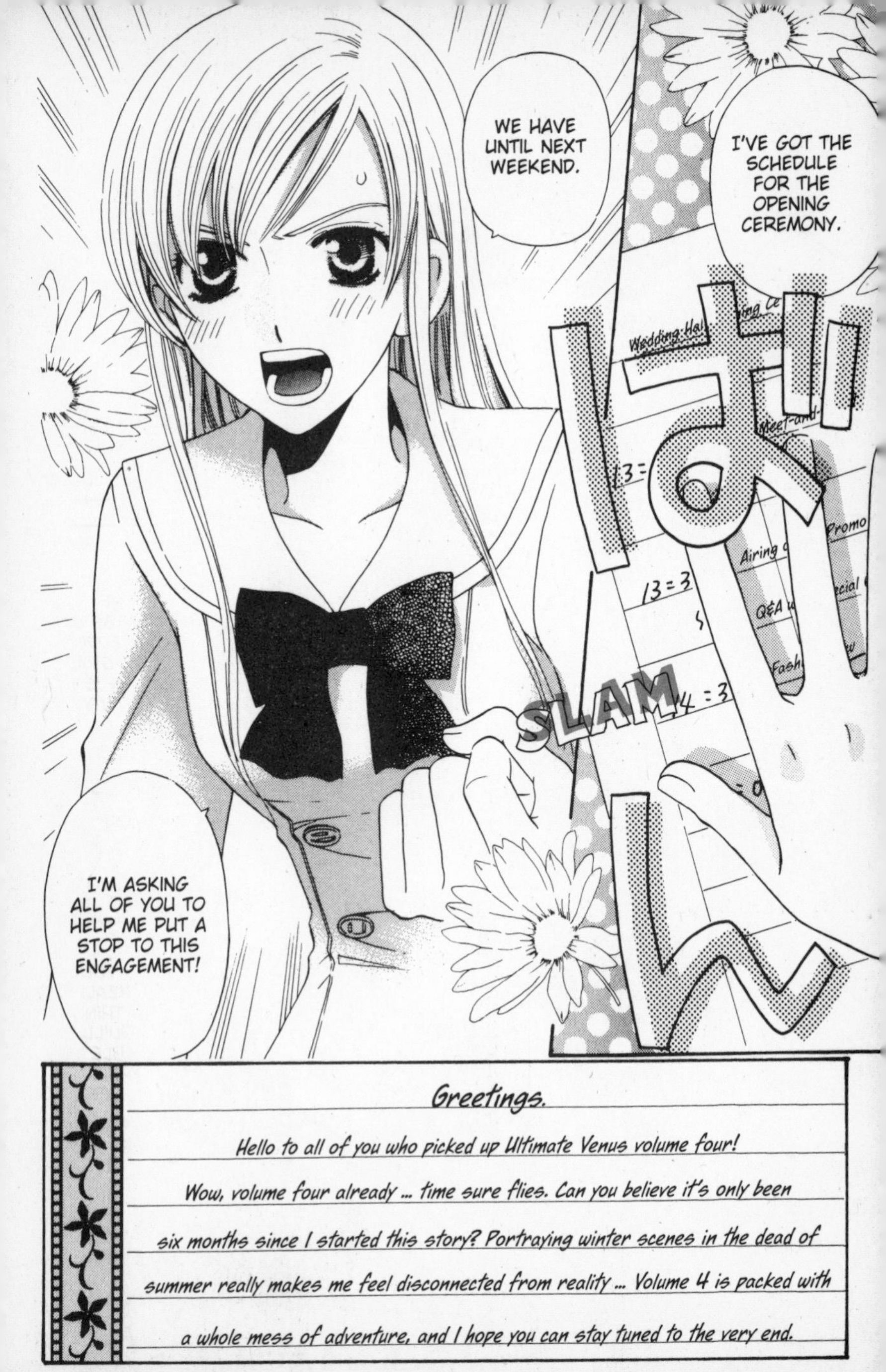
I'VE GOT THE SCHEDULE FOR THE OPENING CEREMONY.
WE HAVE UNTIL NEXT WEEKEND.
SLAM
I'M ASKING ALL OF YOU TO HELP ME PUT A STOP TO THIS ENGAGEMENT!

Greetings.

Hello to all of you who picked up Ultimate Venus volume four!

Wow, volume four already ... time sure flies. Can you believe it's only been six months since I started this story? Portraying winter scenes in the dead of summer really makes me feel disconnected from reality ... Volume 4 is packed with a whole mess of adventure, and I hope you can stay tuned to the very end.

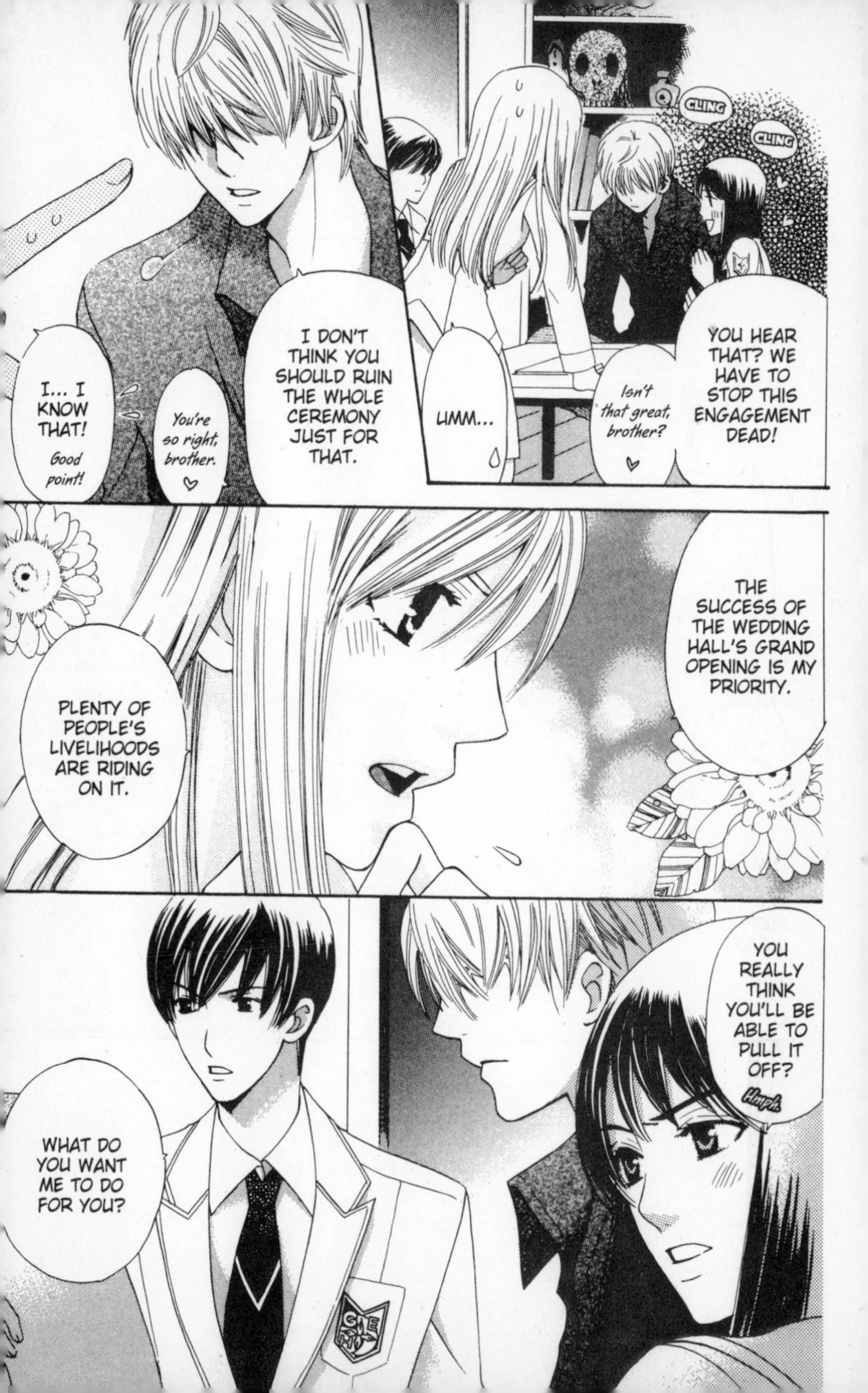
CLING
CLING
YOU HEAR THAT? WE HAVE TO STOP THIS ENGAGEMENT DEAD!
Isn't that great, brother?
UMM...
I DON'T THINK YOU SHOULD RUIN THE WHOLE CEREMONY JUST FOR THAT.
You're so right, brother.
I... I KNOW THAT!
Good point!
THE SUCCESS OF THE WEDDING HALL'S GRAND OPENING IS MY PRIORITY.
PLENTY OF PEOPLE'S LIVELIHOODS ARE RIDING ON IT.
YOU REALLY THINK YOU'LL BE ABLE TO PULL IT OFF?
Hmph.
WHAT DO YOU WANT ME TO DO FOR YOU?

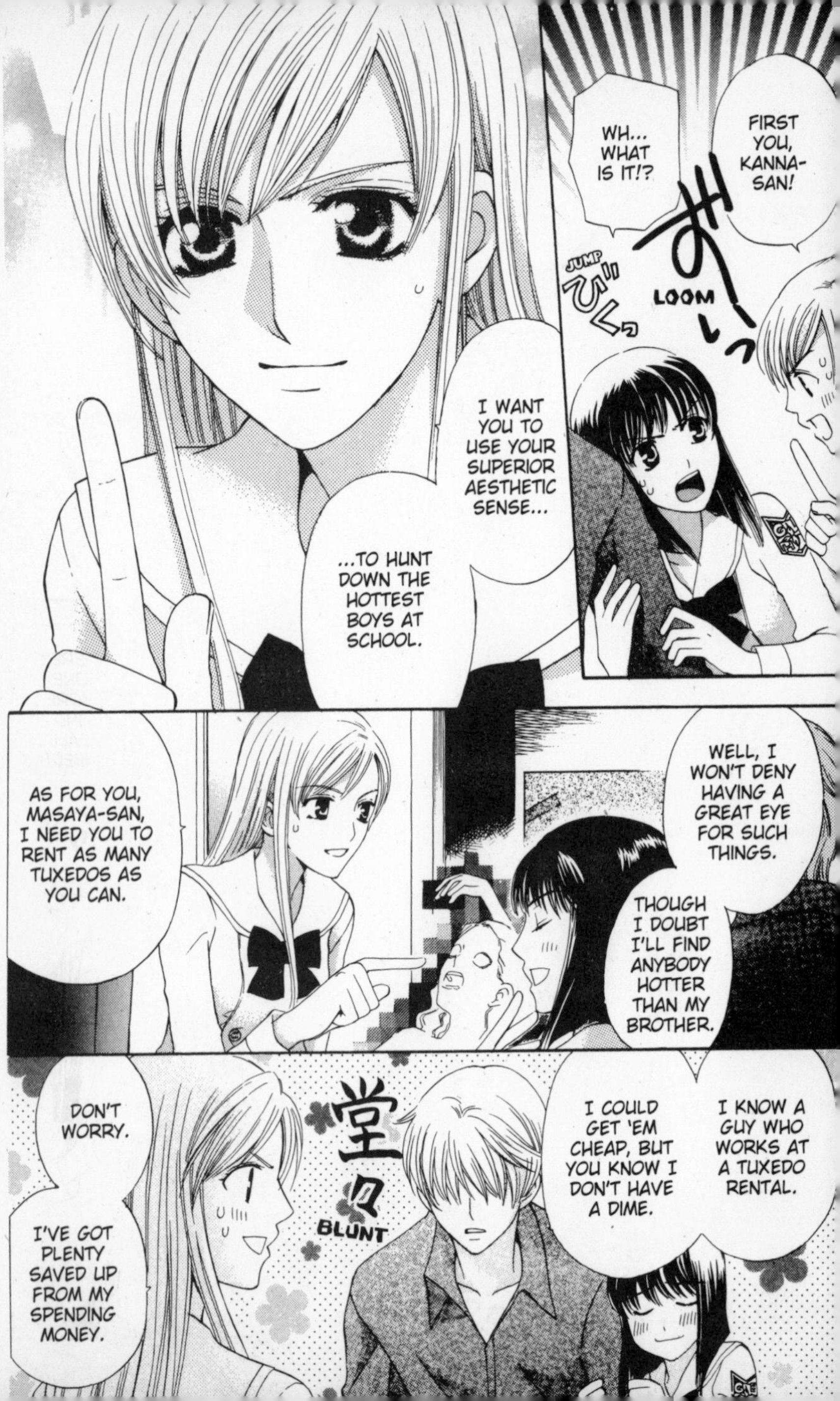
FIRST YOU, KANNA-SAN!
WH... WHAT IS IT!?
LOOM
JUMP
I WANT YOU TO USE YOUR SUPERIOR AESTHETIC SENSE...
...TO HUNT DOWN THE HOTTEST BOYS AT SCHOOL.
WELL, I WON'T DENY HAVING A GREAT EYE FOR SUCH THINGS.
THOUGH I DOUBT I'LL FIND ANYBODY HOTTER THAN MY BROTHER.
AS FOR YOU, MASAYA-SAN, I NEED YOU TO RENT AS MANY TUXEDOS AS YOU CAN.
I KNOW A GUY WHO WORKS AT A TUXEDO RENTAL.
I COULD GET 'EM CHEAP, BUT YOU KNOW I DON'T HAVE A DIME.
堂々
BLUNT
DON'T WORRY.
I'VE GOT PLENTY SAVED UP FROM MY SPENDING MONEY.

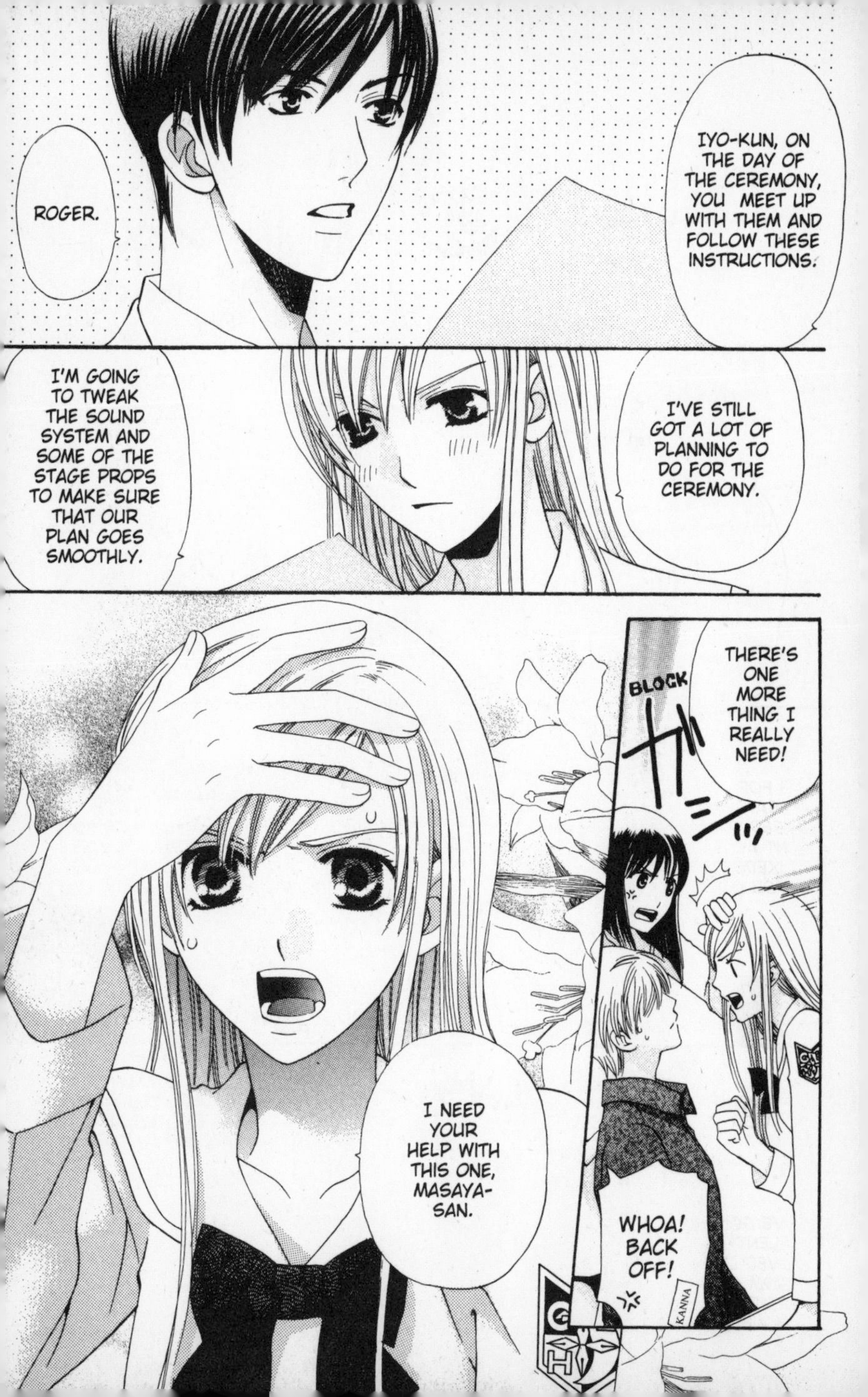
IYO-KUN, ON THE DAY OF THE CEREMONY, YOU MEET UP WITH THEM AND FOLLOW THESE INSTRUCTIONS.
ROGER.
I'VE STILL GOT A LOT OF PLANNING TO DO FOR THE CEREMONY.
I'M GOING TO TWEAK THE SOUND SYSTEM AND SOME OF THE STAGE PROPS TO MAKE SURE THAT OUR PLAN GOES SMOOTHLY.
THERE'S ONE MORE THING I REALLY NEED!
BLOCK
WHOA! BACK OFF!
KANNA
I NEED YOUR HELP WITH THIS ONE, MASAYA-SAN.

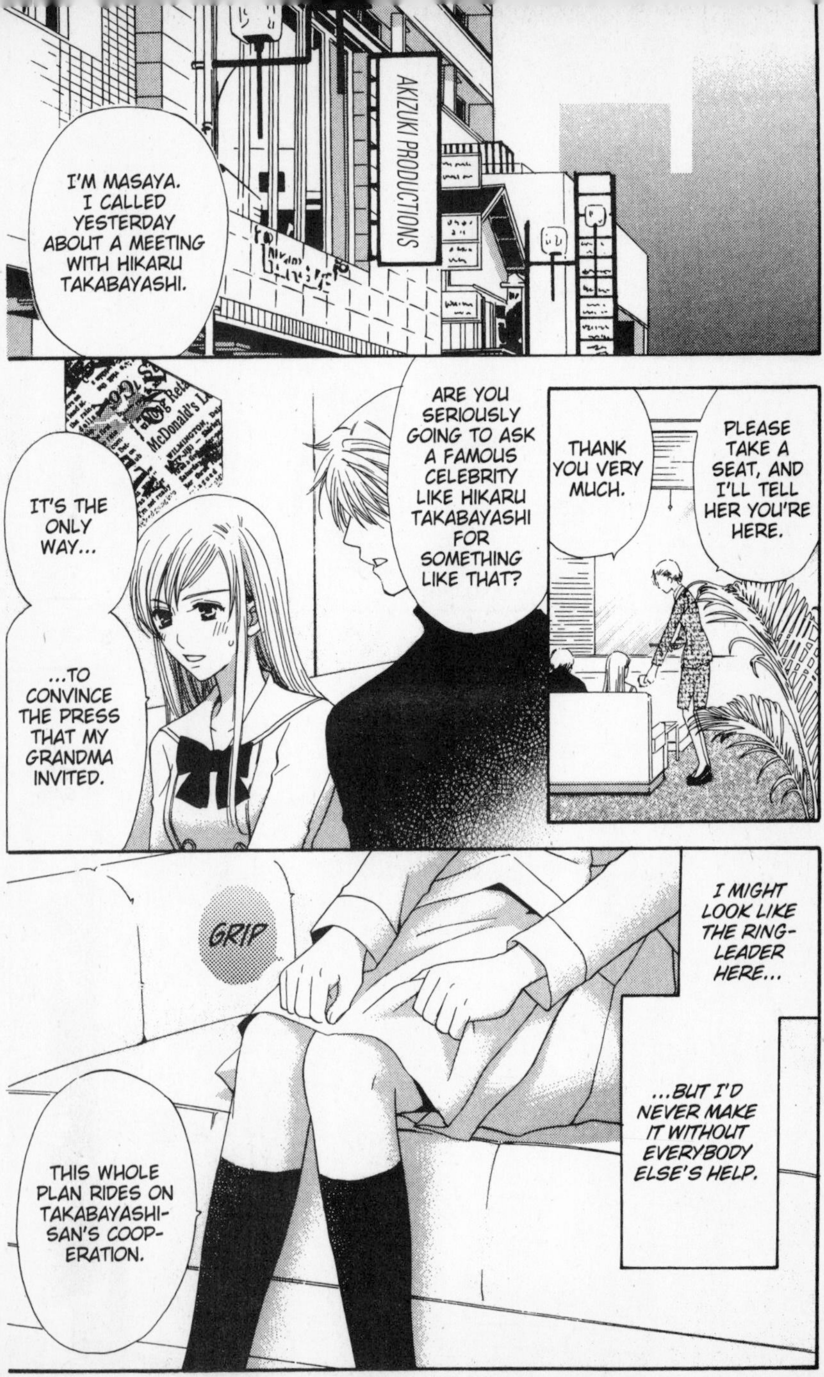
AKIZUKI PRODUCTIONS
I'M MASAYA. I CALLED YESTERDAY ABOUT A MEETING WITH HIKARU TAKABAYASHI.
PLEASE TAKE A SEAT, AND I'LL TELL HER YOU'RE HERE.
THANK YOU VERY MUCH.
ARE YOU SERIOUSLY GOING TO ASK A FAMOUS CELEBRITY LIKE HIKARU TAKABAYASHI FOR SOMETHING LIKE THAT?
IT'S THE ONLY WAY...
...TO CONVINCE THE PRESS THAT MY GRANDMA INVITED.
I MIGHT LOOK LIKE THE RING-LEADER HERE...
...BUT I'D NEVER MAKE IT WITHOUT EVERYBODY ELSE'S HELP.
GRIP
THIS WHOLE PLAN RIDES ON TAKABAYASHI-SAN'S COOP-ERATION.

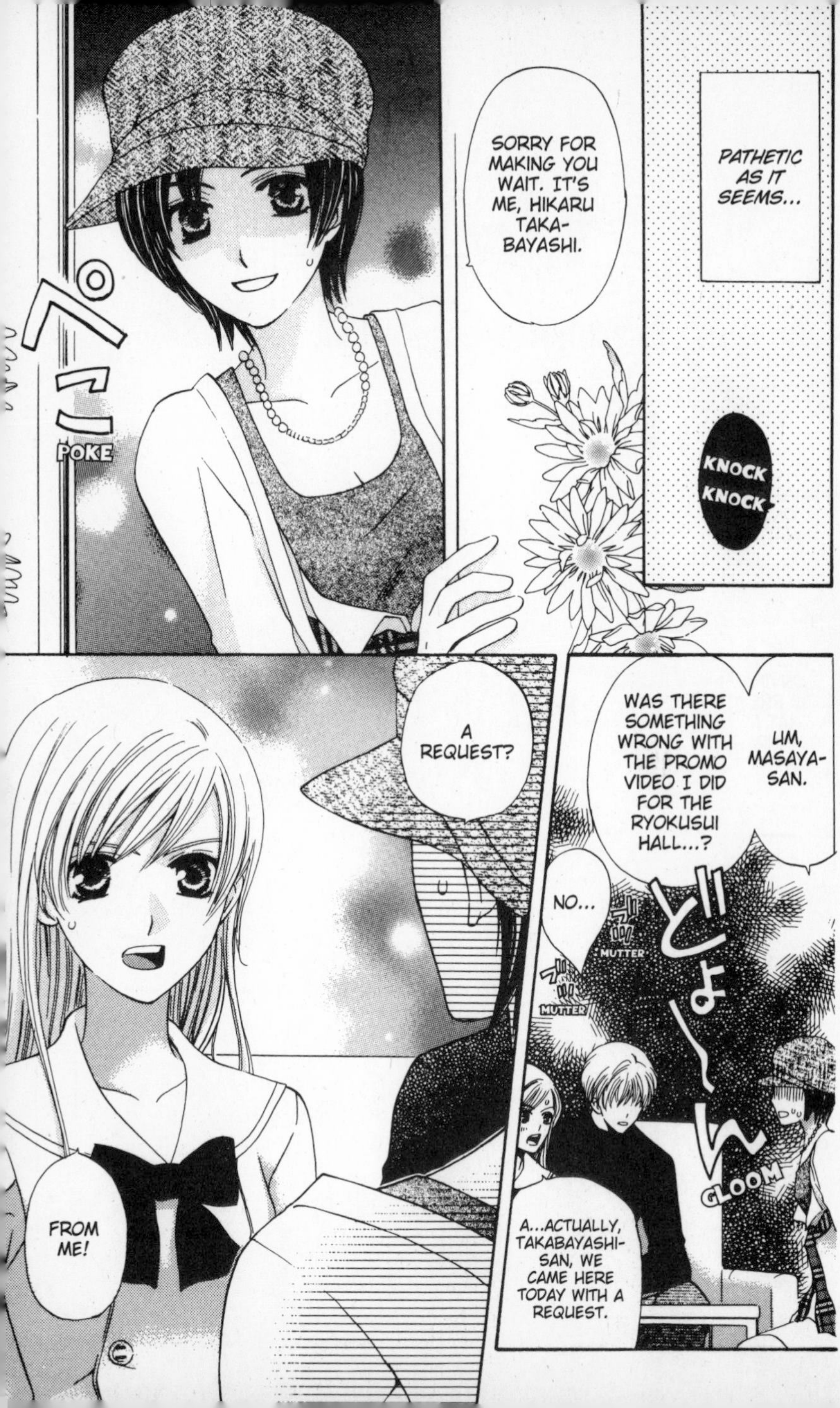
PATHETIC AS IT SEEMS...
KNOCK KNOCK
SORRY FOR MAKING YOU WAIT. IT'S ME, HIKARU TAKA-BAYASHI.
POKE
UM, MASAYA-SAN.
WAS THERE SOMETHING WRONG WITH THE PROMO VIDEO I DID FOR THE RYOKUSUI HALL...?
NO...
MUTTER
MUTTER
GLOOM
A...ACTUALLY, TAKABAYASHI-SAN, WE CAME HERE TODAY WITH A REQUEST.
A REQUEST?
FROM ME!

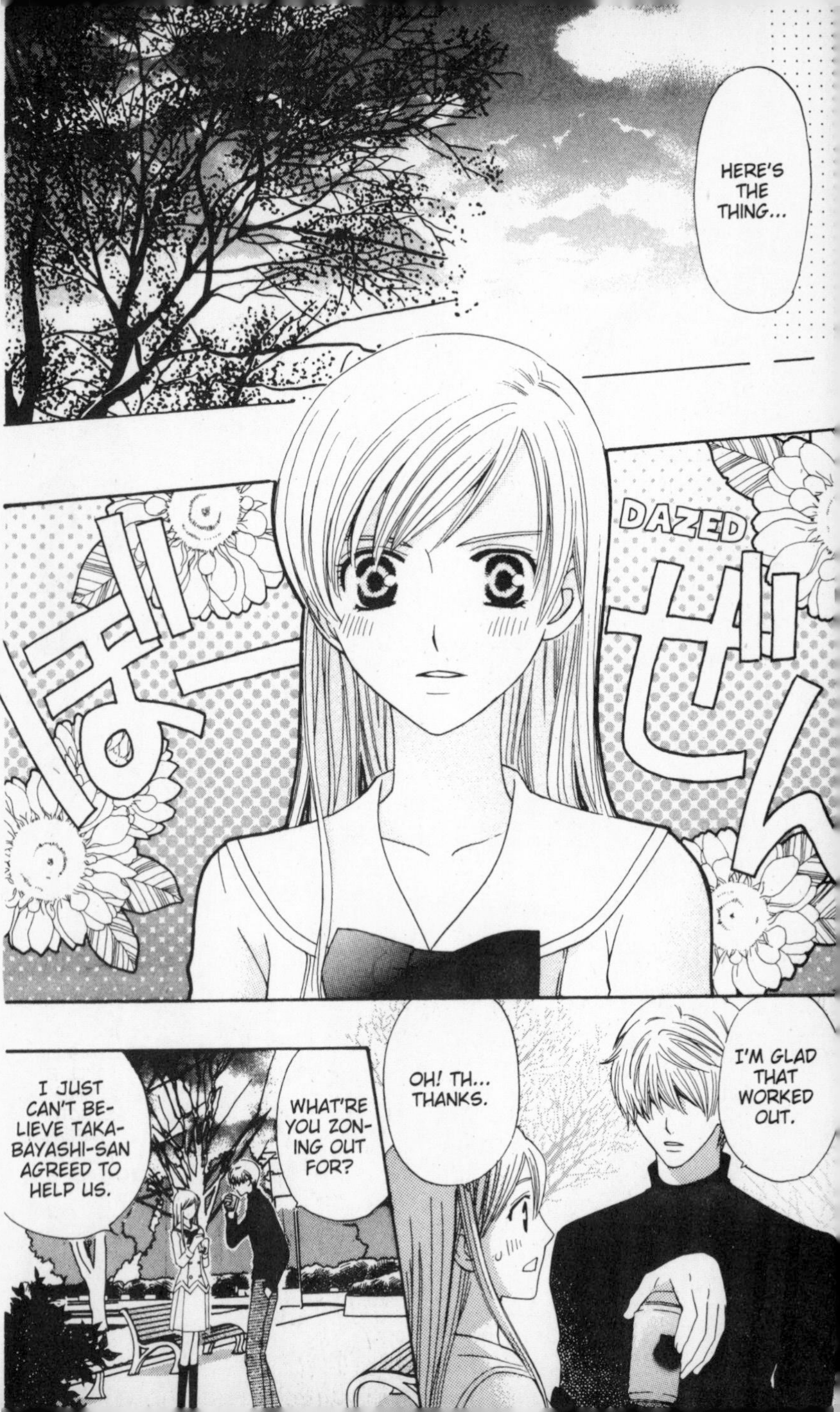
HERE'S THE THING...
DAZED
ぼーぜん
I'M GLAD THAT WORKED OUT.
OH! TH... THANKS.
WHAT'RE YOU ZONING OUT FOR?
I JUST CAN'T BELIEVE TAKABAYASHI-SAN AGREED TO HELP US.

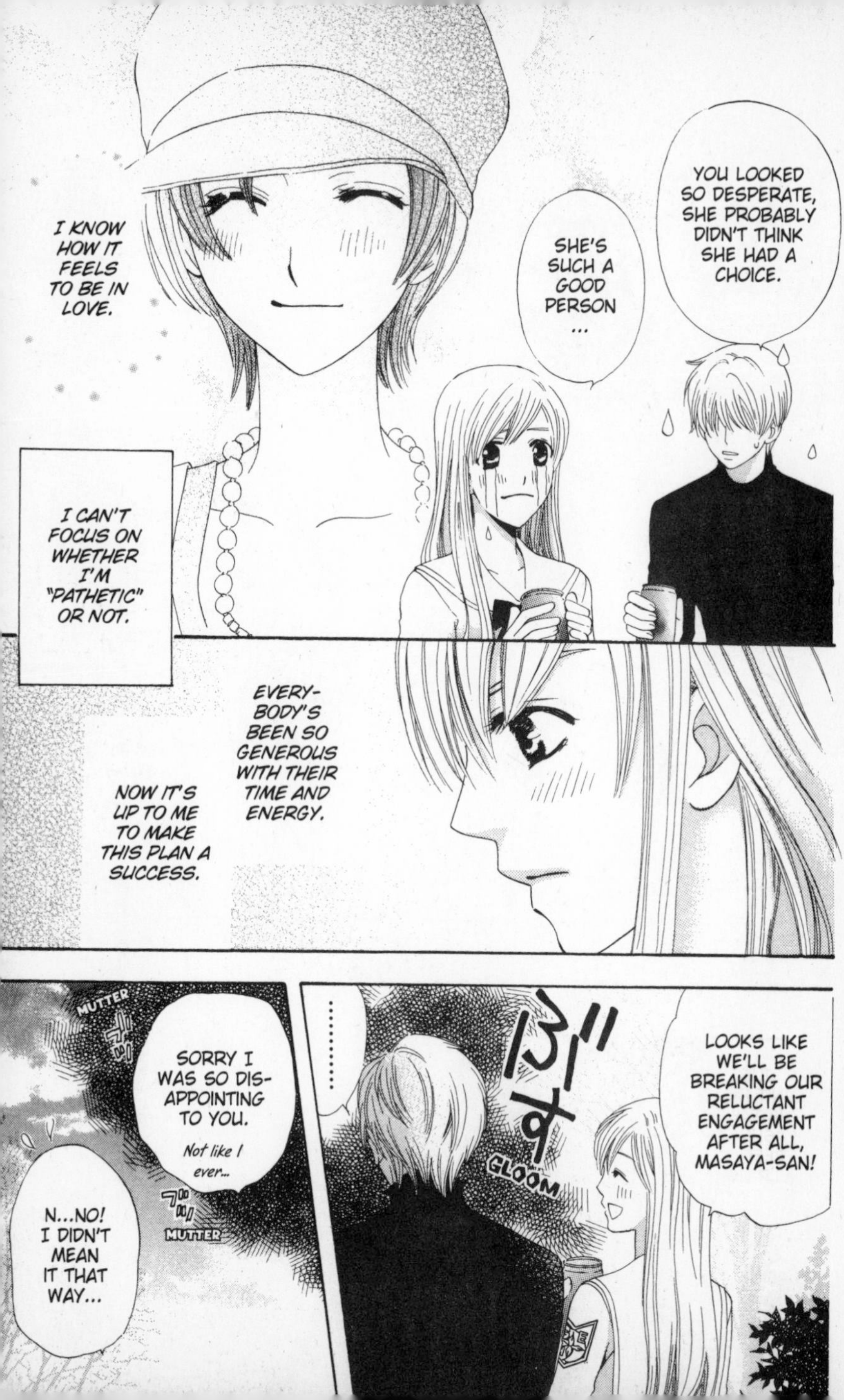

YOU LOOKED SO DESPERATE, SHE PROBABLY DIDN'T THINK SHE HAD A CHOICE.
SHE'S SUCH A GOOD PERSON ...
I KNOW HOW IT FEELS TO BE IN LOVE.
I CAN'T FOCUS ON WHETHER I'M "PATHETIC" OR NOT.
EVERY-BODY'S BEEN SO GENEROUS WITH THEIR TIME AND ENERGY.
NOW IT'S UP TO ME TO MAKE THIS PLAN A SUCCESS.
LOOKS LIKE WE'LL BE BREAKING OUR RELUCTANT ENGAGEMENT AFTER ALL, MASAYA-SAN!
GLOOM
....
MUTTER
SORRY I WAS SO DIS-APPOINTING TO YOU.
Not like I ever...
MUTTER
N...NO! I DIDN'T MEAN IT THAT WAY...

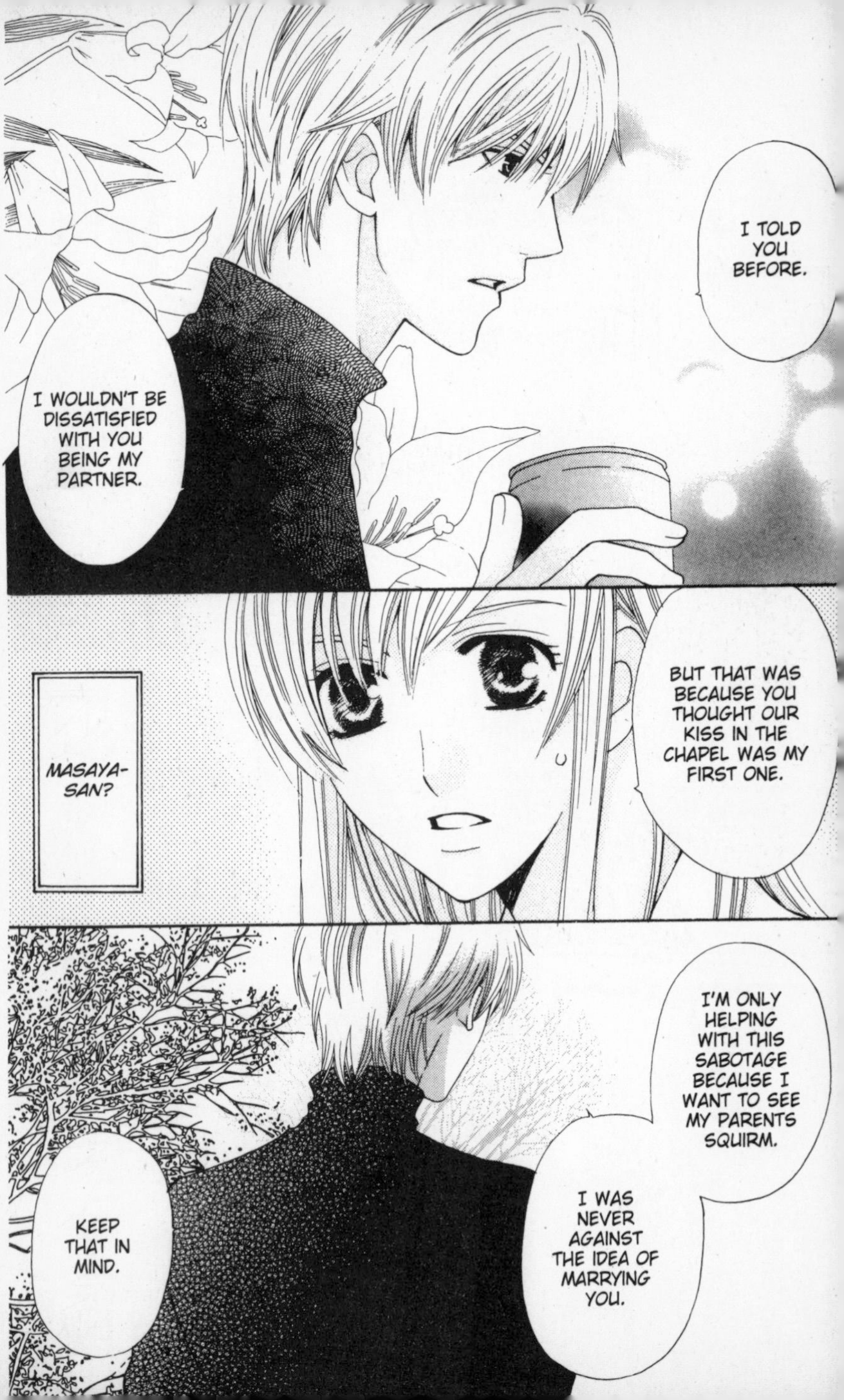
I TOLD YOU BEFORE.
I WOULDN'T BE DISSATISFIED WITH YOU BEING MY PARTNER.
BUT THAT WAS BECAUSE YOU THOUGHT OUR KISS IN THE CHAPEL WAS MY FIRST ONE.
MASAYA-SAN?
I'M ONLY HELPING WITH THIS SABOTAGE BECAUSE I WANT TO SEE MY PARENTS SQUIRM.
I WAS NEVER AGAINST THE IDEA OF MARRYING YOU.
KEEP THAT IN MIND.

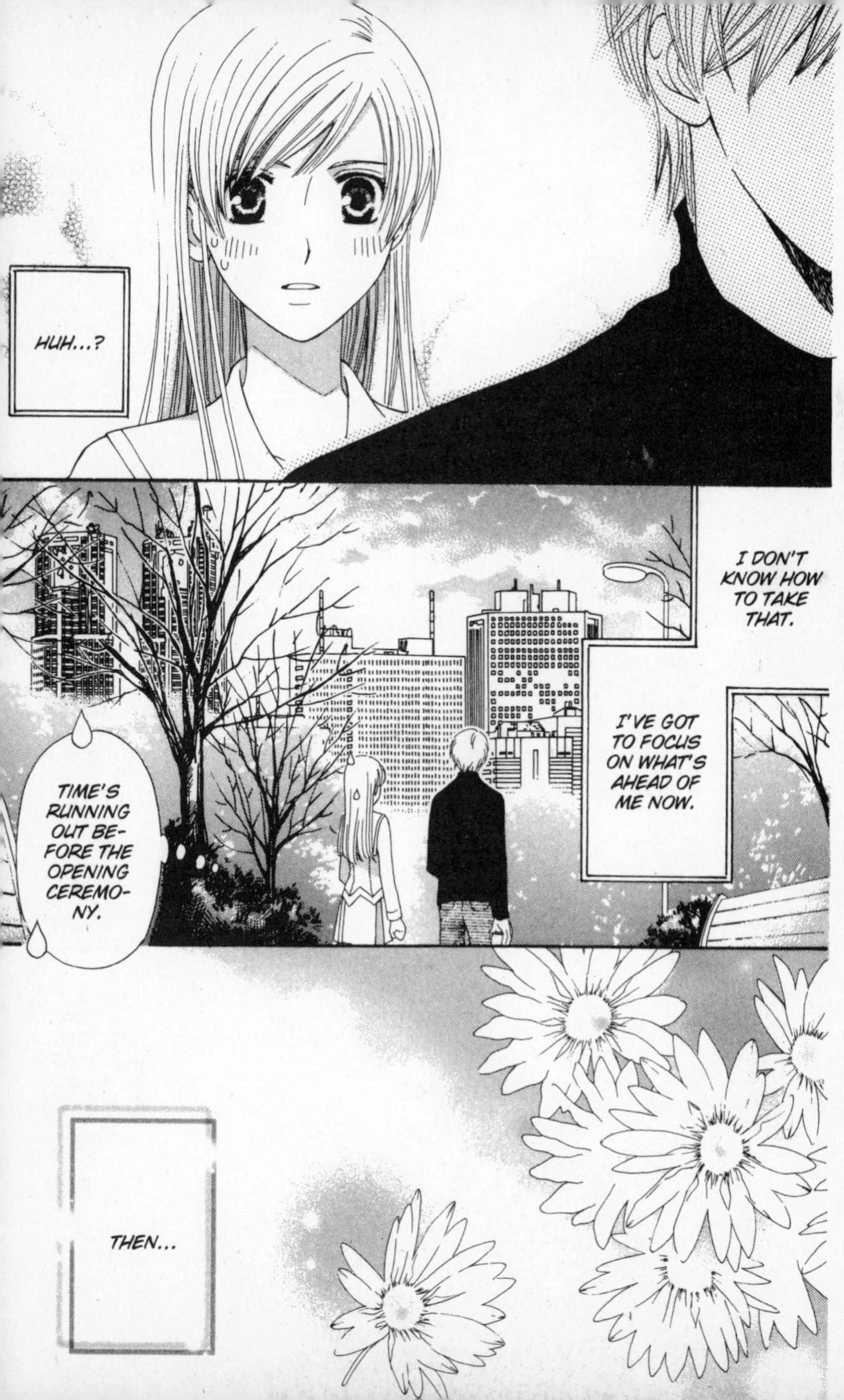
HUH...?
I DON'T KNOW HOW TO TAKE THAT.
I'VE GOT TO FOCUS ON WHAT'S AHEAD OF ME NOW.
TIME'S RUNNING OUT BE-FORE THE OPENING CEREMO-NY.
THEN...

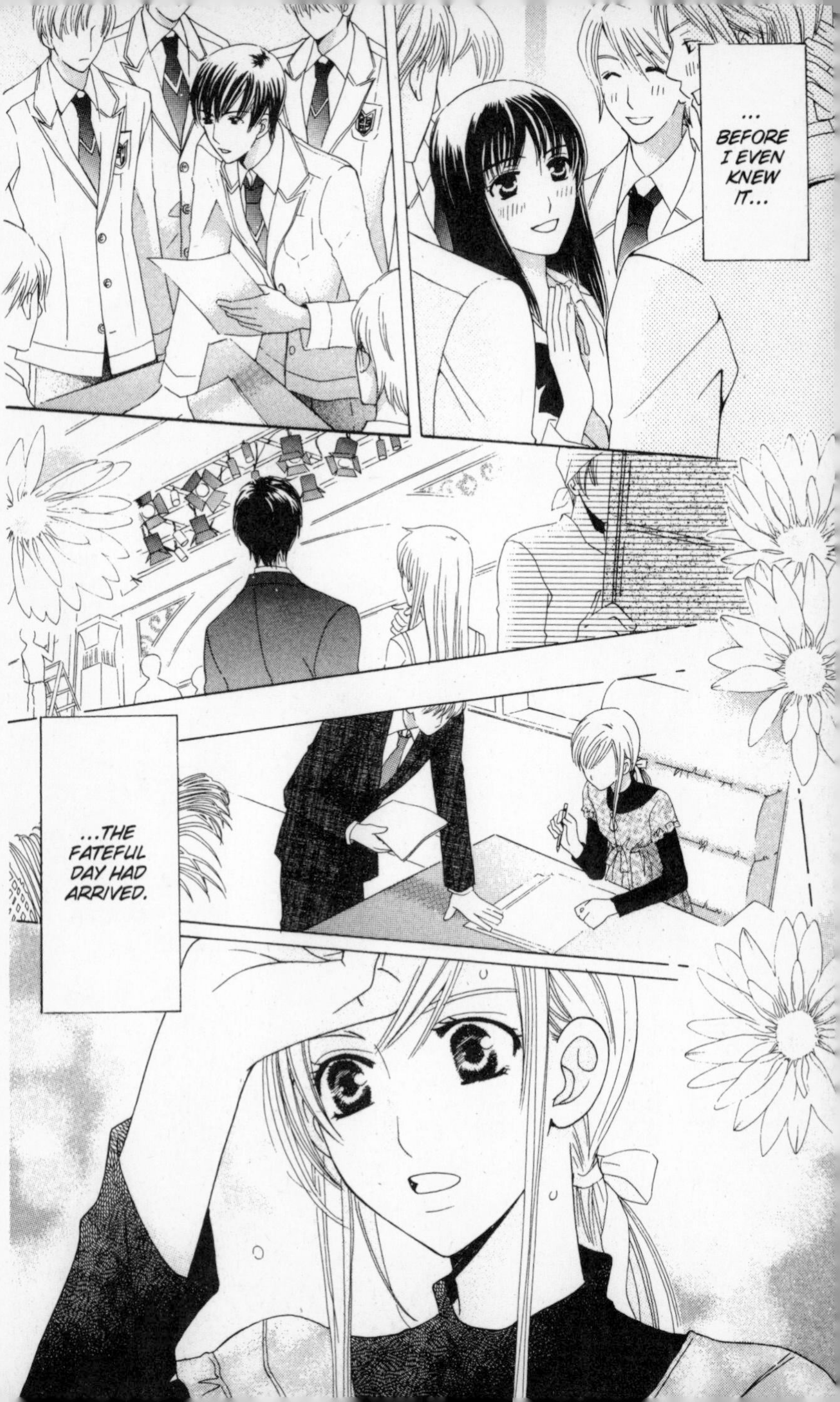
...BEFORE I EVEN KNEW IT...
...THE FATEFUL DAY HAD ARRIVED.

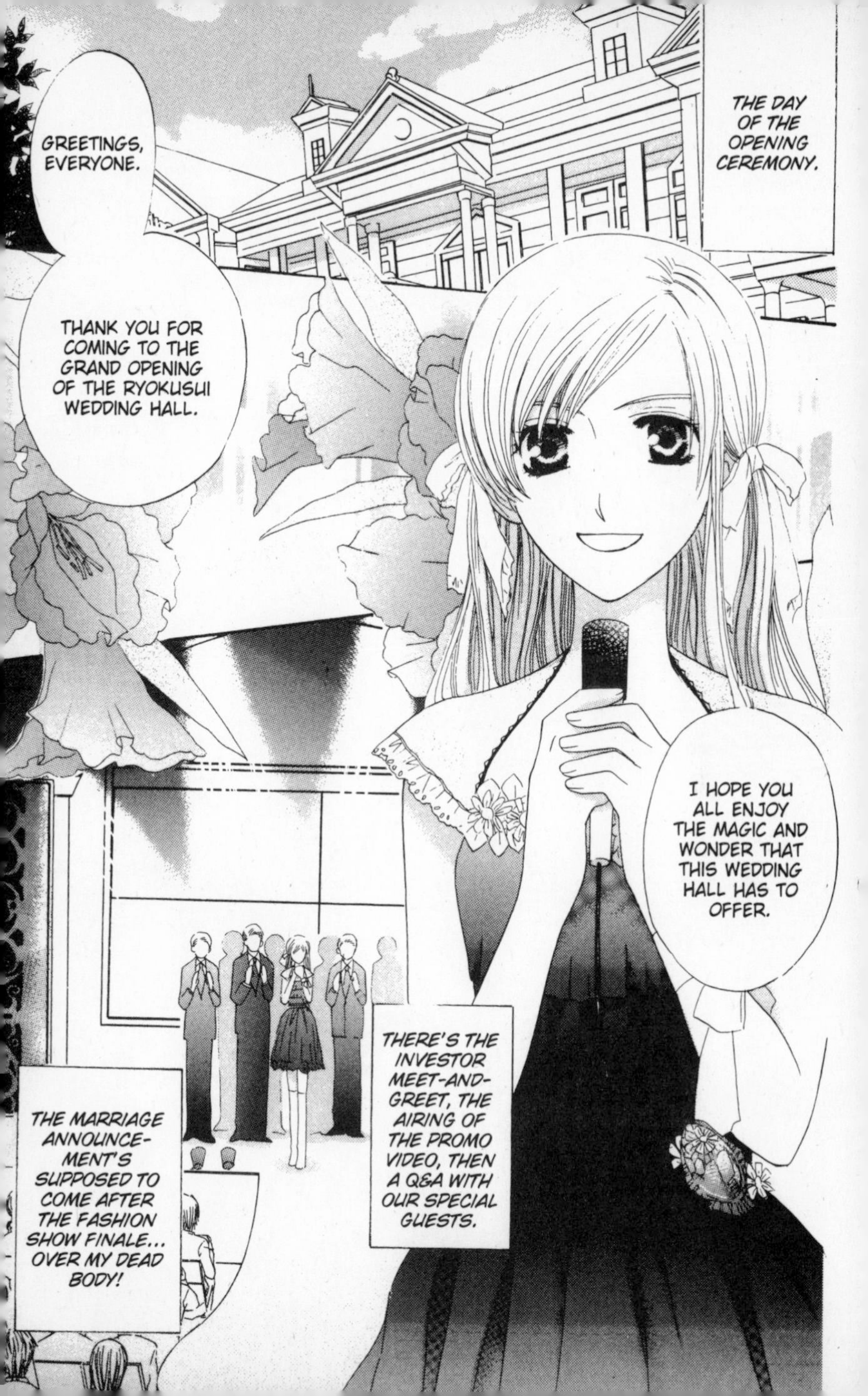
THE DAY OF THE OPENING CEREMONY.
GREETINGS, EVERYONE.
THANK YOU FOR COMING TO THE GRAND OPENING OF THE RYOKUSUI WEDDING HALL.
I HOPE YOU ALL ENJOY THE MAGIC AND WONDER THAT THIS WEDDING HALL HAS TO OFFER.
THERE'S THE INVESTOR MEET-AND-GREET, THE AIRING OF THE PROMO VIDEO, THEN A Q&A WITH OUR SPECIAL GUESTS.
THE MARRIAGE ANNOUNCE-MENT'S SUPPOSED TO COME AFTER THE FASHION SHOW FINALE... OVER MY DEAD BODY!

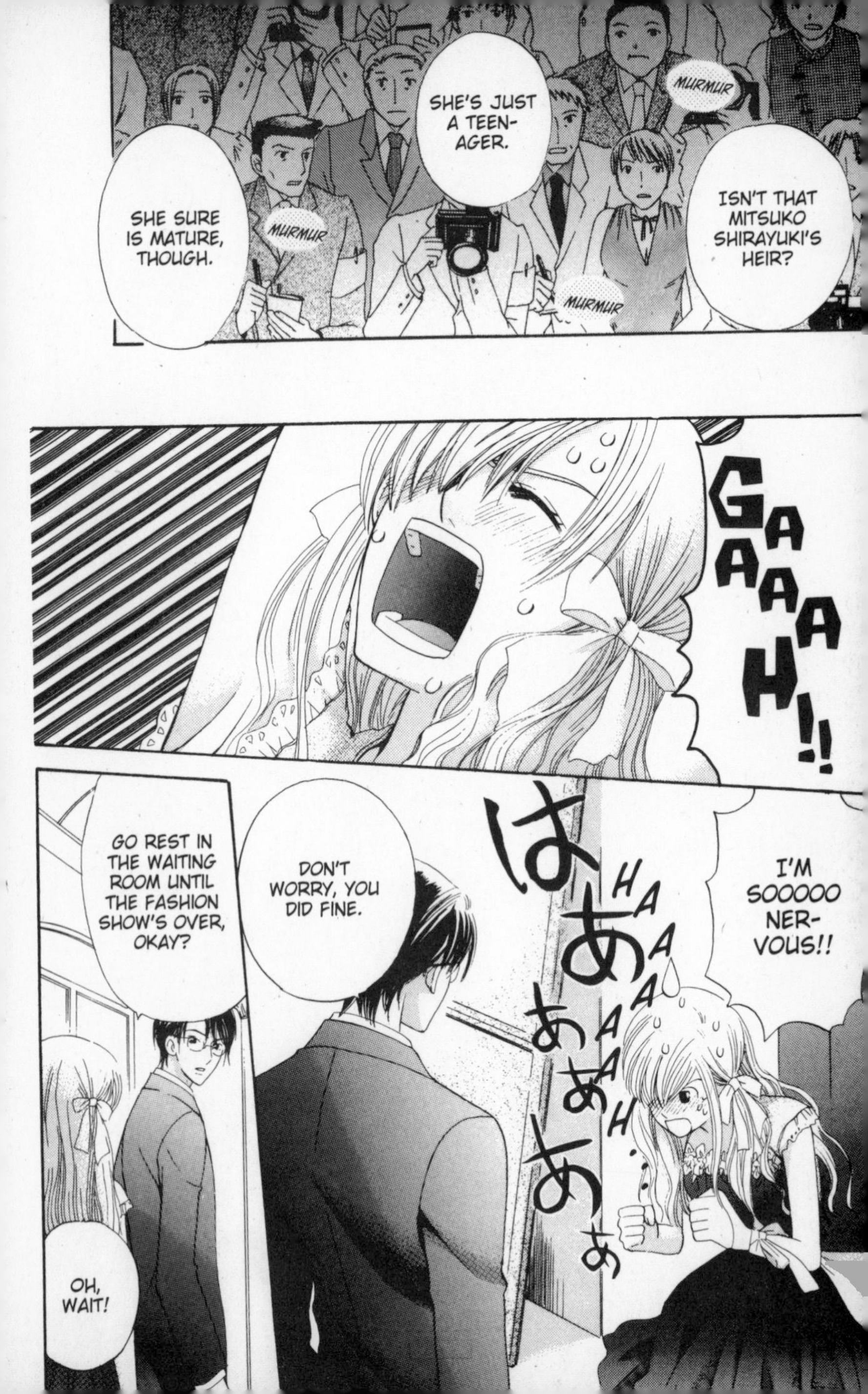
MURMUR
ISN'T THAT MITSUKO SHIRAYUKI'S HEIR?
MURMUR
SHE'S JUST A TEEN-AGER.
MURMUR
SHE SURE IS MATURE, THOUGH.
GAAAAH!!
I'M SOOOOO NER-VOUS!!
HAAAAAAH...
はあああああ
DON'T WORRY, YOU DID FINE.
GO REST IN THE WAITING ROOM UNTIL THE FASHION SHOW'S OVER, OKAY?
OH, WAIT!

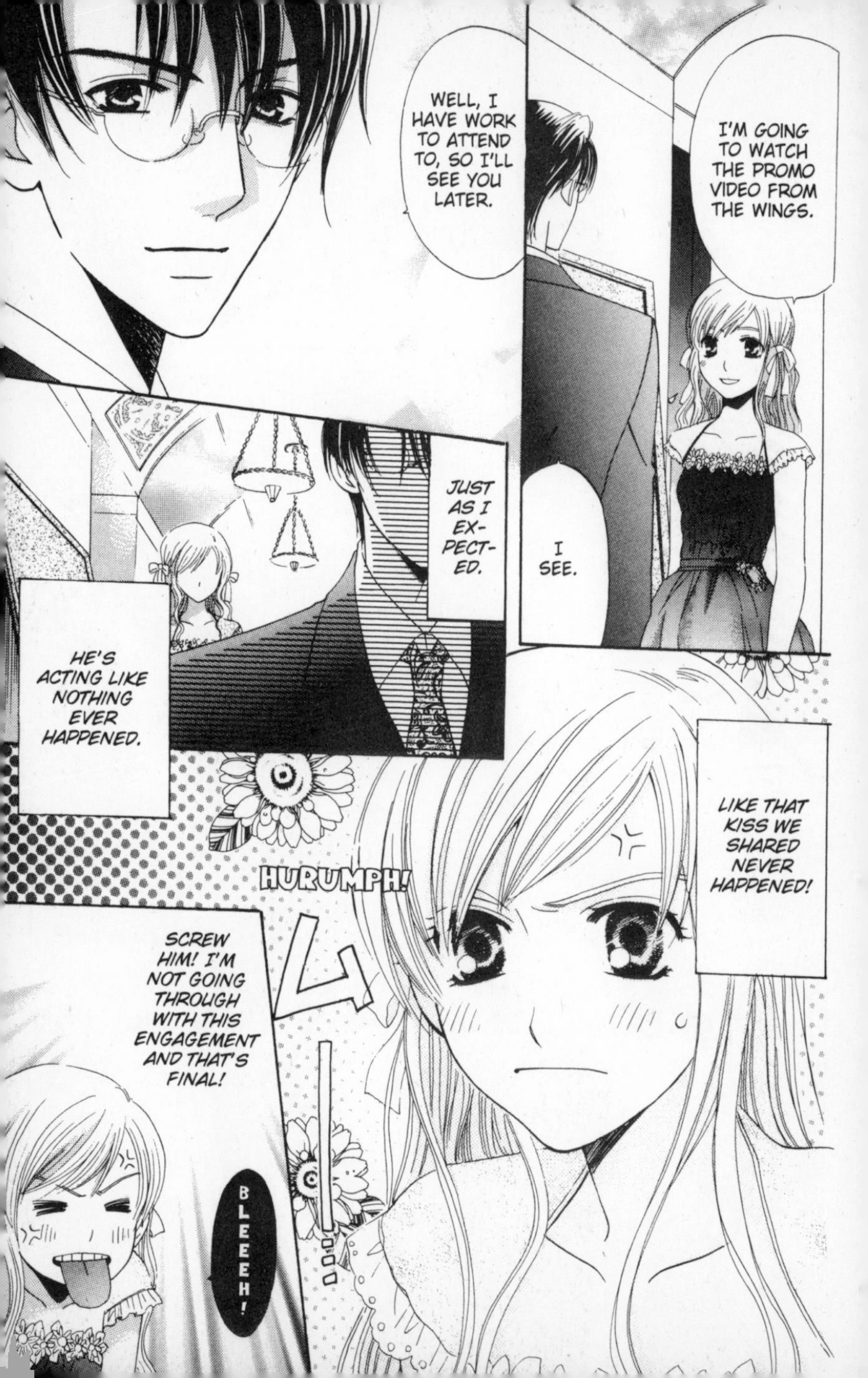
I'M GOING TO WATCH THE PROMO VIDEO FROM THE WINGS.
I SEE.
WELL, I HAVE WORK TO ATTEND TO, SO I'LL SEE YOU LATER.
JUST AS I EX-PECT-ED.
HE'S ACTING LIKE NOTHING EVER HAPPENED.
LIKE THAT KISS WE SHARED NEVER HAPPENED!
HURUMPH!
SCREW HIM! I'M NOT GOING THROUGH WITH THIS ENGAGEMENT AND THAT'S FINAL!
BLEEEH!

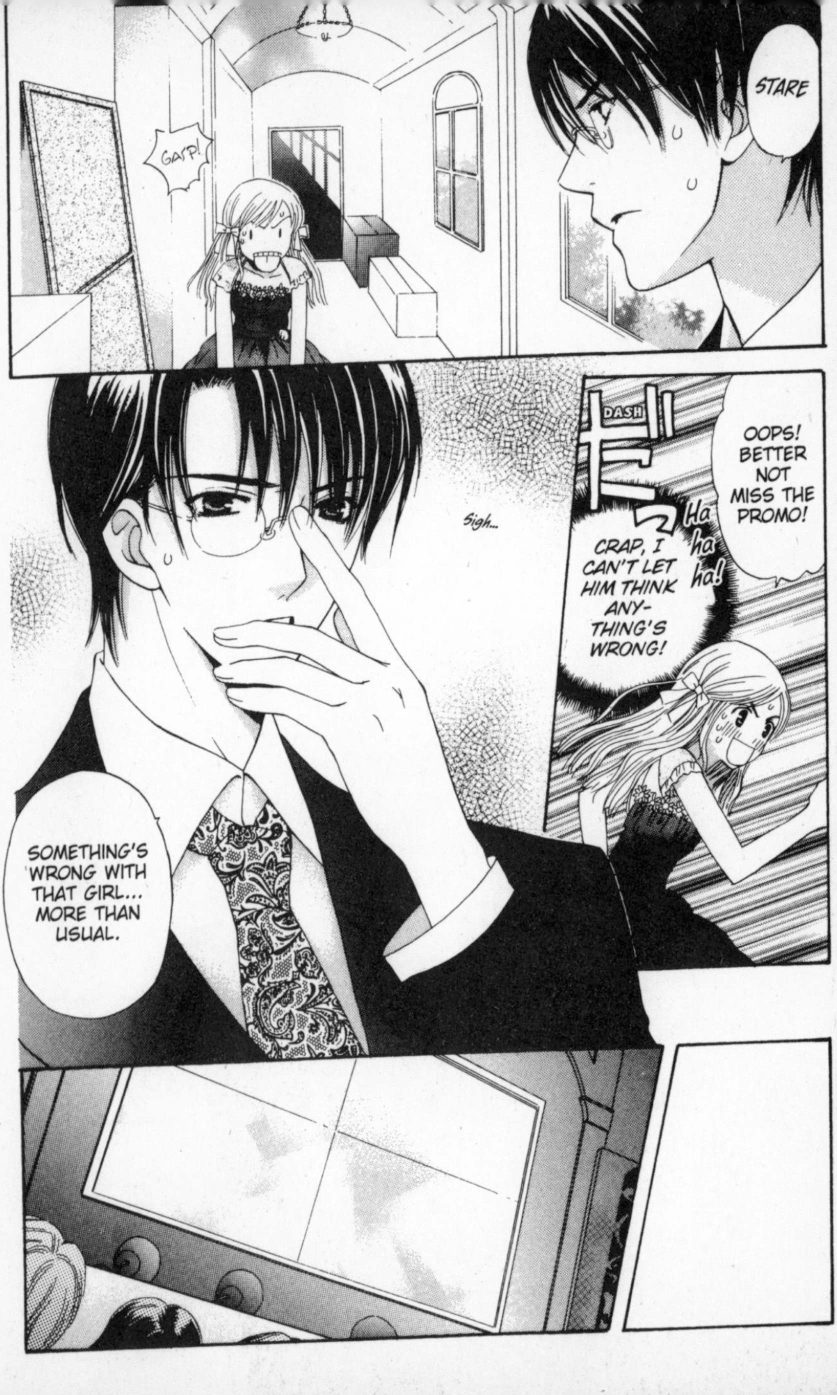
STARE
GASP!
DASH
だっ
OOPS! BETTER NOT MISS THE PROMO!
Ha ha ha!
CRAP, I CAN'T LET HIM THINK ANY-THING'S WRONG!
Sigh...
SOMETHING'S WRONG WITH THAT GIRL... MORE THAN USUAL.

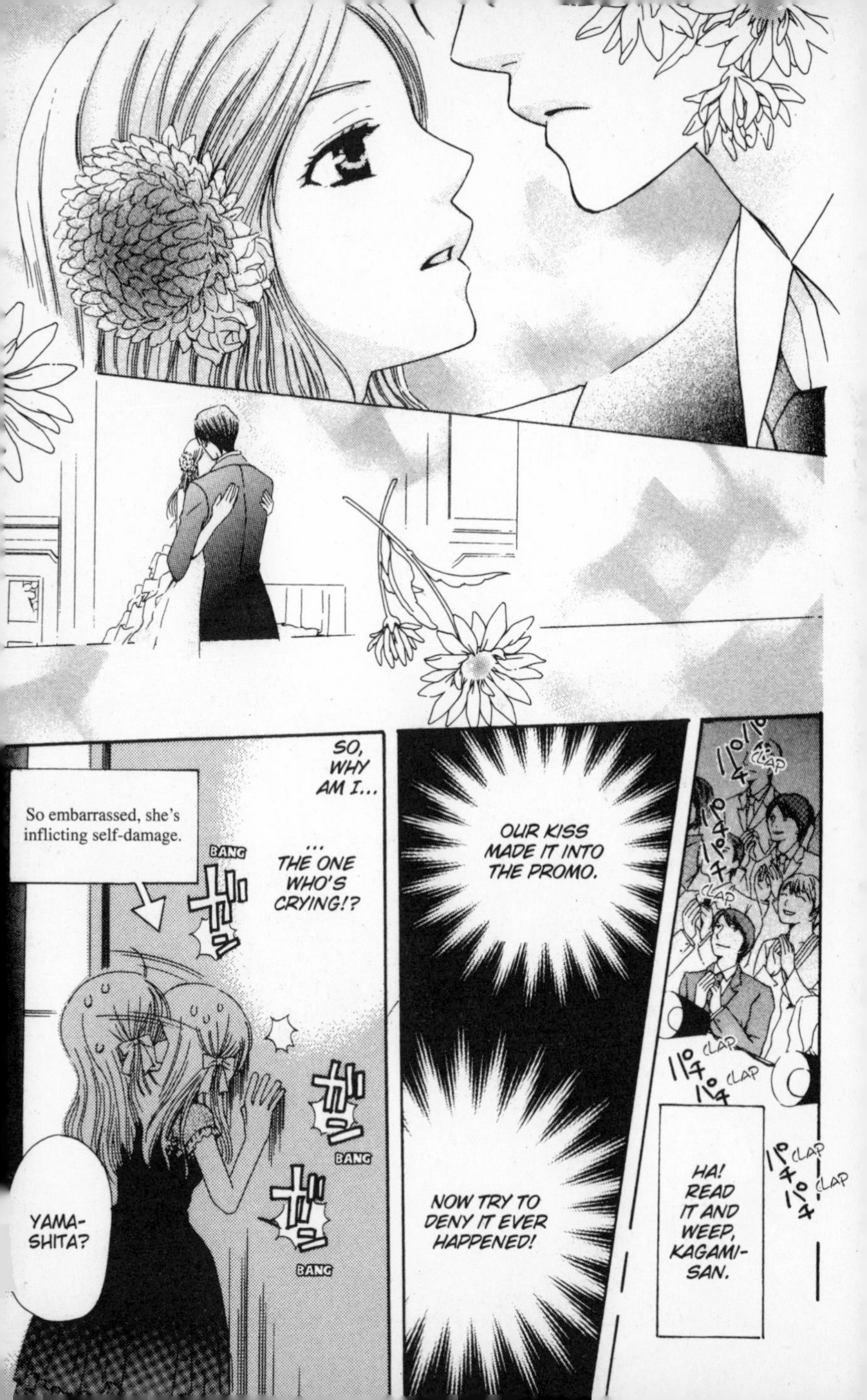

CLAP
CLAP
CLAP CLAP
CLAP CLAP
HA! READ IT AND WEEP, KAGAMI-SAN.
OUR KISS MADE IT INTO THE PROMO.
NOW TRY TO DENY IT EVER HAPPENED!
SO, WHY AM I...
... THE ONE WHO'S CRYING!?
BANG
BANG
BANG
So embarrassed, she's inflicting self-damage.
YAMA-SHITA?

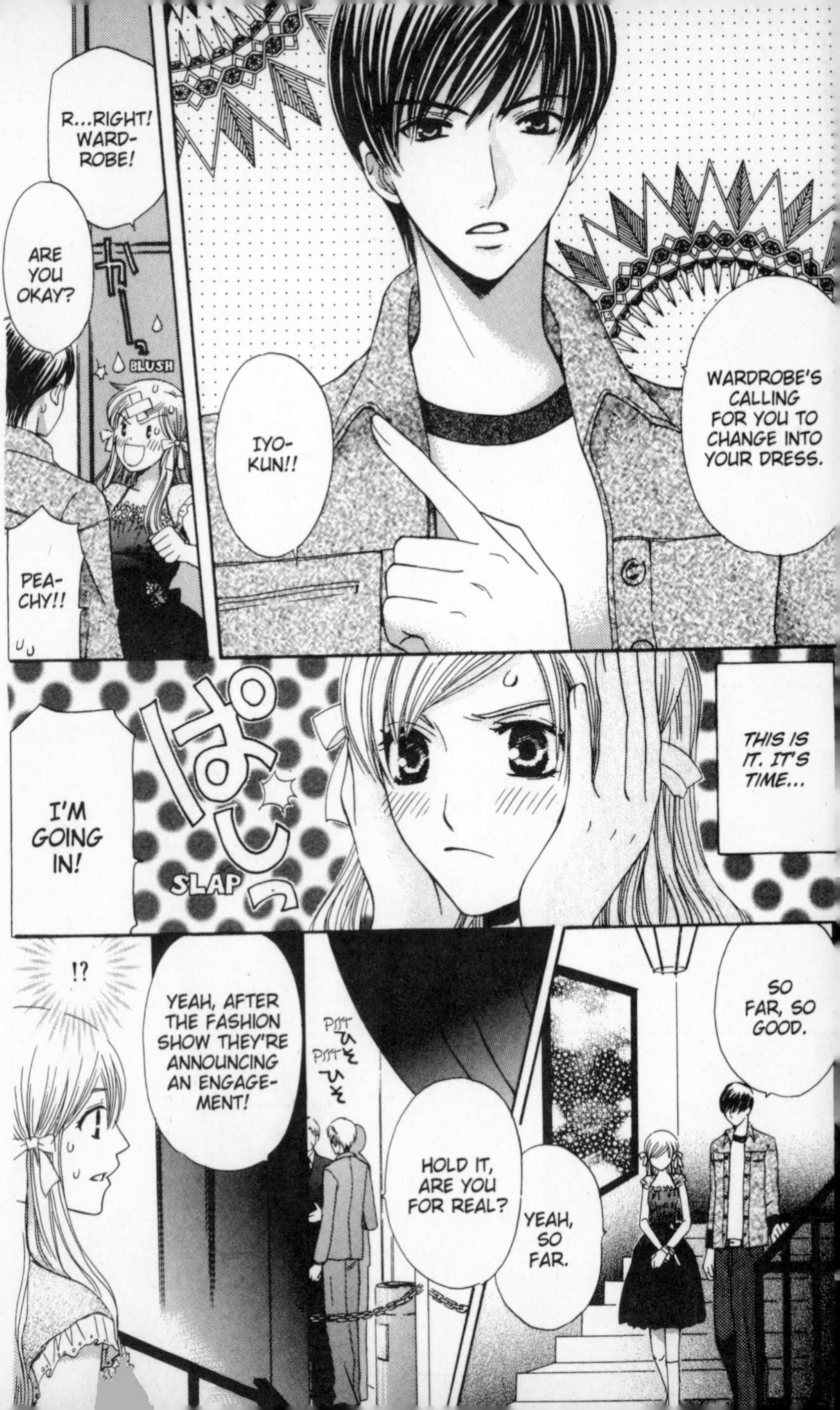
WARDROBE'S CALLING FOR YOU TO CHANGE INTO YOUR DRESS.
IYO-KUN!!
R...RIGHT! WARD-ROBE!
ARE YOU OKAY?
BLUSH
PEA-CHY!!
THIS IS IT. IT'S TIME...
SLAP
I'M GOING IN!
SO FAR, SO GOOD.
YEAH, SO FAR.
HOLD IT, ARE YOU FOR REAL?
PSST
PSST
YEAH, AFTER THE FASHION SHOW THEY'RE ANNOUNCING AN ENGAGE-MENT!
!?

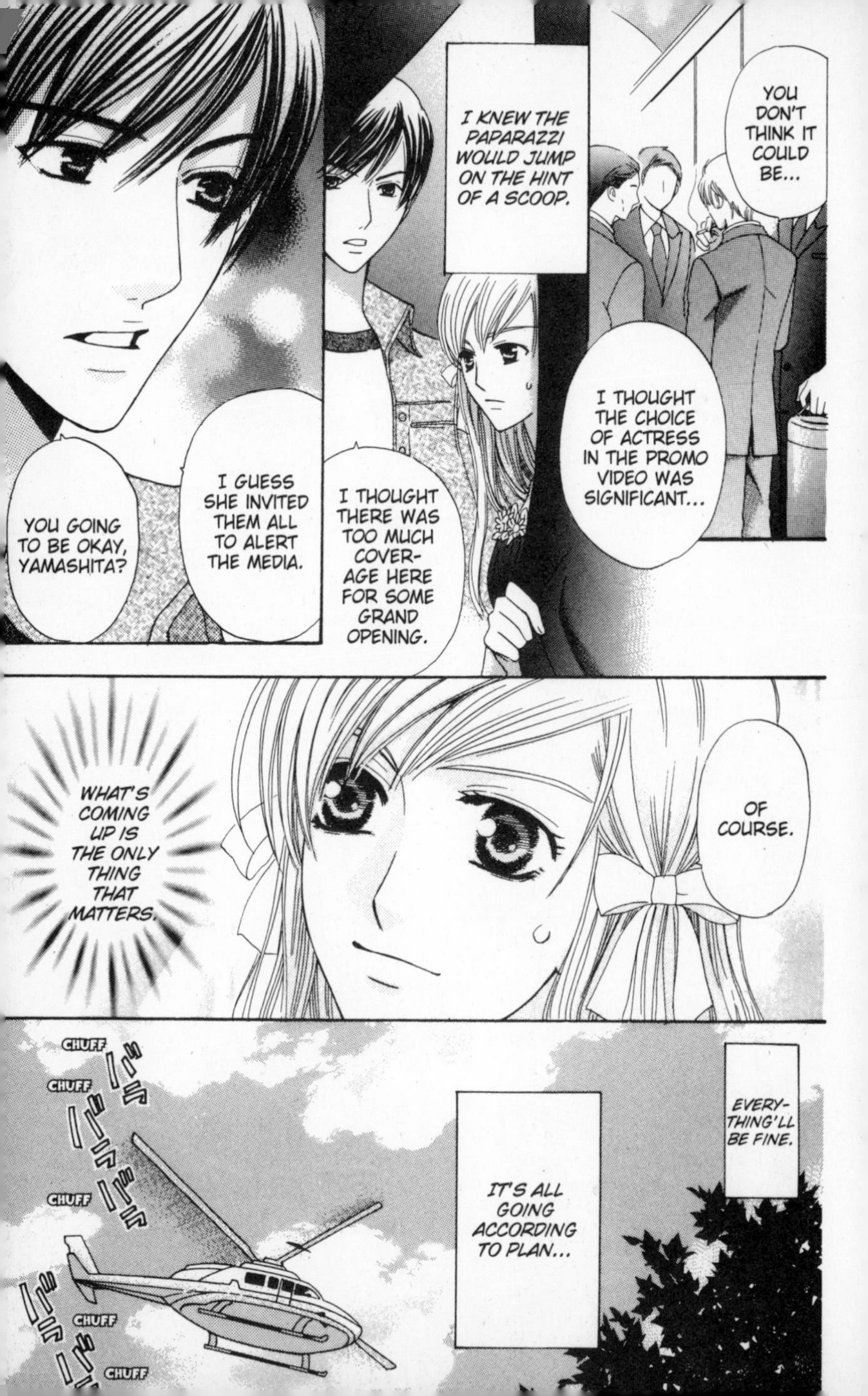
YOU DON'T THINK IT COULD BE...
I THOUGHT THE CHOICE OF ACTRESS IN THE PROMO VIDEO WAS SIGNIFICANT...
I KNEW THE PAPARAZZI WOULD JUMP ON THE HINT OF A SCOOP.
I THOUGHT THERE WAS TOO MUCH COVER-AGE HERE FOR SOME GRAND OPENING.
I GUESS SHE INVITED THEM ALL TO ALERT THE MEDIA.
YOU GOING TO BE OKAY, YAMASHITA?
OF COURSE.
WHAT'S COMING UP IS THE ONLY THING THAT MATTERS.
EVERY-THING'LL BE FINE.
IT'S ALL GOING ACCORDING TO PLAN...
CHUFF
CHUFF
CHUFF
CHUFF
CHUFF

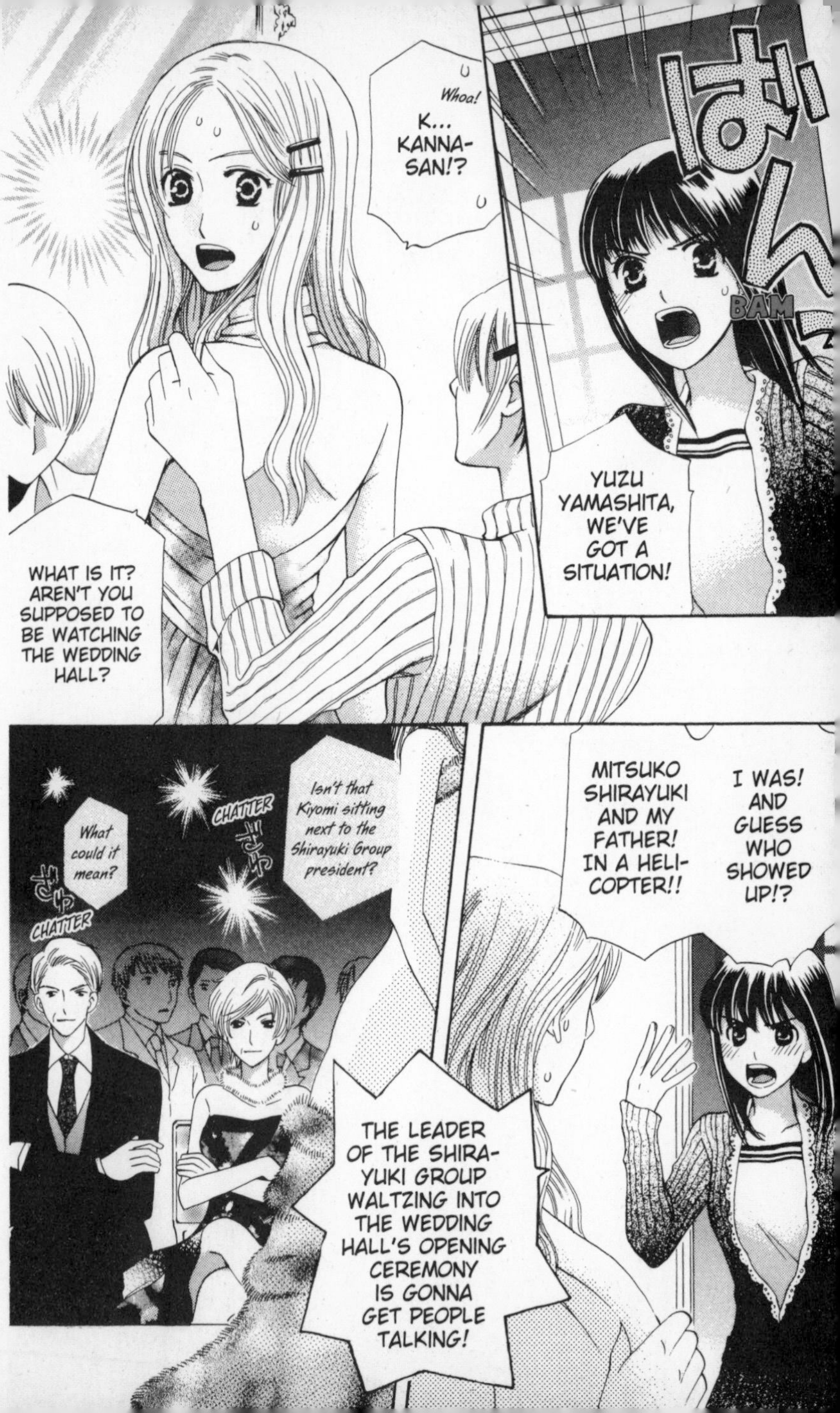
ばん
BAM
YUZU YAMASHITA, WE'VE GOT A SITUATION!
Whoa!
K... KANNA-SAN!?
WHAT IS IT? AREN'T YOU SUPPOSED TO BE WATCHING THE WEDDING HALL?
I WAS! AND GUESS WHO SHOWED UP!?
MITSUKO SHIRAYUKI AND MY FATHER! IN A HELI-COPTER!!
THE LEADER OF THE SHIRA-YUKI GROUP WALTZING INTO THE WEDDING HALL'S OPENING CEREMONY IS GONNA GET PEOPLE TALKING!
Isn't that Kiyomi sitting next to the Shirayuki Group president?
CHATTER
What could it mean?
CHATTER

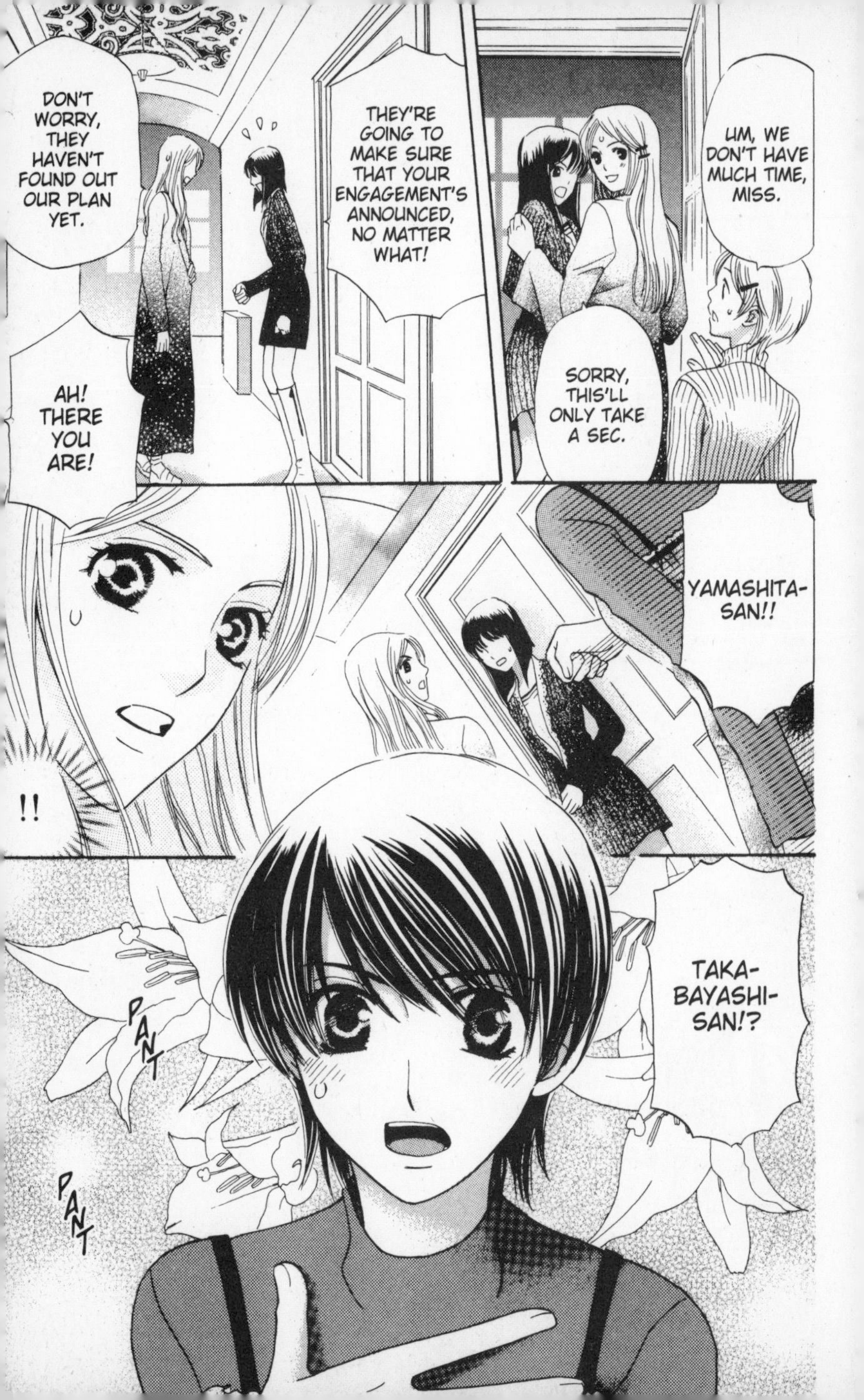
UM, WE DON'T HAVE MUCH TIME, MISS.
SORRY, THIS'LL ONLY TAKE A SEC.
THEY'RE GOING TO MAKE SURE THAT YOUR ENGAGEMENT'S ANNOUNCED, NO MATTER WHAT!
DON'T WORRY, THEY HAVEN'T FOUND OUT OUR PLAN YET.
AH! THERE YOU ARE!
YAMASHITA-SAN!!
!!
TAKA-BAYASHI-SAN!?
PANT
PANT

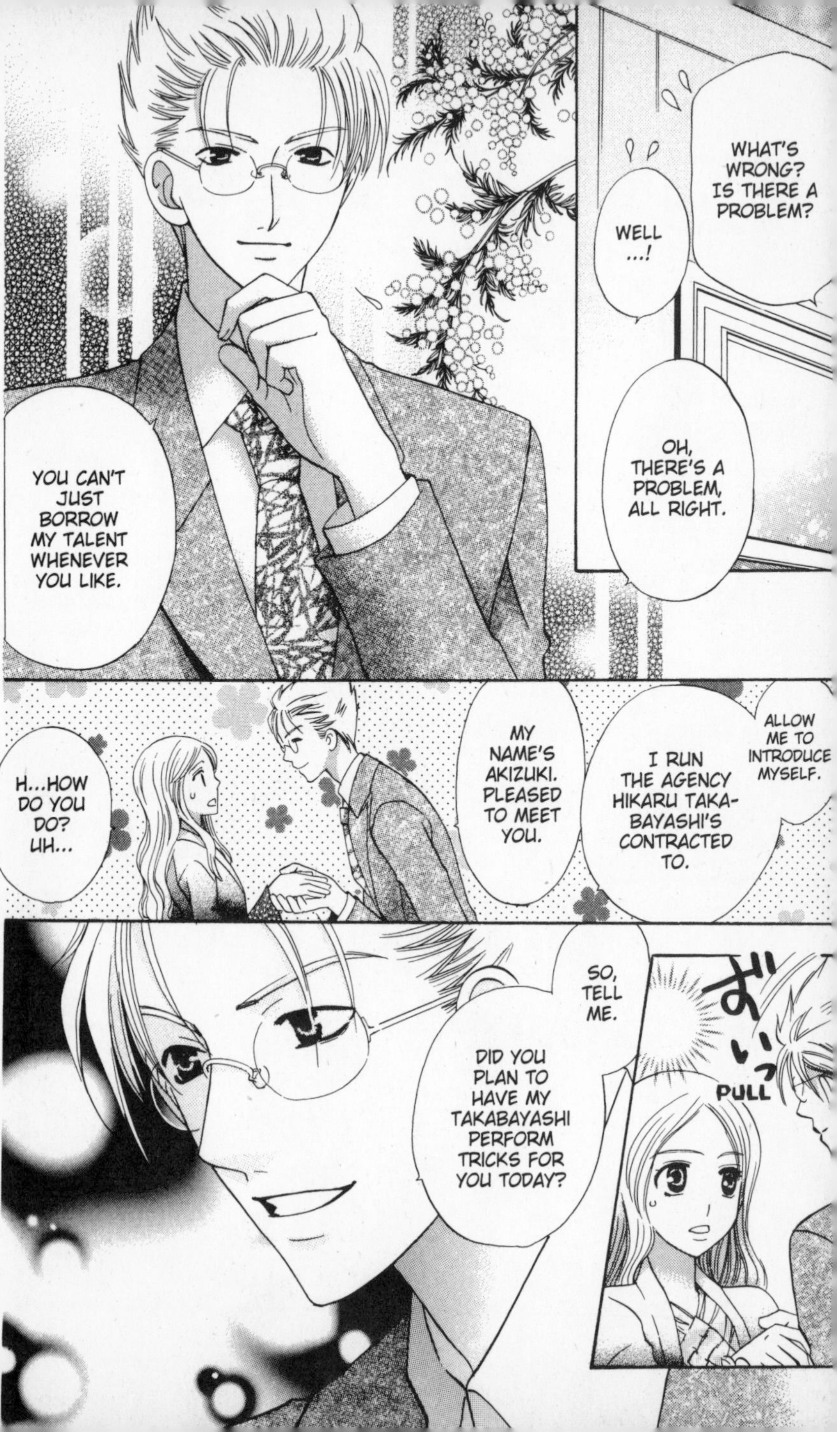
WHAT'S WRONG? IS THERE A PROBLEM?
WELL ...!
OH, THERE'S A PROBLEM, ALL RIGHT.
YOU CAN'T JUST BORROW MY TALENT WHENEVER YOU LIKE.
ALLOW ME TO INTRODUCE MYSELF.
I RUN THE AGENCY HIKARU TAKA-BAYASHI'S CONTRACTED TO.
MY NAME'S AKIZUKI. PLEASED TO MEET YOU.
H...HOW DO YOU DO? UH...
PULL
SO, TELL ME.
DID YOU PLAN TO HAVE MY TAKABAYASHI PERFORM TRICKS FOR YOU TODAY?

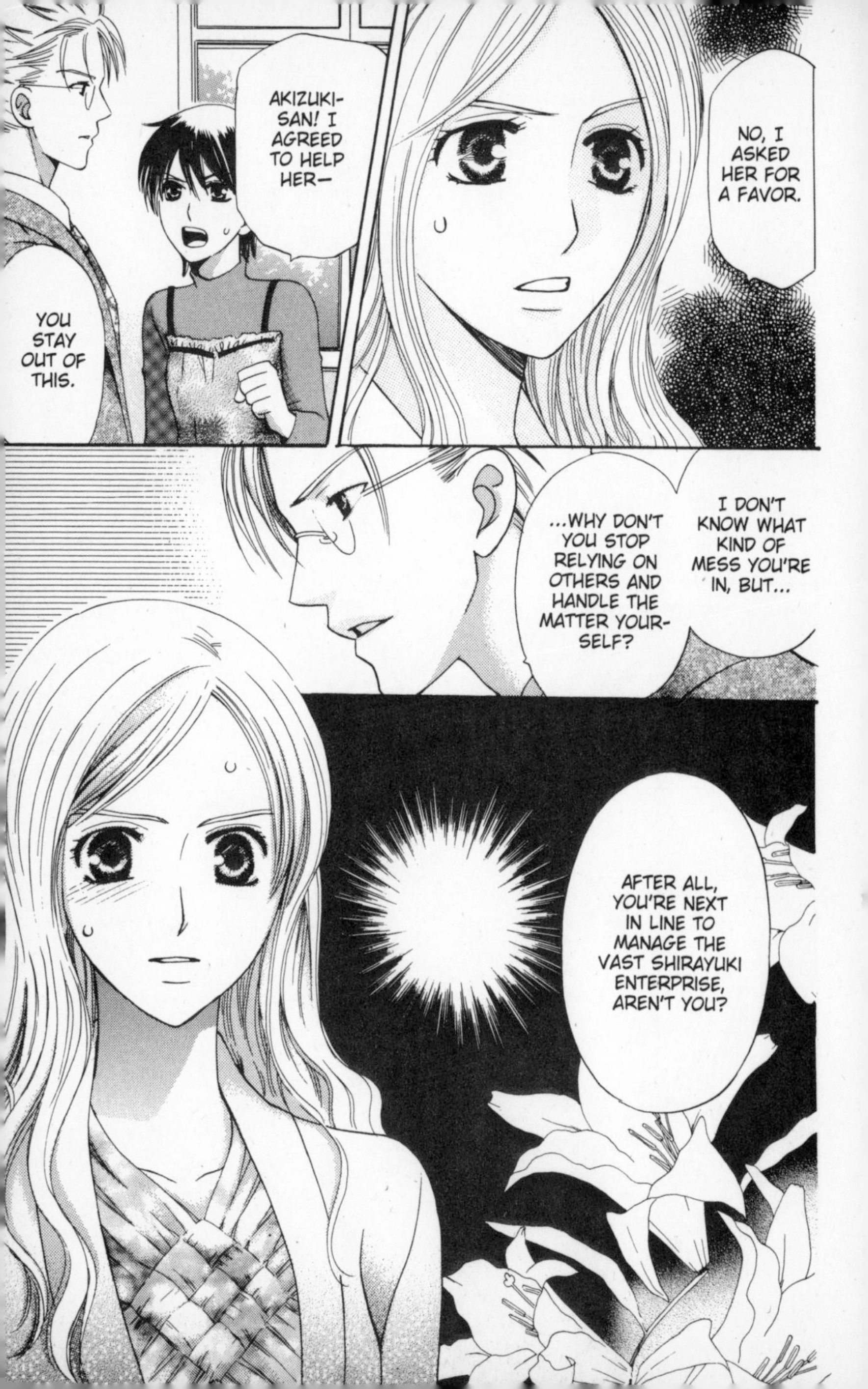
NO, I ASKED HER FOR A FAVOR.
AKIZUKI-SAN! I AGREED TO HELP HER—
YOU STAY OUT OF THIS.
I DON'T KNOW WHAT KIND OF MESS YOU'RE IN, BUT...
...WHY DON'T YOU STOP RELYING ON OTHERS AND HANDLE THE MATTER YOURSELF?
AFTER ALL, YOU'RE NEXT IN LINE TO MANAGE THE VAST SHIRAYUKI ENTERPRISE, AREN'T YOU?

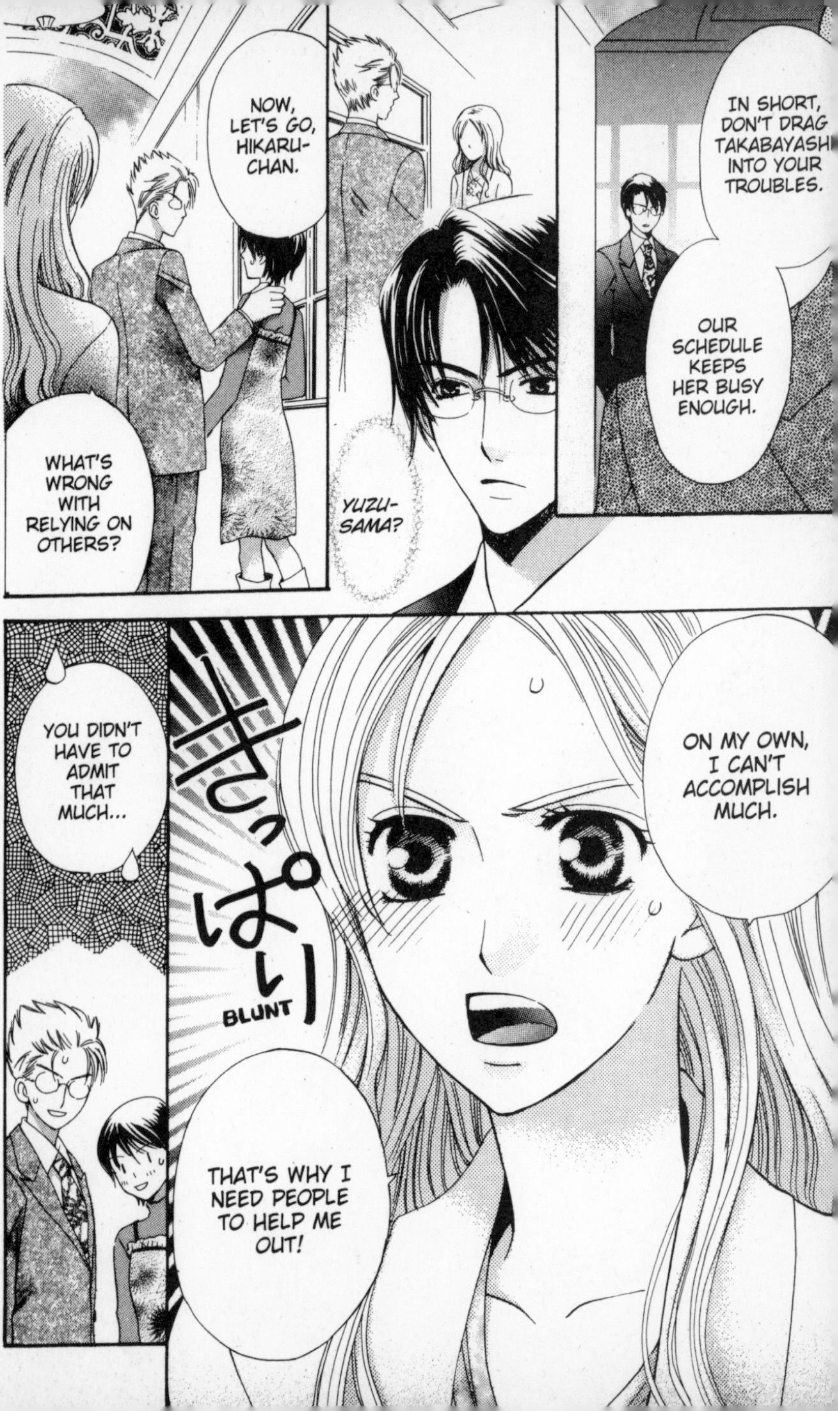
IN SHORT, DON'T DRAG TAKABAYASHI INTO YOUR TROUBLES.
OUR SCHEDULE KEEPS HER BUSY ENOUGH.
YUZU-SAMA?
NOW, LET'S GO, HIKARU-CHAN.
WHAT'S WRONG WITH RELYING ON OTHERS?
ON MY OWN, I CAN'T ACCOMPLISH MUCH.
きっぱり
BLUNT
THAT'S WHY I NEED PEOPLE TO HELP ME OUT!
YOU DIDN'T HAVE TO ADMIT THAT MUCH...

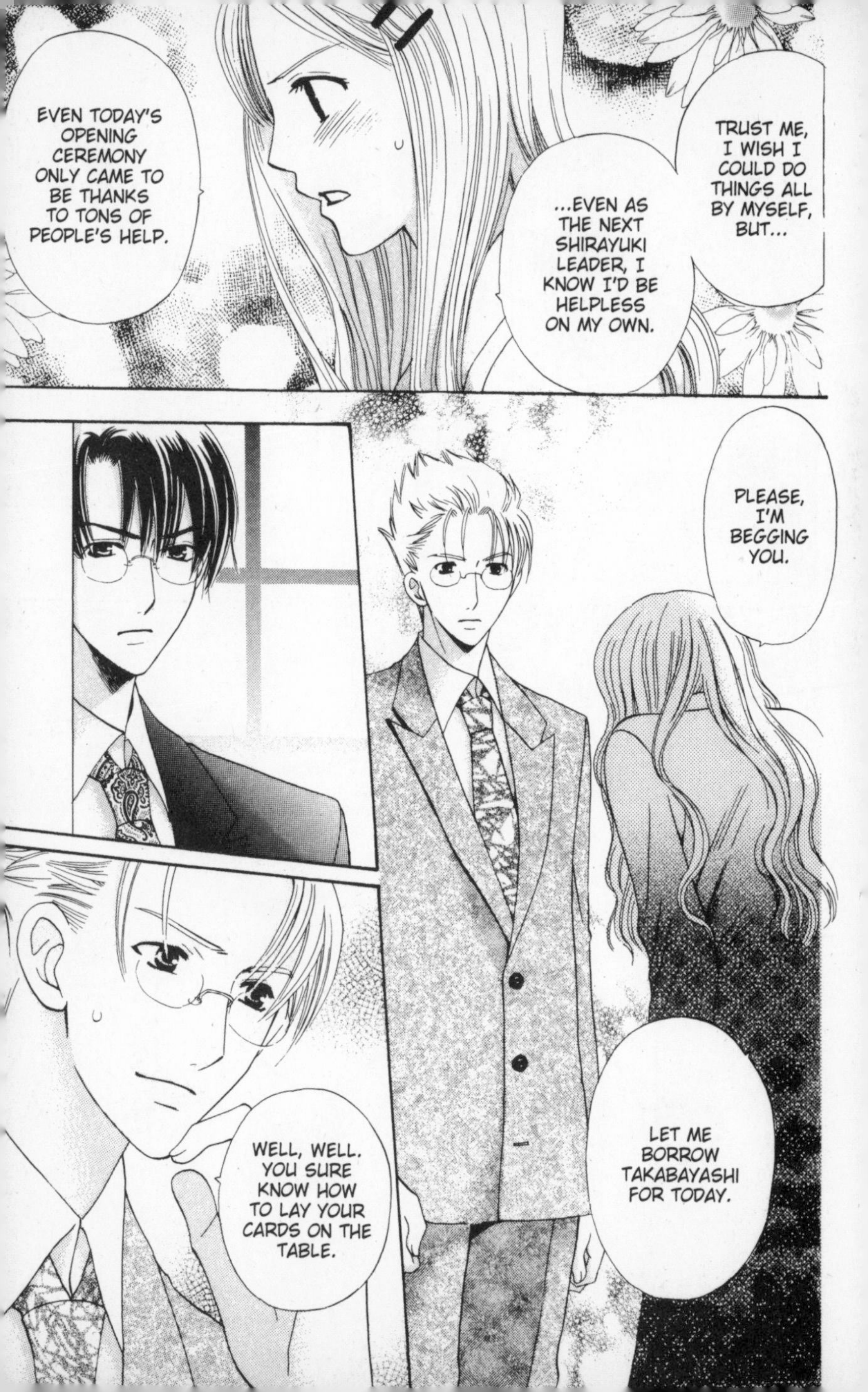
TRUST ME, I WISH I COULD DO THINGS ALL BY MYSELF, BUT...
...EVEN AS THE NEXT SHIRAYUKI LEADER, I KNOW I'D BE HELPLESS ON MY OWN.
EVEN TODAY'S OPENING CEREMONY ONLY CAME TO BE THANKS TO TONS OF PEOPLE'S HELP.
PLEASE, I'M BEGGING YOU.
LET ME BORROW TAKABAYASHI FOR TODAY.
WELL, WELL. YOU SURE KNOW HOW TO LAY YOUR CARDS ON THE TABLE.

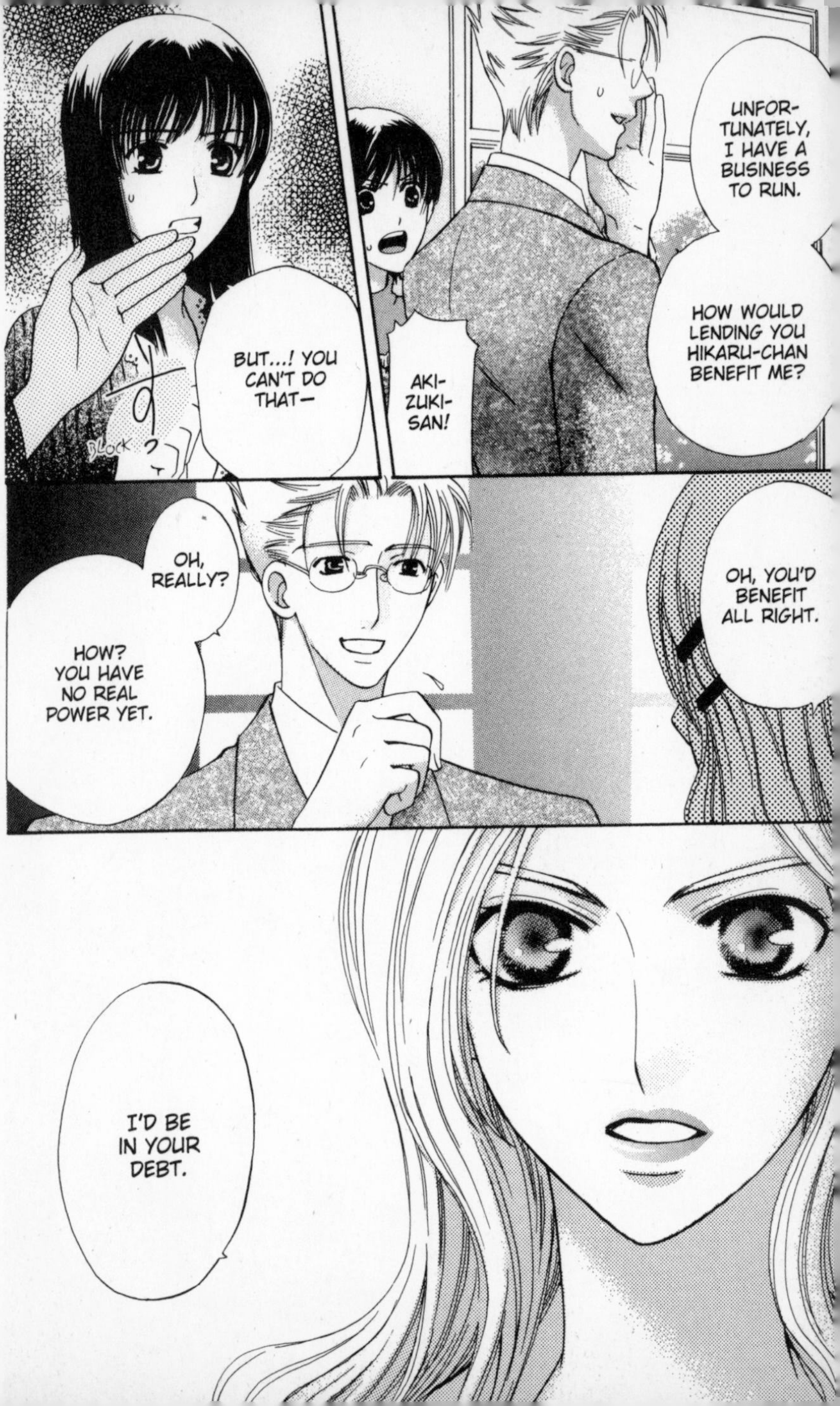
UNFOR-TUNATELY, I HAVE A BUSINESS TO RUN.
HOW WOULD LENDING YOU HIKARU-CHAN BENEFIT ME?
AKI-ZUKI-SAN!
BUT...! YOU CAN'T DO THAT—
BLOCK
OH, YOU'D BENEFIT ALL RIGHT.
OH, REALLY?
HOW? YOU HAVE NO REAL POWER YET.
I'D BE IN YOUR DEBT.

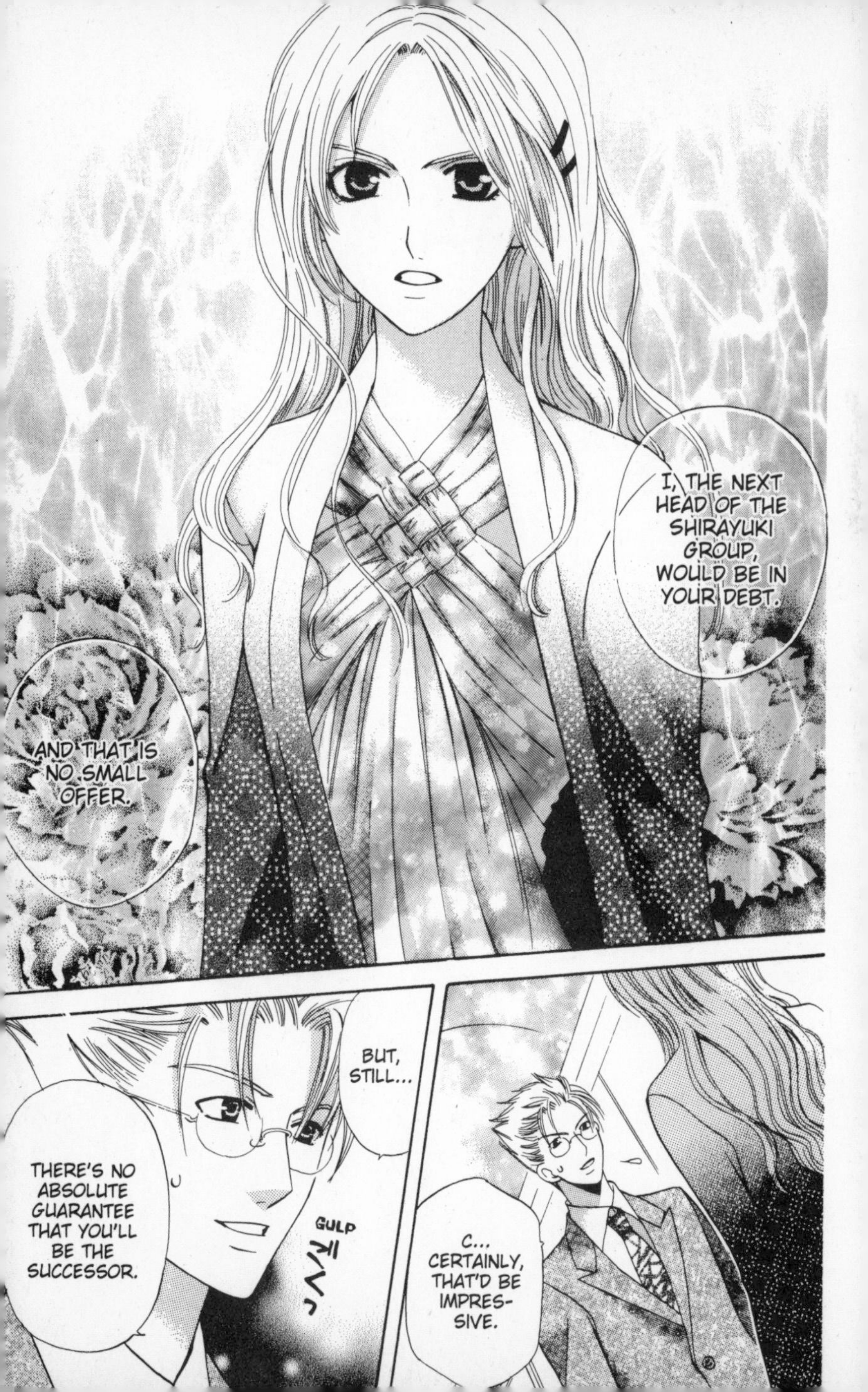

I, THE NEXT HEAD OF THE SHIRAYUKI GROUP, WOULD BE IN YOUR DEBT.
AND THAT IS NO SMALL OFFER.
C... CERTAINLY, THAT'D BE IMPRES-SIVE.
BUT, STILL...
THERE'S NO ABSOLUTE GUARANTEE THAT YOU'LL BE THE SUCCESSOR.
GULP

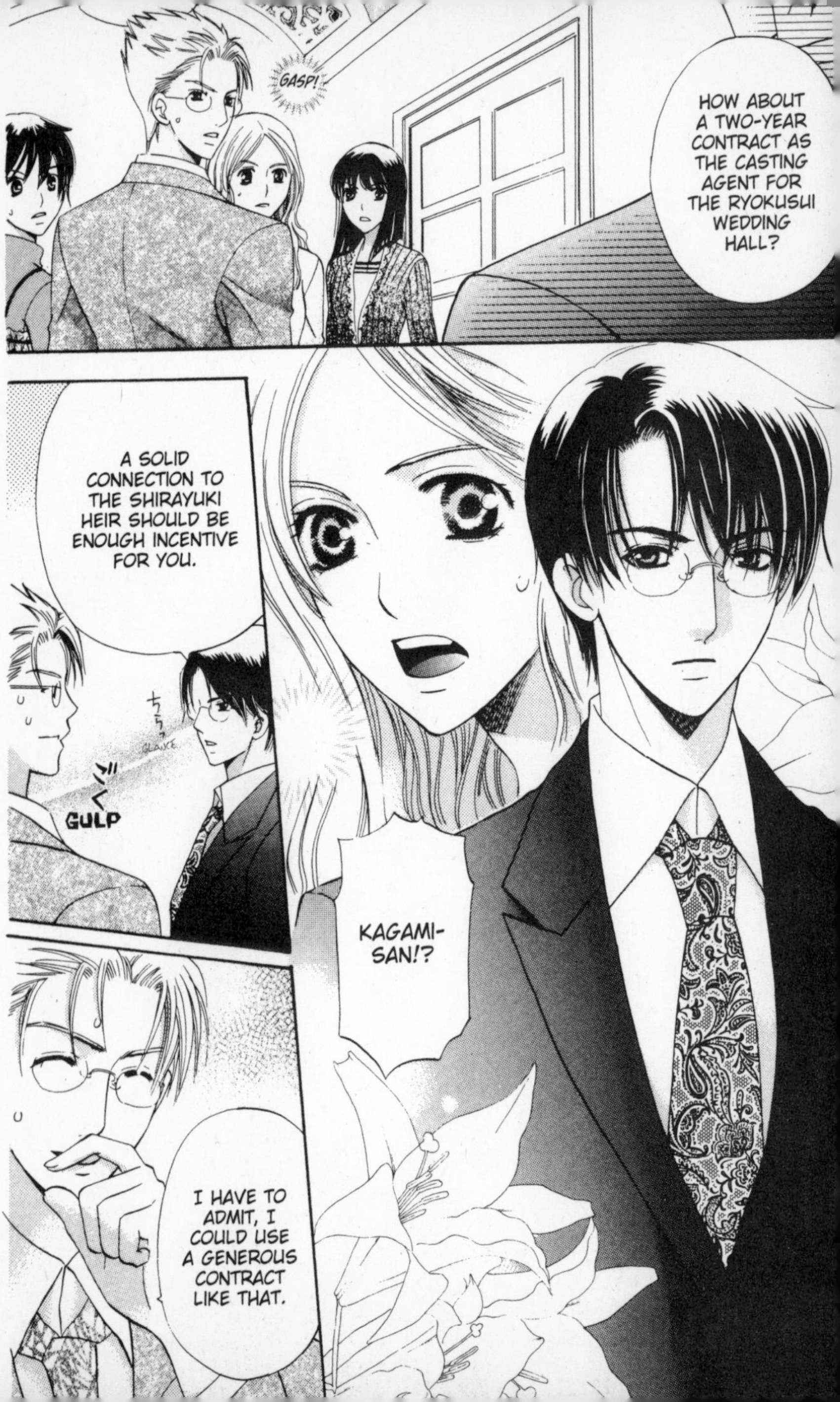
HOW ABOUT A TWO-YEAR CONTRACT AS THE CASTING AGENT FOR THE RYOKUSUI WEDDING HALL?
GASP!
KAGAMI-SAN!?
A SOLID CONNECTION TO THE SHIRAYUKI HEIR SHOULD BE ENOUGH INCENTIVE FOR YOU.
GULP
I HAVE TO ADMIT, I COULD USE A GENEROUS CONTRACT LIKE THAT.

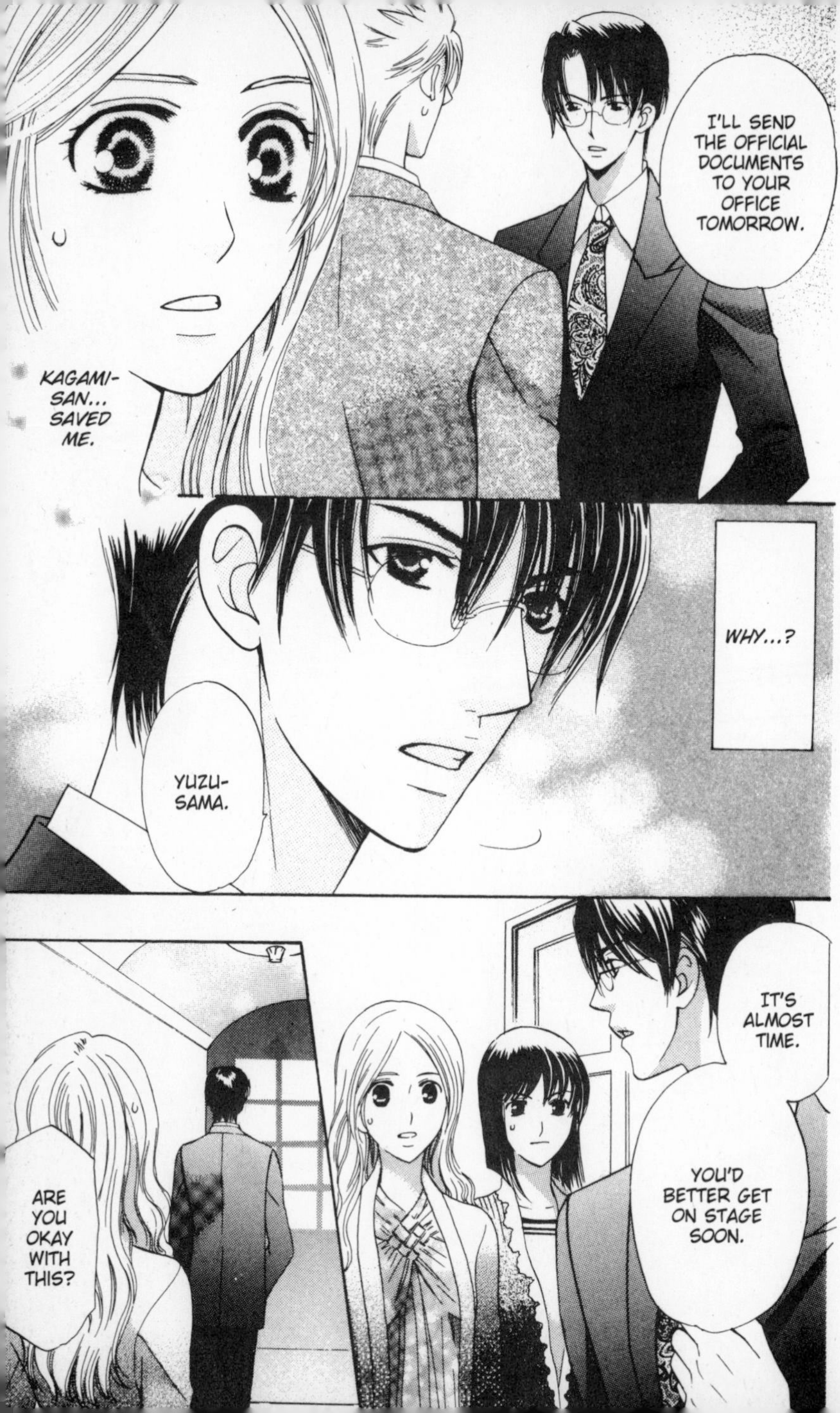
I'LL SEND THE OFFICIAL DOCUMENTS TO YOUR OFFICE TOMORROW.
KAGAMI-SAN... SAVED ME.
WHY...?
YUZU-SAMA.
IT'S ALMOST TIME.
YOU'D BETTER GET ON STAGE SOON.
ARE YOU OKAY WITH THIS?

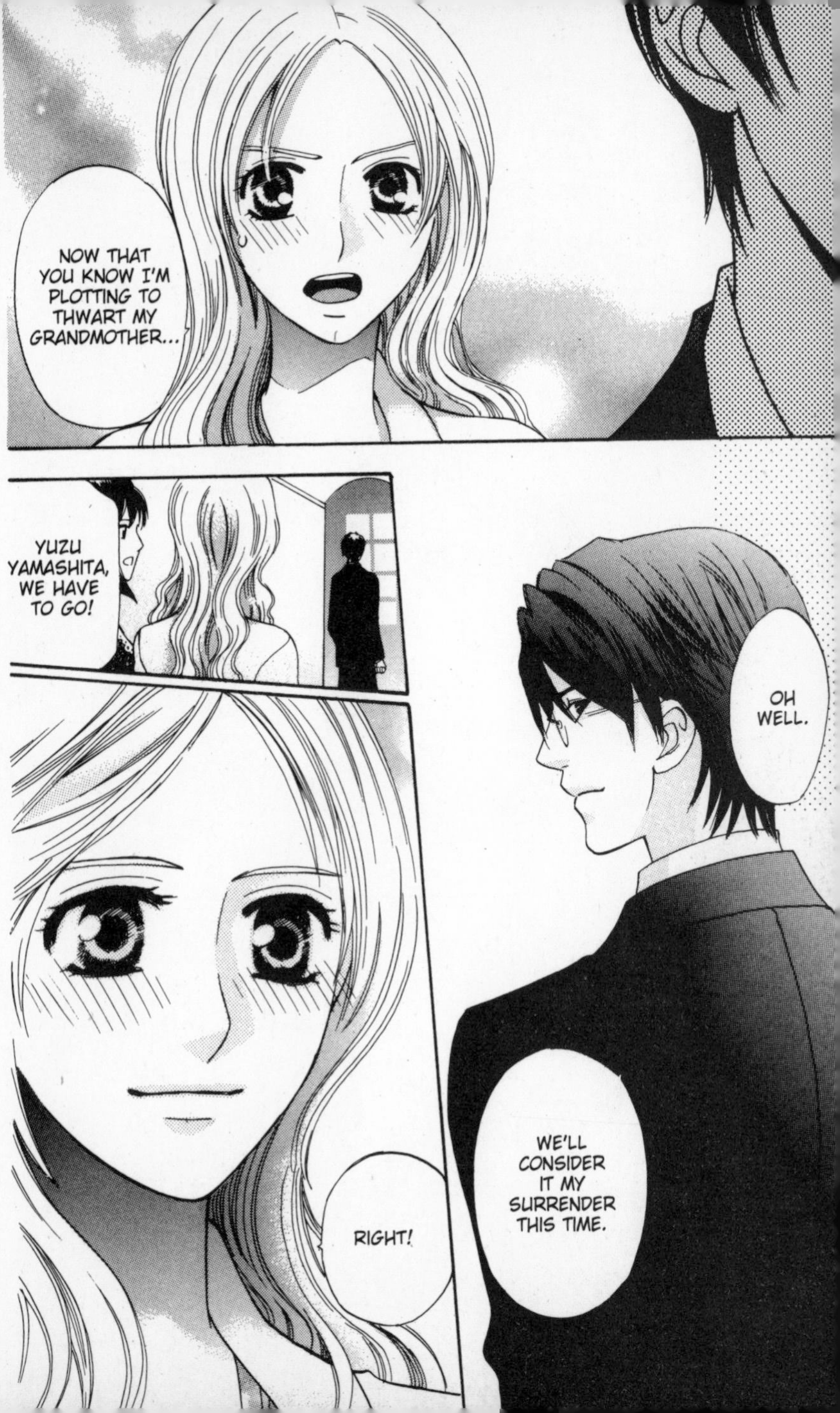
NOW THAT YOU KNOW I'M PLOTTING TO THWART MY GRANDMOTHER...
OH WELL.
WE'LL CONSIDER IT MY SURRENDER THIS TIME.
YUZU YAMASHITA, WE HAVE TO GO!
RIGHT!

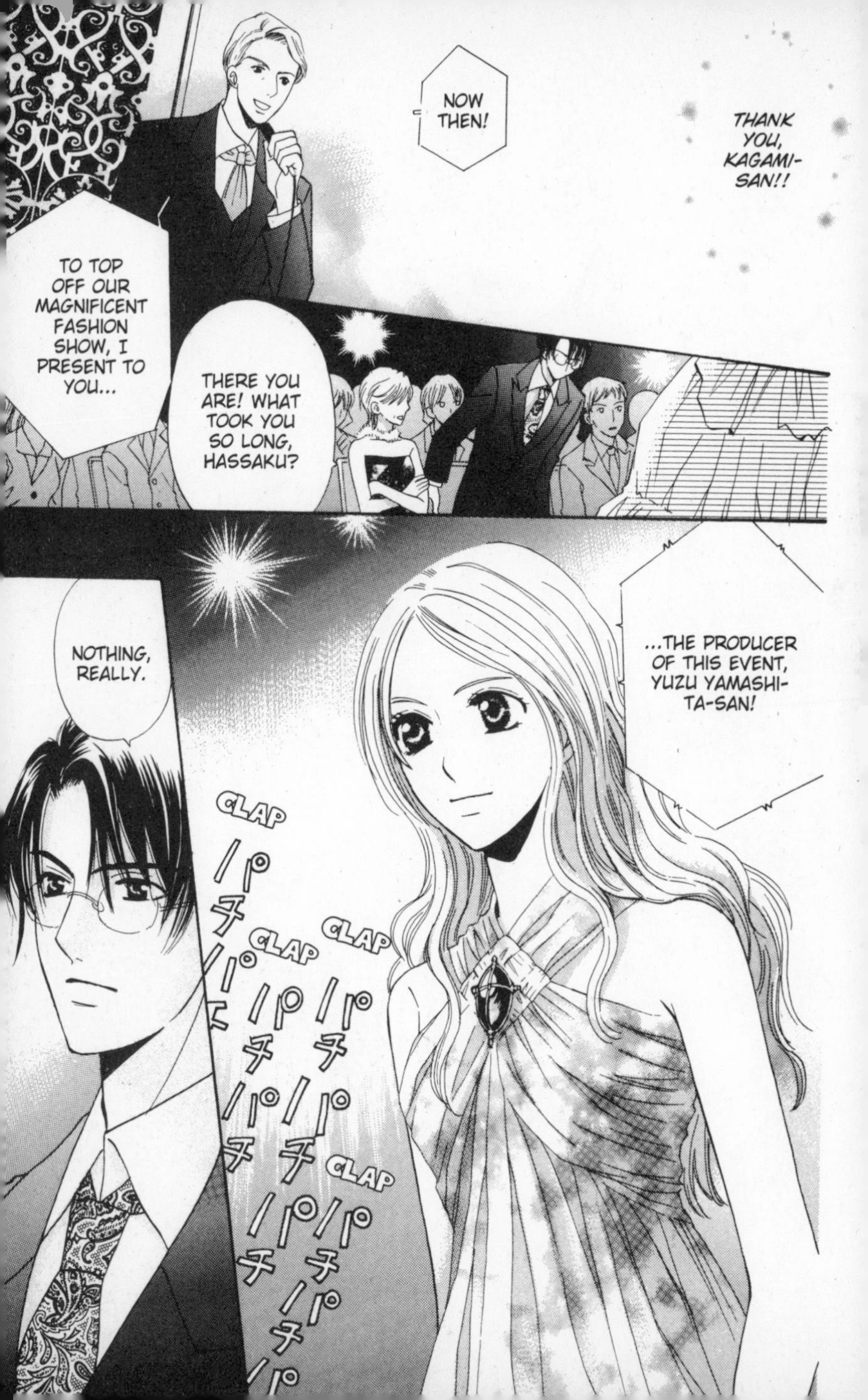
THANK YOU, KAGAMI-SAN!!
NOW THEN!
TO TOP OFF OUR MAGNIFICENT FASHION SHOW, I PRESENT TO YOU...
THERE YOU ARE! WHAT TOOK YOU SO LONG, HASSAKU?
...THE PRODUCER OF THIS EVENT, YUZU YAMASHITA-SAN!
NOTHING, REALLY.
CLAP
CLAP
CLAP
CLAP
パチパチパチパチ
パチパチパチパチ
パチパチパチパチ
パチパチ

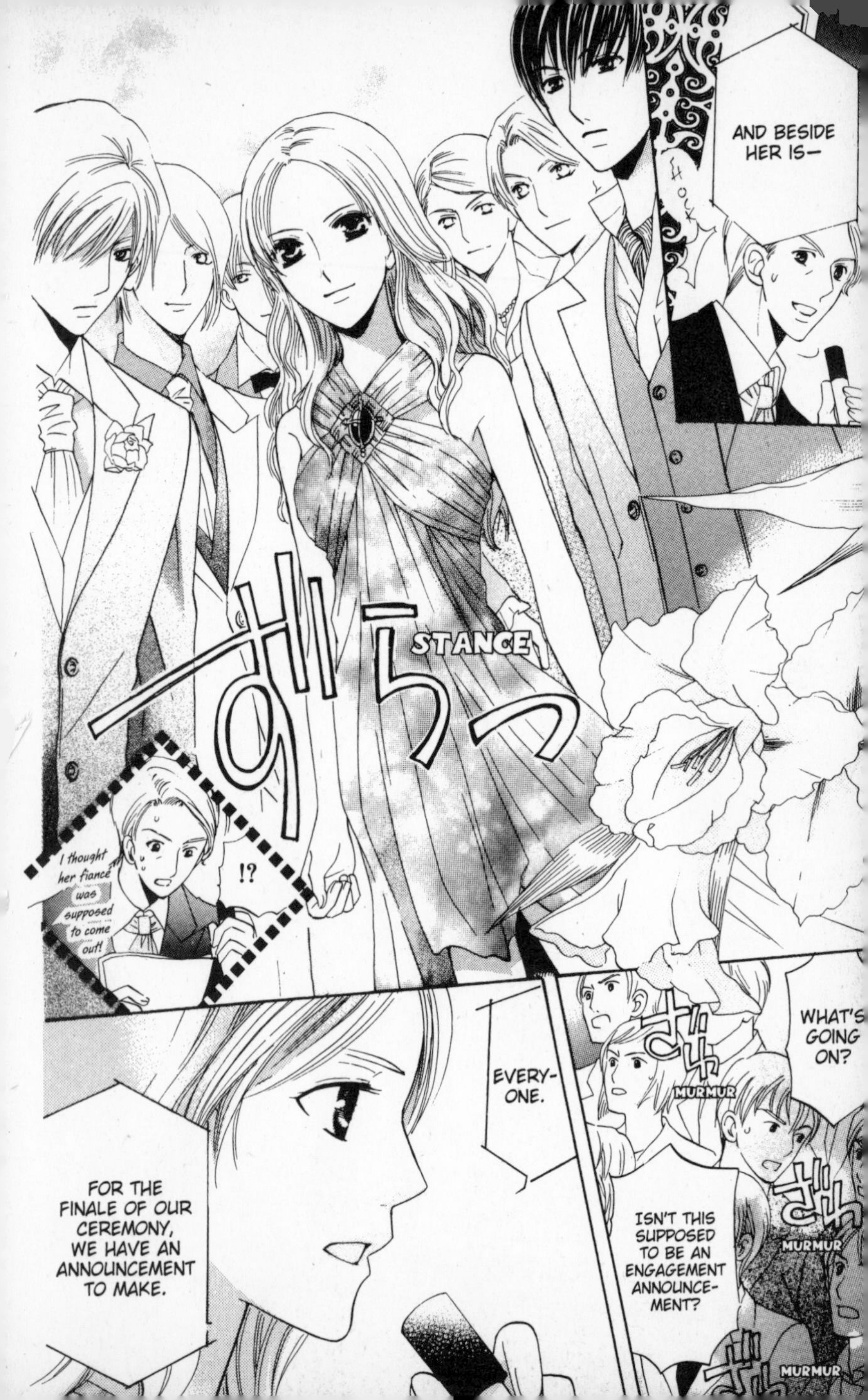
AND BESIDE HER IS—
SHOCK
すらっ
STANCE
!?
I thought her fiance was supposed to come out!
WHAT'S GOING ON?
ざわ
MURMUR
ざわ
MURMUR
ISN'T THIS SUPPOSED TO BE AN ENGAGEMENT ANNOUNCE-MENT?
MURMUR
EVERY-ONE.
FOR THE FINALE OF OUR CEREMONY, WE HAVE AN ANNOUNCEMENT TO MAKE.

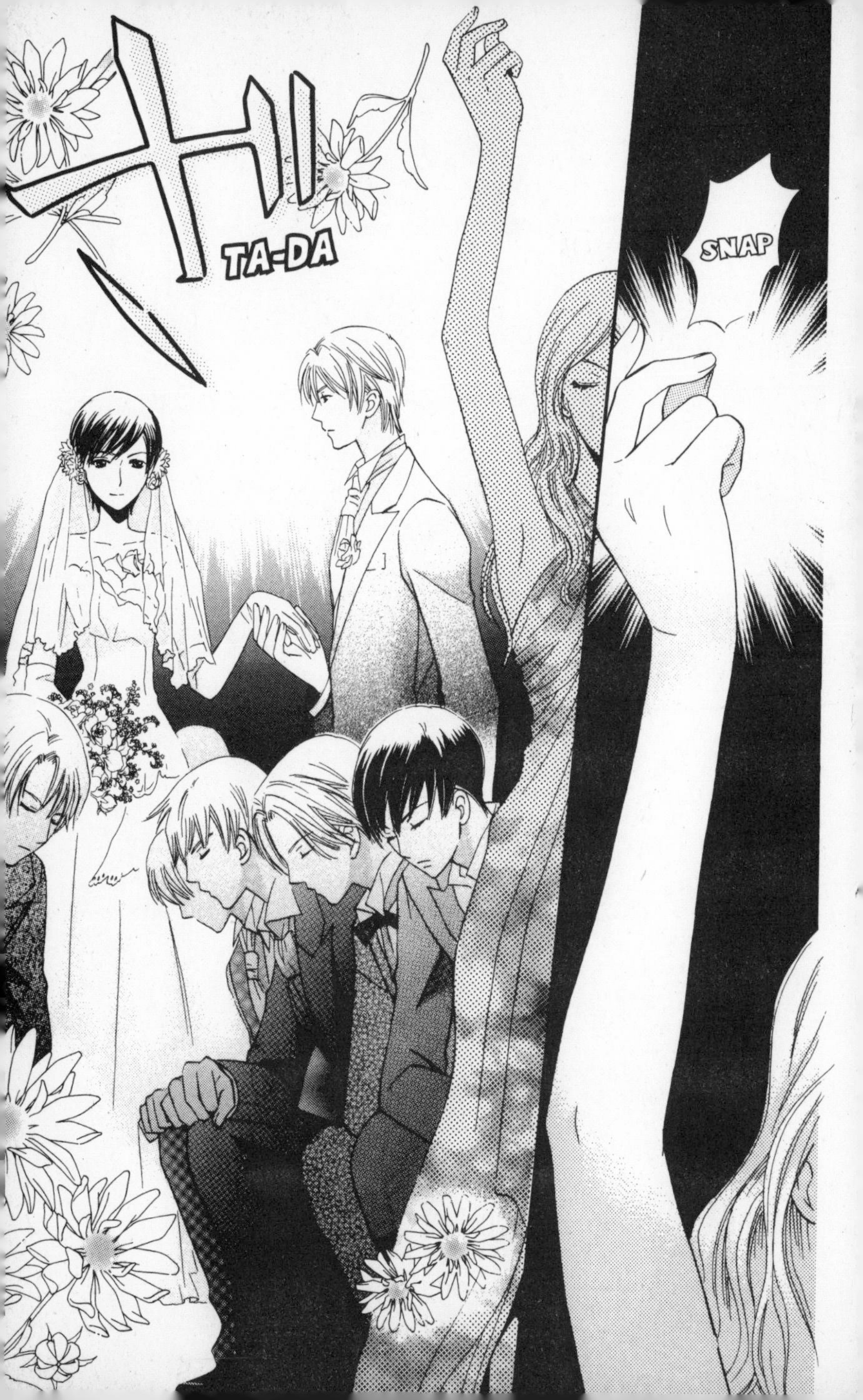
SNAP
TA-DA

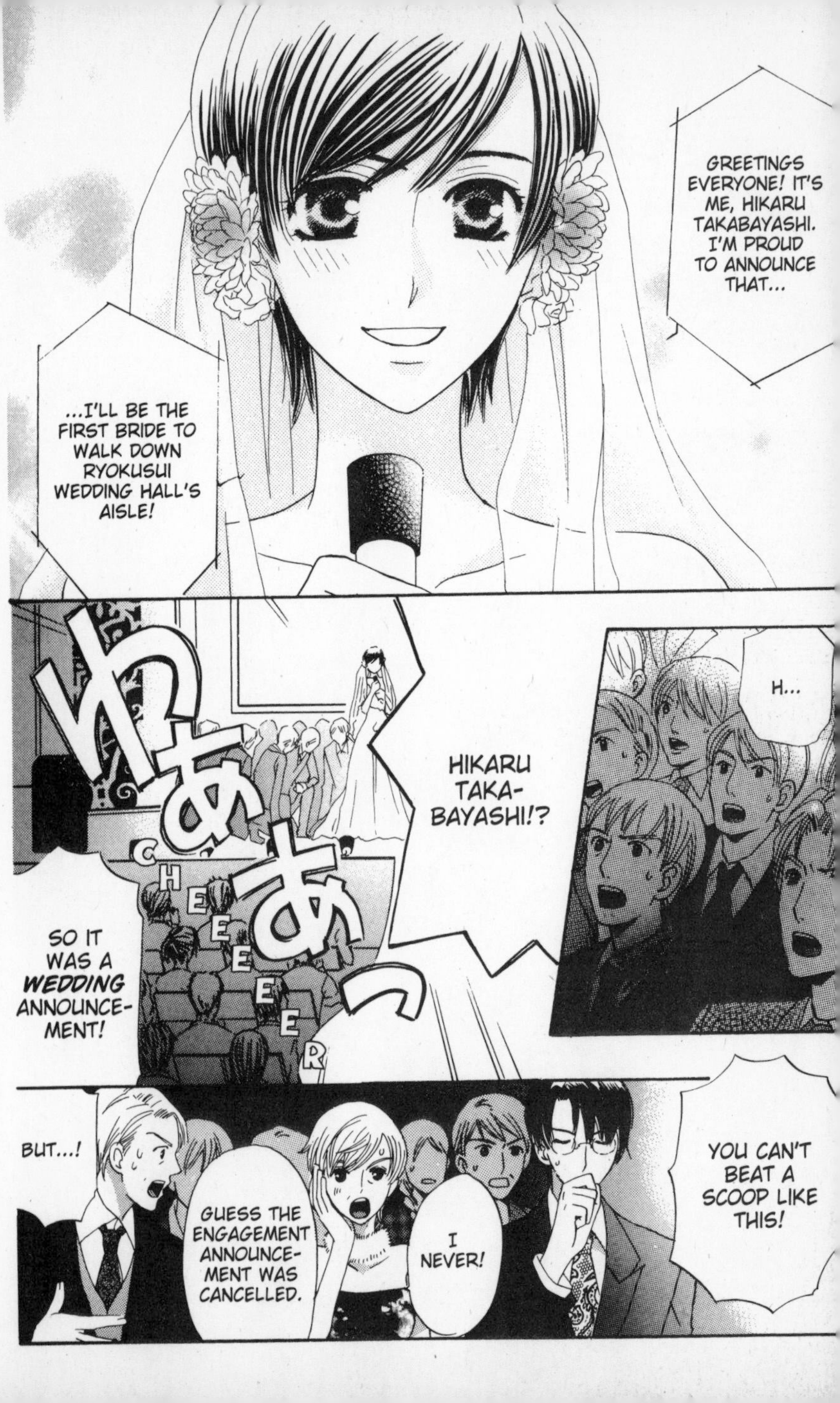
GREETINGS EVERYONE! IT'S ME, HIKARU TAKABAYASHI. I'M PROUD TO ANNOUNCE THAT...
...I'LL BE THE FIRST BRIDE TO WALK DOWN RYOKUSUI WEDDING HALL'S AISLE!
H...
HIKARU TAKA-BAYASHI!?
わああっ
CHEEEEER
SO IT WAS A ***WEDDING*** ANNOUNCE-MENT!
YOU CAN'T BEAT A SCOOP LIKE THIS!
I NEVER!
GUESS THE ENGAGEMENT ANNOUNCE-MENT WAS CANCELLED.
BUT...!

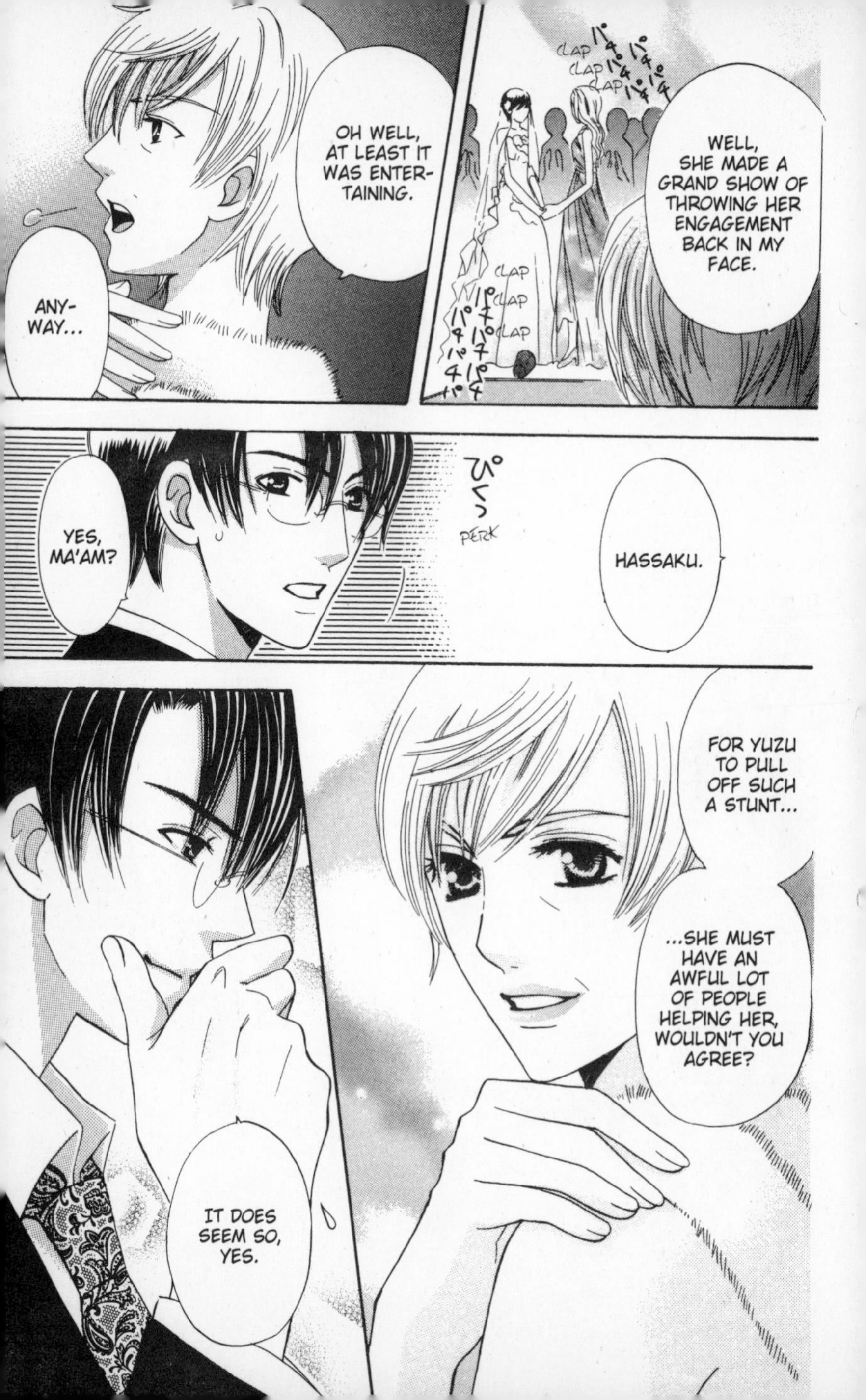
CLAP CLAP CLAP
WELL, SHE MADE A GRAND SHOW OF THROWING HER ENGAGEMENT BACK IN MY FACE.
CLAP CLAP CLAP
OH WELL, AT LEAST IT WAS ENTER-TAINING.
ANY-WAY...
HASSAKU.
ぴくっ
PERK
YES, MA'AM?
FOR YUZU TO PULL OFF SUCH A STUNT...
...SHE MUST HAVE AN AWFUL LOT OF PEOPLE HELPING HER, WOULDN'T YOU AGREE?
IT DOES SEEM SO, YES.

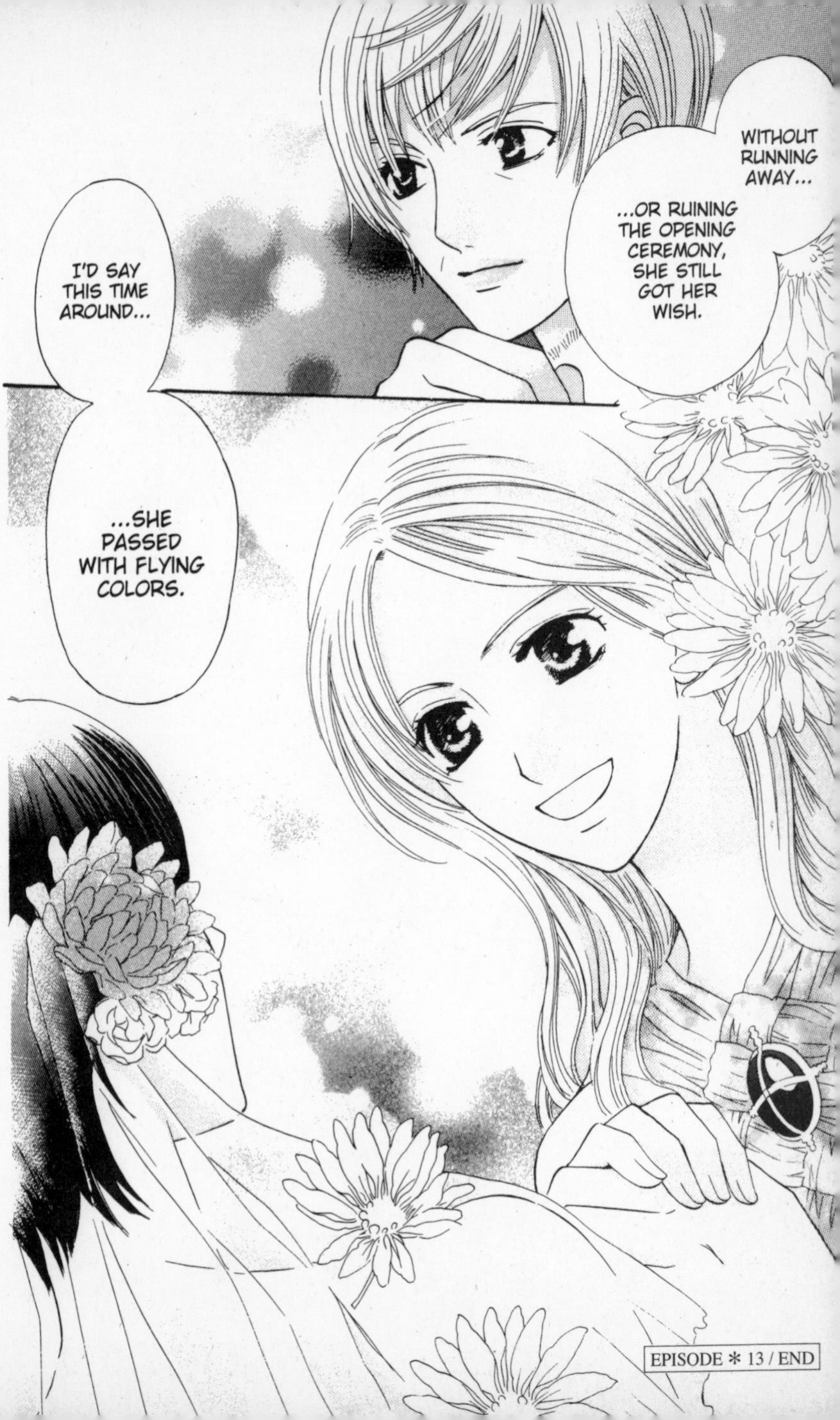
WITHOUT RUNNING AWAY...
...OR RUINING THE OPENING CEREMONY, SHE STILL GOT HER WISH.
I'D SAY THIS TIME AROUND...
...SHE PASSED WITH FLYING COLORS.

EPISODE ✻ 13 / END

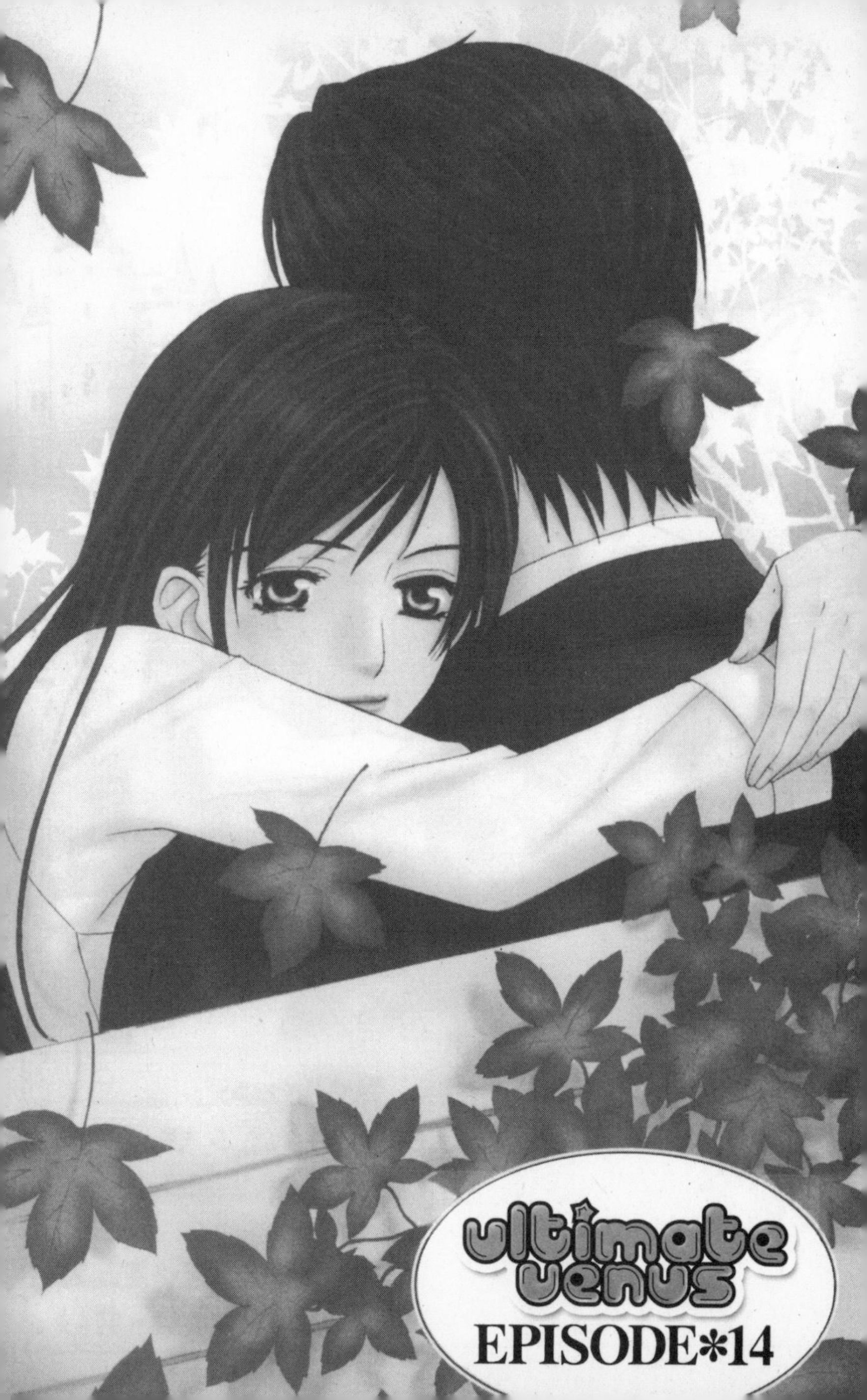
ultimate venus
EPISODE*14

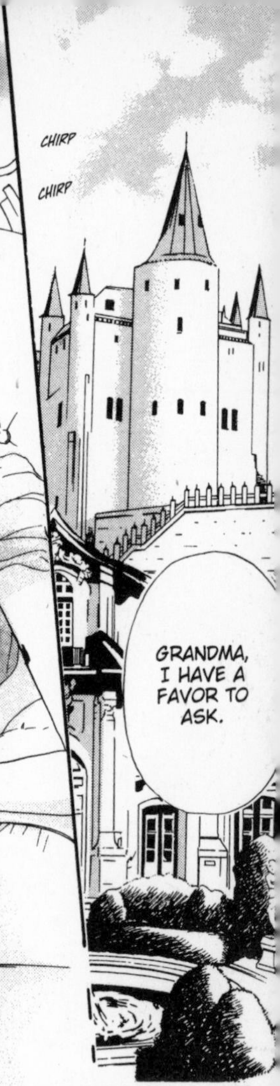
CHIRP
CHIRP
GRANDMA, I HAVE A FAVOR TO ASK.

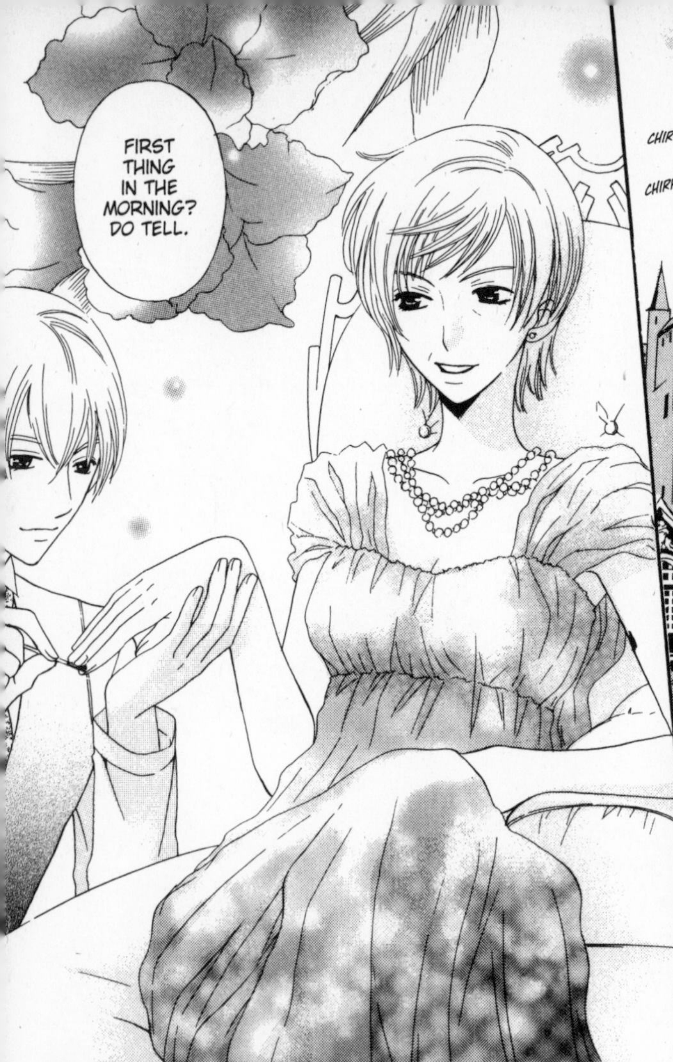
FIRST THING IN THE MORNING? DO TELL.

Masaya Kiyomi (age 22)

Birthday: March 13th

Blood Type: AB

Hobbies: 24-hour horror flick marathons

Favorite Food: Curry and rice

He has a super negative mindset and always carries a cloud over him. But under it all, he's dazzlingly beautiful.

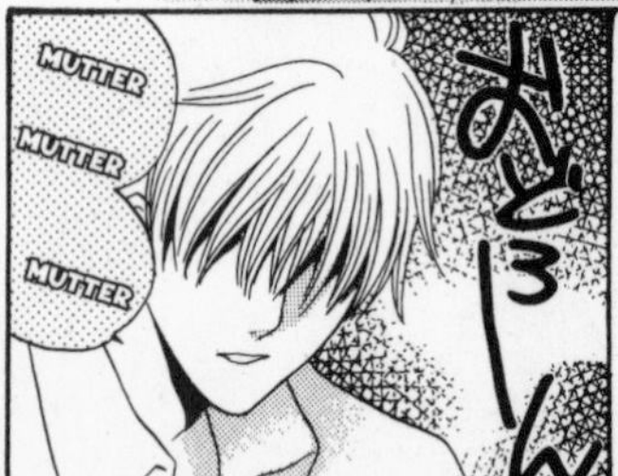
MUTTER
MUTTER
MUTTER
どよ〜ん
GLOOM

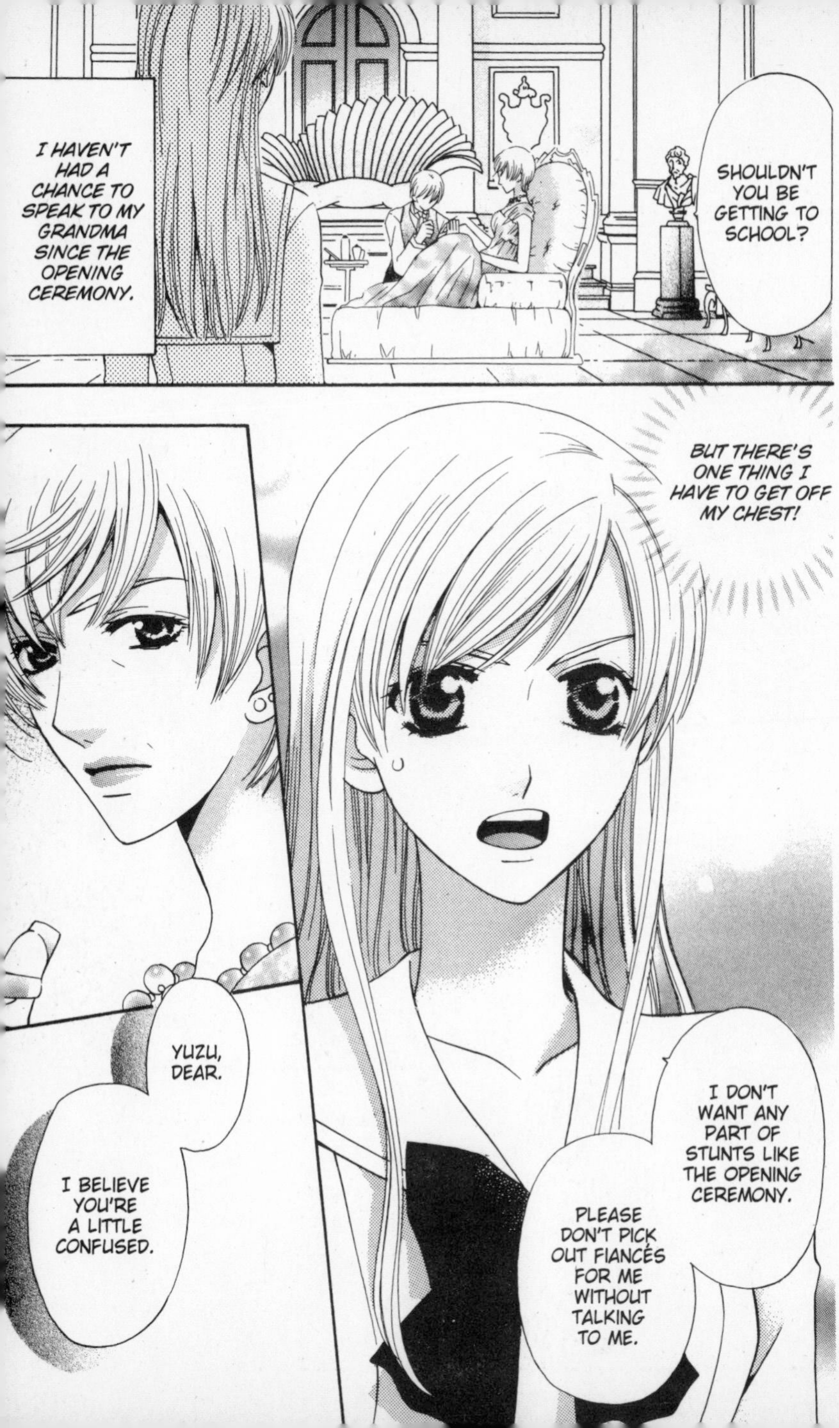
SHOULDN'T YOU BE GETTING TO SCHOOL?
I HAVEN'T HAD A CHANCE TO SPEAK TO MY GRANDMA SINCE THE OPENING CEREMONY.
BUT THERE'S ONE THING I HAVE TO GET OFF MY CHEST!
I DON'T WANT ANY PART OF STUNTS LIKE THE OPENING CEREMONY.
PLEASE DON'T PICK OUT FIANCÉS FOR ME WITHOUT TALKING TO ME.
YUZU, DEAR.
I BELIEVE YOU'RE A LITTLE CONFUSED.

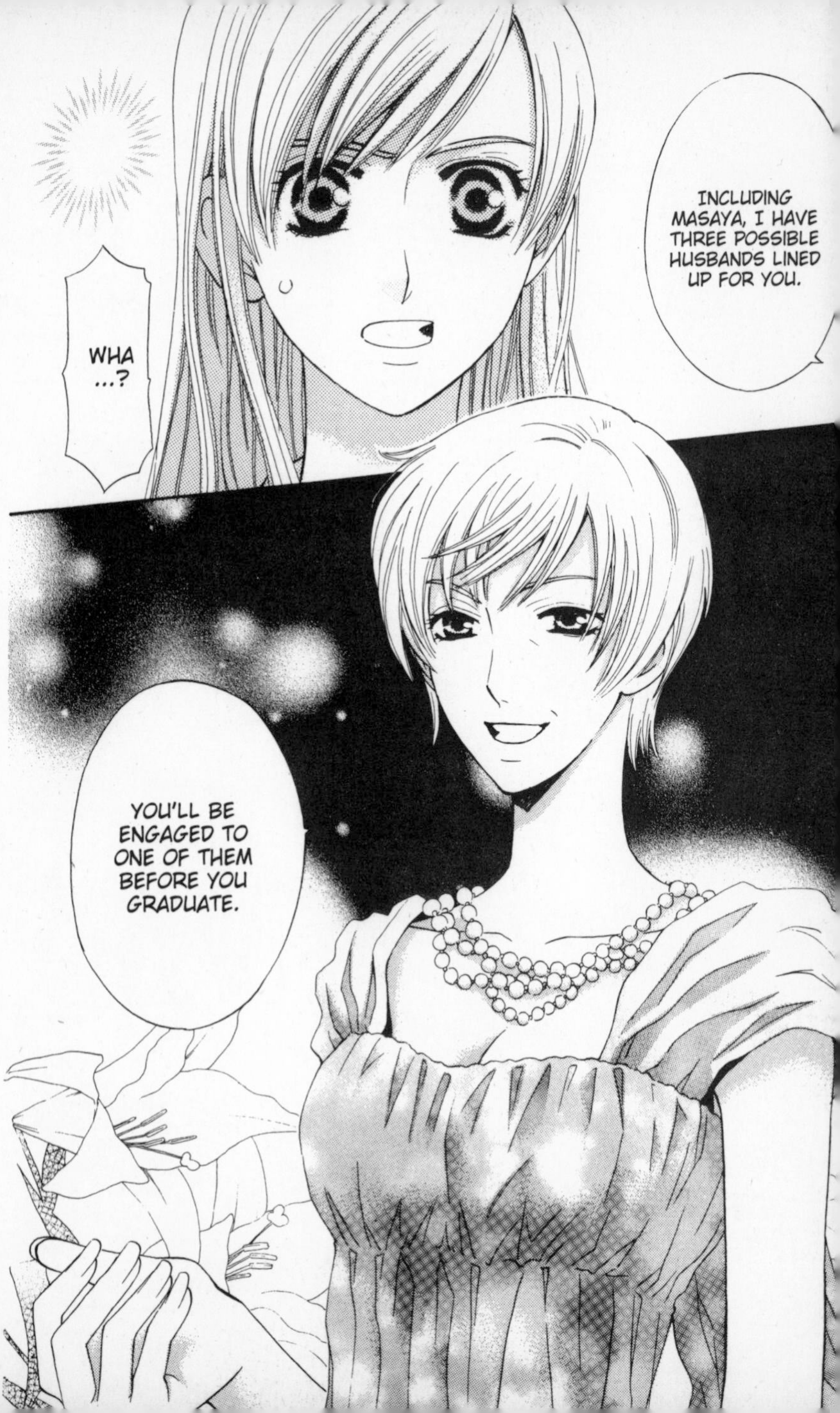
INCLUDING MASAYA, I HAVE THREE POSSIBLE HUSBANDS LINED UP FOR YOU.
WHA ...?
YOU'LL BE ENGAGED TO ONE OF THEM BEFORE YOU GRADUATE.

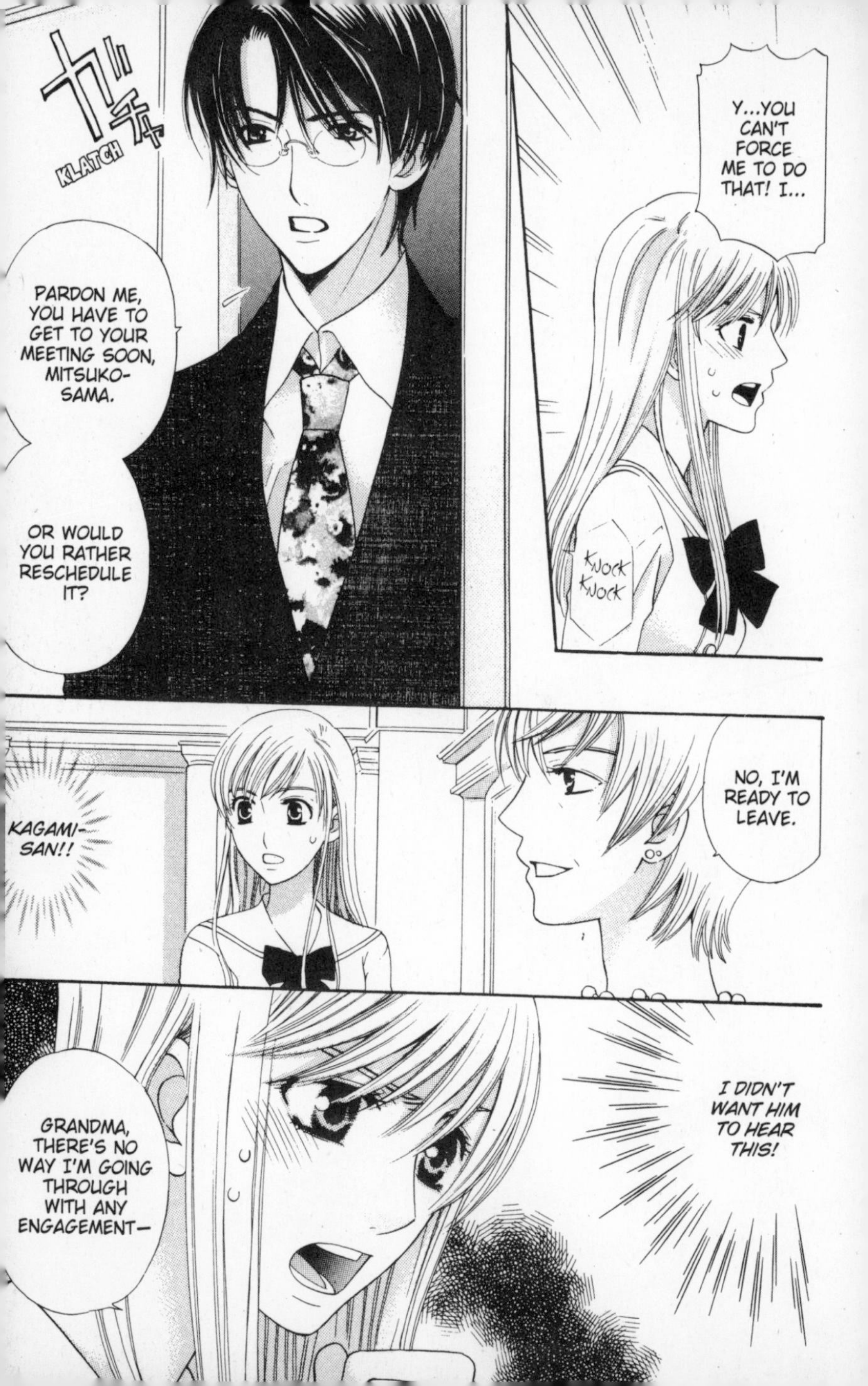
Y...YOU CAN'T FORCE ME TO DO THAT! I...
KNOCK KNOCK
KLATCH
PARDON ME, YOU HAVE TO GET TO YOUR MEETING SOON, MITSUKO-SAMA.
OR WOULD YOU RATHER RESCHEDULE IT?
NO, I'M READY TO LEAVE.
KAGAMI-SAN!!
I DIDN'T WANT HIM TO HEAR THIS!
GRANDMA, THERE'S NO WAY I'M GOING THROUGH WITH ANY ENGAGEMENT—

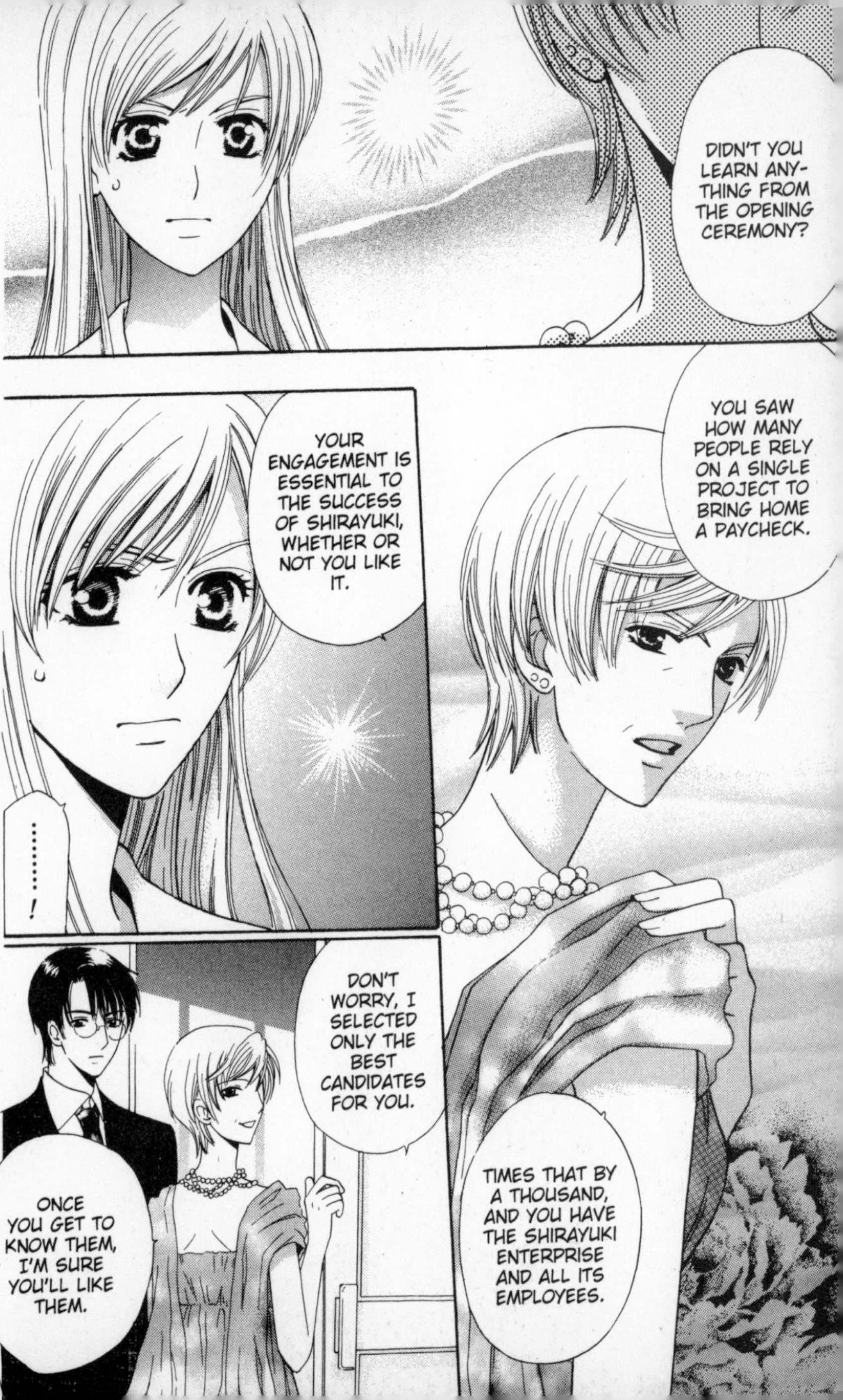
DIDN'T YOU LEARN ANY-THING FROM THE OPENING CEREMONY?
YOU SAW HOW MANY PEOPLE RELY ON A SINGLE PROJECT TO BRING HOME A PAYCHECK.
TIMES THAT BY A THOUSAND, AND YOU HAVE THE SHIRAYUKI ENTERPRISE AND ALL ITS EMPLOYEES.
YOUR ENGAGEMENT IS ESSENTIAL TO THE SUCCESS OF SHIRAYUKI, WHETHER OR NOT YOU LIKE IT.
......!
DON'T WORRY, I SELECTED ONLY THE BEST CANDIDATES FOR YOU.
ONCE YOU GET TO KNOW THEM, I'M SURE YOU'LL LIKE THEM.

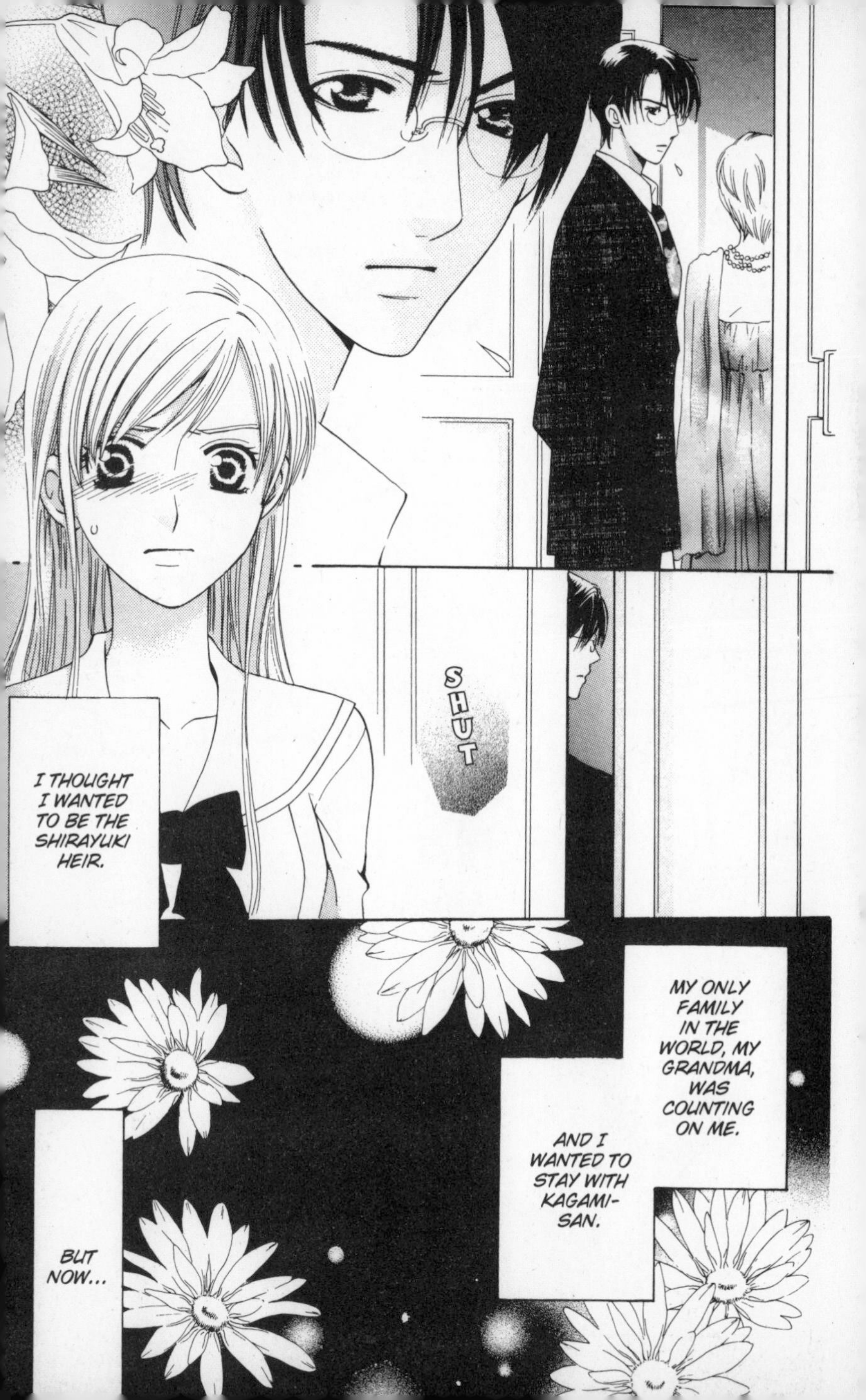
SHUT
I THOUGHT I WANTED TO BE THE SHIRAYUKI HEIR.
MY ONLY FAMILY IN THE WORLD, MY GRANDMA, WAS COUNTING ON ME.
AND I WANTED TO STAY WITH KAGAMI-SAN.
BUT NOW...

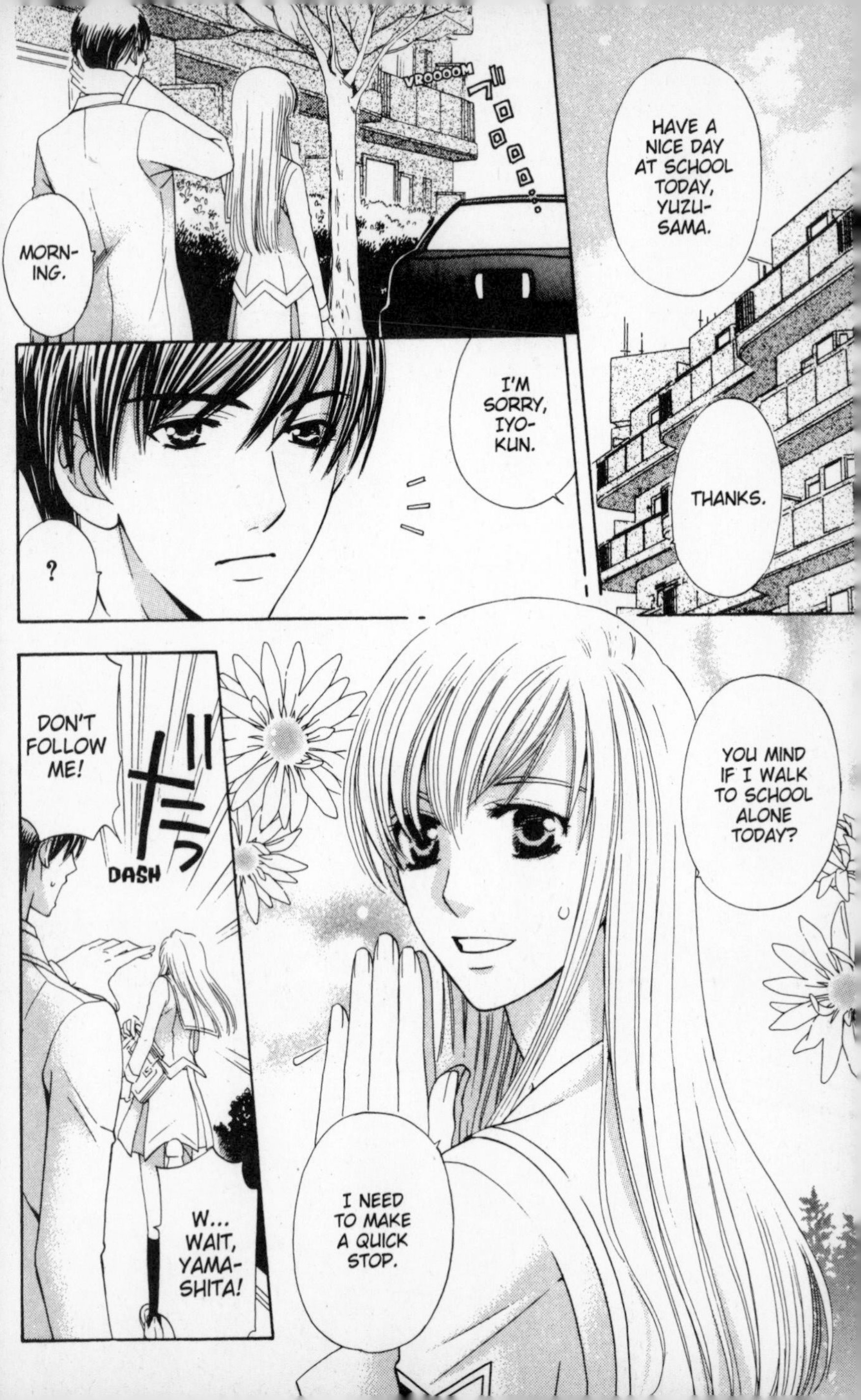
HAVE A NICE DAY AT SCHOOL TODAY, YUZU-SAMA.
THANKS.
VROOOOM
MORN-ING.
I'M SORRY, IYO-KUN.
?
YOU MIND IF I WALK TO SCHOOL ALONE TODAY?
I NEED TO MAKE A QUICK STOP.
DON'T FOLLOW ME!
DASH
W... WAIT, YAMA-SHITA!

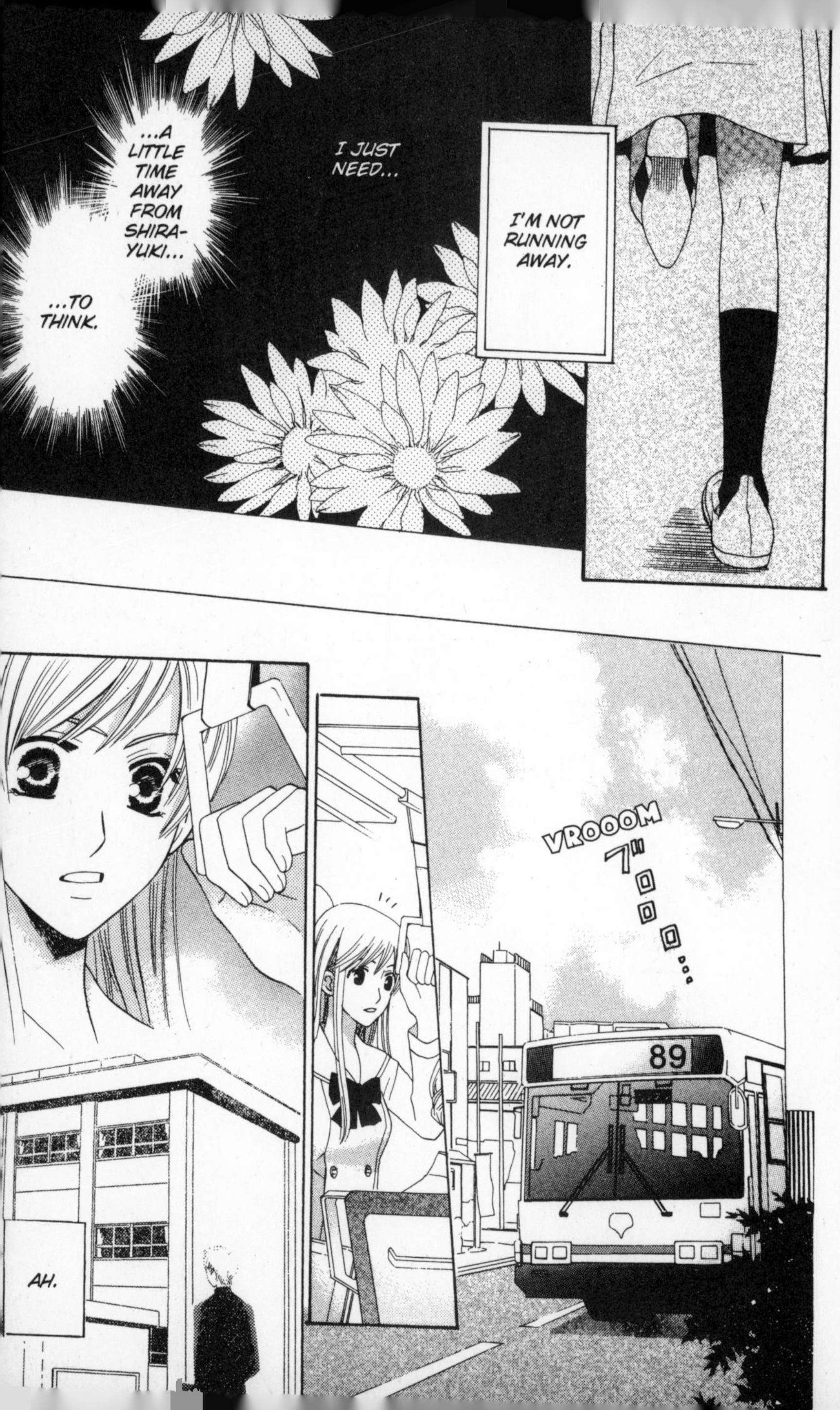
I'M NOT RUNNING AWAY.
I JUST NEED...
...A LITTLE TIME AWAY FROM SHIRA-YUKI...
...TO THINK.
VROOOM
ブロロロ...
89
AH.

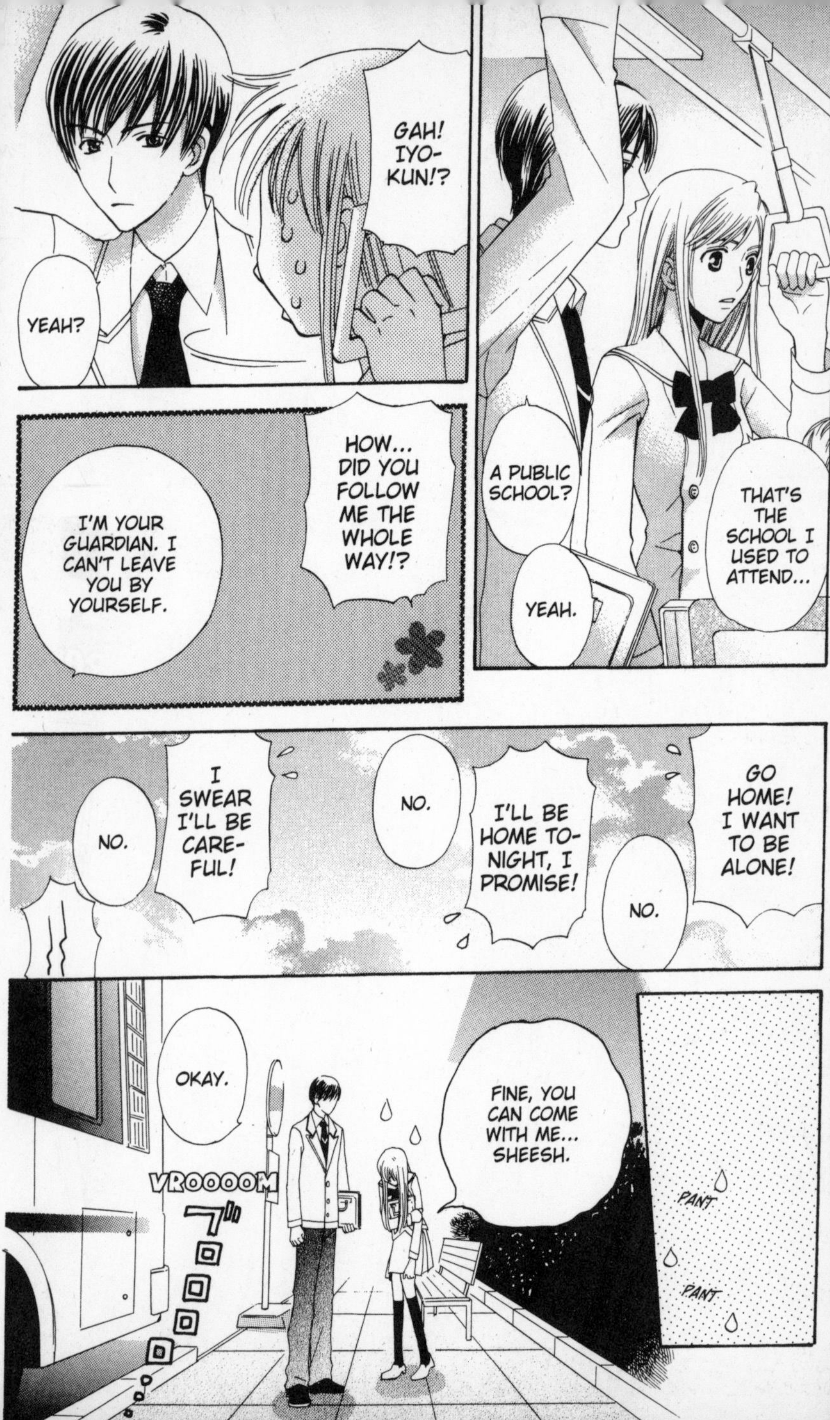
A PUBLIC SCHOOL?
THAT'S THE SCHOOL I USED TO ATTEND...
YEAH.
GAH! IYO-KUN!?
YEAH?
HOW... DID YOU FOLLOW ME THE WHOLE WAY!?
I'M YOUR GUARDIAN. I CAN'T LEAVE YOU BY YOURSELF.
GO HOME! I WANT TO BE ALONE!
NO.
I'LL BE HOME TO-NIGHT, I PROMISE!
NO.
I SWEAR I'LL BE CARE-FUL!
NO.
PANT
PANT
FINE, YOU CAN COME WITH ME... SHEESH.
OKAY.
VROOOOM

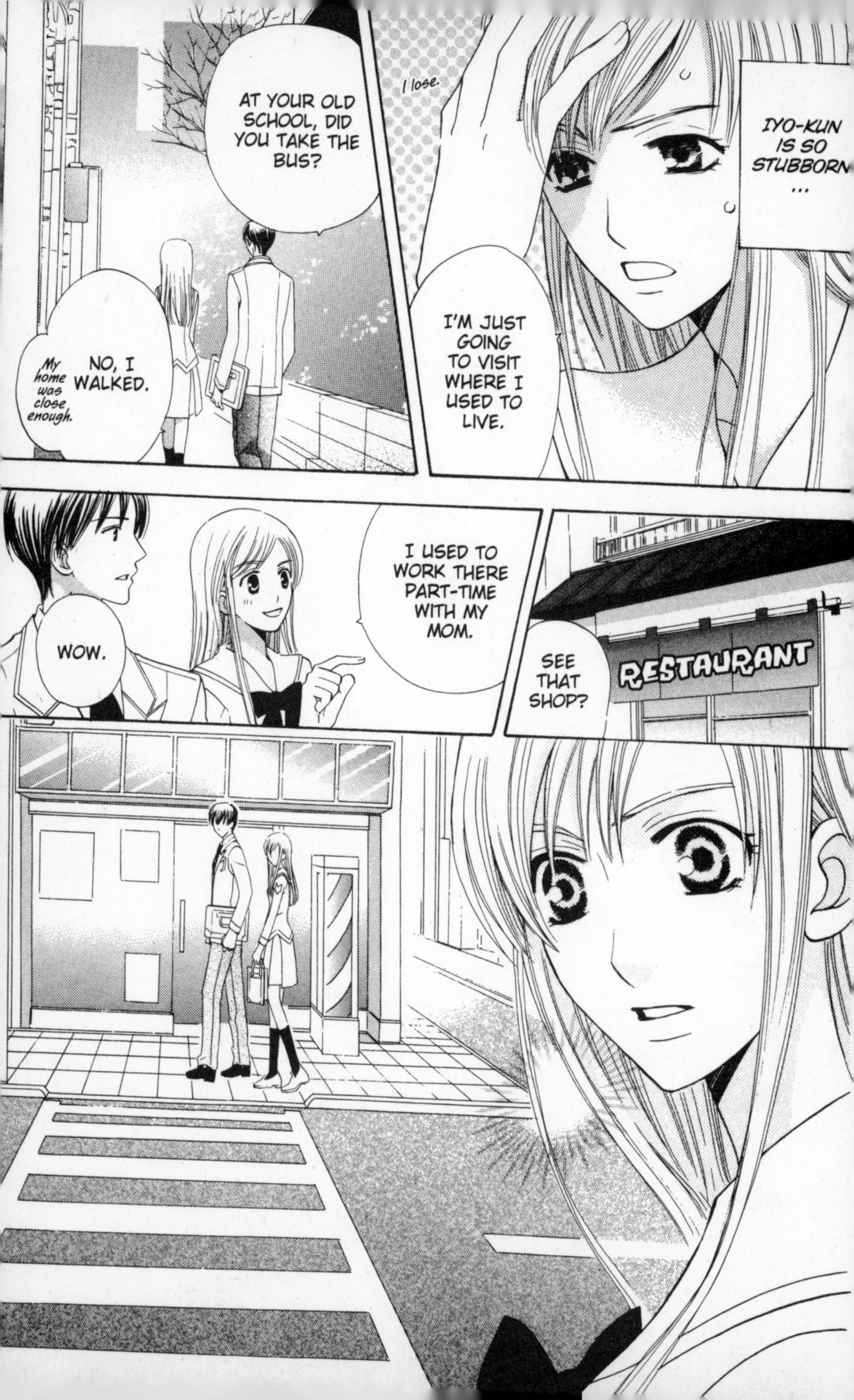

IYO-KUN IS SO STUBBORN...
I lose.
I'M JUST GOING TO VISIT WHERE I USED TO LIVE.
AT YOUR OLD SCHOOL, DID YOU TAKE THE BUS?
NO, I WALKED.
My home was close enough.
SEE THAT SHOP?
RESTAURANT
I USED TO WORK THERE PART-TIME WITH MY MOM.
WOW.

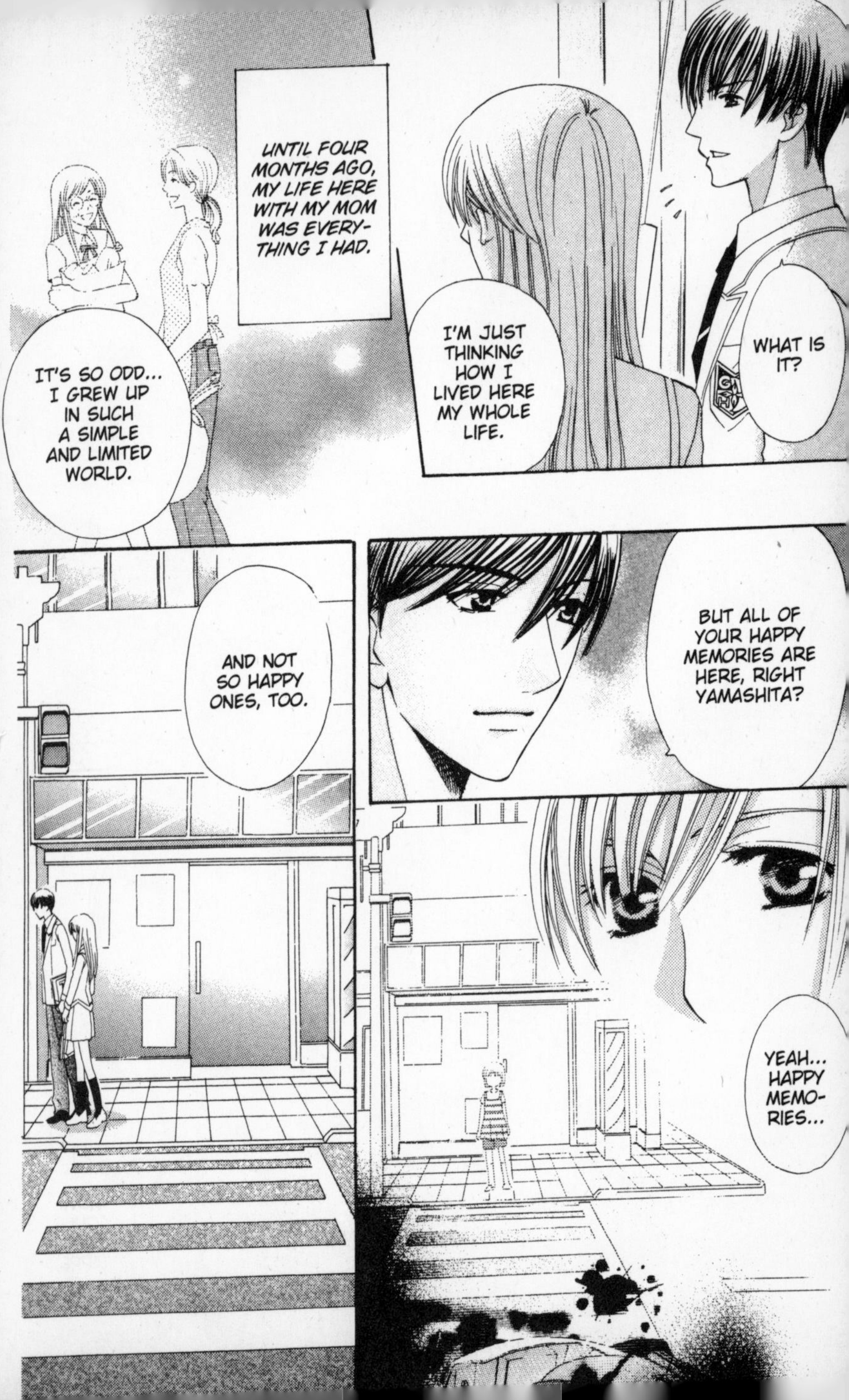
WHAT IS IT?
I'M JUST THINKING HOW I LIVED HERE MY WHOLE LIFE.
UNTIL FOUR MONTHS AGO, MY LIFE HERE WITH MY MOM WAS EVERY-THING I HAD.
IT'S SO ODD... I GREW UP IN SUCH A SIMPLE AND LIMITED WORLD.
BUT ALL OF YOUR HAPPY MEMORIES ARE HERE, RIGHT YAMASHITA?
YEAH... HAPPY MEMO-RIES...
AND NOT SO HAPPY ONES, TOO.

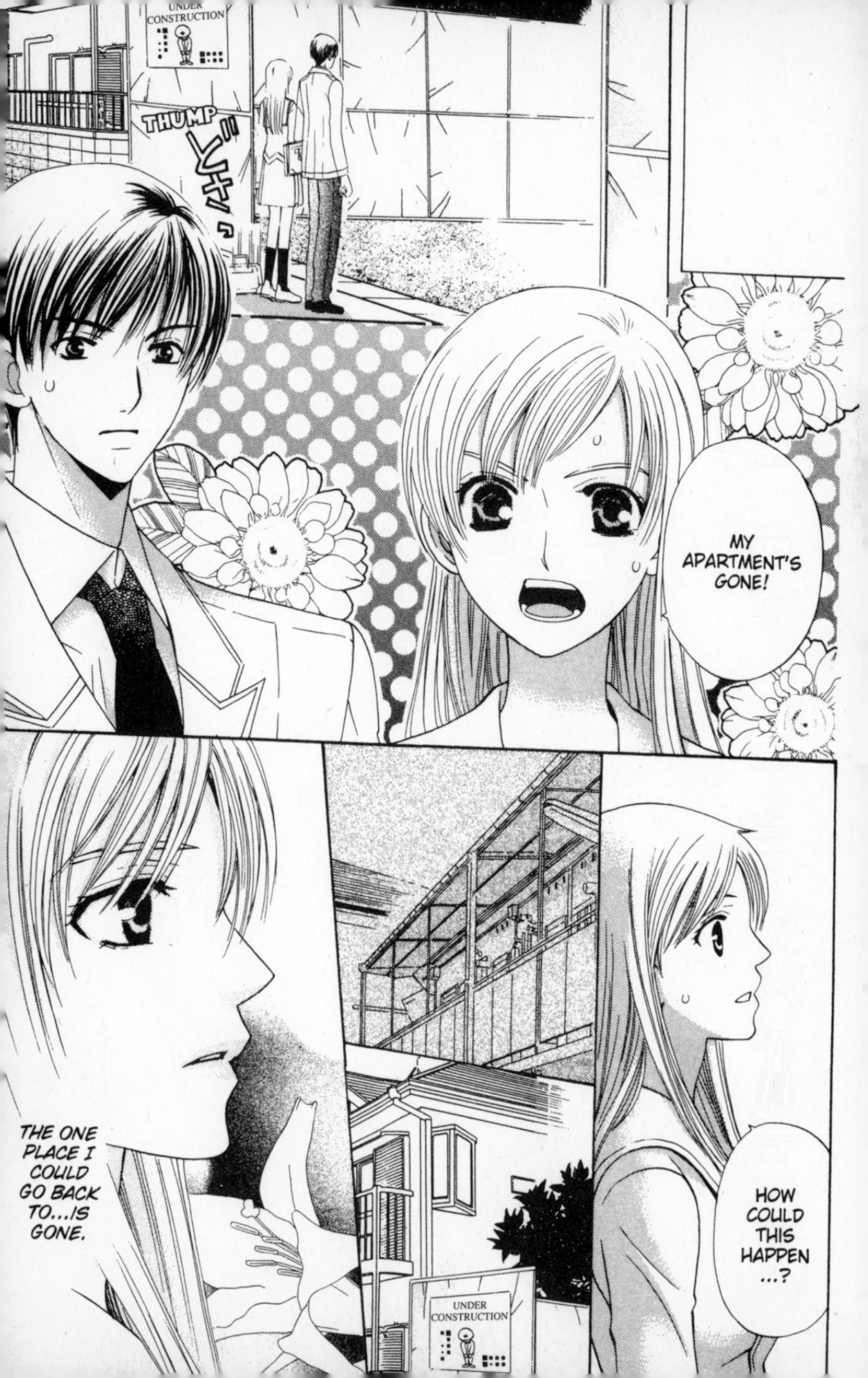
UNDER CONSTRUCTION
THUMP
MY APARTMENT'S GONE!
HOW COULD THIS HAPPEN ...?
UNDER CONSTRUCTION
THE ONE PLACE I COULD GO BACK TO...IS GONE.

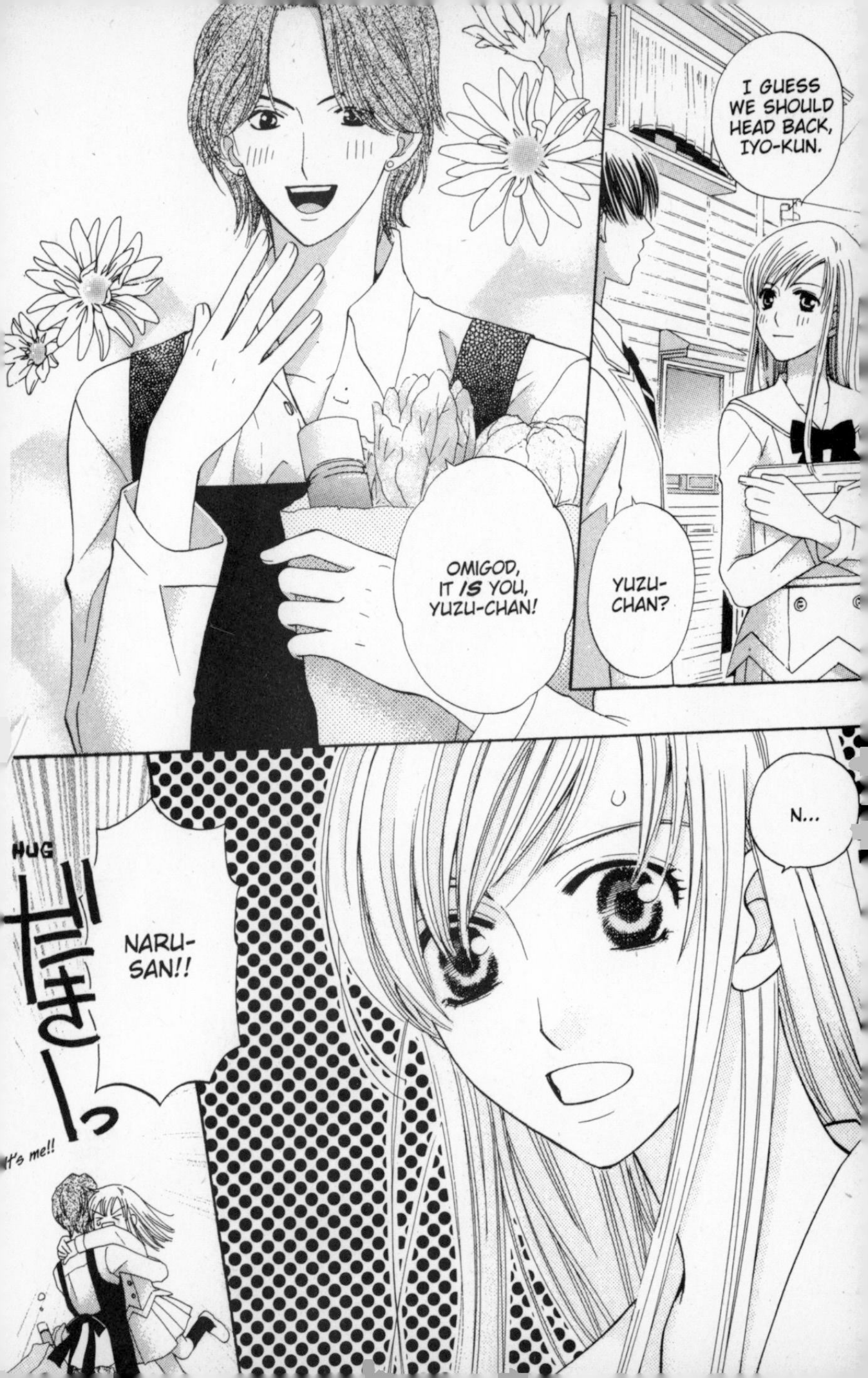
I GUESS WE SHOULD HEAD BACK, IYO-KUN.
YUZU-CHAN?
OMIGOD, IT *IS* YOU, YUZU-CHAN!
N...
NARU-SAN!!
HUG
It's me!!

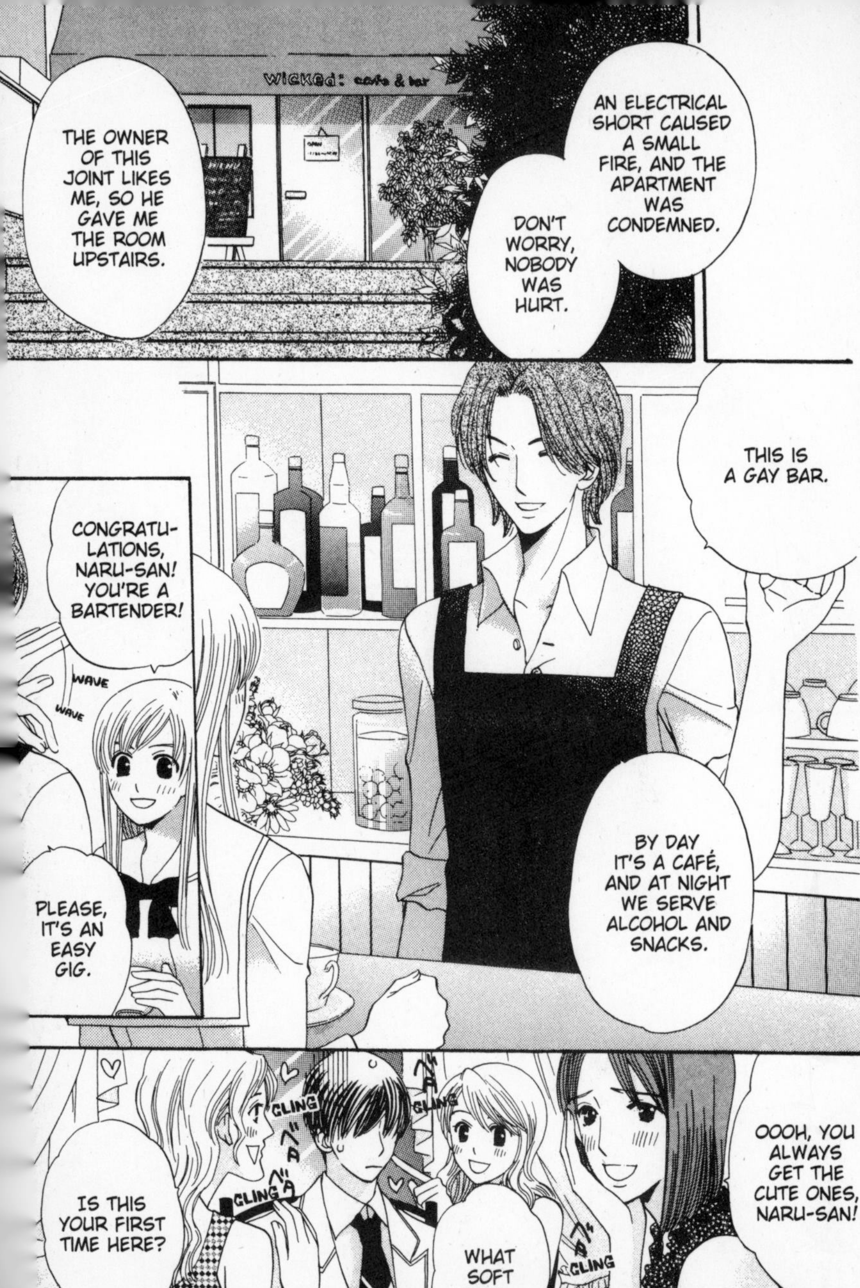
wicked: cafe & bar
AN ELECTRICAL SHORT CAUSED A SMALL FIRE, AND THE APARTMENT WAS CONDEMNED.
DON'T WORRY, NOBODY WAS HURT.
THE OWNER OF THIS JOINT LIKES ME, SO HE GAVE ME THE ROOM UPSTAIRS.
THIS IS A GAY BAR.
BY DAY IT'S A CAFÉ, AND AT NIGHT WE SERVE ALCOHOL AND SNACKS.
CONGRATULATIONS, NARU-SAN! YOU'RE A BARTENDER!
WAVE
WAVE
PLEASE, IT'S AN EASY GIG.
OOOH, YOU ALWAYS GET THE CUTE ONES, NARU-SAN!
CLING
CLING
WHAT SOFT SKIN...
CLING
CLING
IS THIS YOUR FIRST TIME HERE?

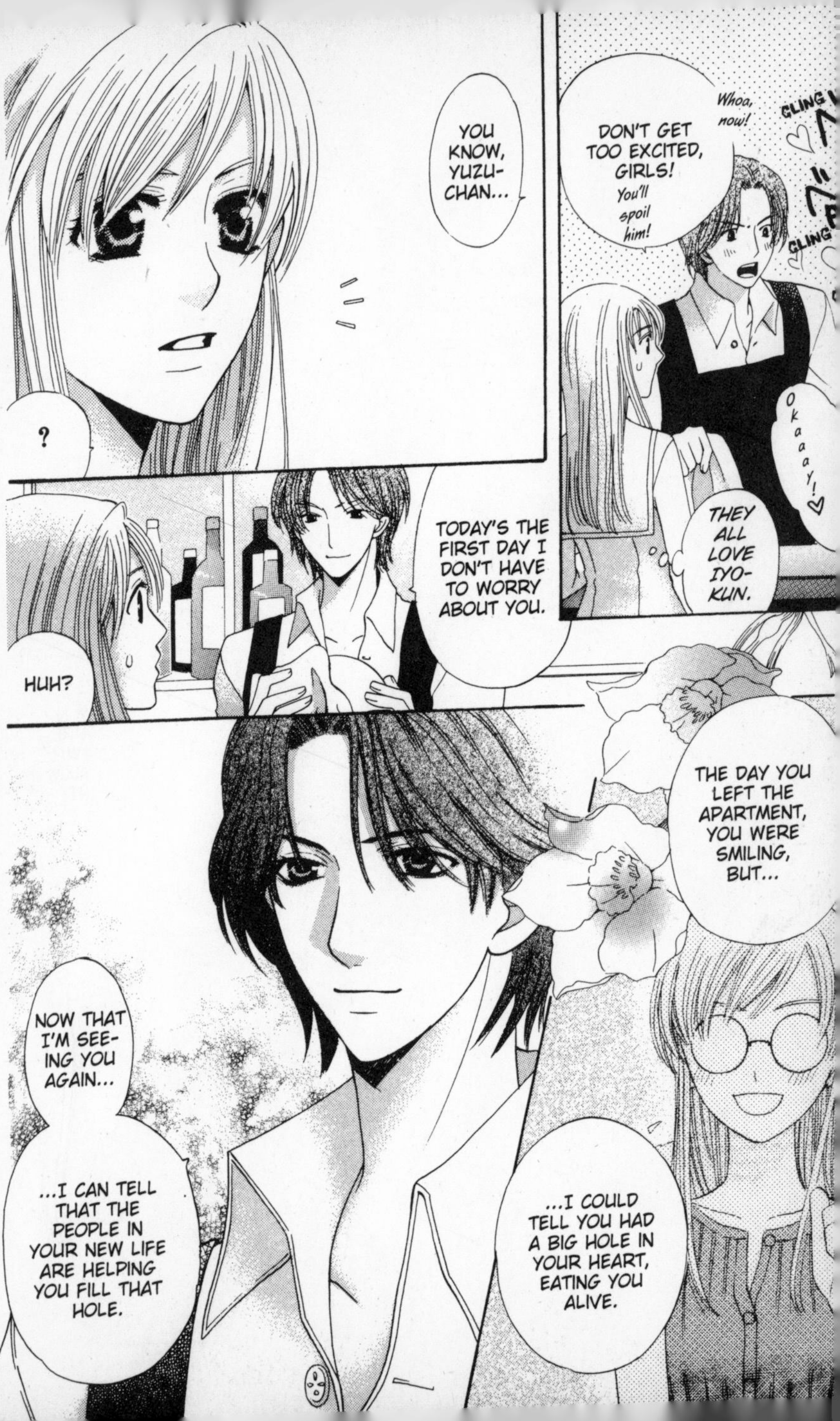
Whoa, now!
DON'T GET TOO EXCITED, GIRLS! You'll spoil him!
CLING
CLING
Okaaay!♥
THEY ALL LOVE IYO-KUN.
YOU KNOW, YUZU-CHAN...
?
TODAY'S THE FIRST DAY I DON'T HAVE TO WORRY ABOUT YOU.
HUH?
THE DAY YOU LEFT THE APARTMENT, YOU WERE SMILING, BUT...
...I COULD TELL YOU HAD A BIG HOLE IN YOUR HEART, EATING YOU ALIVE.
NOW THAT I'M SEEING YOU AGAIN...
...I CAN TELL THAT THE PEOPLE IN YOUR NEW LIFE ARE HELPING YOU FILL THAT HOLE.

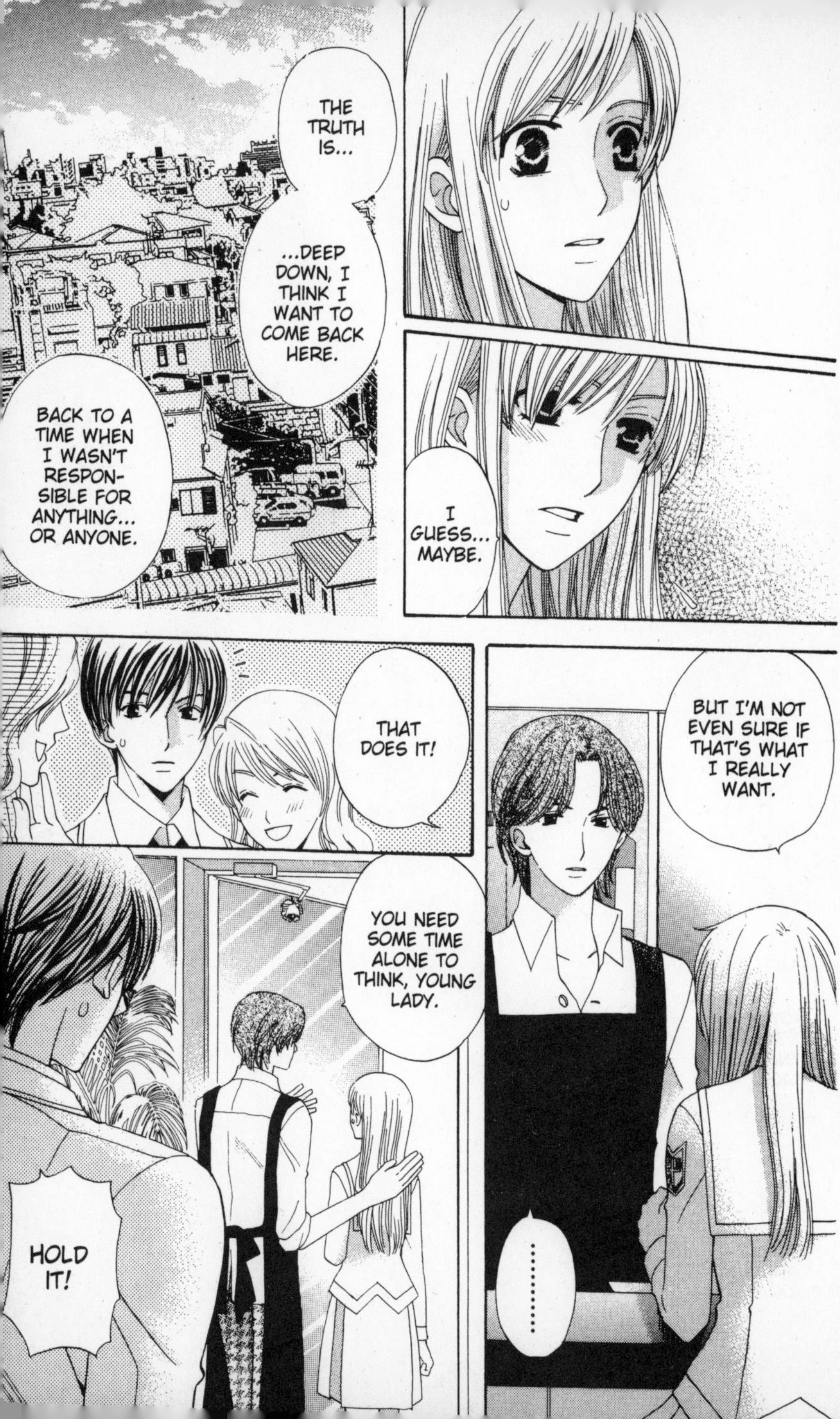
I GUESS... MAYBE.
THE TRUTH IS...
...DEEP DOWN, I THINK I WANT TO COME BACK HERE.
BACK TO A TIME WHEN I WASN'T RESPONSIBLE FOR ANYTHING... OR ANYONE.
BUT I'M NOT EVEN SURE IF THAT'S WHAT I REALLY WANT.
......
THAT DOES IT!
YOU NEED SOME TIME ALONE TO THINK, YOUNG LADY.
HOLD IT!

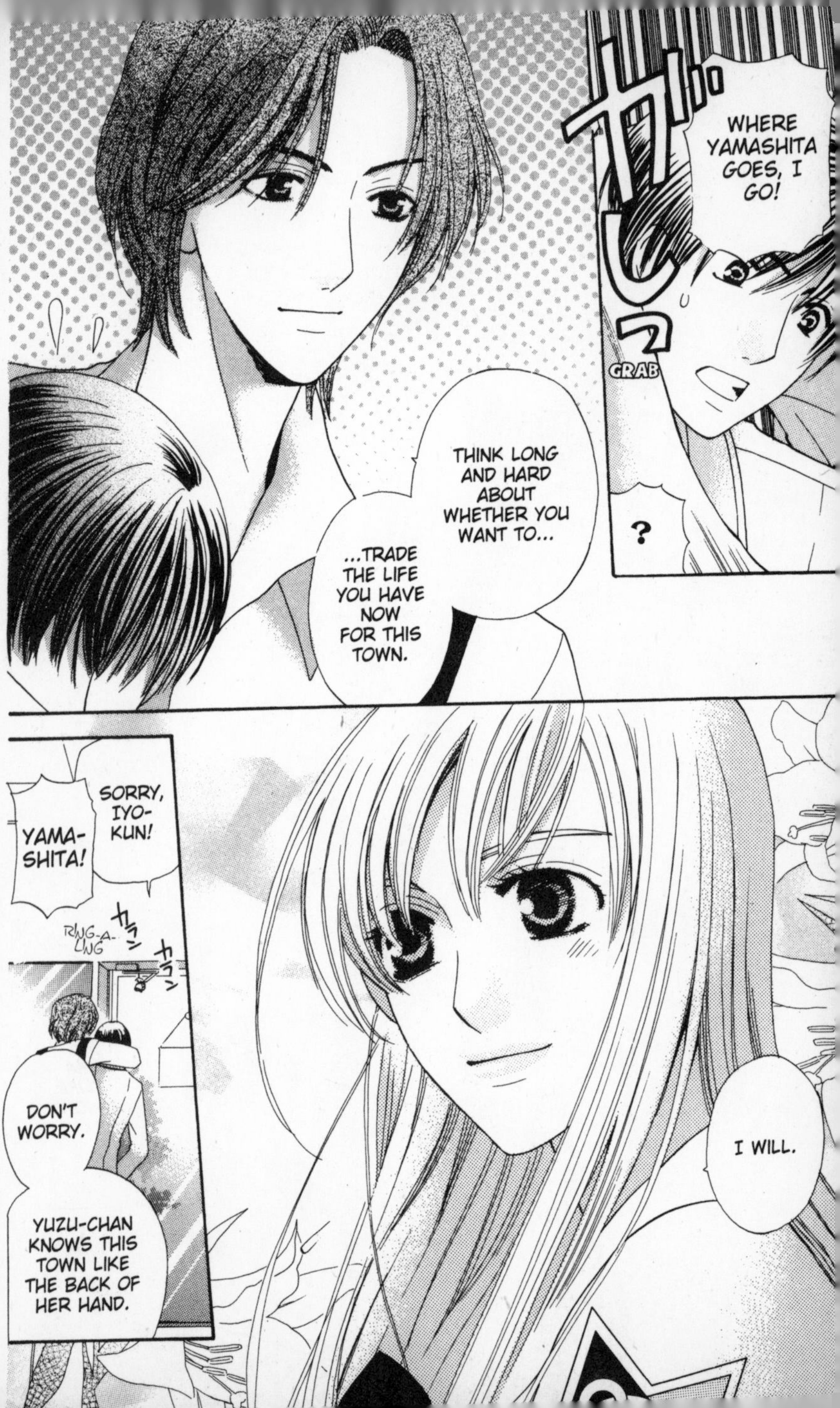
WHERE YAMASHITA GOES, I GO!
GRAB
?
THINK LONG AND HARD ABOUT WHETHER YOU WANT TO...
...TRADE THE LIFE YOU HAVE NOW FOR THIS TOWN.
I WILL.
SORRY, IYO-KUN!
YAMA-SHITA!
RING-A-LING
DON'T WORRY.
YUZU-CHAN KNOWS THIS TOWN LIKE THE BACK OF HER HAND.

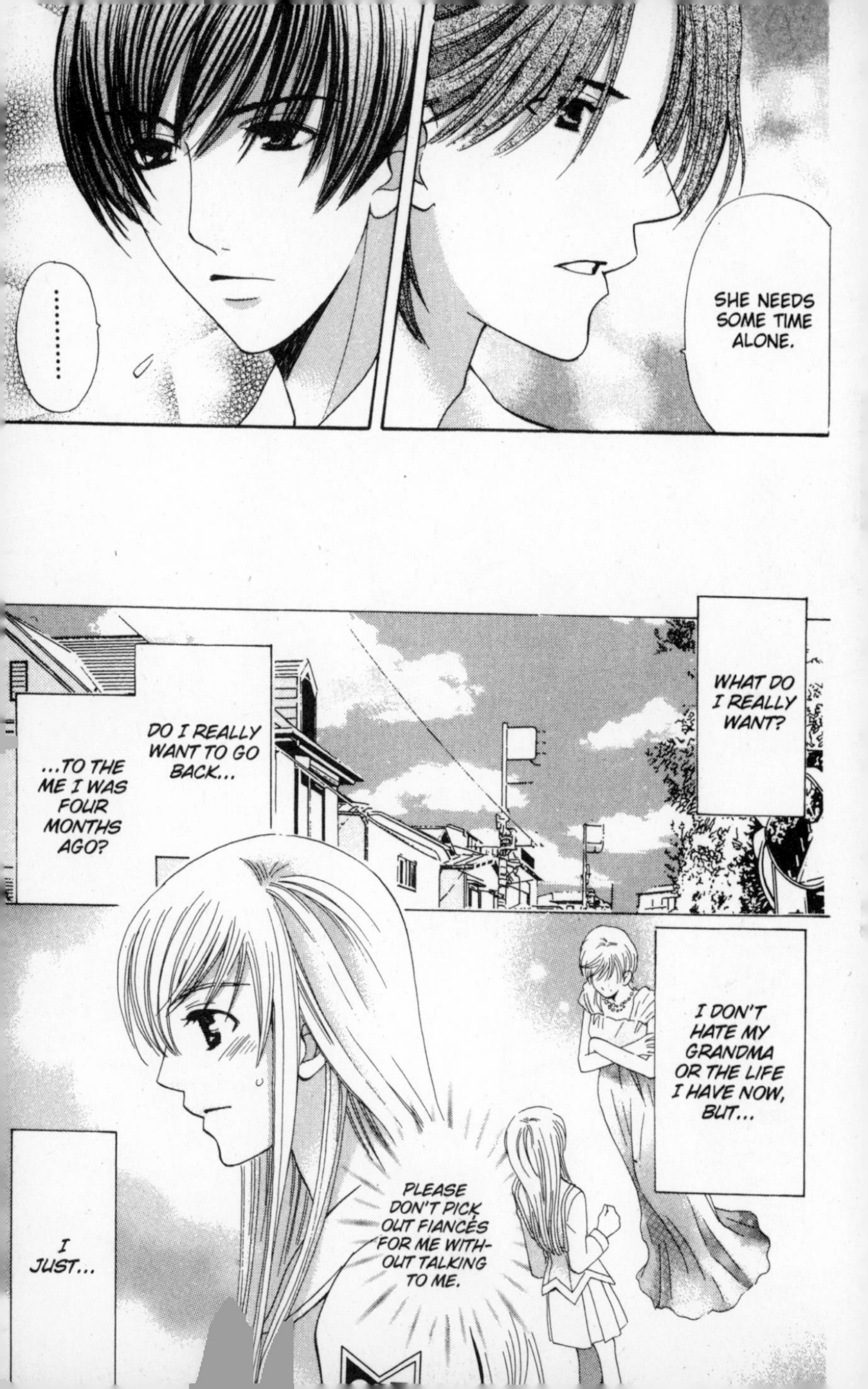
SHE NEEDS SOME TIME ALONE.
......
WHAT DO I REALLY WANT?
DO I REALLY WANT TO GO BACK...
...TO THE ME I WAS FOUR MONTHS AGO?
I DON'T HATE MY GRANDMA OR THE LIFE I HAVE NOW, BUT...
PLEASE DON'T PICK OUT FIANCÉS FOR ME WITH-OUT TALKING TO ME.
I JUST...

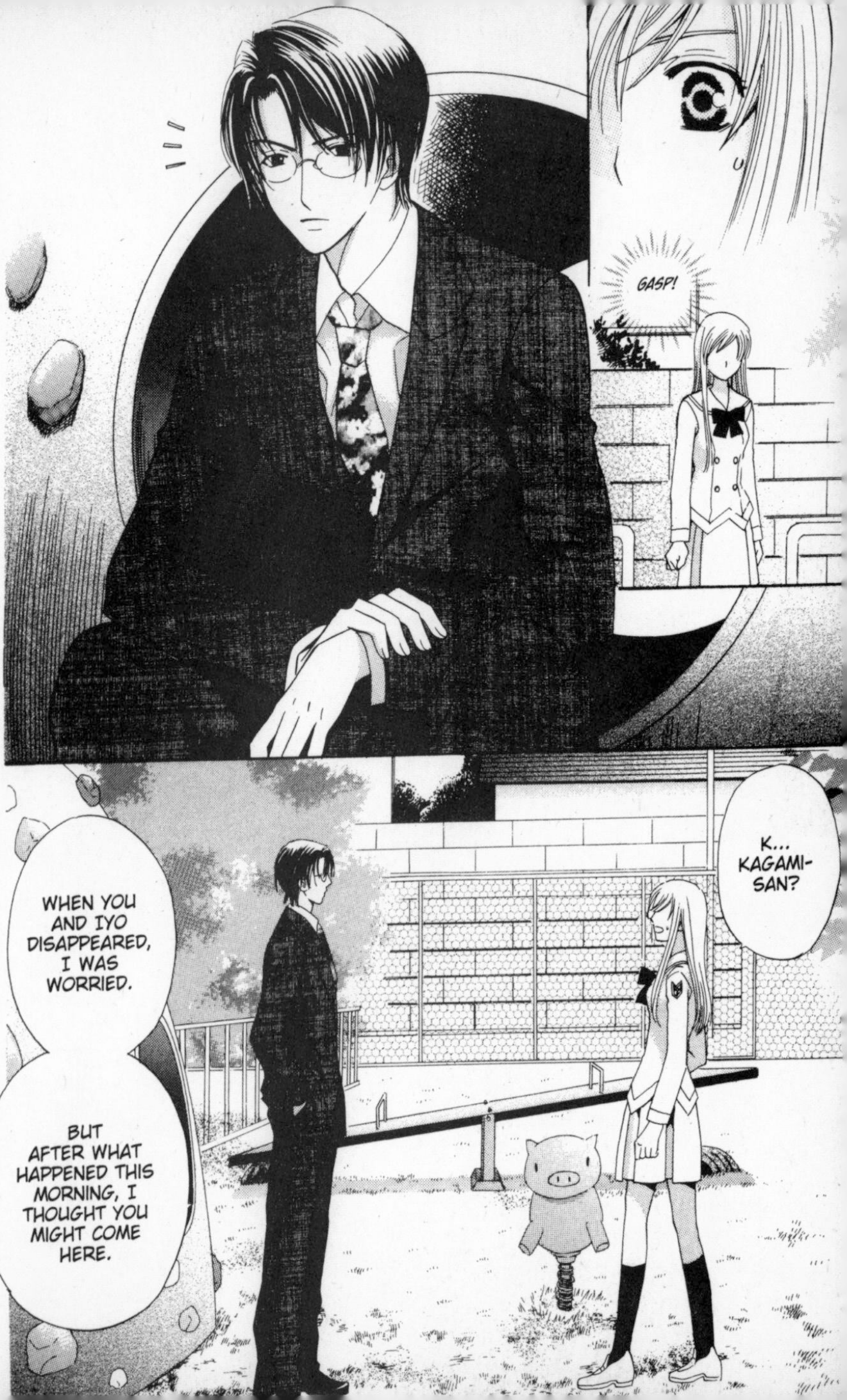
GASP!
K... KAGAMI-SAN?
WHEN YOU AND IYO DISAPPEARED, I WAS WORRIED.
BUT AFTER WHAT HAPPENED THIS MORNING, I THOUGHT YOU MIGHT COME HERE.

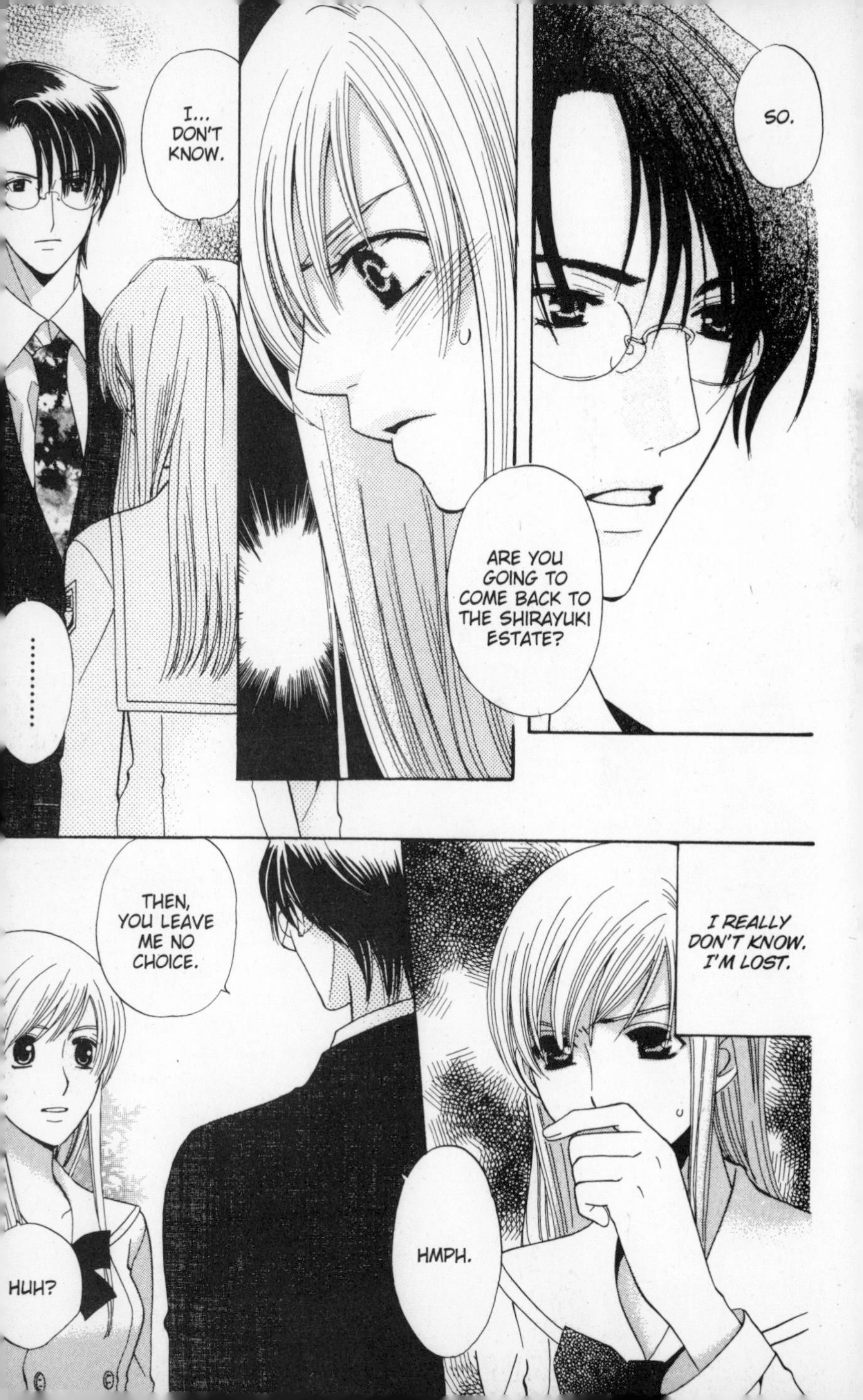
SO.
ARE YOU GOING TO COME BACK TO THE SHIRAYUKI ESTATE?
I... DON'T KNOW.
....
I REALLY DON'T KNOW. I'M LOST.
HMPH.
THEN, YOU LEAVE ME NO CHOICE.
HUH?

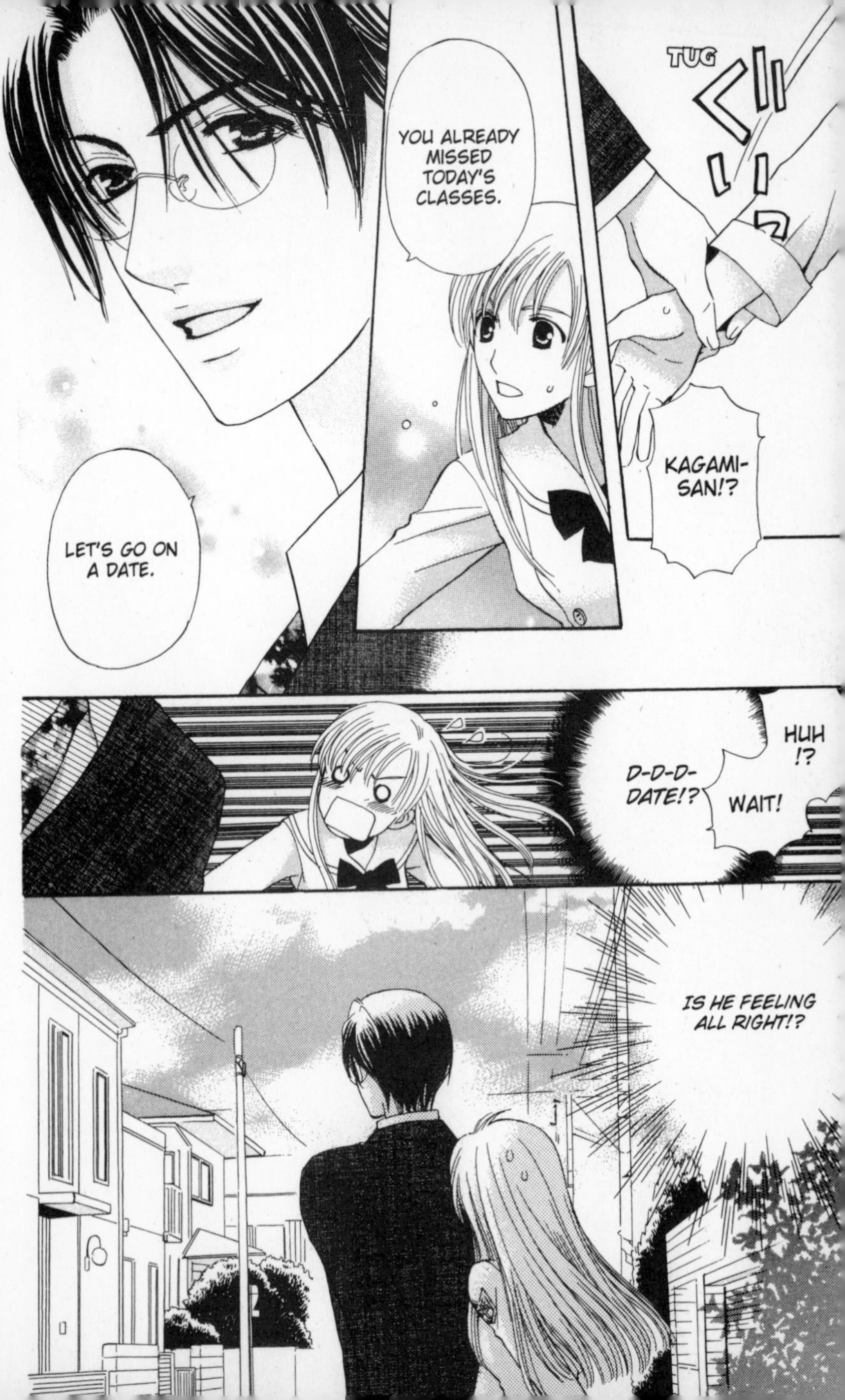
TUG
YOU ALREADY MISSED TODAY'S CLASSES.
KAGAMI-SAN!?
LET'S GO ON A DATE.
HUH!?
WAIT!
D-D-D-DATE!?
IS HE FEELING ALL RIGHT!?

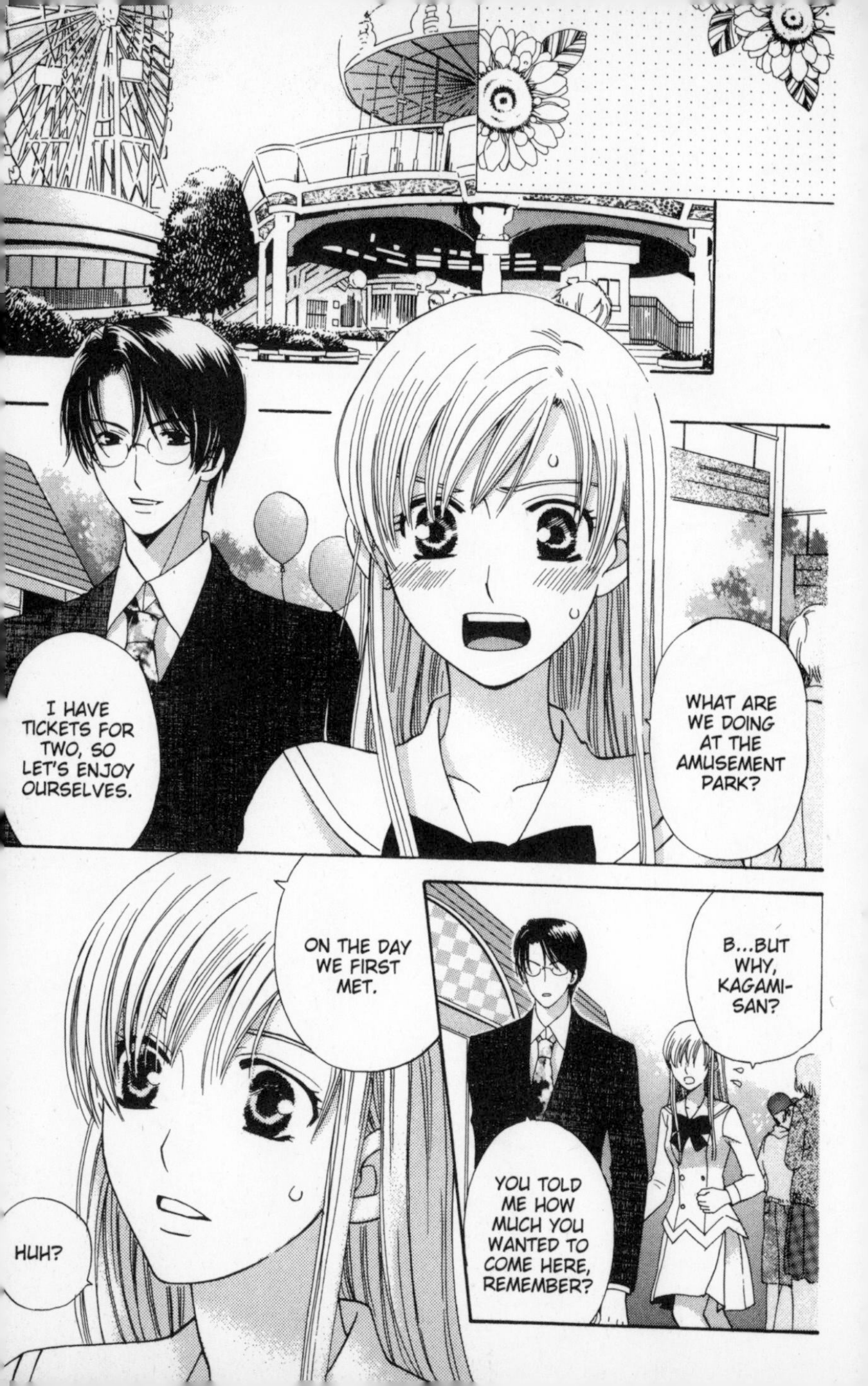
WHAT ARE WE DOING AT THE AMUSEMENT PARK?
I HAVE TICKETS FOR TWO, SO LET'S ENJOY OURSELVES.
B...BUT WHY, KAGAMI-SAN?
YOU TOLD ME HOW MUCH YOU WANTED TO COME HERE, REMEMBER?
ON THE DAY WE FIRST MET.
HUH?

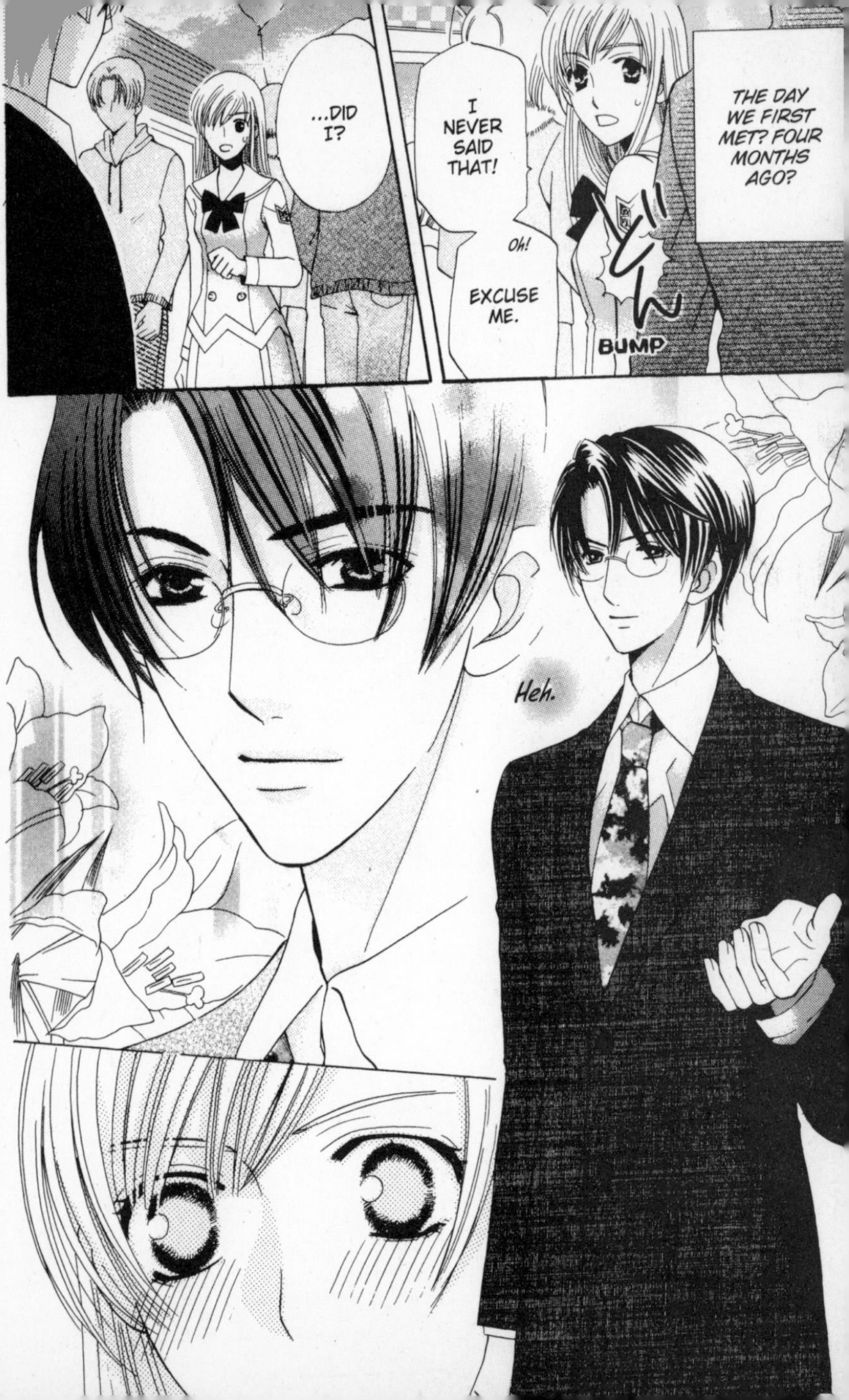
THE DAY WE FIRST MET? FOUR MONTHS AGO?
I NEVER SAID THAT!
BUMP
Oh!
EXCUSE ME.
...DID I?
Heh.

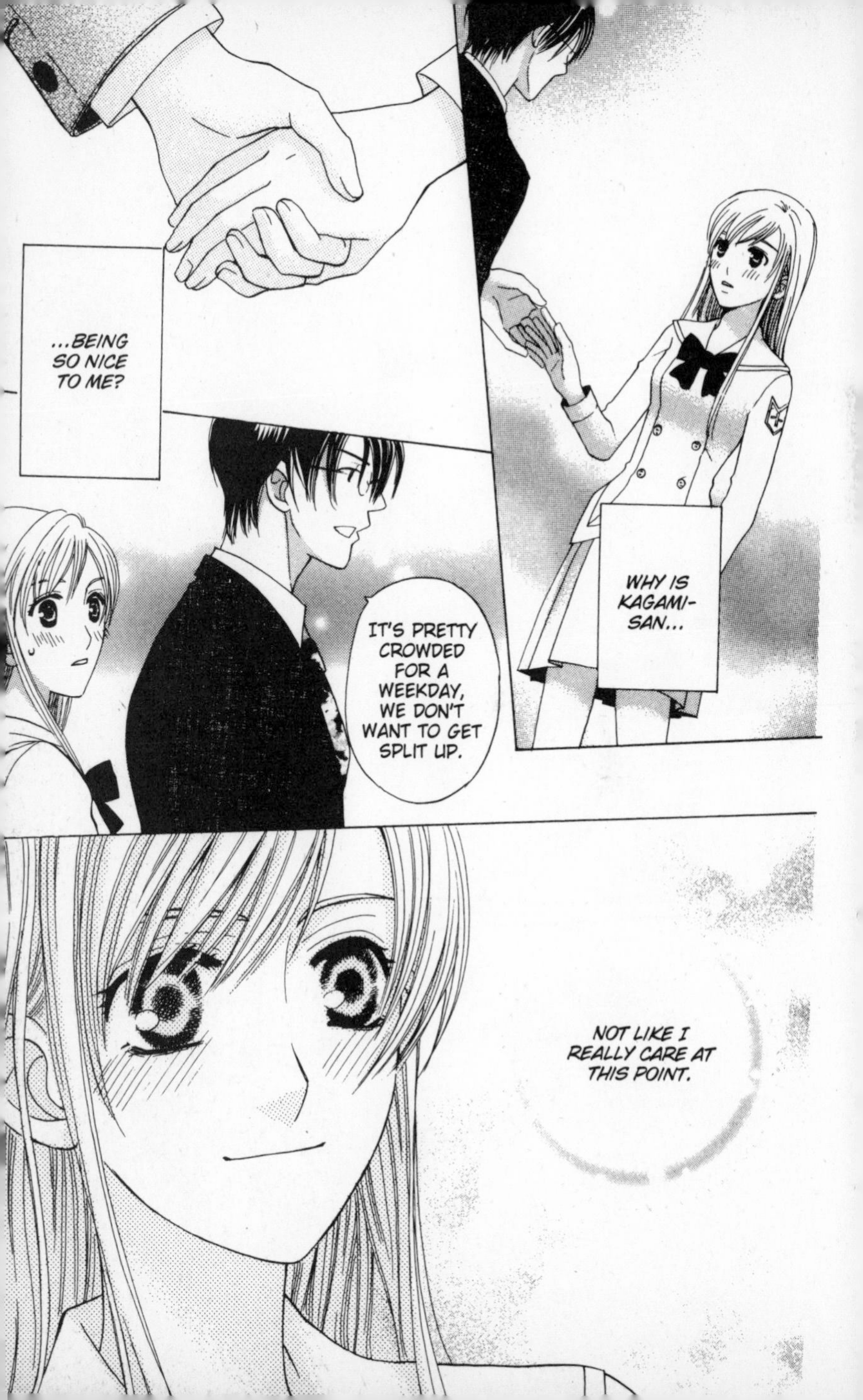
WHY IS KAGAMI-SAN...
...BEING SO NICE TO ME?
IT'S PRETTY CROWDED FOR A WEEKDAY, WE DON'T WANT TO GET SPLIT UP.
NOT LIKE I REALLY CARE AT THIS POINT.

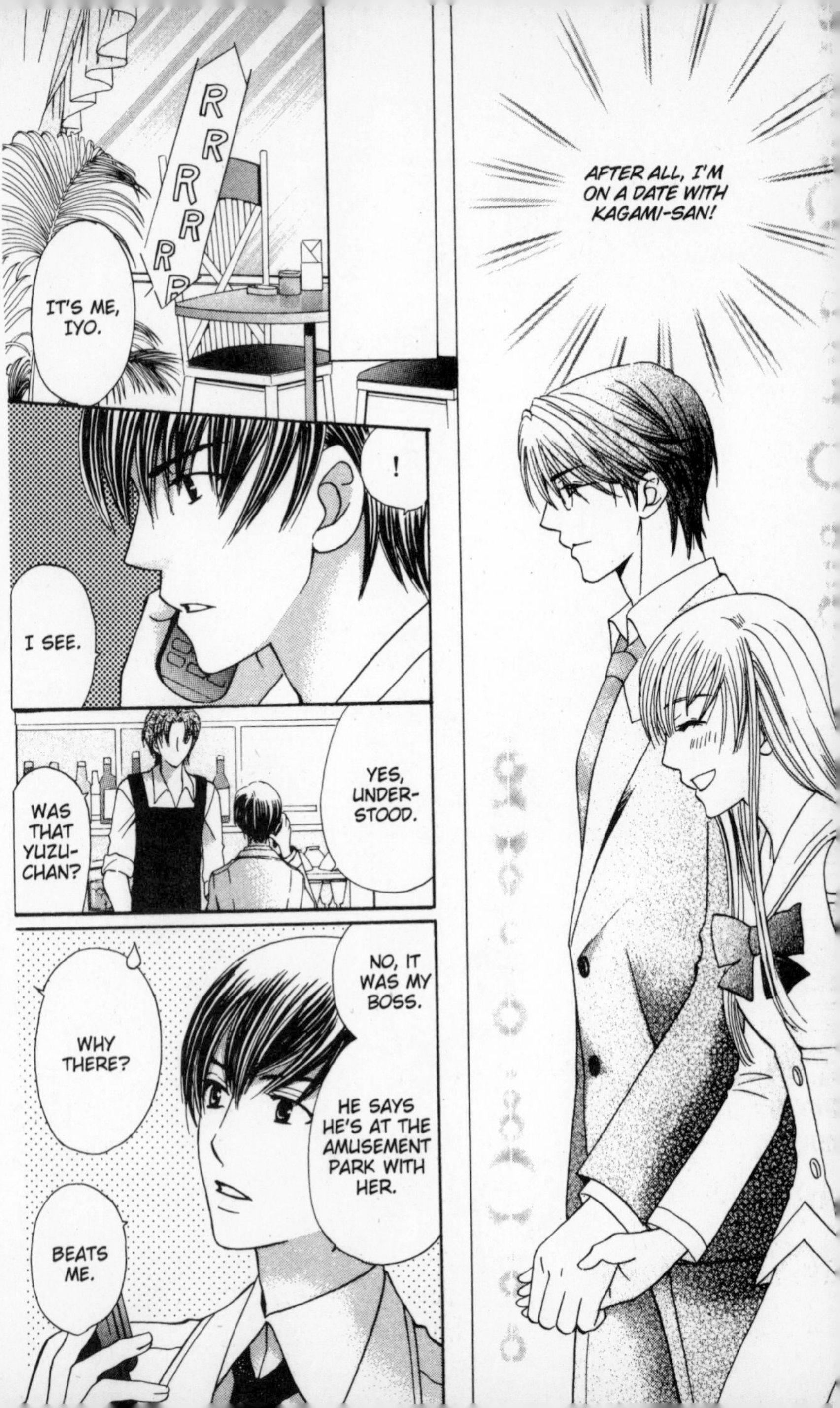
AFTER ALL, I'M ON A DATE WITH KAGAMI-SAN!
RRRRRR
IT'S ME, IYO.
!
I SEE.
YES, UNDER-STOOD.
WAS THAT YUZU-CHAN?
NO, IT WAS MY BOSS.
HE SAYS HE'S AT THE AMUSEMENT PARK WITH HER.
WHY THERE?
BEATS ME.

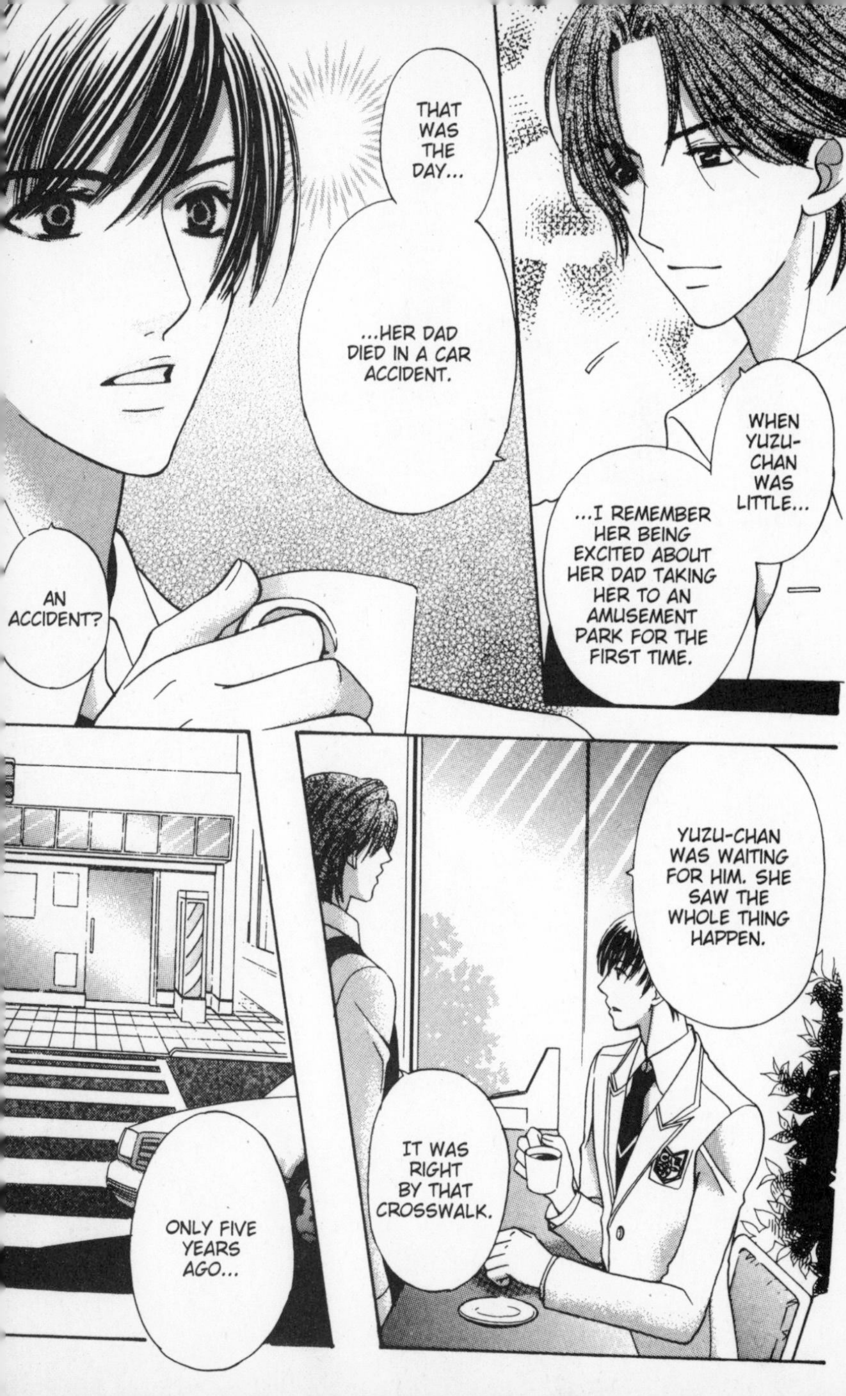
WHEN YUZU-CHAN WAS LITTLE...
...I REMEMBER HER BEING EXCITED ABOUT HER DAD TAKING HER TO AN AMUSEMENT PARK FOR THE FIRST TIME.
THAT WAS THE DAY...
...HER DAD DIED IN A CAR ACCIDENT.
AN ACCIDENT?
YUZU-CHAN WAS WAITING FOR HIM. SHE SAW THE WHOLE THING HAPPEN.
IT WAS RIGHT BY THAT CROSSWALK.
ONLY FIVE YEARS AGO...

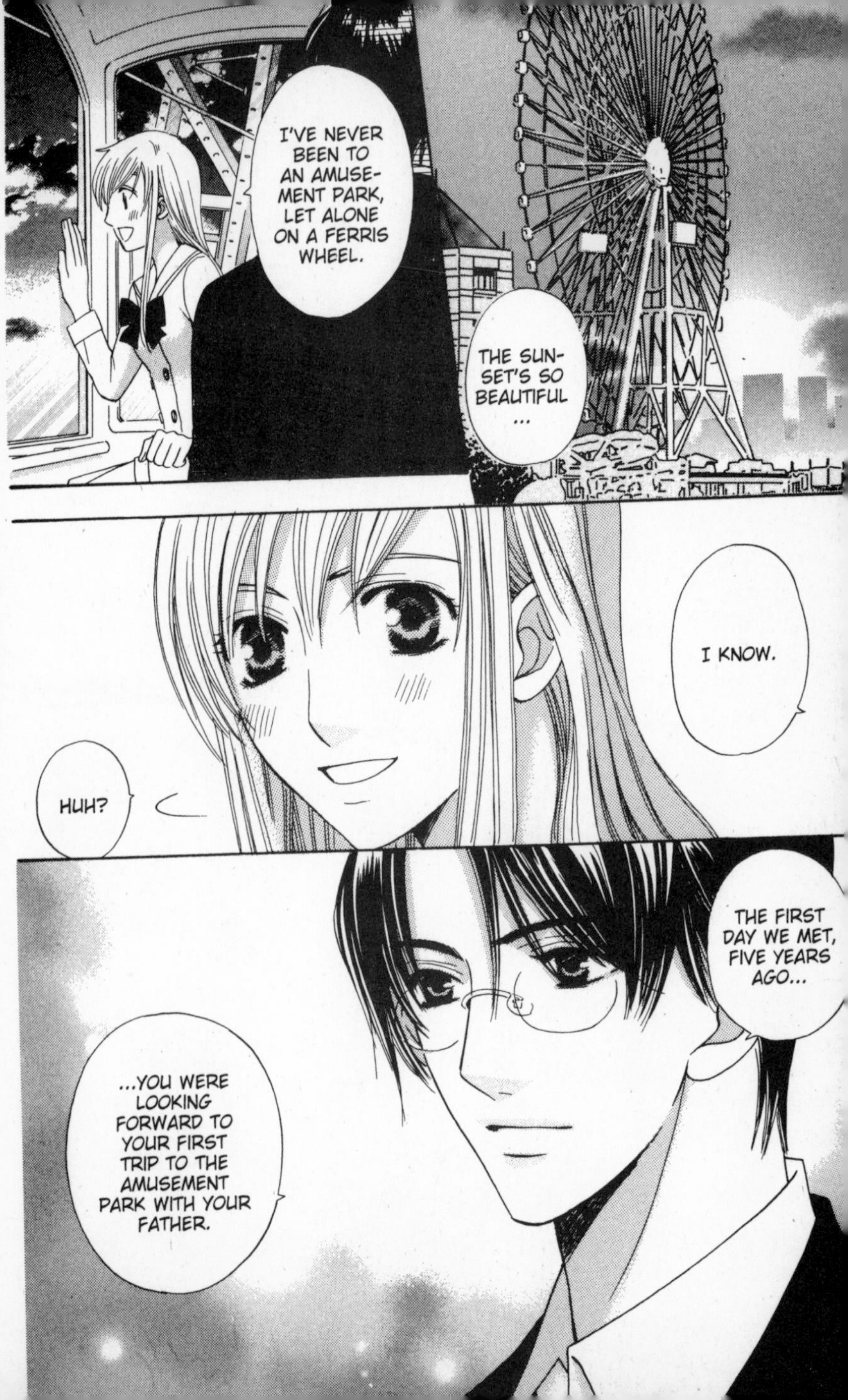
I'VE NEVER BEEN TO AN AMUSEMENT PARK, LET ALONE ON A FERRIS WHEEL.
THE SUNSET'S SO BEAUTIFUL ...
I KNOW.
HUH?
THE FIRST DAY WE MET, FIVE YEARS AGO...
...YOU WERE LOOKING FORWARD TO YOUR FIRST TRIP TO THE AMUSEMENT PARK WITH YOUR FATHER.

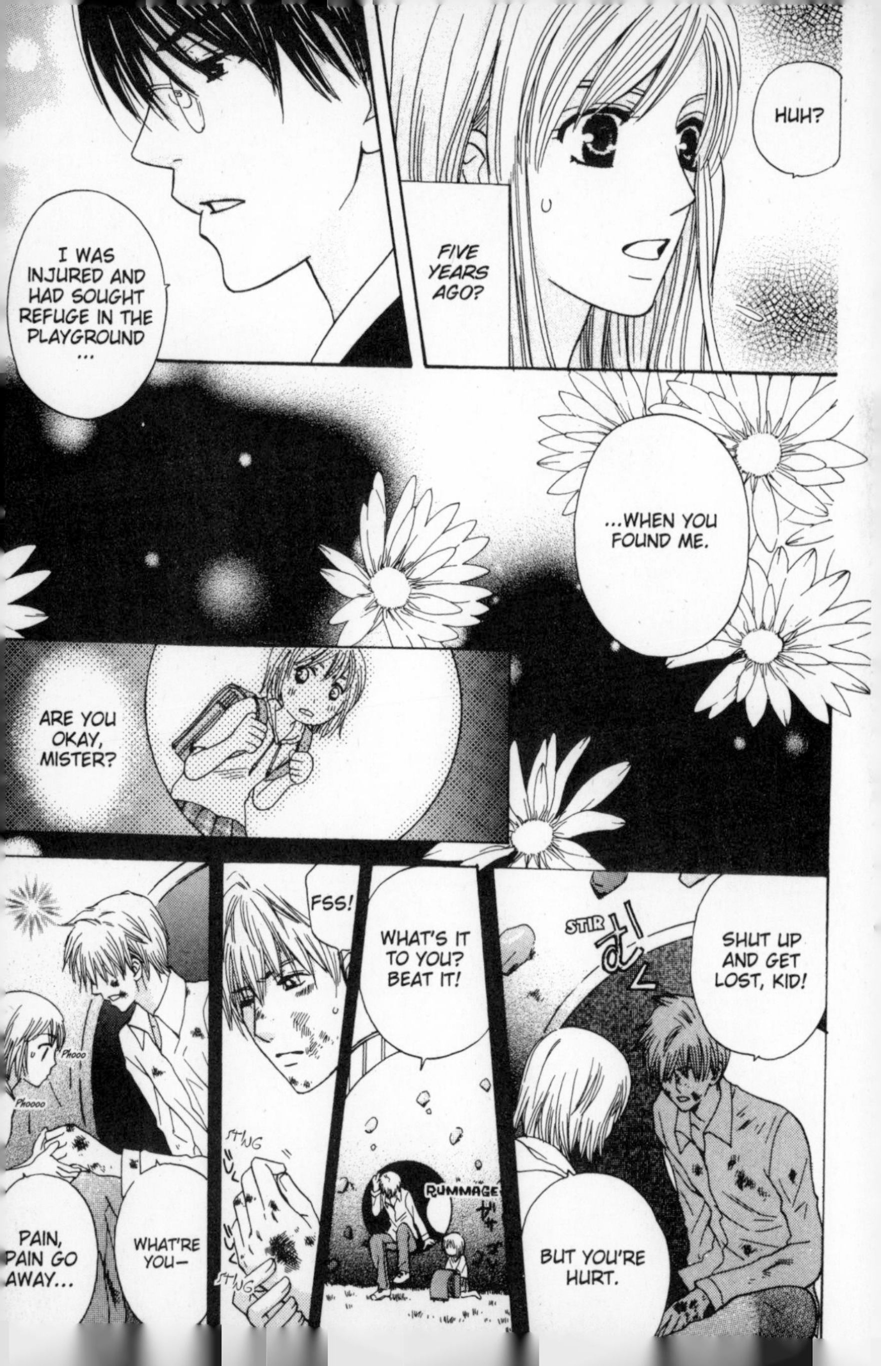
HUH?
FIVE YEARS AGO?
I WAS INJURED AND HAD SOUGHT REFUGE IN THE PLAYGROUND ...
...WHEN YOU FOUND ME.
ARE YOU OKAY, MISTER?
STIR
SHUT UP AND GET LOST, KID!
BUT YOU'RE HURT.
RUMMAGE
WHAT'S IT TO YOU? BEAT IT!
FSS!
STING
STING
WHAT'RE YOU—
Phooo
Phoooo
PAIN, PAIN GO AWAY...

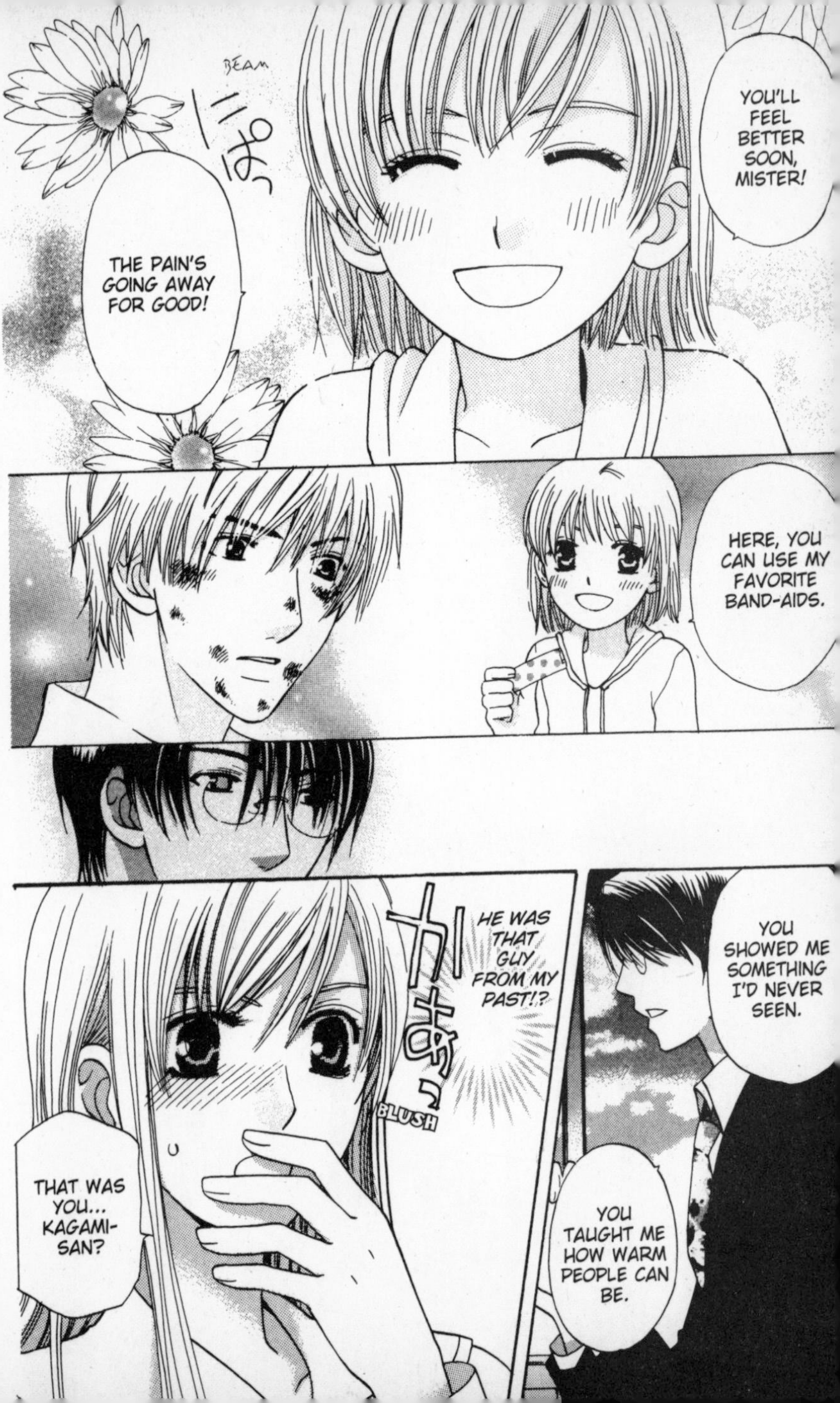
YOU'LL FEEL BETTER SOON, MISTER!
にぱっ
BEAM
THE PAIN'S GOING AWAY FOR GOOD!
HERE, YOU CAN USE MY FAVORITE BAND-AIDS.
YOU SHOWED ME SOMETHING I'D NEVER SEEN.
YOU TAUGHT ME HOW WARM PEOPLE CAN BE.
HE WAS THAT GUY FROM MY PAST!?
かあっ
BLUSH
THAT WAS YOU... KAGAMI-SAN?

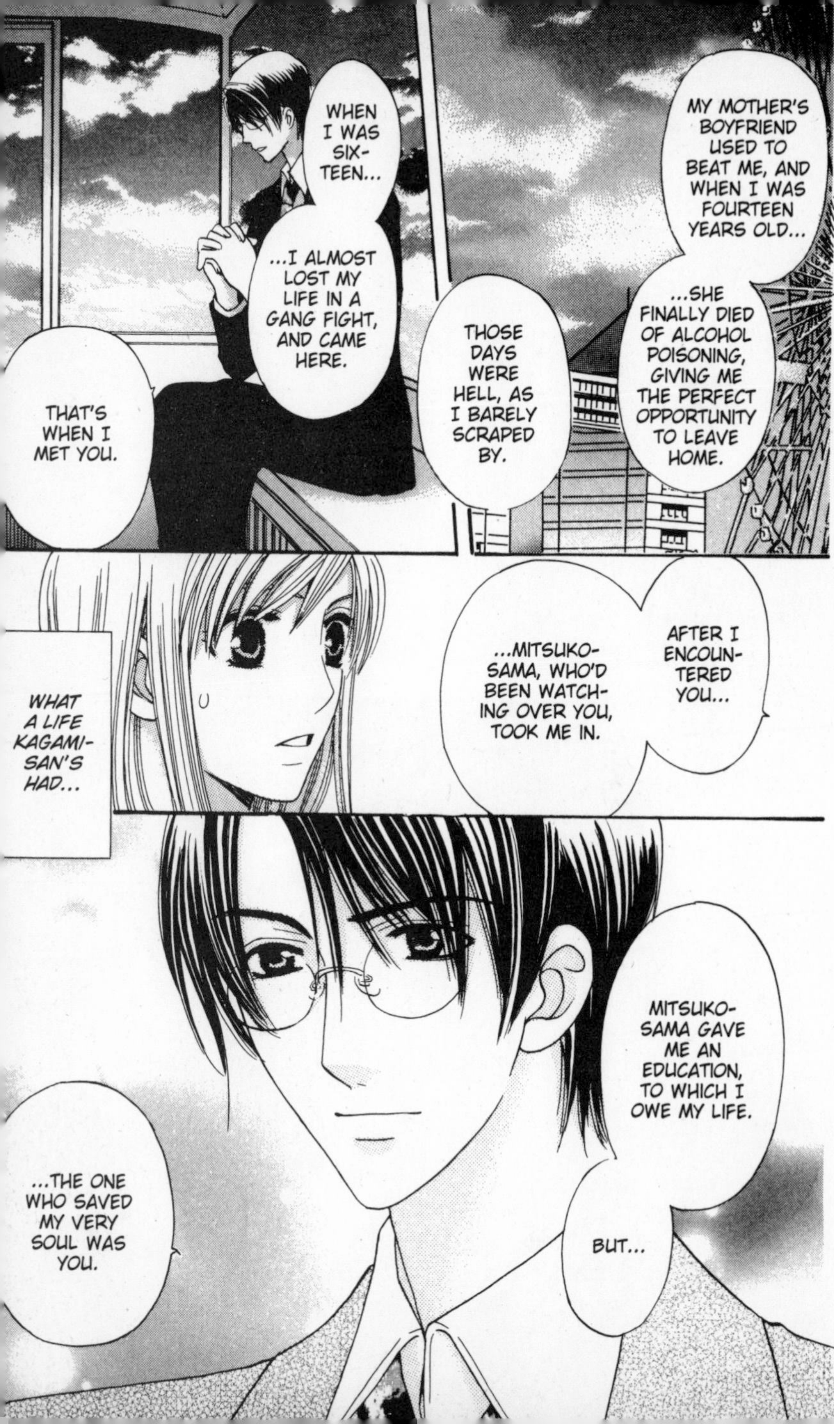
MY MOTHER'S BOYFRIEND USED TO BEAT ME, AND WHEN I WAS FOURTEEN YEARS OLD...
...SHE FINALLY DIED OF ALCOHOL POISONING, GIVING ME THE PERFECT OPPORTUNITY TO LEAVE HOME.
THOSE DAYS WERE HELL, AS I BARELY SCRAPED BY.
WHEN I WAS SIX-TEEN...
...I ALMOST LOST MY LIFE IN A GANG FIGHT, AND CAME HERE.
THAT'S WHEN I MET YOU.
AFTER I ENCOUN-TERED YOU...
...MITSUKO-SAMA, WHO'D BEEN WATCH-ING OVER YOU, TOOK ME IN.
WHAT A LIFE KAGAMI-SAN'S HAD...
MITSUKO-SAMA GAVE ME AN EDUCATION, TO WHICH I OWE MY LIFE.
BUT...
...THE ONE WHO SAVED MY VERY SOUL WAS YOU.

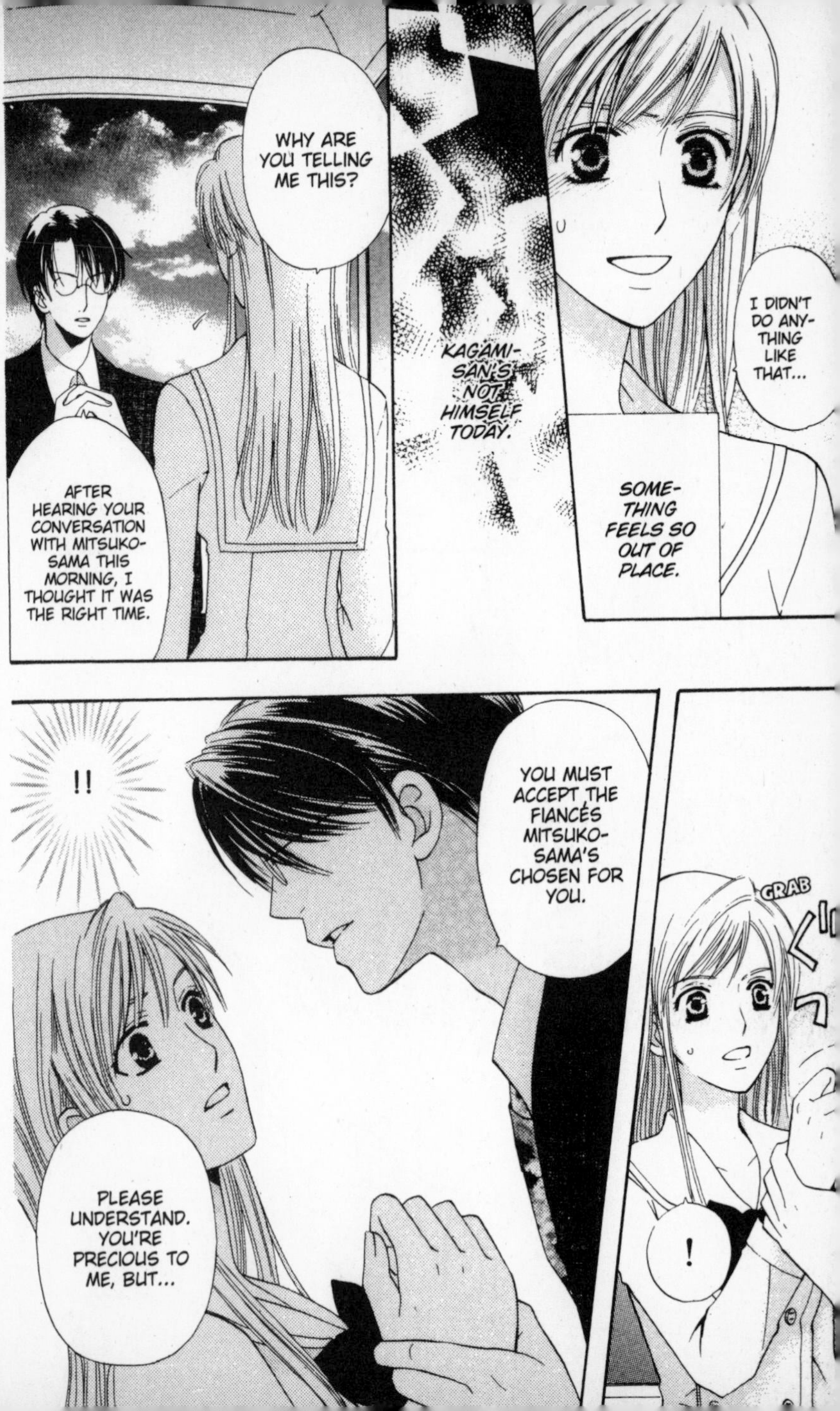
I DIDN'T DO ANYTHING LIKE THAT...
SOMETHING FEELS SO OUT OF PLACE.
KAGAMI-SAN'S NOT HIMSELF TODAY.
WHY ARE YOU TELLING ME THIS?
AFTER HEARING YOUR CONVERSATION WITH MITSUKO-SAMA THIS MORNING, I THOUGHT IT WAS THE RIGHT TIME.
GRAB
!
YOU MUST ACCEPT THE FIANCÉS MITSUKO-SAMA'S CHOSEN FOR YOU.
!!
PLEASE UNDERSTAND. YOU'RE PRECIOUS TO ME, BUT...

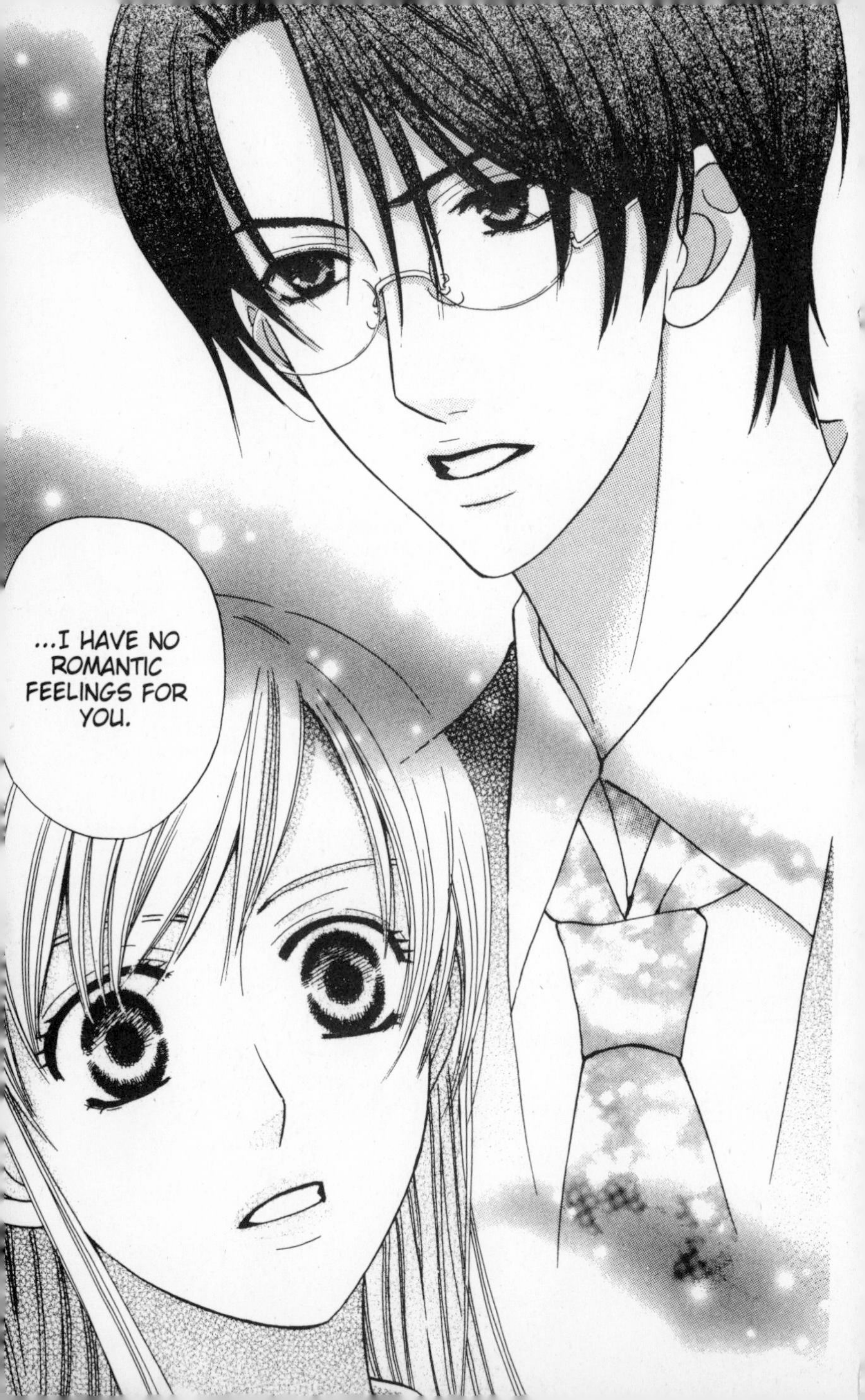
...I HAVE NO ROMANTIC FEELINGS FOR YOU.

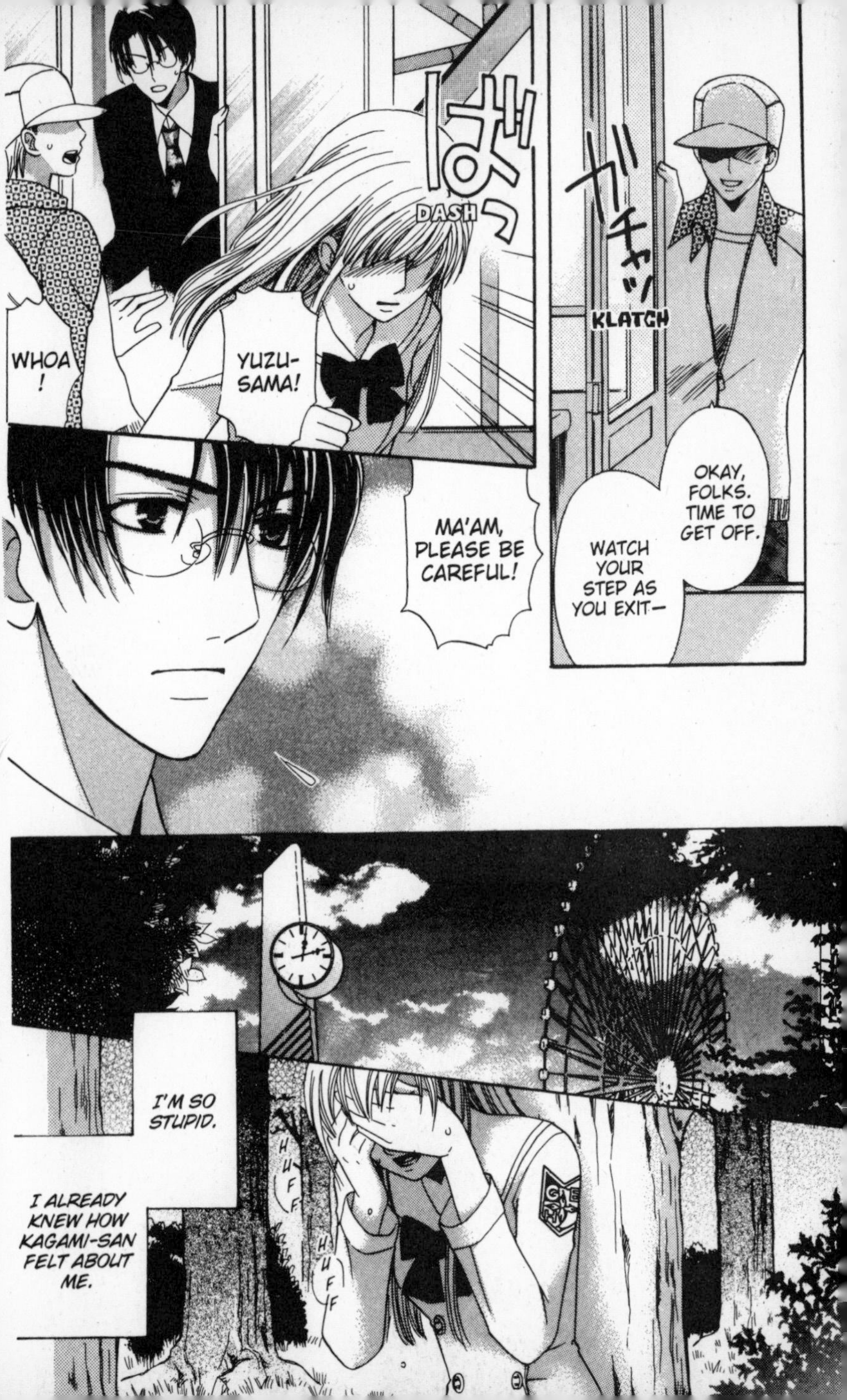
ガチャッ
KLATCH
OKAY, FOLKS. TIME TO GET OFF.
WATCH YOUR STEP AS YOU EXIT—
ぱっ
DASH
YUZU-SAMA!
WHOA!
MA'AM, PLEASE BE CAREFUL!
I'M SO STUPID.
I ALREADY KNEW HOW KAGAMI-SAN FELT ABOUT ME.
HUFF
HUFF

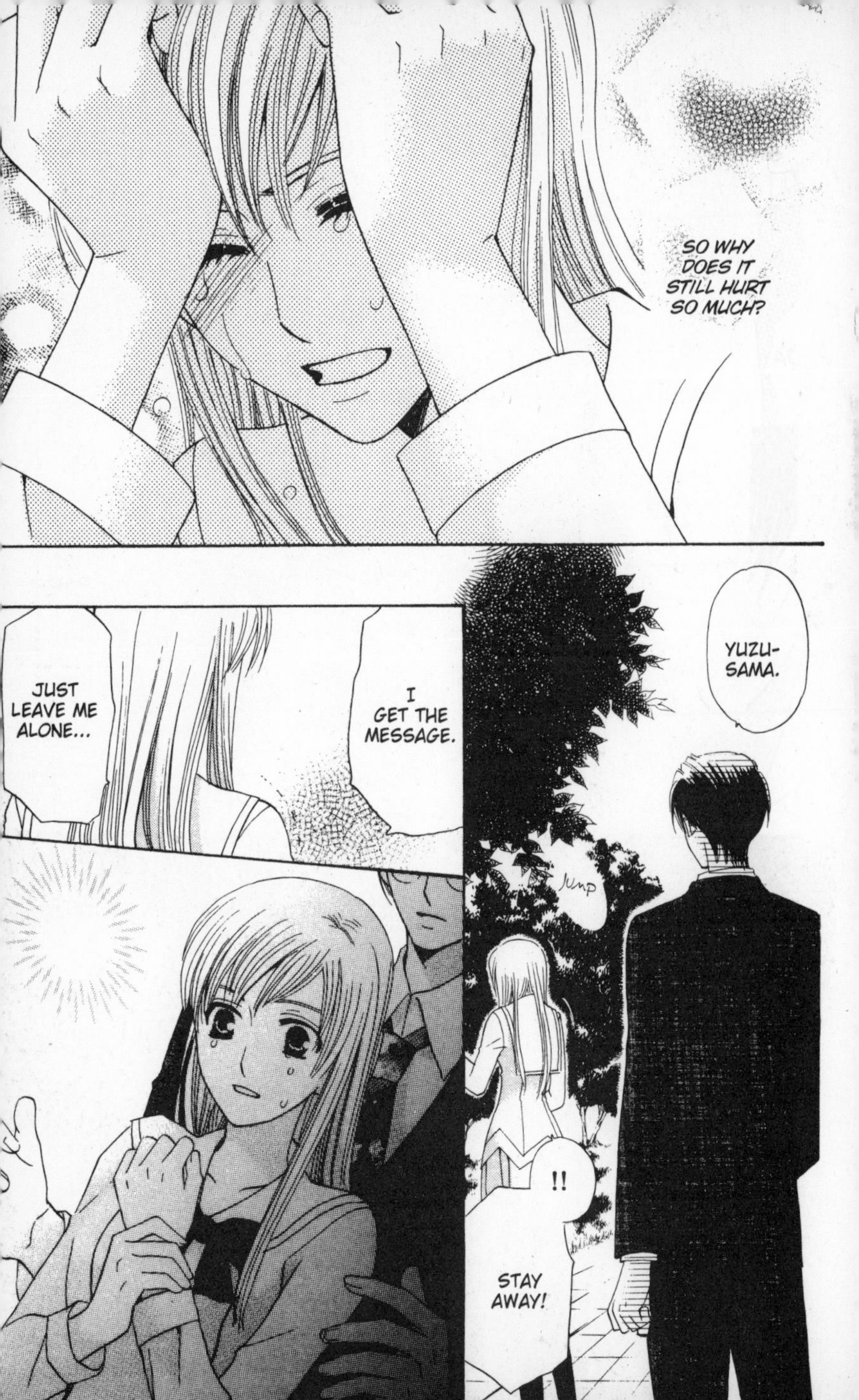
SO WHY DOES IT STILL HURT SO MUCH?
YUZU-SAMA.
JUMP
!!
STAY AWAY!
I GET THE MESSAGE.
JUST LEAVE ME ALONE...

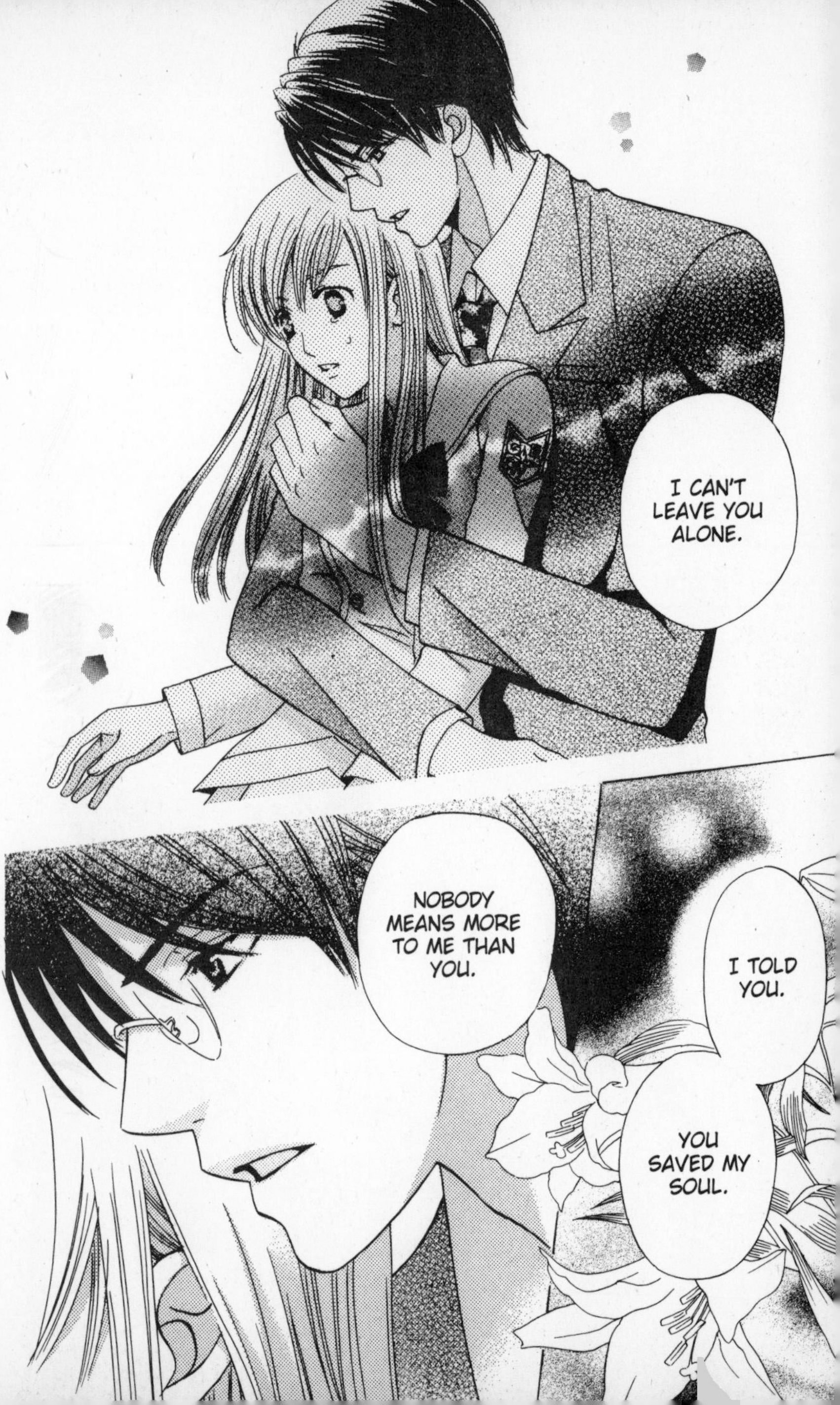
I CAN'T LEAVE YOU ALONE.
I TOLD YOU.
YOU SAVED MY SOUL.
NOBODY MEANS MORE TO ME THAN YOU.

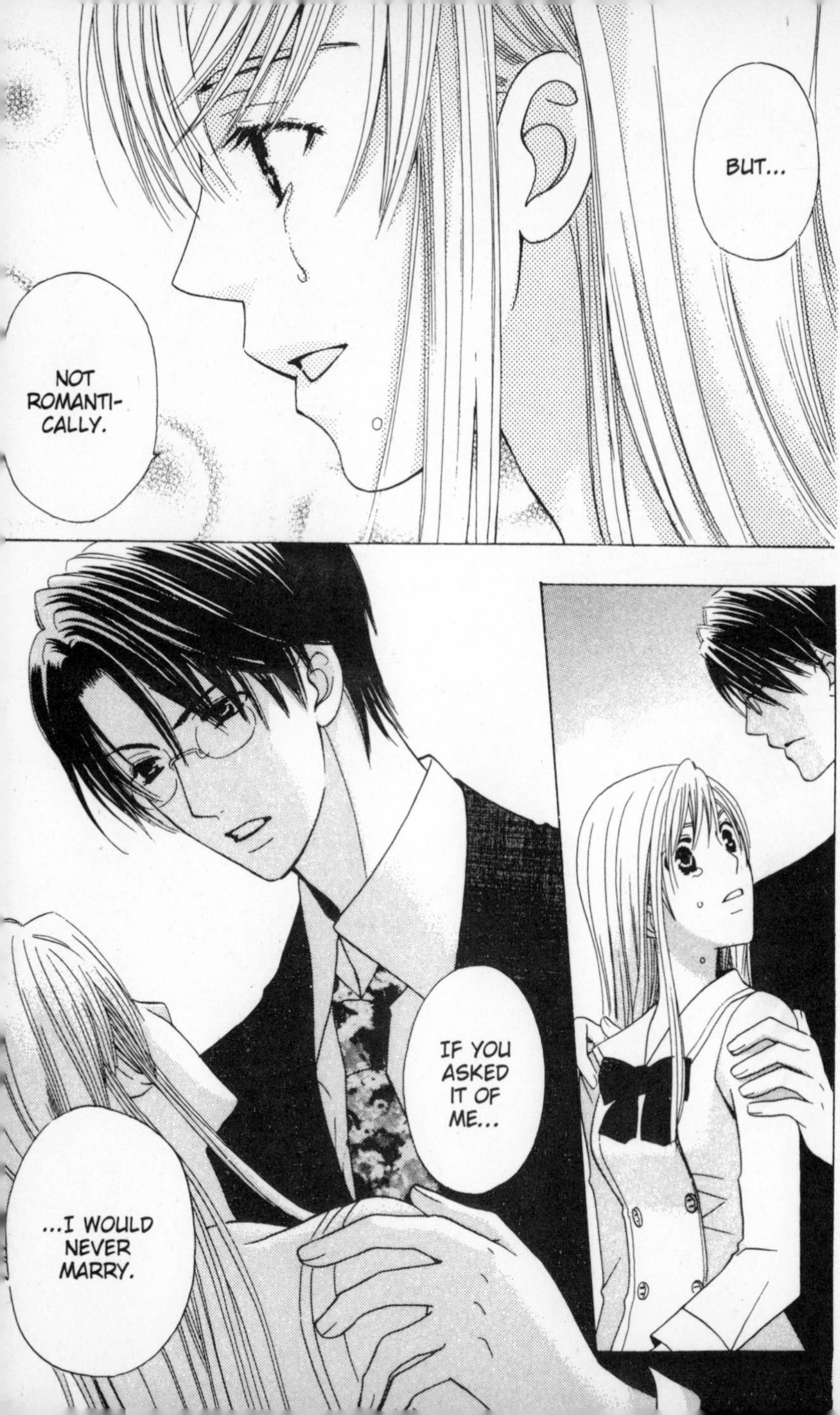
BUT...
NOT ROMANTI-CALLY.
IF YOU ASKED IT OF ME...
...I WOULD NEVER MARRY.

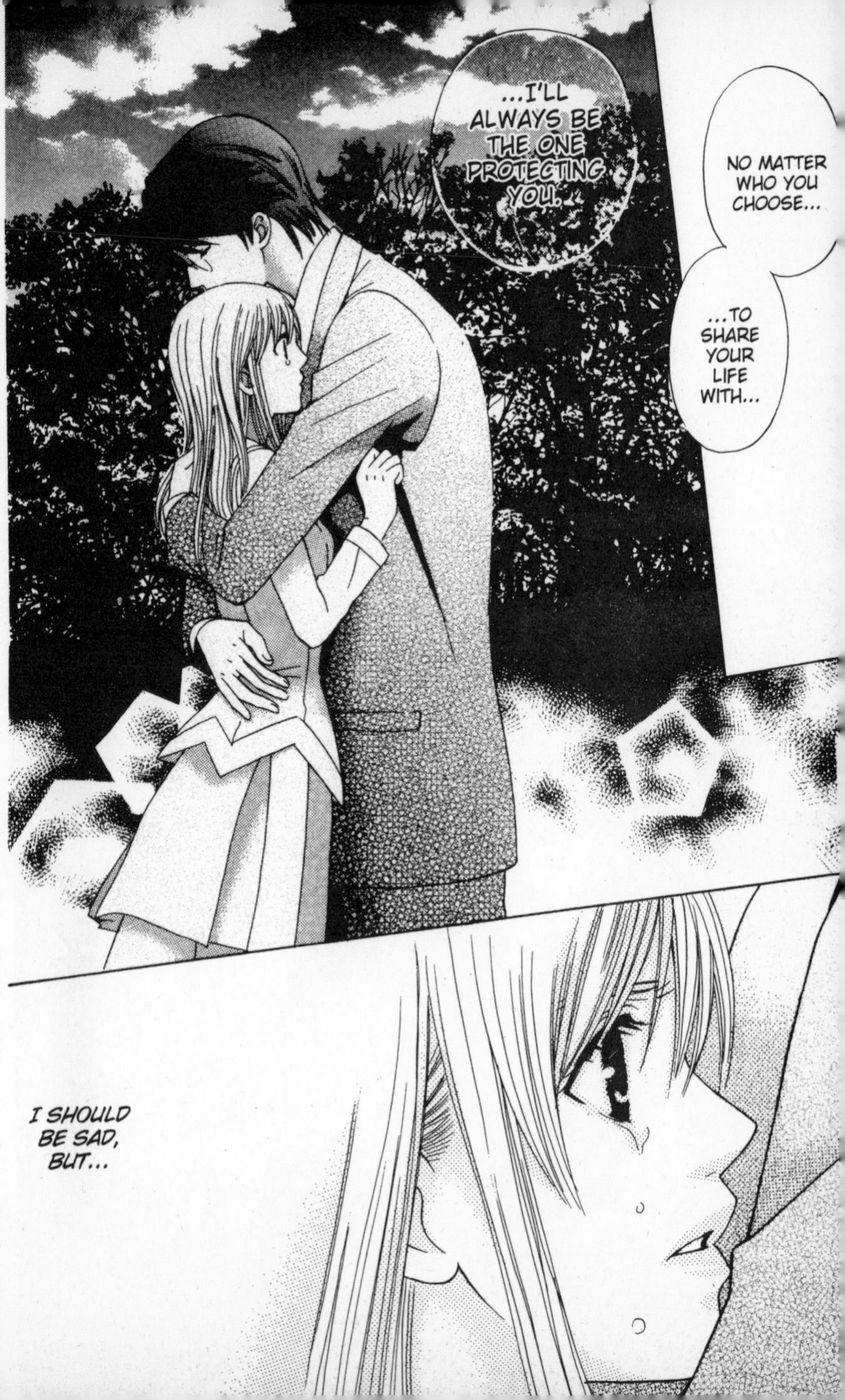
NO MATTER WHO YOU CHOOSE...
...TO SHARE YOUR LIFE WITH...
...I'LL ALWAYS BE THE ONE PROTECTING YOU.
I SHOULD BE SAD, BUT...

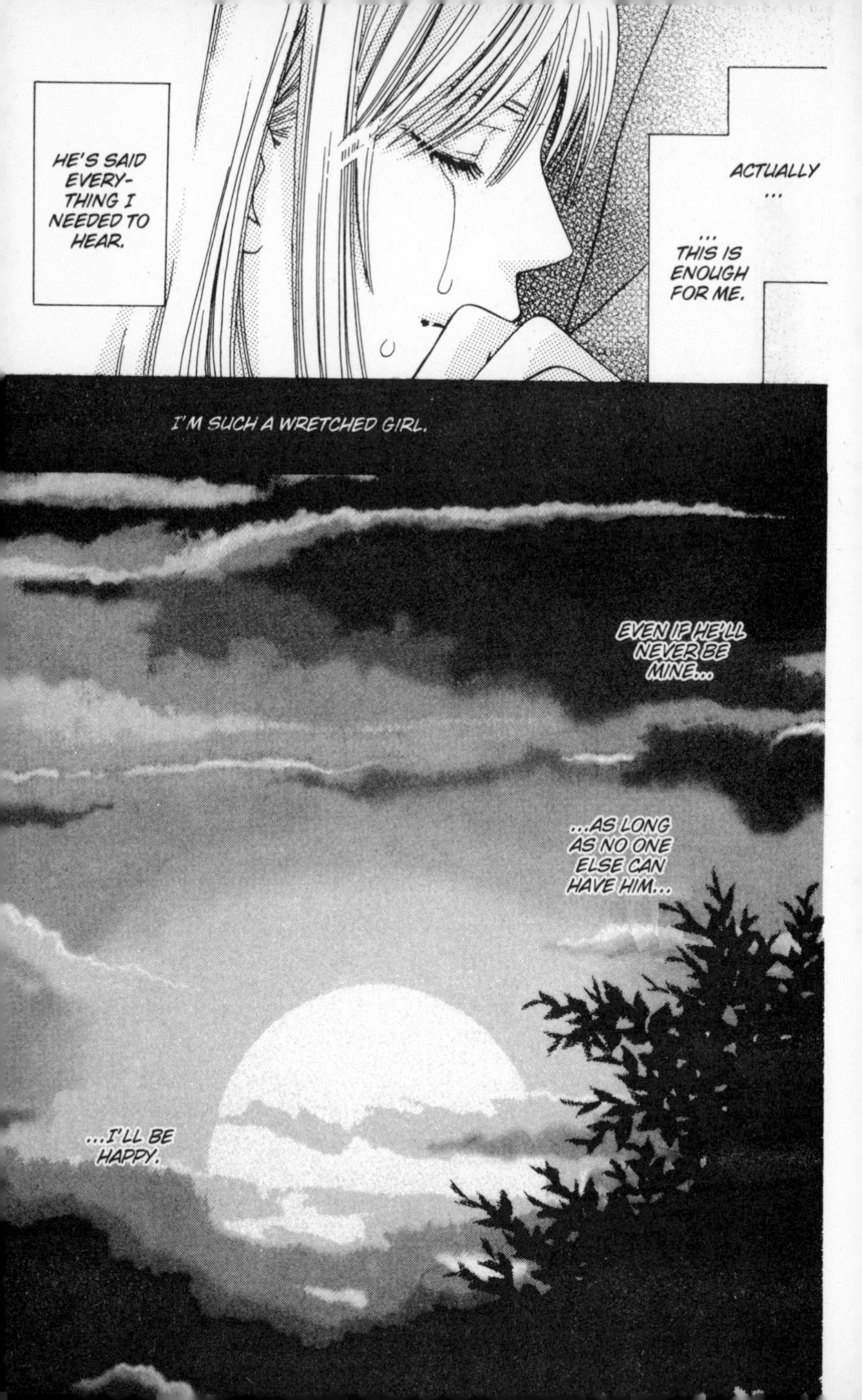
ACTUALLY ...
... THIS IS ENOUGH FOR ME.
HE'S SAID EVERY-THING I NEEDED TO HEAR.
I'M SUCH A WRETCHED GIRL.
EVEN IF HE'LL NEVER BE MINE...
...AS LONG AS NO ONE ELSE CAN HAVE HIM...
...I'LL BE HAPPY.

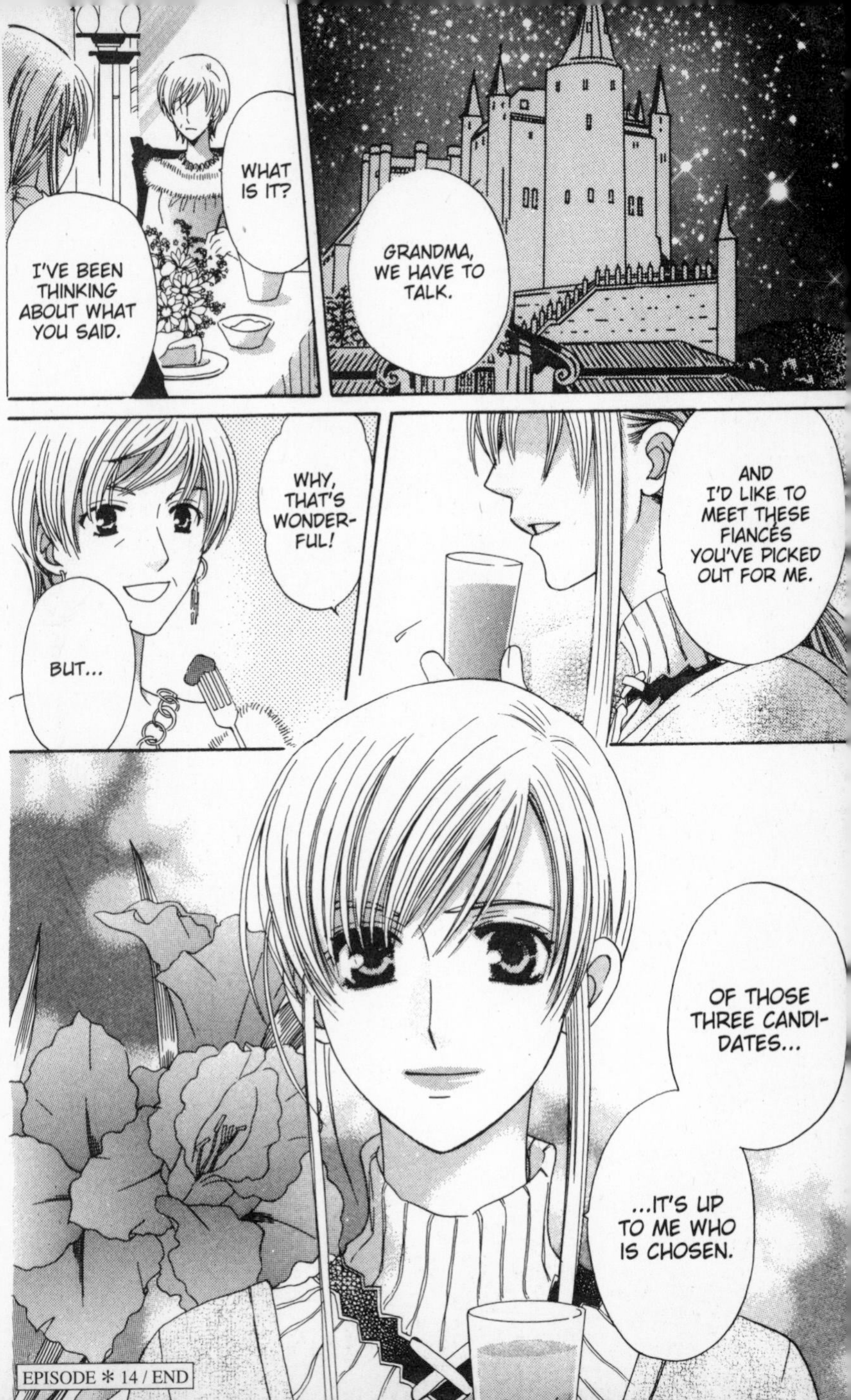
GRANDMA, WE HAVE TO TALK.
WHAT IS IT?
I'VE BEEN THINKING ABOUT WHAT YOU SAID.
AND I'D LIKE TO MEET THESE FIANCÉS YOU'VE PICKED OUT FOR ME.
WHY, THAT'S WONDER-FUL!
BUT...
OF THOSE THREE CANDI-DATES...
...IT'S UP TO ME WHO IS CHOSEN.

EPISODE * 14 / END

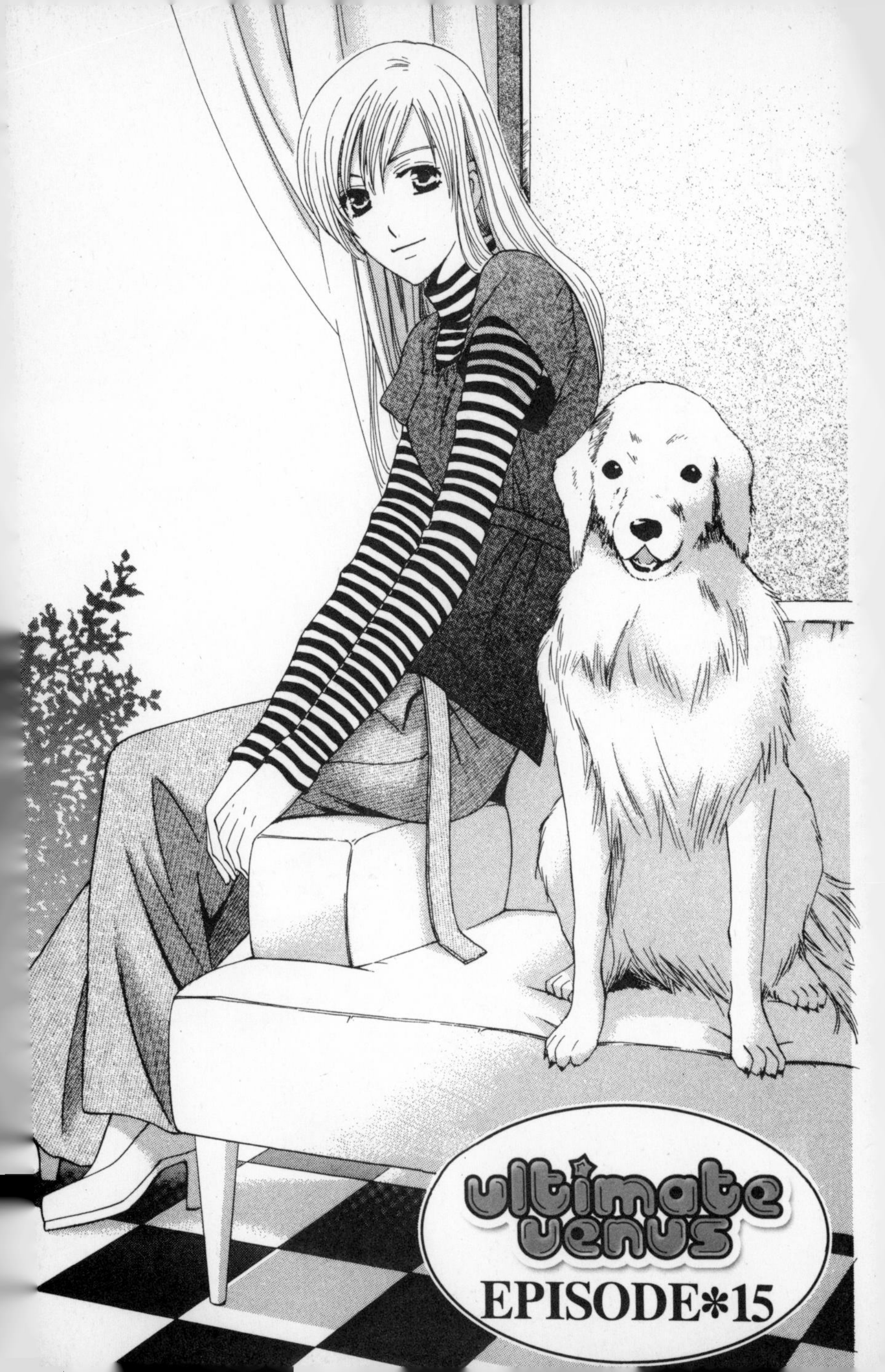
ultimate venus
EPISODE*15

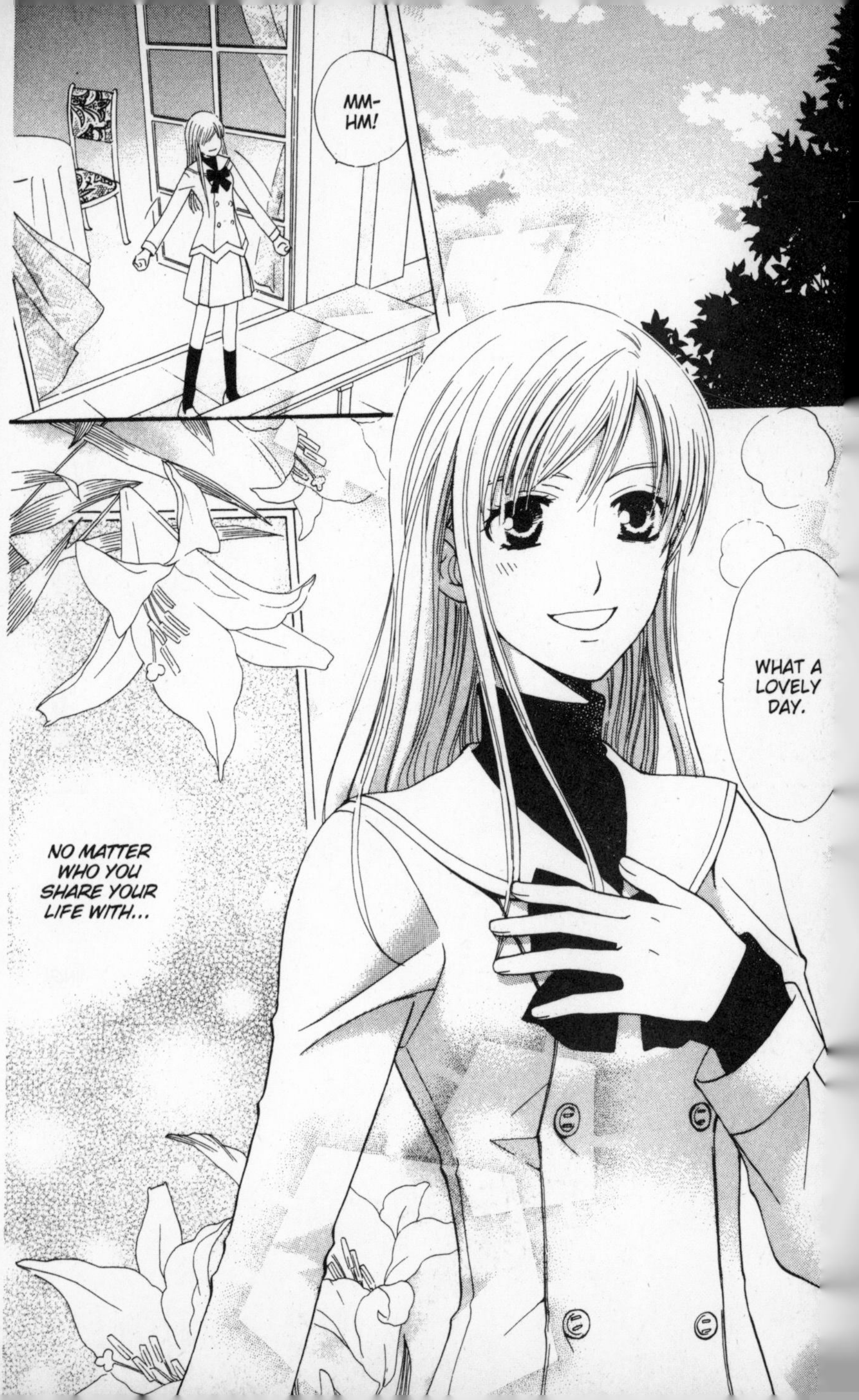
MM-HM!
WHAT A LOVELY DAY.
NO MATTER WHO YOU SHARE YOUR LIFE WITH...

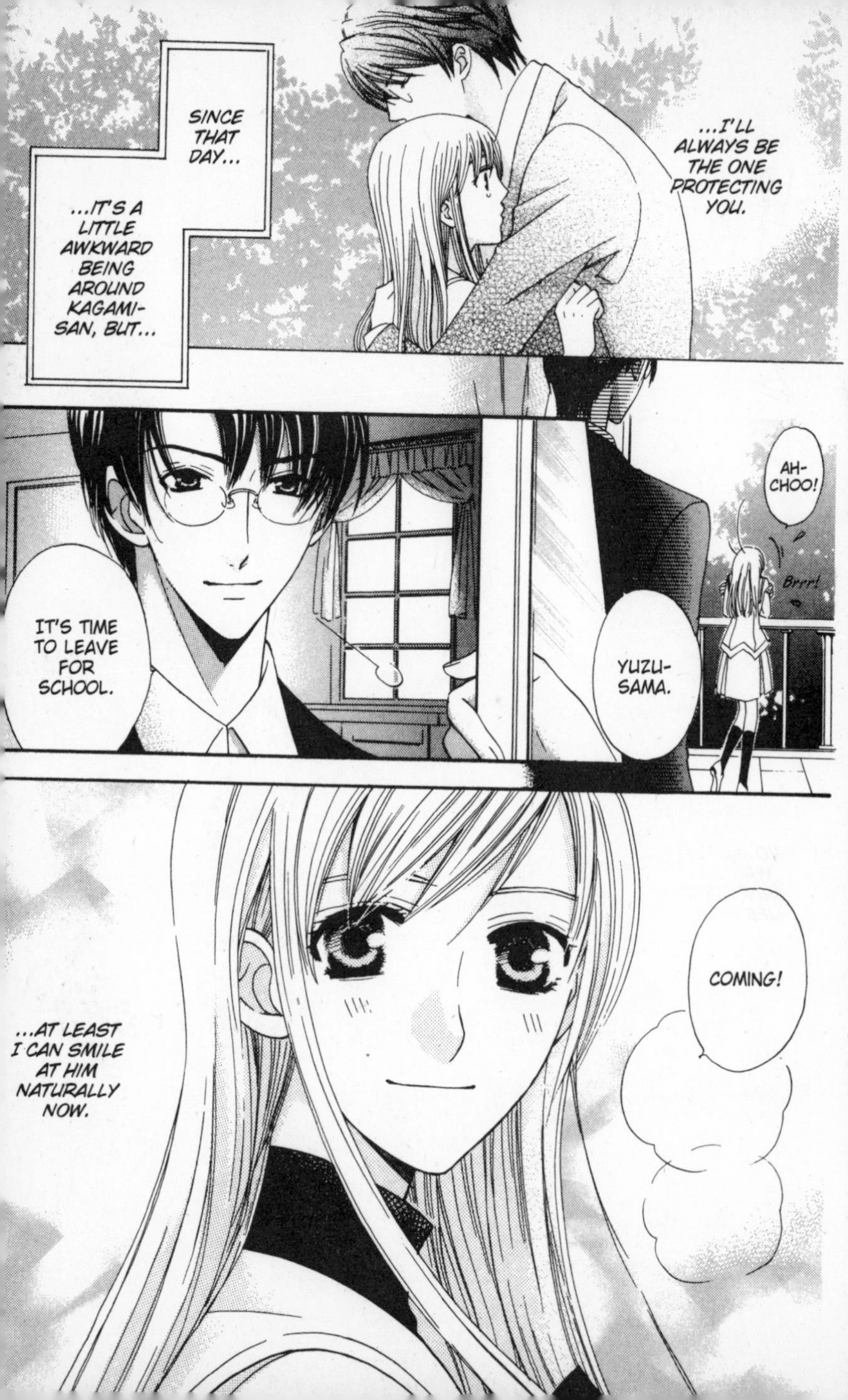
...I'LL ALWAYS BE THE ONE PROTECTING YOU.
SINCE THAT DAY...
...IT'S A LITTLE AWKWARD BEING AROUND KAGAMI-SAN, BUT...
AH-CHOO!
Brrr!
YUZU-SAMA.
IT'S TIME TO LEAVE FOR SCHOOL.
COMING!
...AT LEAST I CAN SMILE AT HIM NATURALLY NOW.

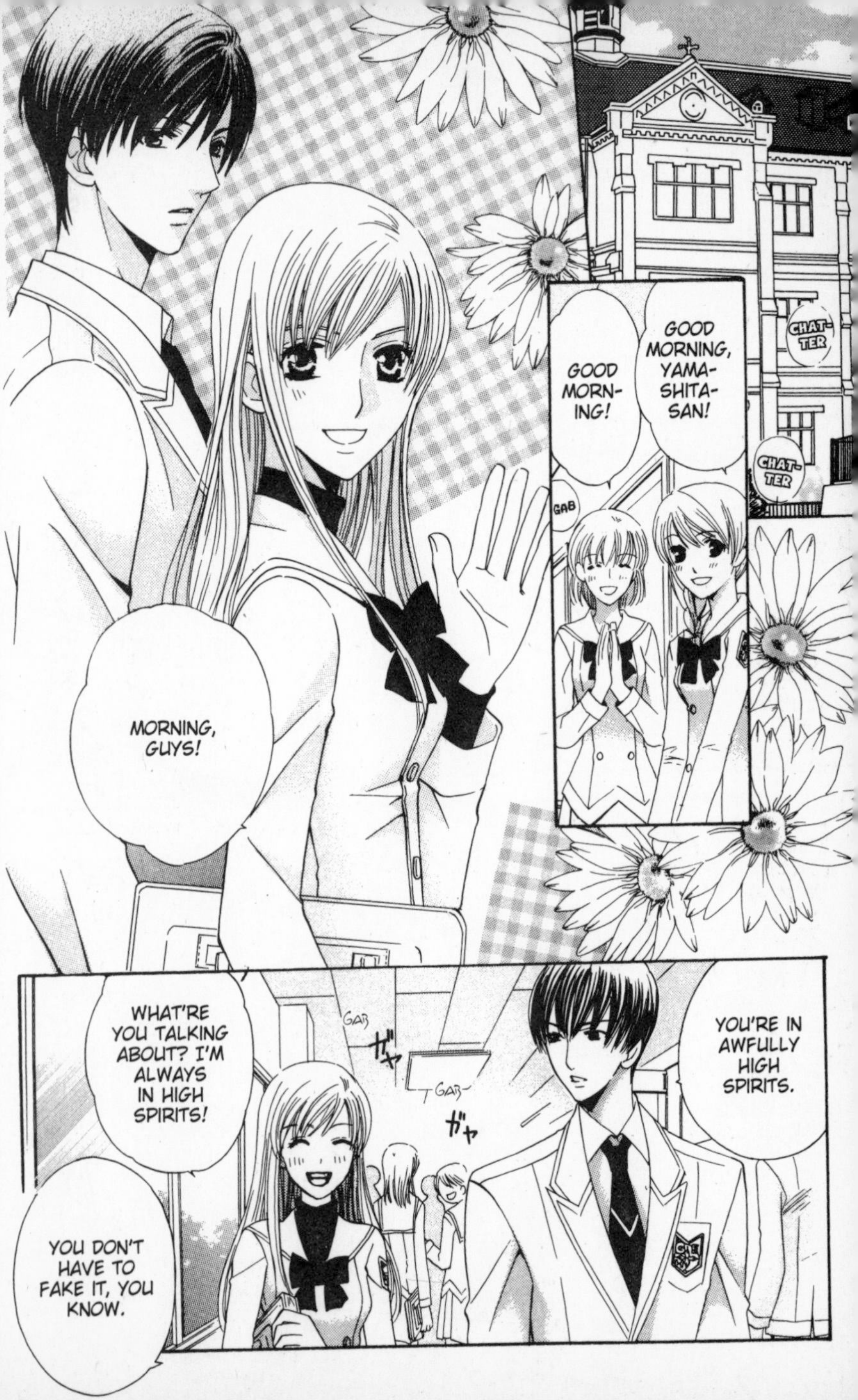
CHAT-TER
CHAT-TER
GOOD MORNING, YAMA-SHITA-SAN!
GOOD MORN-ING!
GAB
MORNING, GUYS!
YOU'RE IN AWFULLY HIGH SPIRITS.
GAB ガヤ
GAB ガヤ
WHAT'RE YOU TALKING ABOUT? I'M ALWAYS IN HIGH SPIRITS!
YOU DON'T HAVE TO FAKE IT, YOU KNOW.

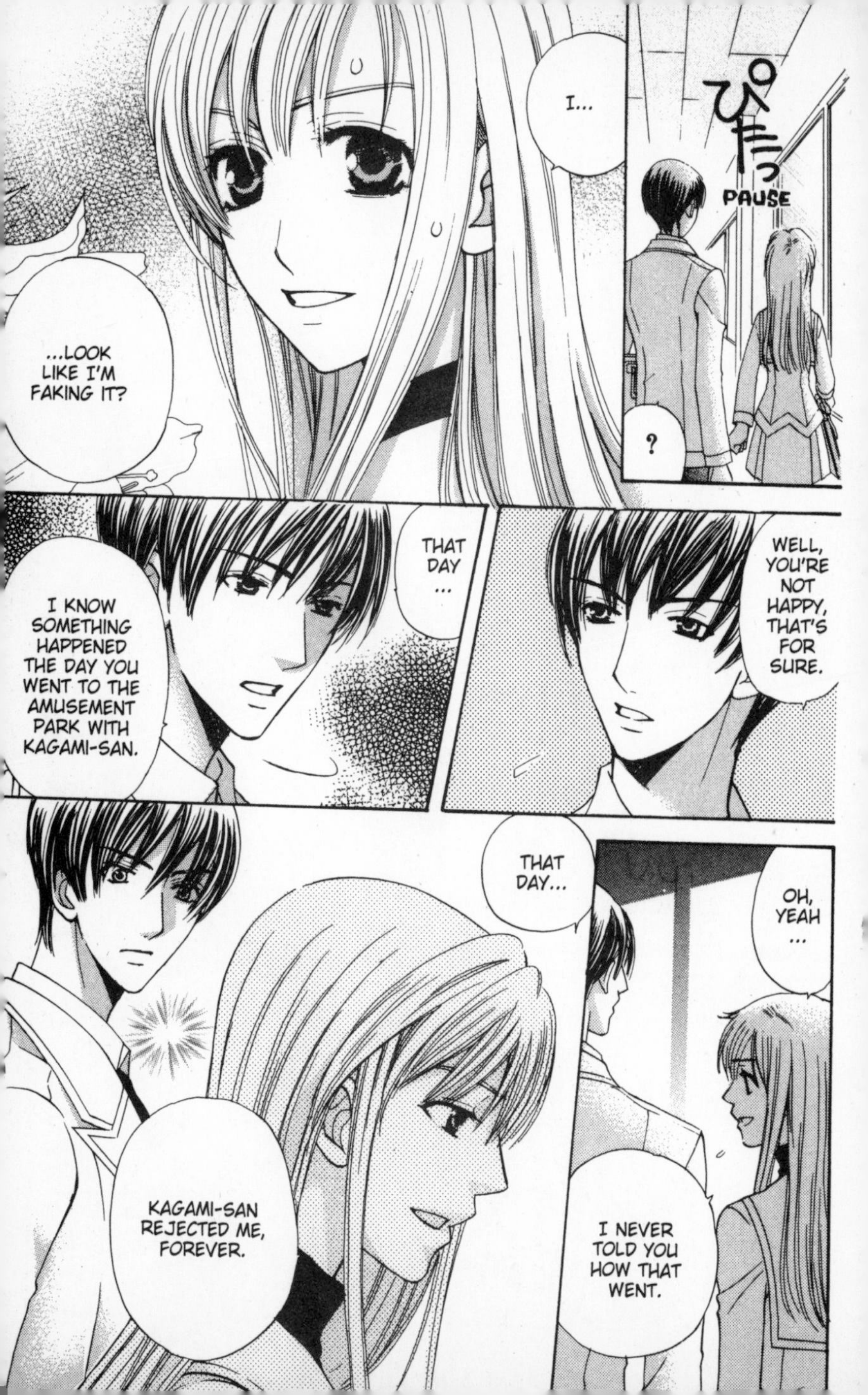
ぴたっ
PAUSE
?
I...
...LOOK LIKE I'M FAKING IT?
WELL, YOU'RE NOT HAPPY, THAT'S FOR SURE.
THAT DAY ...
I KNOW SOMETHING HAPPENED THE DAY YOU WENT TO THE AMUSEMENT PARK WITH KAGAMI-SAN.
OH, YEAH ...
I NEVER TOLD YOU HOW THAT WENT.
THAT DAY...
KAGAMI-SAN REJECTED ME, FOREVER.

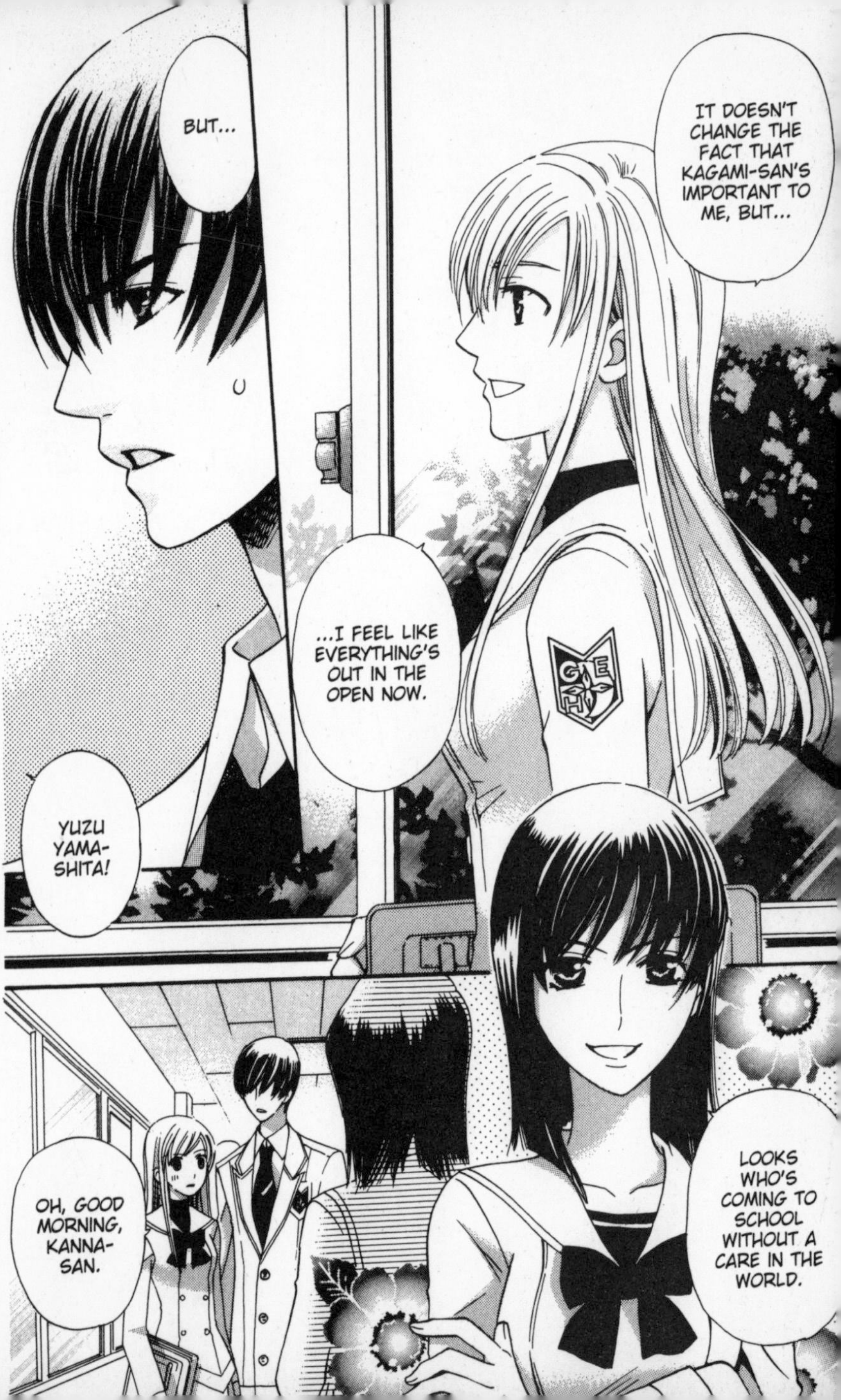
IT DOESN'T CHANGE THE FACT THAT KAGAMI-SAN'S IMPORTANT TO ME, BUT...
...I FEEL LIKE EVERYTHING'S OUT IN THE OPEN NOW.
BUT...
YUZU YAMA-SHITA!
LOOKS WHO'S COMING TO SCHOOL WITHOUT A CARE IN THE WORLD.
OH, GOOD MORNING, KANNA-SAN.

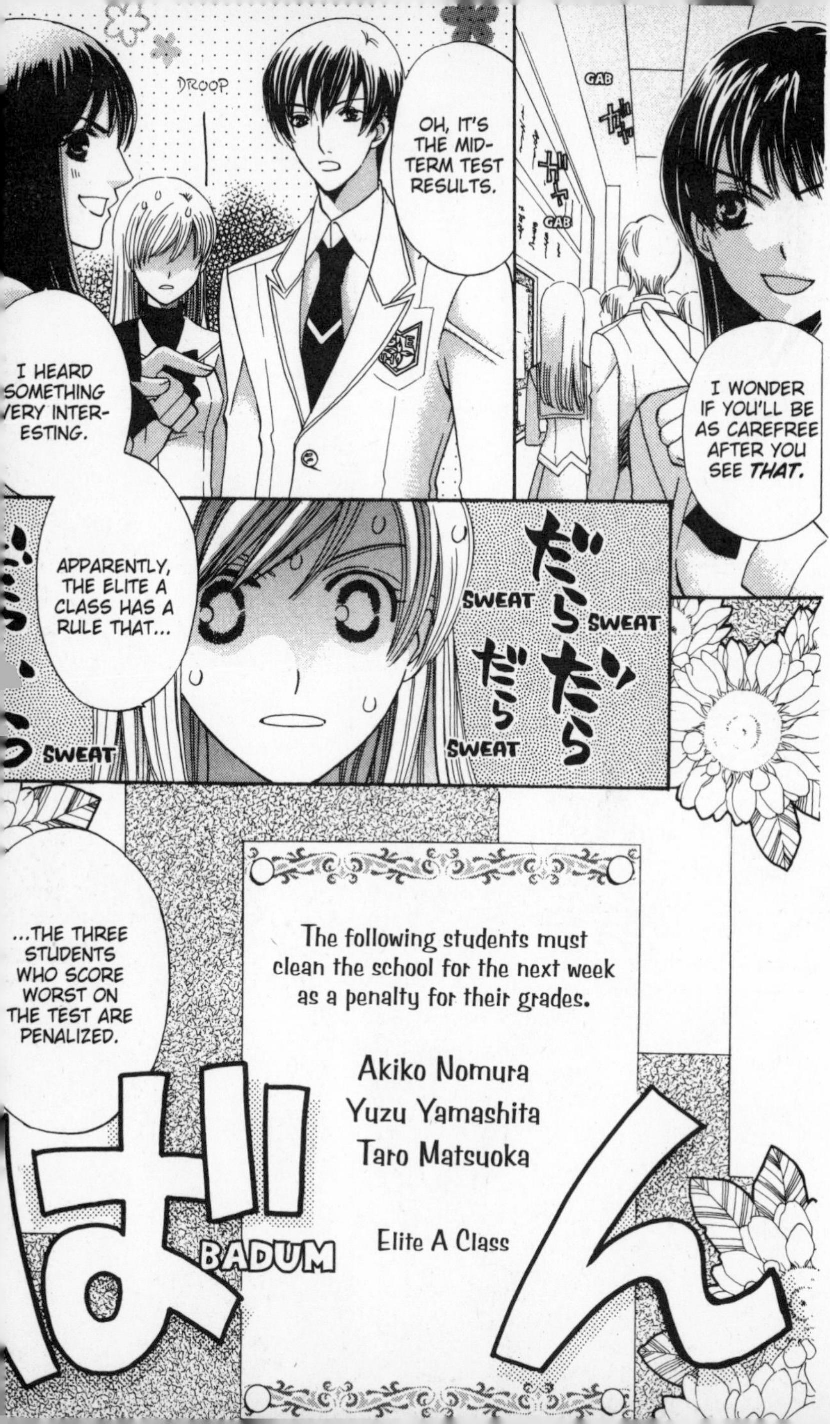
GAB
GAB
I WONDER IF YOU'LL BE AS CAREFREE AFTER YOU SEE *THAT.*
OH, IT'S THE MID-TERM TEST RESULTS.
DROOP
I HEARD SOMETHING VERY INTER-ESTING.
だらだら
SWEAT
SWEAT
だらだら
SWEAT
SWEAT
APPARENTLY, THE ELITE A CLASS HAS A RULE THAT...
The following students must clean the school for the next week as a penalty for their grades.
Akiko Nomura
Yuzu Yamashita
Taro Matsuoka
Elite A Class
...THE THREE STUDENTS WHO SCORE WORST ON THE TEST ARE PENALIZED.
BADUM

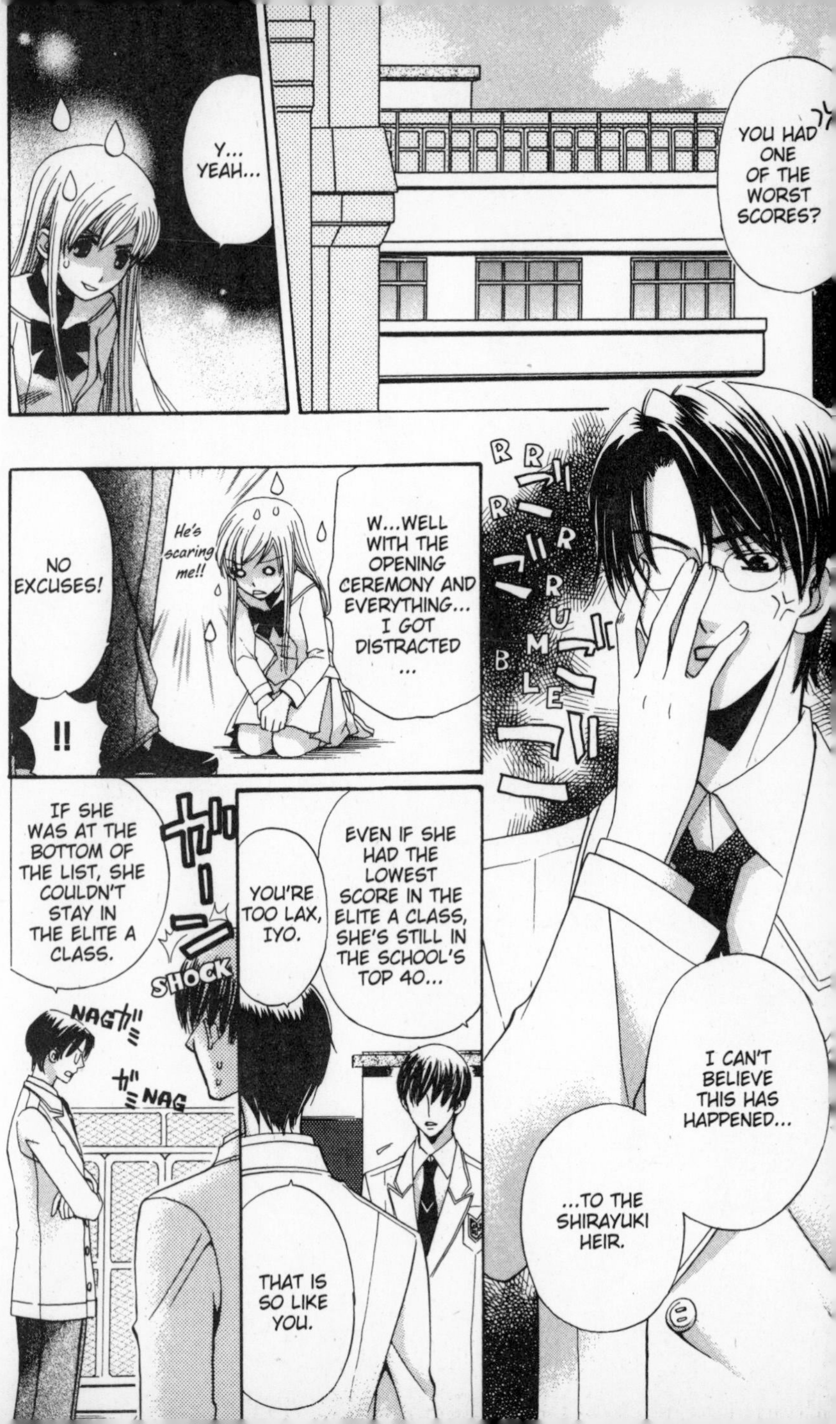
YOU HAD ONE OF THE WORST SCORES?
Y... YEAH...
RRRUMBLE
I CAN'T BELIEVE THIS HAS HAPPENED...
...TO THE SHIRAYUKI HEIR.
W...WELL WITH THE OPENING CEREMONY AND EVERYTHING... I GOT DISTRACTED ...
He's scaring me!!
NO EXCUSES!
!!
EVEN IF SHE HAD THE LOWEST SCORE IN THE ELITE A CLASS, SHE'S STILL IN THE SCHOOL'S TOP 40...
YOU'RE TOO LAX, IYO.
THAT IS SO LIKE YOU.
SHOCK
IF SHE WAS AT THE BOTTOM OF THE LIST, SHE COULDN'T STAY IN THE ELITE A CLASS.
NAG
NAG

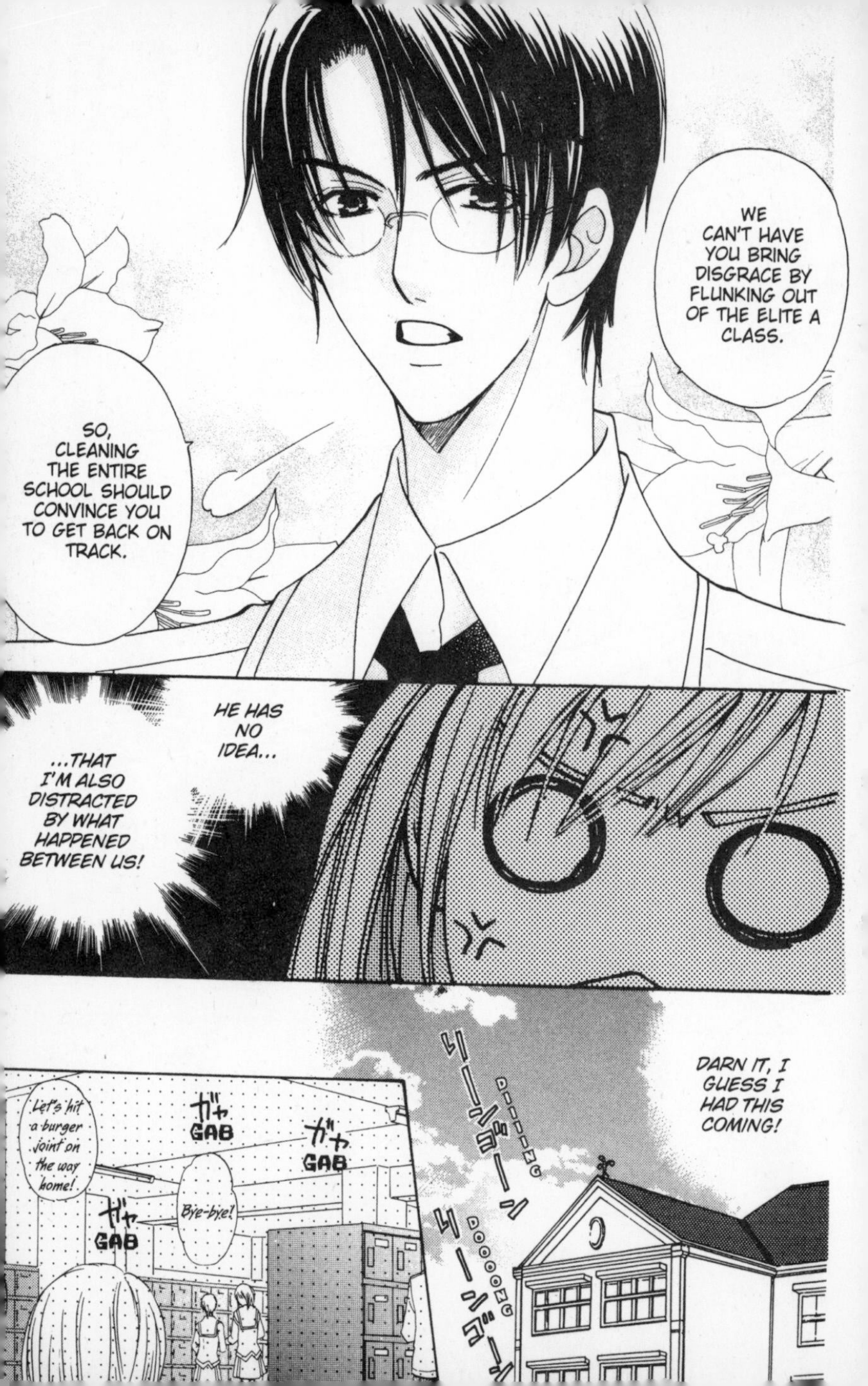

WE CAN'T HAVE YOU BRING DISGRACE BY FLUNKING OUT OF THE ELITE A CLASS.
SO, CLEANING THE ENTIRE SCHOOL SHOULD CONVINCE YOU TO GET BACK ON TRACK.
HE HAS NO IDEA...
...THAT I'M ALSO DISTRACTED BY WHAT HAPPENED BETWEEN US!
DARN IT, I GUESS I HAD THIS COMING!
DIIIING
DOOOONG
GAB
GAB
Let's hit a burger joint on the way home!
Bye-bye!
GAB

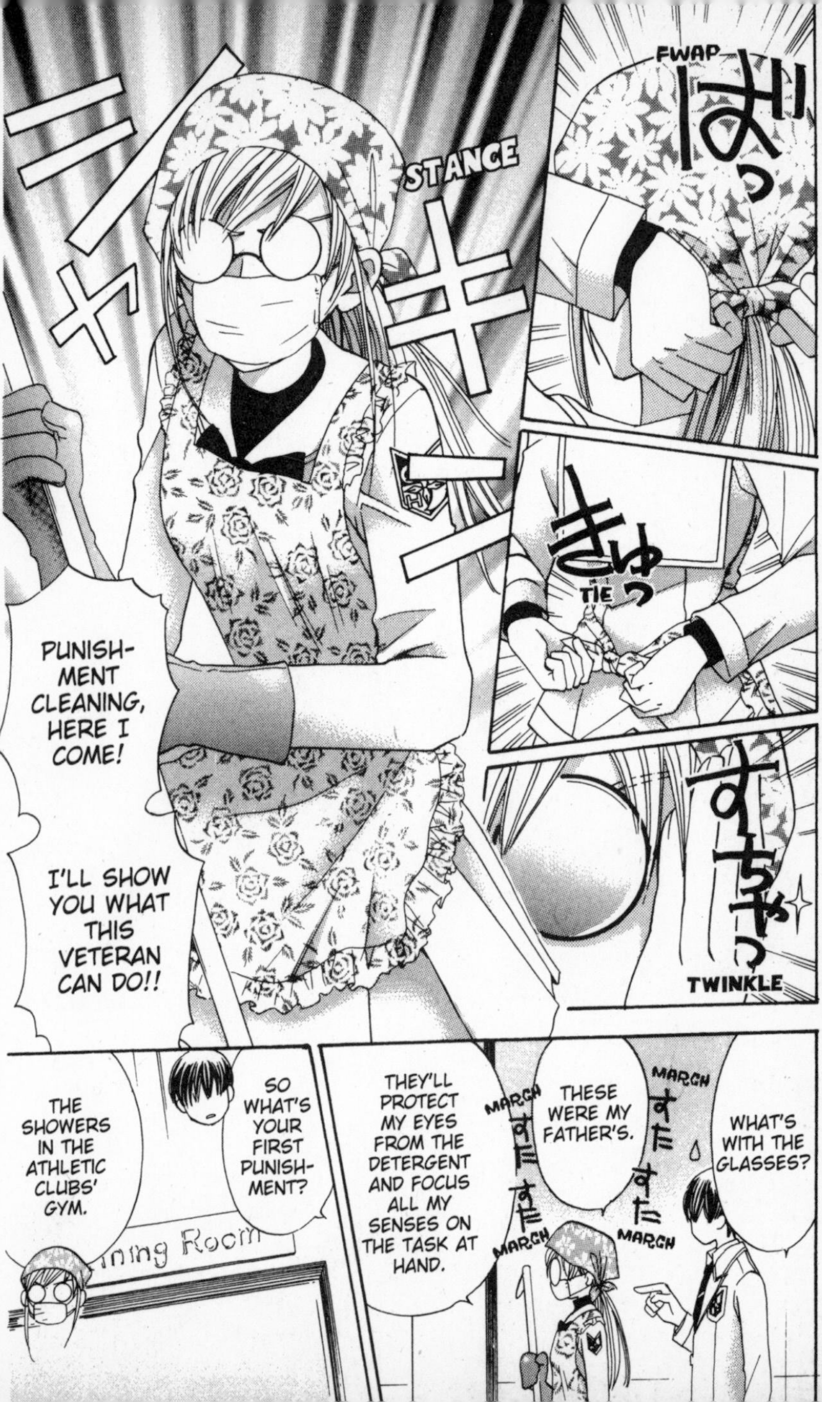

FWAP
ぱっ
きゅっ
TIE
すちゃっ
TWINKLE
STANCE
PUNISHMENT CLEANING, HERE I COME!
I'LL SHOW YOU WHAT THIS VETERAN CAN DO!!
WHAT'S WITH THE GLASSES?
MARCH すた MARCH すた
THESE WERE MY FATHER'S.
MARCH すた MARCH すた
THEY'LL PROTECT MY EYES FROM THE DETERGENT AND FOCUS ALL MY SENSES ON THE TASK AT HAND.
SO WHAT'S YOUR FIRST PUNISHMENT?
THE SHOWERS IN THE ATHLETIC CLUBS' GYM.
ining Room

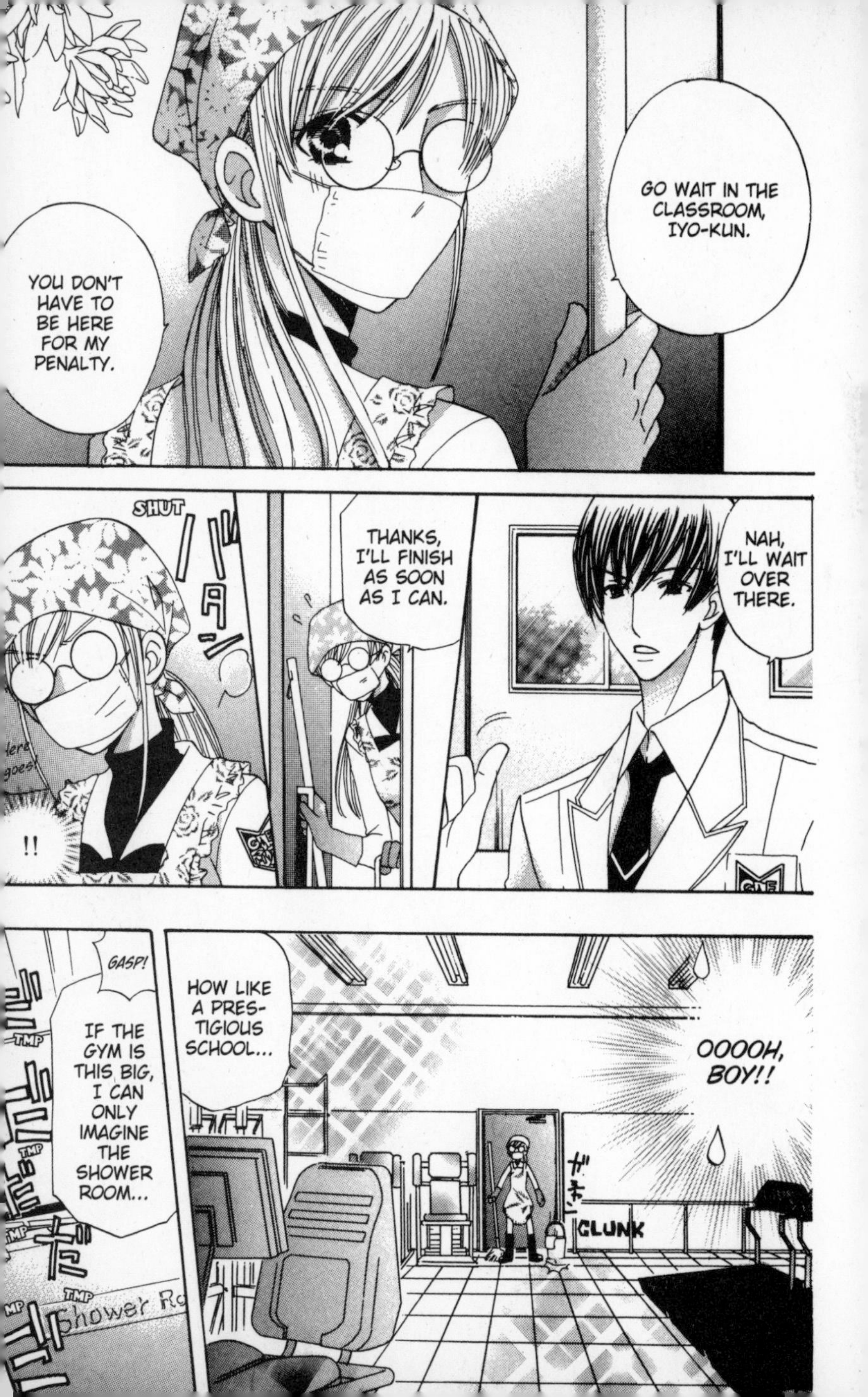
GO WAIT IN THE CLASSROOM, IYO-KUN.
YOU DON'T HAVE TO BE HERE FOR MY PENALTY.
NAH, I'LL WAIT OVER THERE.
THANKS, I'LL FINISH AS SOON AS I CAN.
SHUT
!!
OOOOH, BOY!!
HOW LIKE A PRES-TIGIOUS SCHOOL...
GLUNK
GASP!
IF THE GYM IS THIS BIG, I CAN ONLY IMAGINE THE SHOWER ROOM...
TMP
TMP
TMP
TMP
Shower Ro

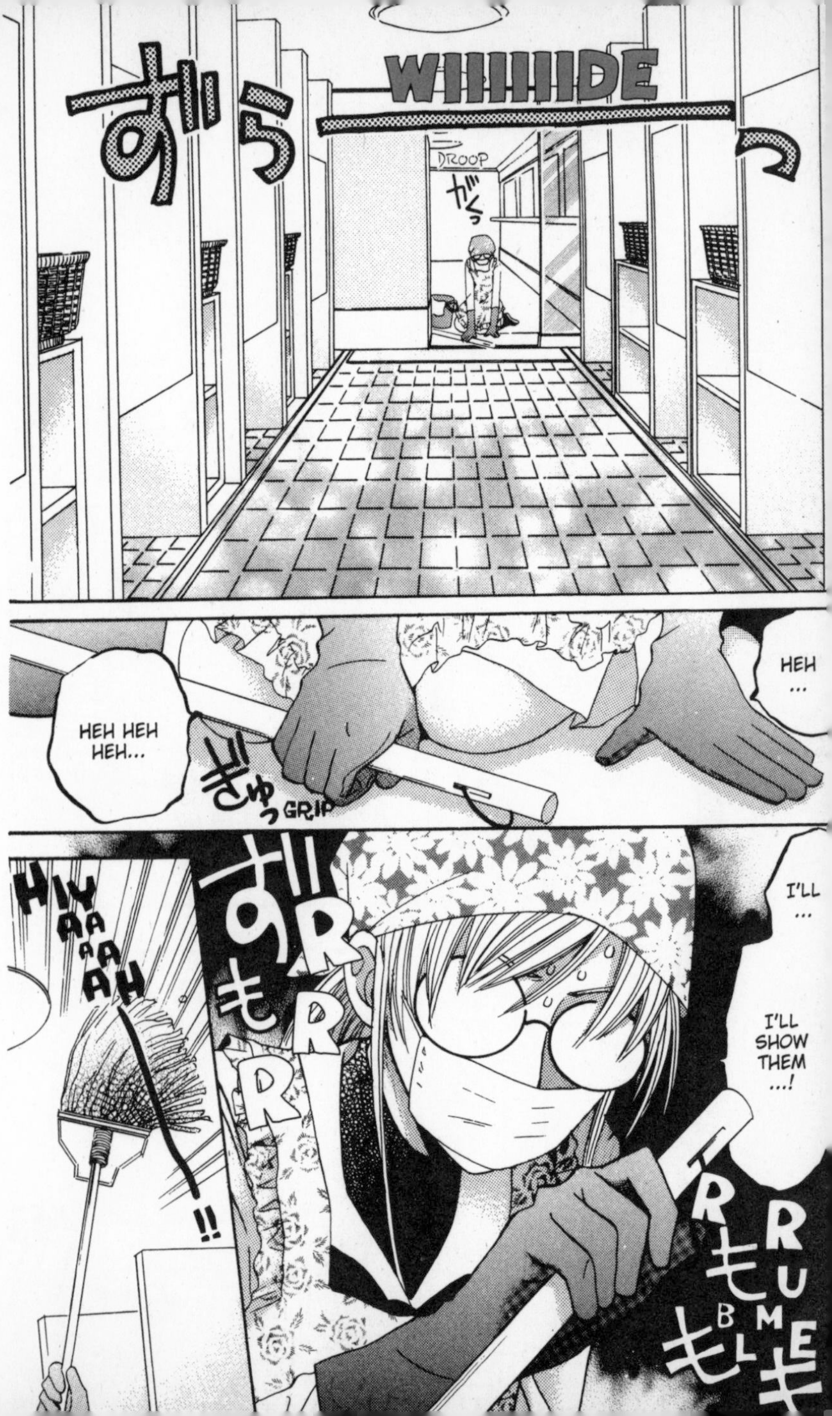

ずらーっ
WIIIIIDE
がくっ
DROOP
HEH ...
HEH HEH HEH...
ぎゅっ
GRIP
I'LL ...
I'LL SHOW THEM ...!
もももも
RUMBLE
ずもも
RRRR
HIYAAAAAH!!

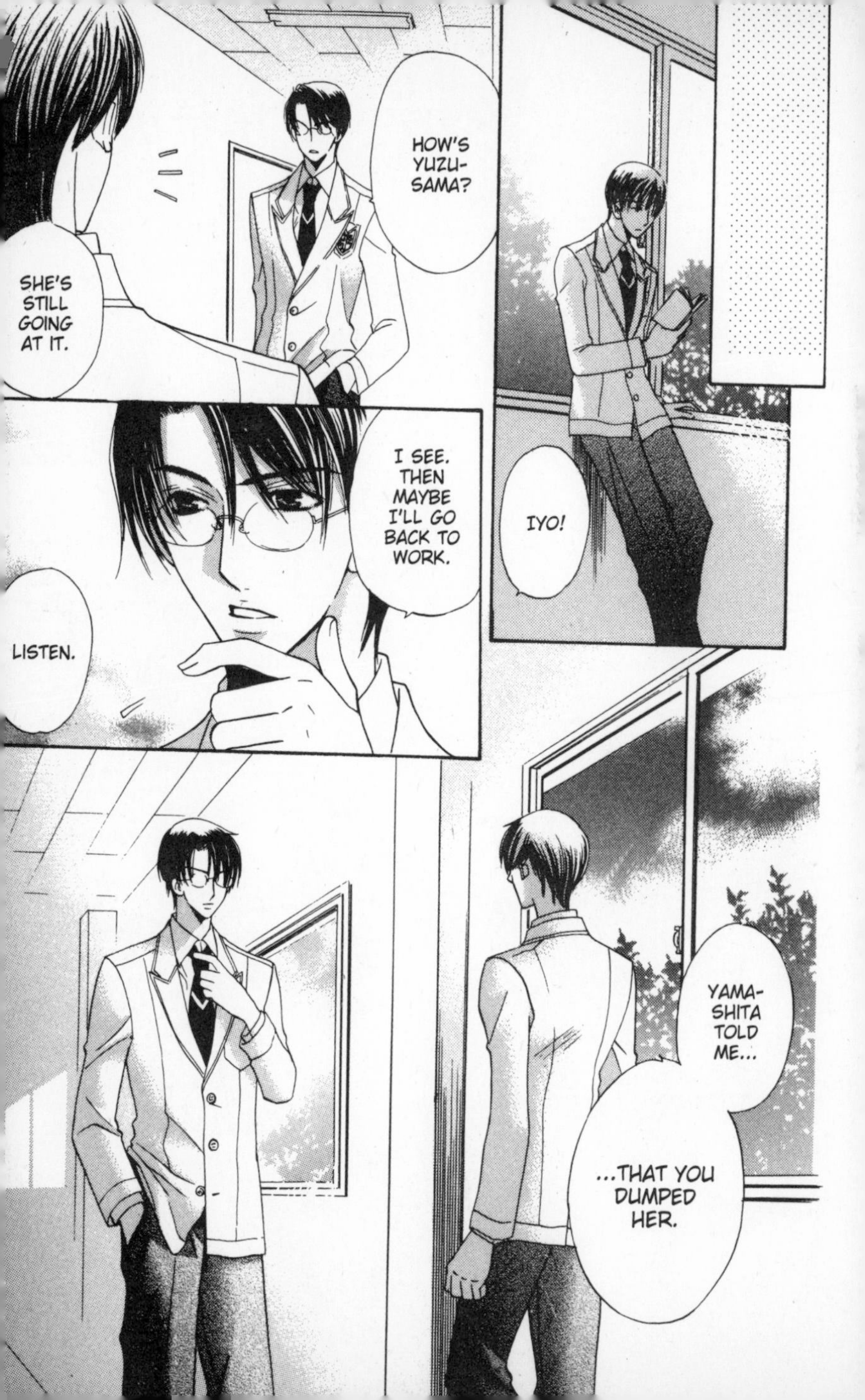
IYO!
HOW'S YUZU-SAMA?
SHE'S STILL GOING AT IT.
I SEE. THEN MAYBE I'LL GO BACK TO WORK.
LISTEN.
YAMASHITA TOLD ME...
...THAT YOU DUMPED HER.

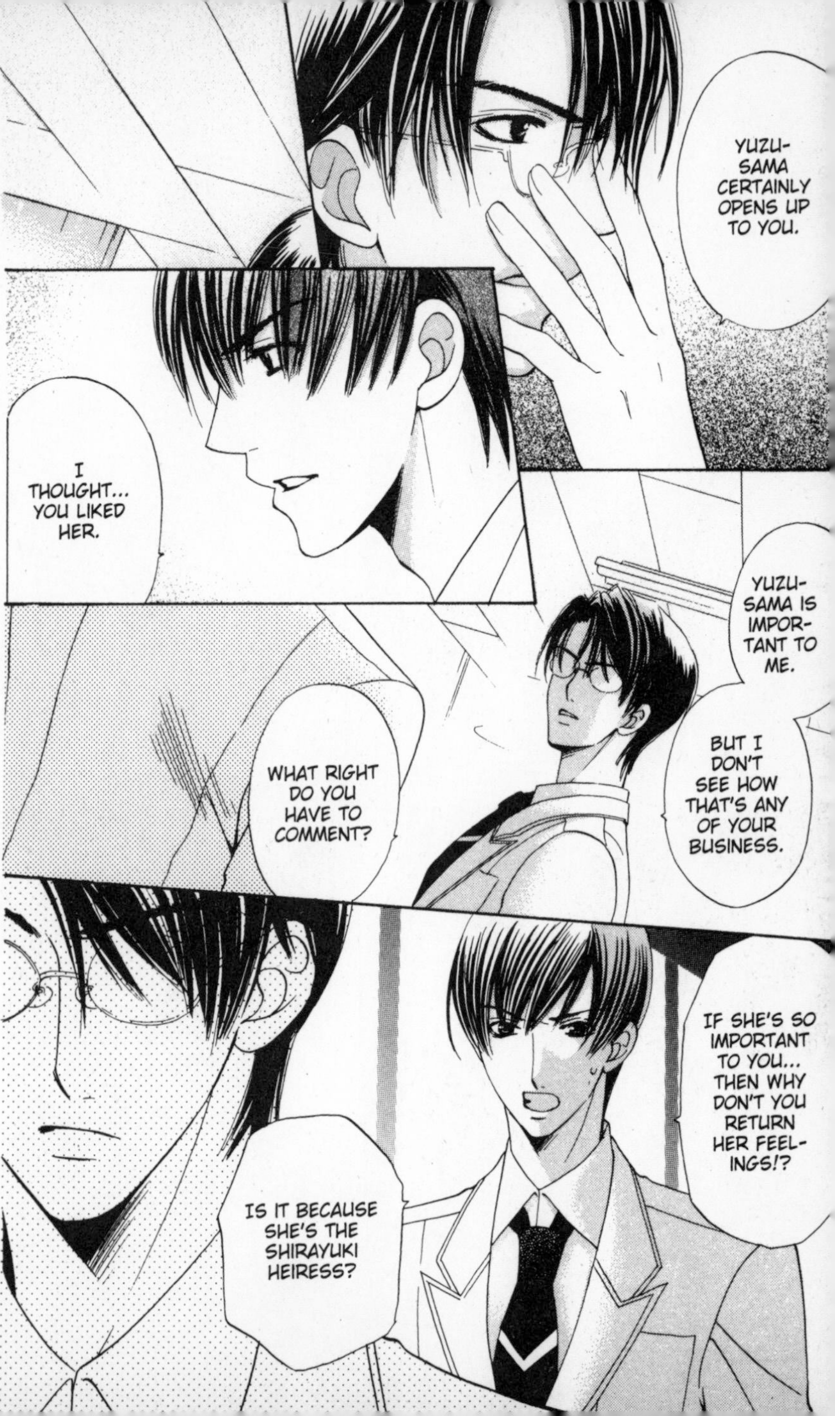
YUZU-SAMA CERTAINLY OPENS UP TO YOU.
I THOUGHT... YOU LIKED HER.
YUZU-SAMA IS IMPORTANT TO ME.
BUT I DON'T SEE HOW THAT'S ANY OF YOUR BUSINESS.
WHAT RIGHT DO YOU HAVE TO COMMENT?
IF SHE'S SO IMPORTANT TO YOU... THEN WHY DON'T YOU RETURN HER FEELINGS!?
IS IT BECAUSE SHE'S THE SHIRAYUKI HEIRESS?

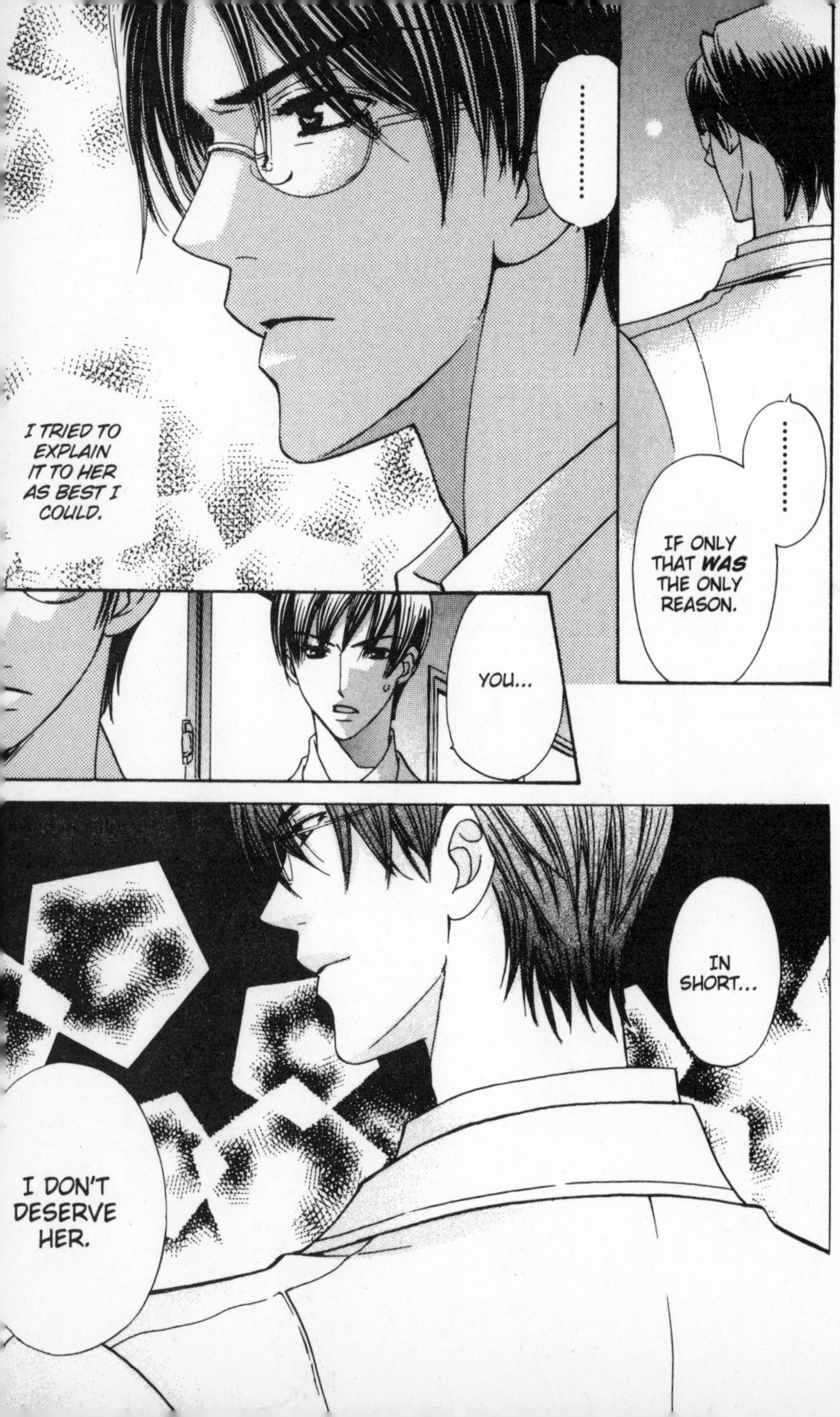
......
IF ONLY THAT ***WAS*** THE ONLY REASON.
......
I TRIED TO EXPLAIN IT TO HER AS BEST I COULD.
YOU...
IN SHORT...
I DON'T DESERVE HER.

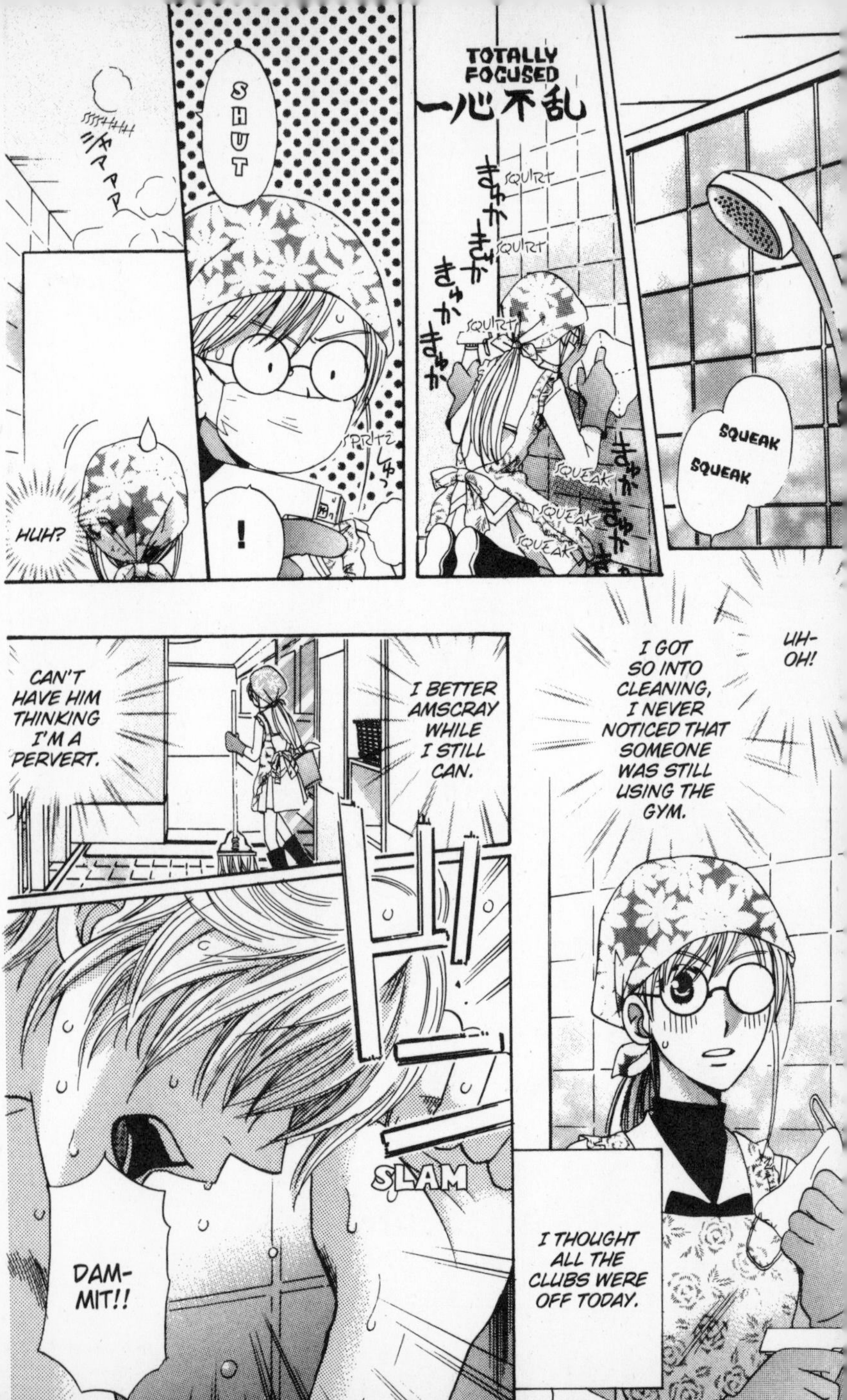
SQUEAK SQUEAK
SQUEAK
SQUEAK
SQUEAK
TOTALLY FOCUSED
一心不乱
SQUIRT
SQUIRT
SQUIRT
SHUT
SPRITZ
しゅっ
!
SSSSHHHH
シャアア
HUH?
UH-OH!
I GOT SO INTO CLEANING, I NEVER NOTICED THAT SOMEONE WAS STILL USING THE GYM.
I THOUGHT ALL THE CLUBS WERE OFF TODAY.
I BETTER AMSCRAY WHILE I STILL CAN.
CAN'T HAVE HIM THINKING I'M A PERVERT.
SLAM
DAM-MIT!!

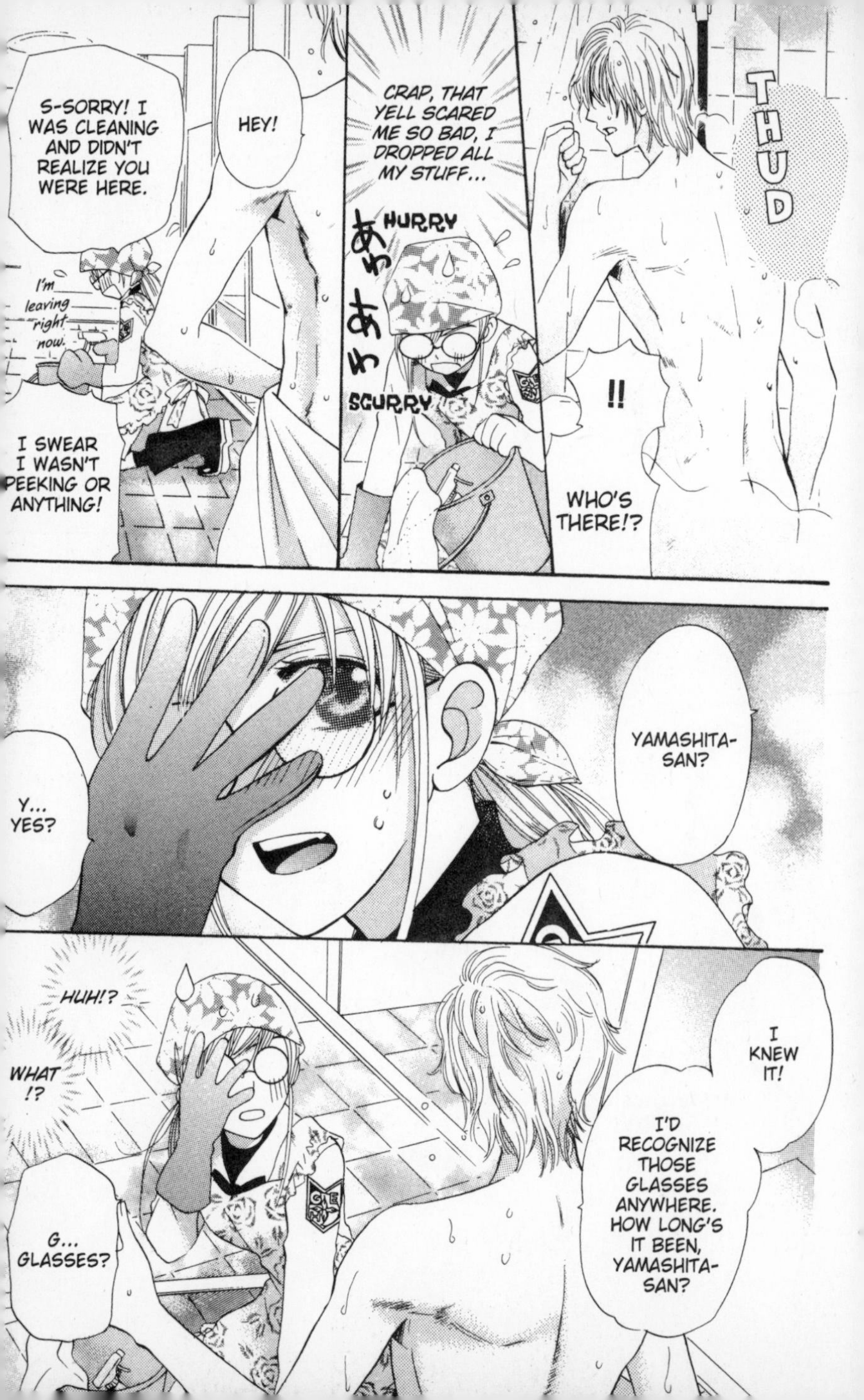
THUD
!!
WHO'S THERE!?
CRAP, THAT YELL SCARED ME SO BAD, I DROPPED ALL MY STUFF...
あわあわ
HURRY
SCURRY
HEY!
S-SORRY! I WAS CLEANING AND DIDN'T REALIZE YOU WERE HERE.
I'm leaving right now.
I SWEAR I WASN'T PEEKING OR ANYTHING!
YAMASHITA-SAN?
Y... YES?
I KNEW IT!
I'D RECOGNIZE THOSE GLASSES ANYWHERE. HOW LONG'S IT BEEN, YAMASHITA-SAN?
HUH!?
WHAT !?
G... GLASSES?

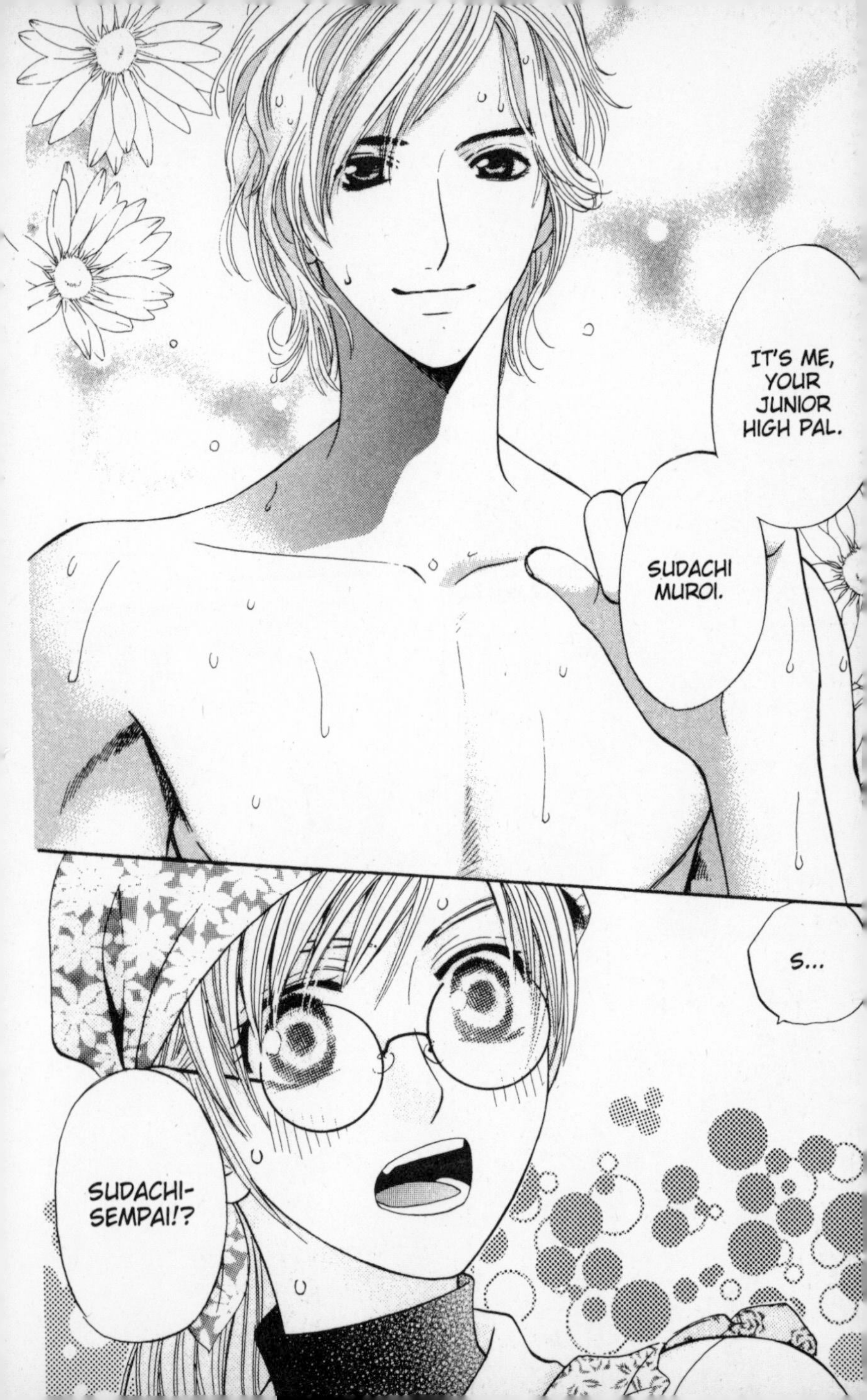
IT'S ME, YOUR JUNIOR HIGH PAL.
SUDACHI MUROI.
S...
SUDACHI-SEMPAI!?

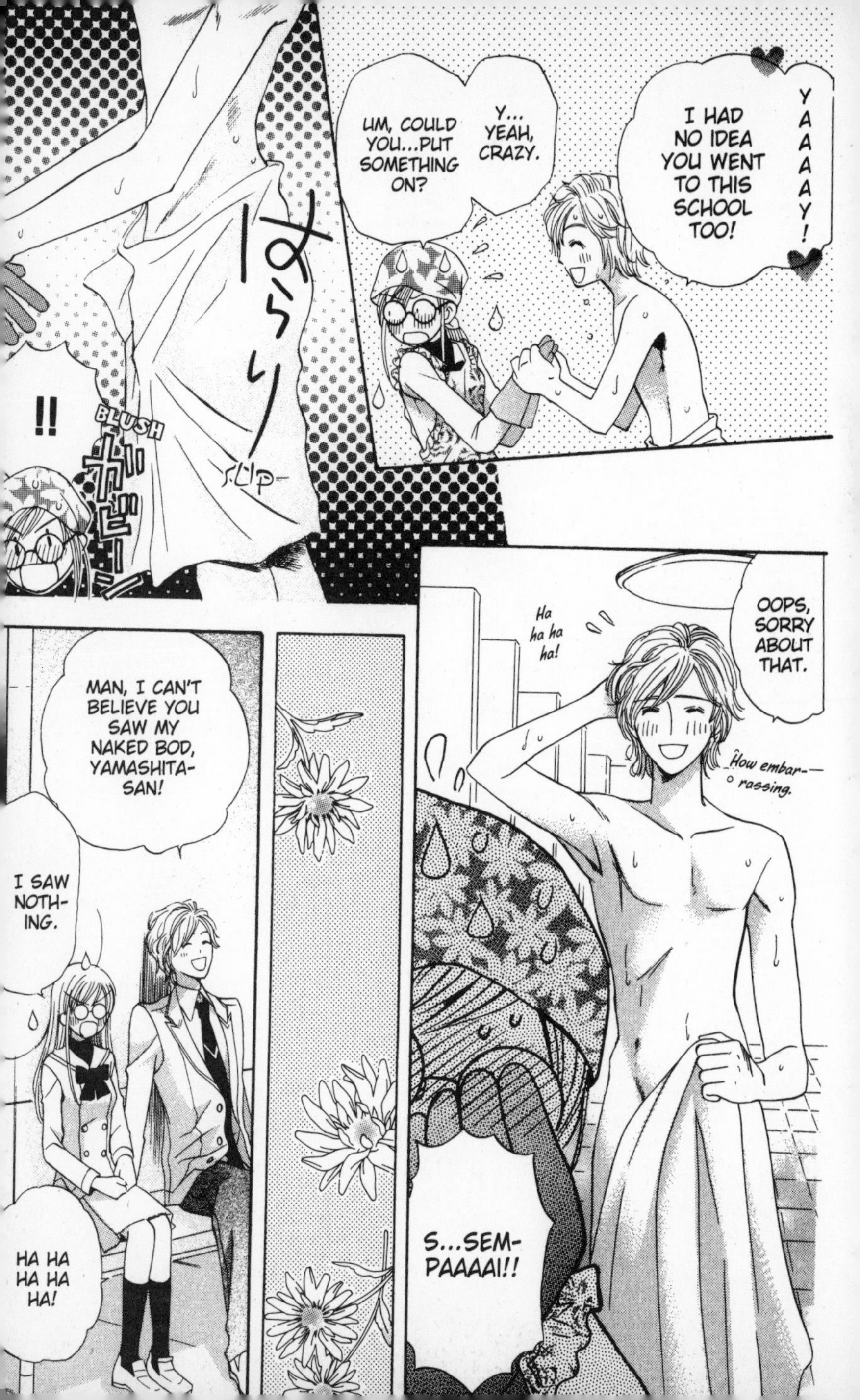
YAAAAAY!
I HAD NO IDEA YOU WENT TO THIS SCHOOL TOO!
Y... YEAH, CRAZY.
UM, COULD YOU...PUT SOMETHING ON?
はらり
SLIP
BLUSH
!!
OOPS, SORRY ABOUT THAT.
Ha ha ha ha!
How embarrassing.
S...SEMPAAAAI!!
MAN, I CAN'T BELIEVE YOU SAW MY NAKED BOD, YAMASHITA-SAN!
I SAW NOTHING.
HA HA HA HA HA!

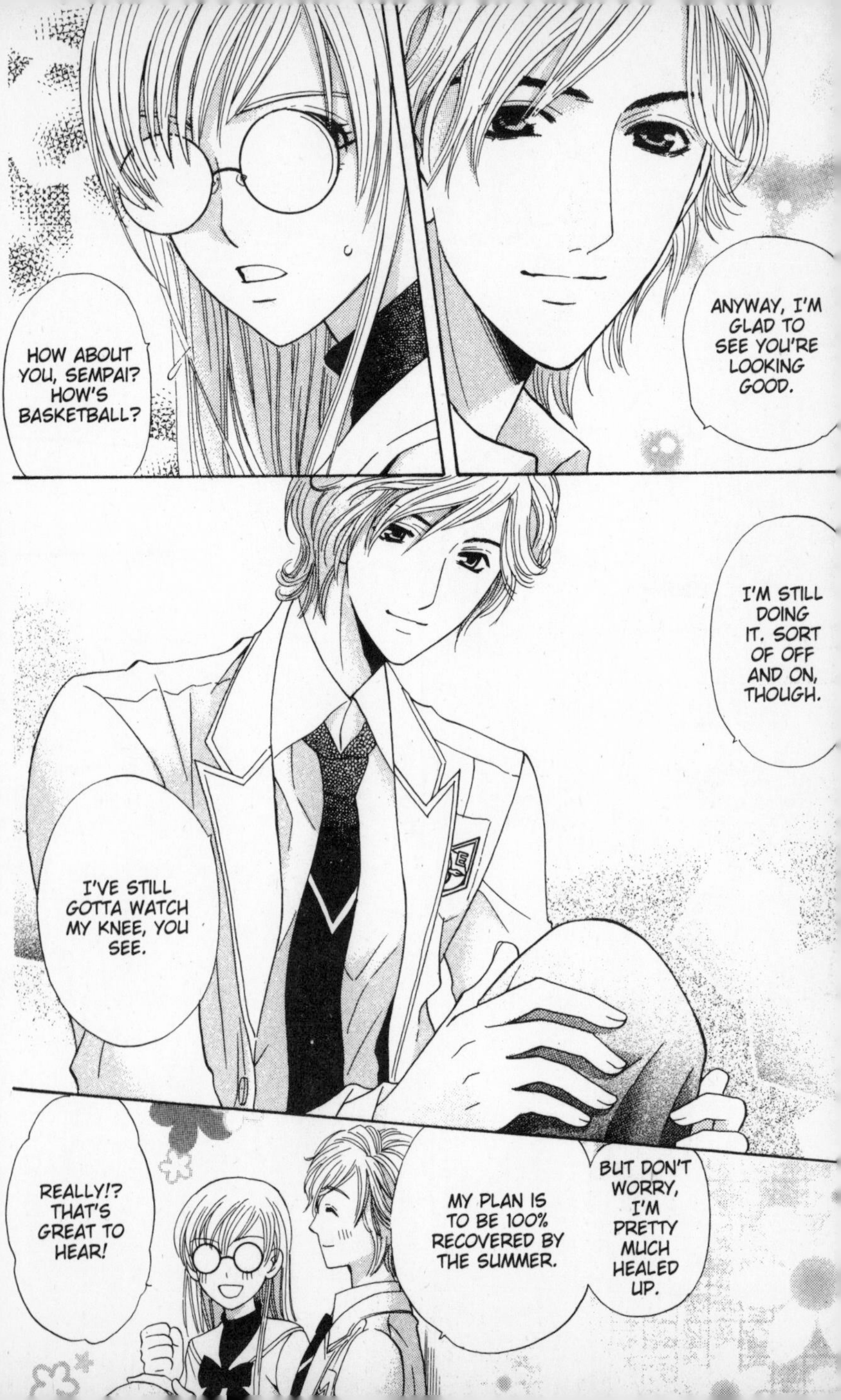
ANYWAY, I'M GLAD TO SEE YOU'RE LOOKING GOOD.
HOW ABOUT YOU, SEMPAI? HOW'S BASKETBALL?
I'M STILL DOING IT. SORT OF OFF AND ON, THOUGH.
I'VE STILL GOTTA WATCH MY KNEE, YOU SEE.
BUT DON'T WORRY, I'M PRETTY MUCH HEALED UP.
MY PLAN IS TO BE 100% RECOVERED BY THE SUMMER.
REALLY!? THAT'S GREAT TO HEAR!

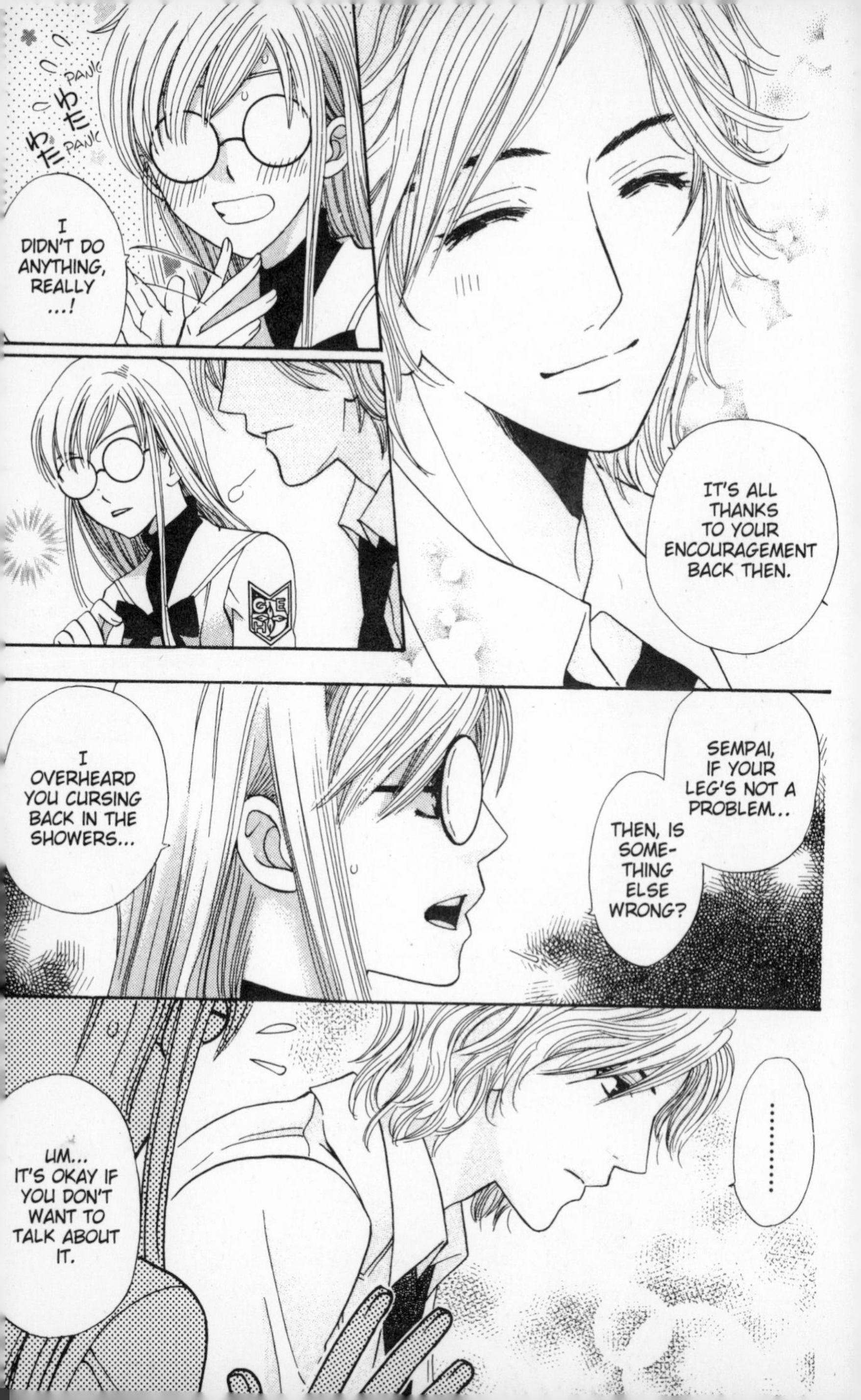
IT'S ALL THANKS TO YOUR ENCOURAGEMENT BACK THEN.
わたわた
PANIC PANIC
I DIDN'T DO ANYTHING, REALLY ...!
SEMPAI, IF YOUR LEG'S NOT A PROBLEM...
THEN, IS SOME-THING ELSE WRONG?
I OVERHEARD YOU CURSING BACK IN THE SHOWERS...
......
UM... IT'S OKAY IF YOU DON'T WANT TO TALK ABOUT IT.

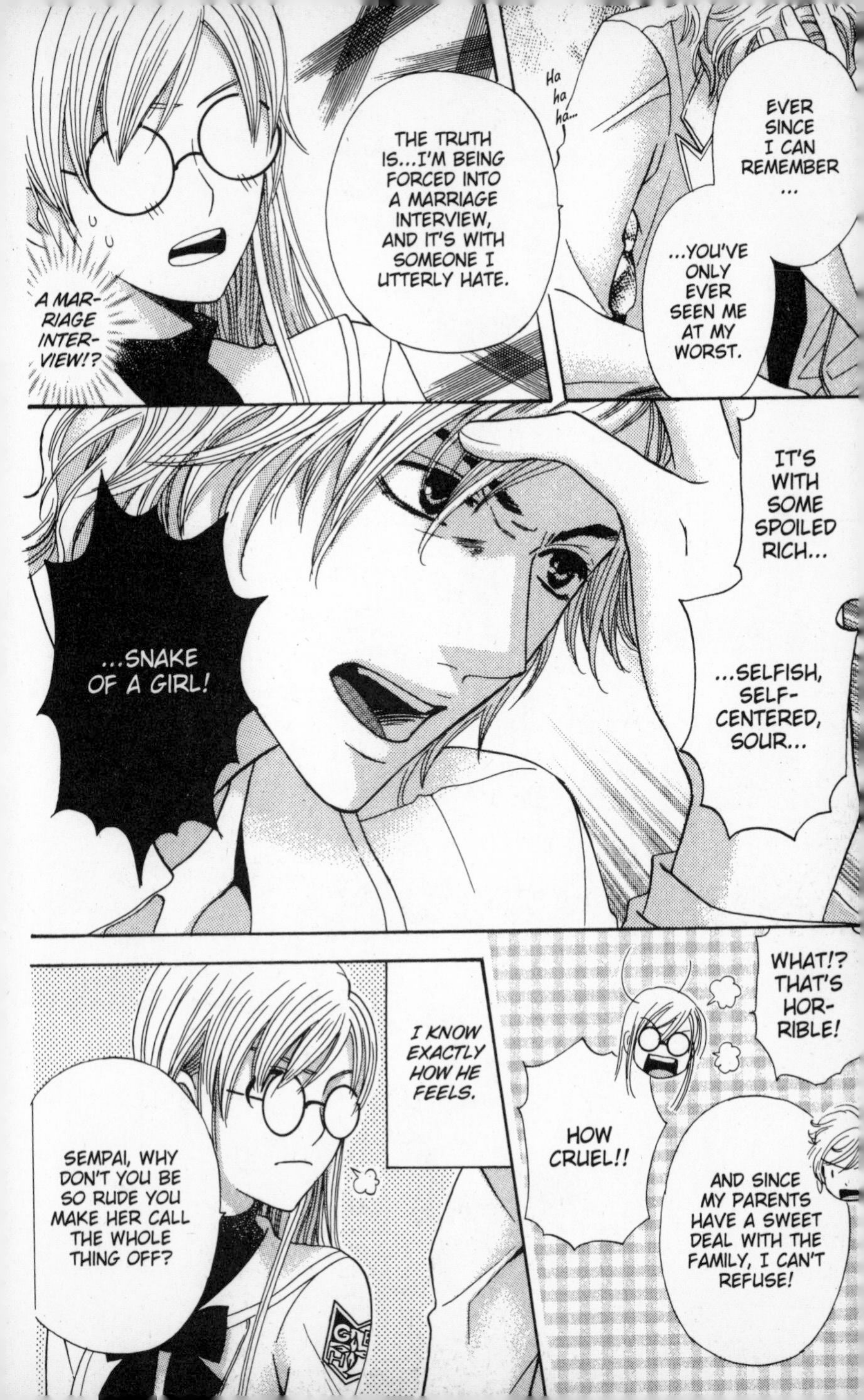
Ha ha ha...
EVER SINCE I CAN REMEMBER...
...YOU'VE ONLY EVER SEEN ME AT MY WORST.
THE TRUTH IS...I'M BEING FORCED INTO A MARRIAGE INTERVIEW, AND IT'S WITH SOMEONE I UTTERLY HATE.
A MAR-RIAGE INTER-VIEW!?
IT'S WITH SOME SPOILED RICH...
...SELFISH, SELF-CENTERED, SOUR...
...SNAKE OF A GIRL!
WHAT!? THAT'S HOR-RIBLE!
HOW CRUEL!!
AND SINCE MY PARENTS HAVE A SWEET DEAL WITH THE FAMILY, I CAN'T REFUSE!
I KNOW EXACTLY HOW HE FEELS.
SEMPAI, WHY DON'T YOU BE SO RUDE YOU MAKE HER CALL THE WHOLE THING OFF?

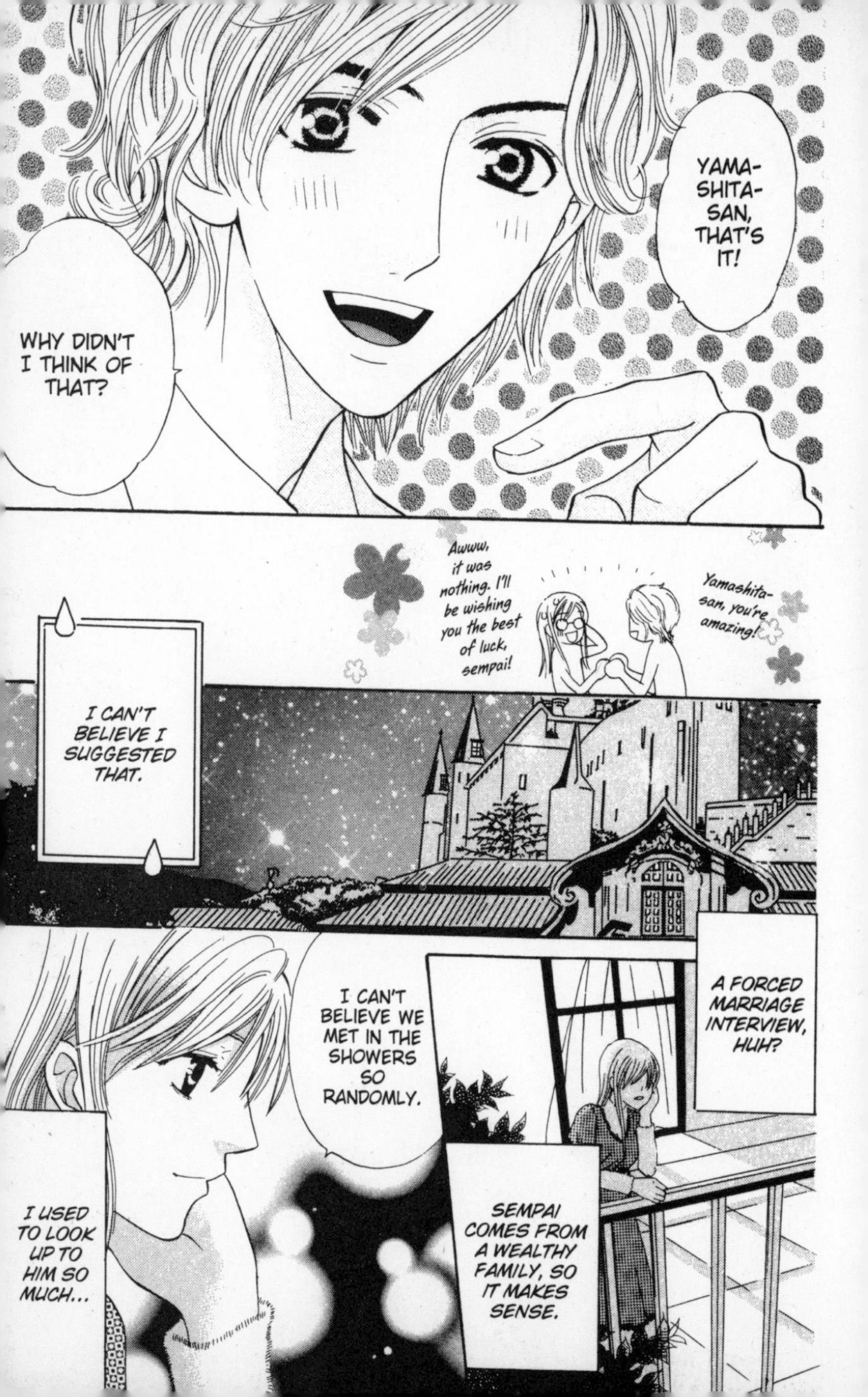

YAMASHITA-SAN, THAT'S IT!
WHY DIDN'T I THINK OF THAT?
Yamashita-san, you're amazing!
Awww, it was nothing. I'll be wishing you the best of luck, sempai!
I CAN'T BELIEVE I SUGGESTED THAT.
A FORCED MARRIAGE INTERVIEW, HUH?
SEMPAI COMES FROM A WEALTHY FAMILY, SO IT MAKES SENSE.
I CAN'T BELIEVE WE MET IN THE SHOWERS SO RANDOMLY.
I USED TO LOOK UP TO HIM SO MUCH...

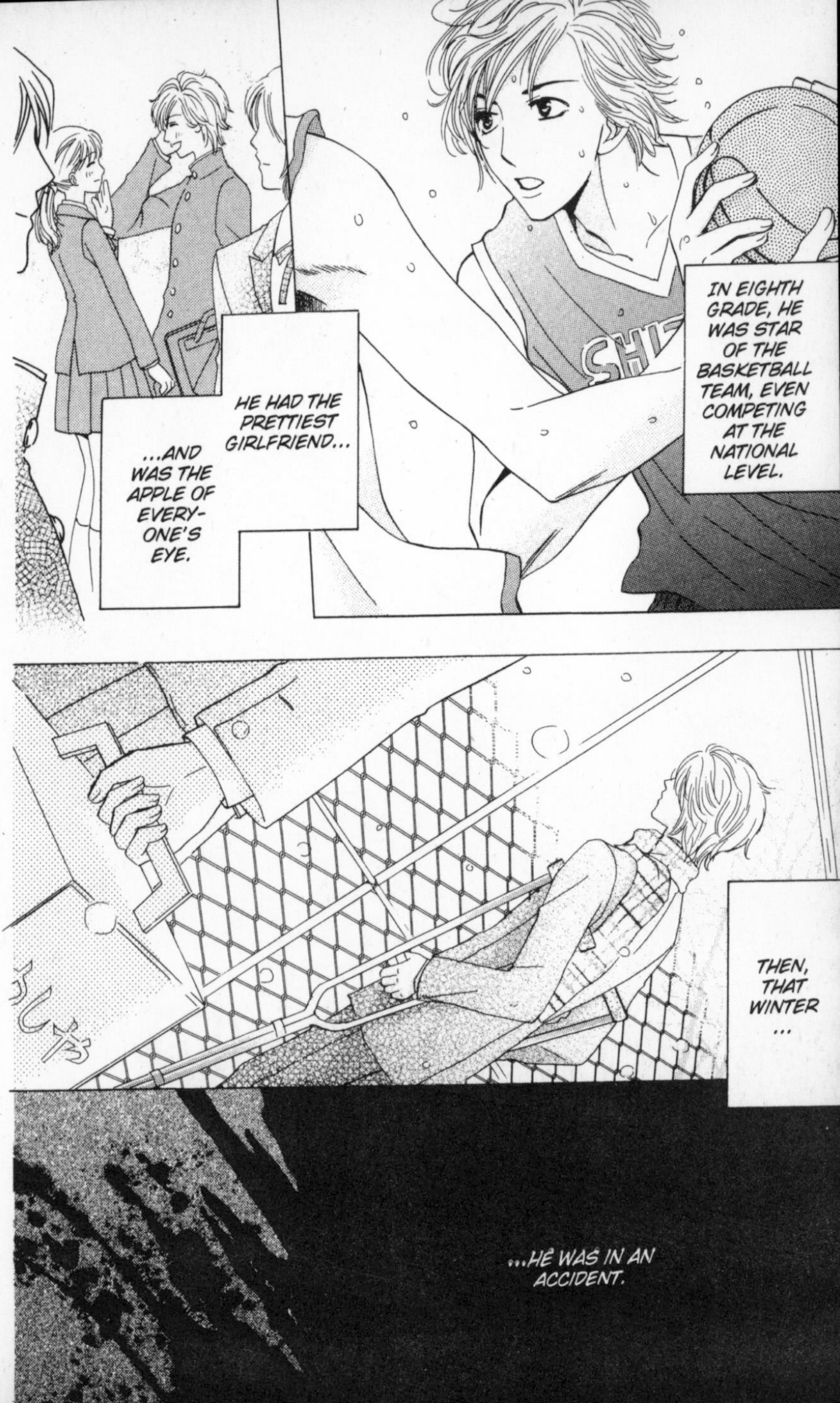
IN EIGHTH GRADE, HE WAS STAR OF THE BASKETBALL TEAM, EVEN COMPETING AT THE NATIONAL LEVEL.
HE HAD THE PRETTIEST GIRLFRIEND...
...AND WAS THE APPLE OF EVERY-ONE'S EYE.
THEN, THAT WINTER ...
...HE WAS IN AN ACCIDENT.

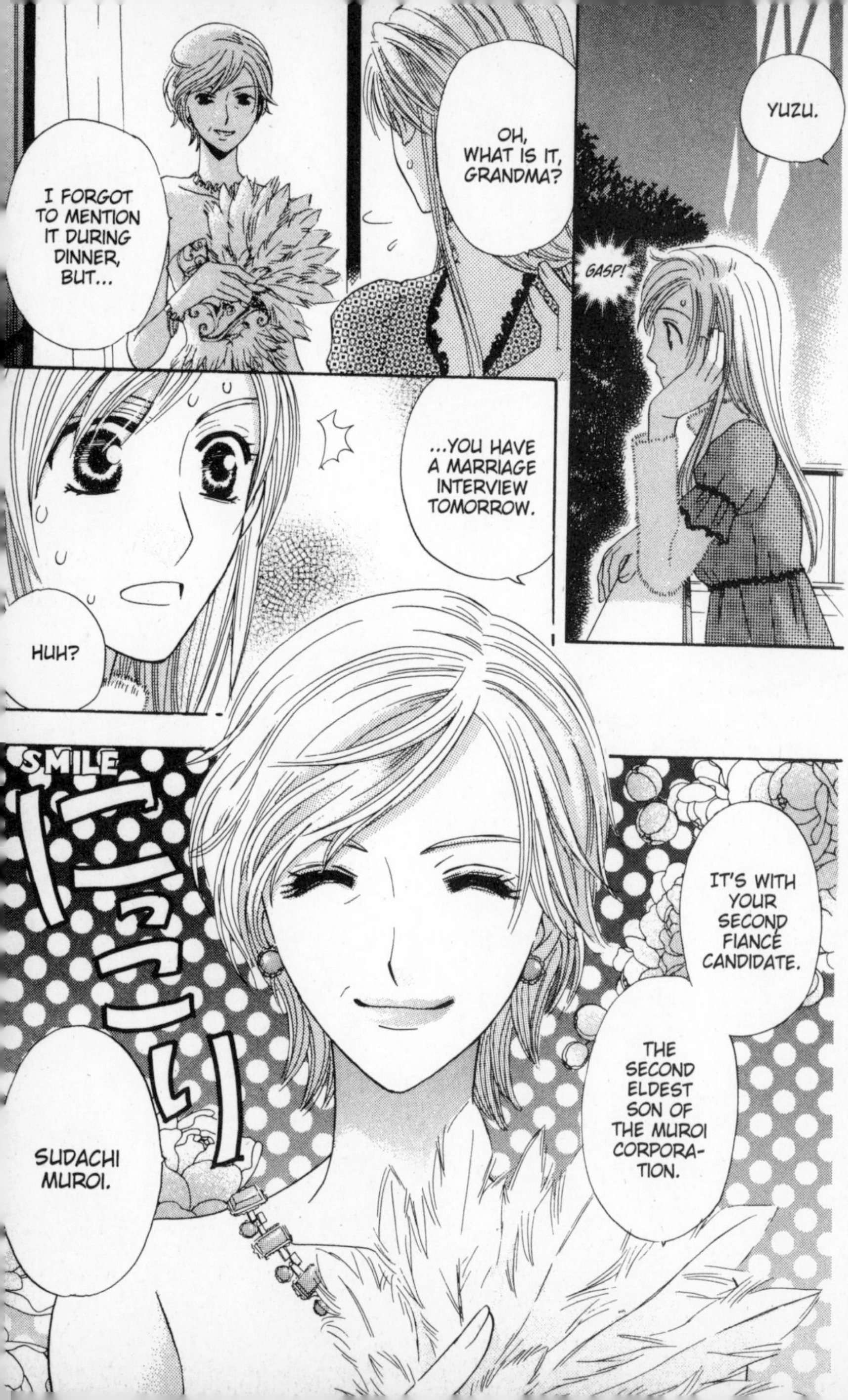
YUZU.
GASP!
OH, WHAT IS IT, GRANDMA?
I FORGOT TO MENTION IT DURING DINNER, BUT...
...YOU HAVE A MARRIAGE INTERVIEW TOMORROW.
HUH?
IT'S WITH YOUR SECOND FIANCÉ CANDIDATE.
THE SECOND ELDEST SON OF THE MUROI CORPORATION.
SMILE
SUDACHI MUROI.

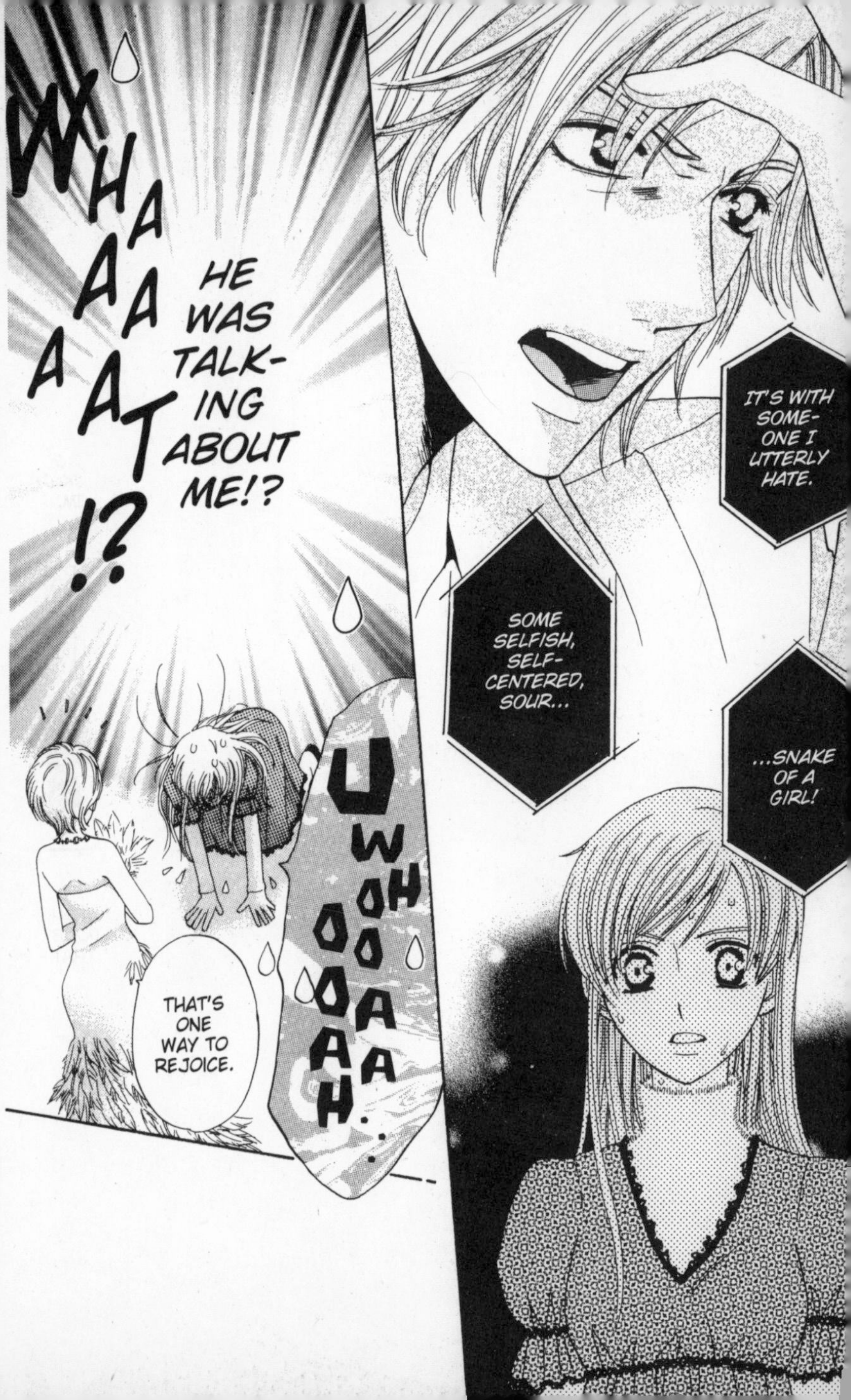
IT'S WITH SOMEONE I UTTERLY HATE.
SOME SELFISH, SELF-CENTERED, SOUR...
...SNAKE OF A GIRL!
WHAAAAAT!?
HE WAS TALKING ABOUT ME!?
UWHOOOOOOAAAAH...
THAT'S ONE WAY TO REJOICE.

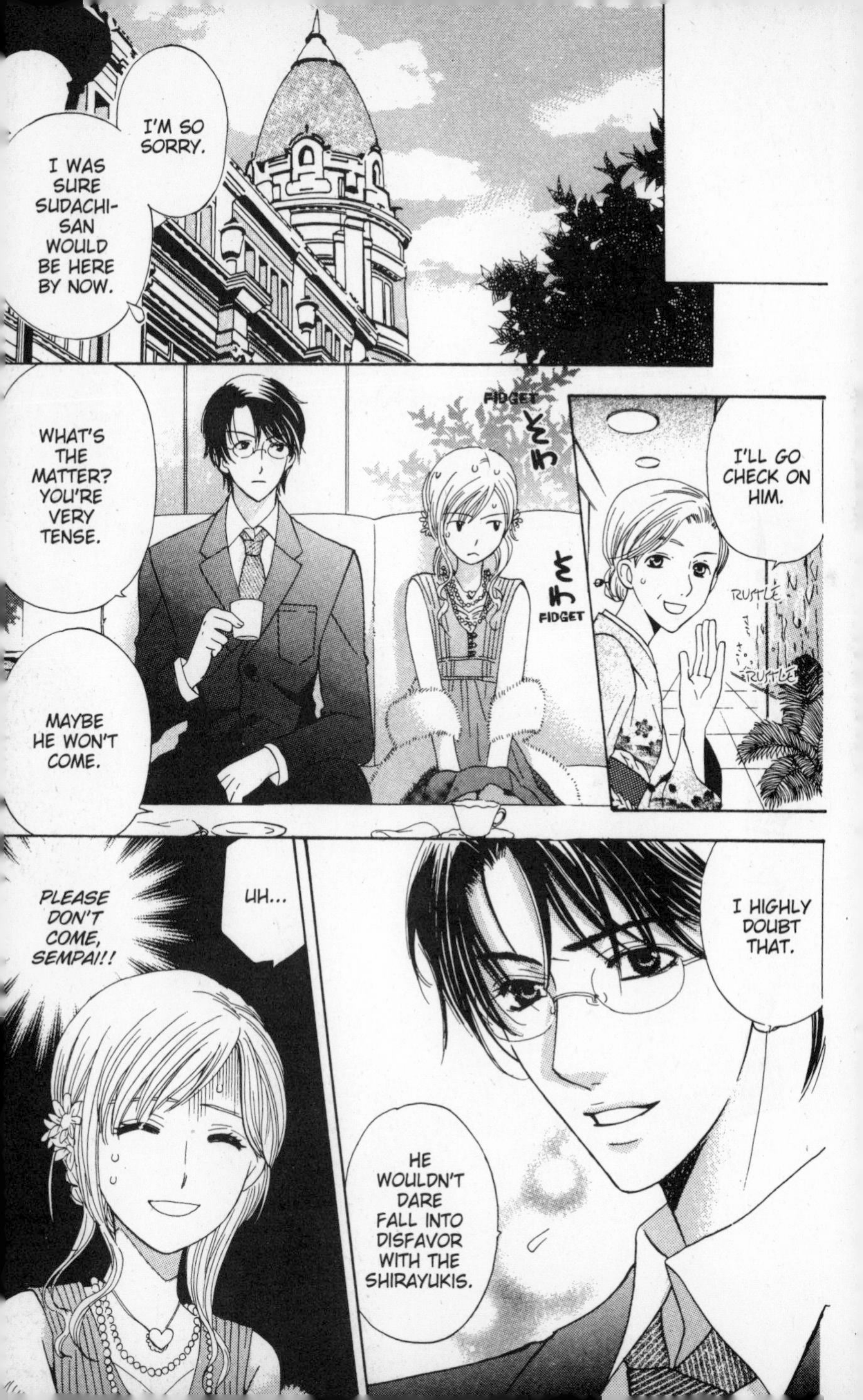
I'M SO SORRY.
I WAS SURE SUDACHI-SAN WOULD BE HERE BY NOW.
I'LL GO CHECK ON HIM.
RUSTLE
RUSTLE
FIDGET
FIDGET
WHAT'S THE MATTER? YOU'RE VERY TENSE.
MAYBE HE WON'T COME.
I HIGHLY DOUBT THAT.
HE WOULDN'T DARE FALL INTO DISFAVOR WITH THE SHIRAYUKIS.
UH...
PLEASE DON'T COME, SEMPAI!!

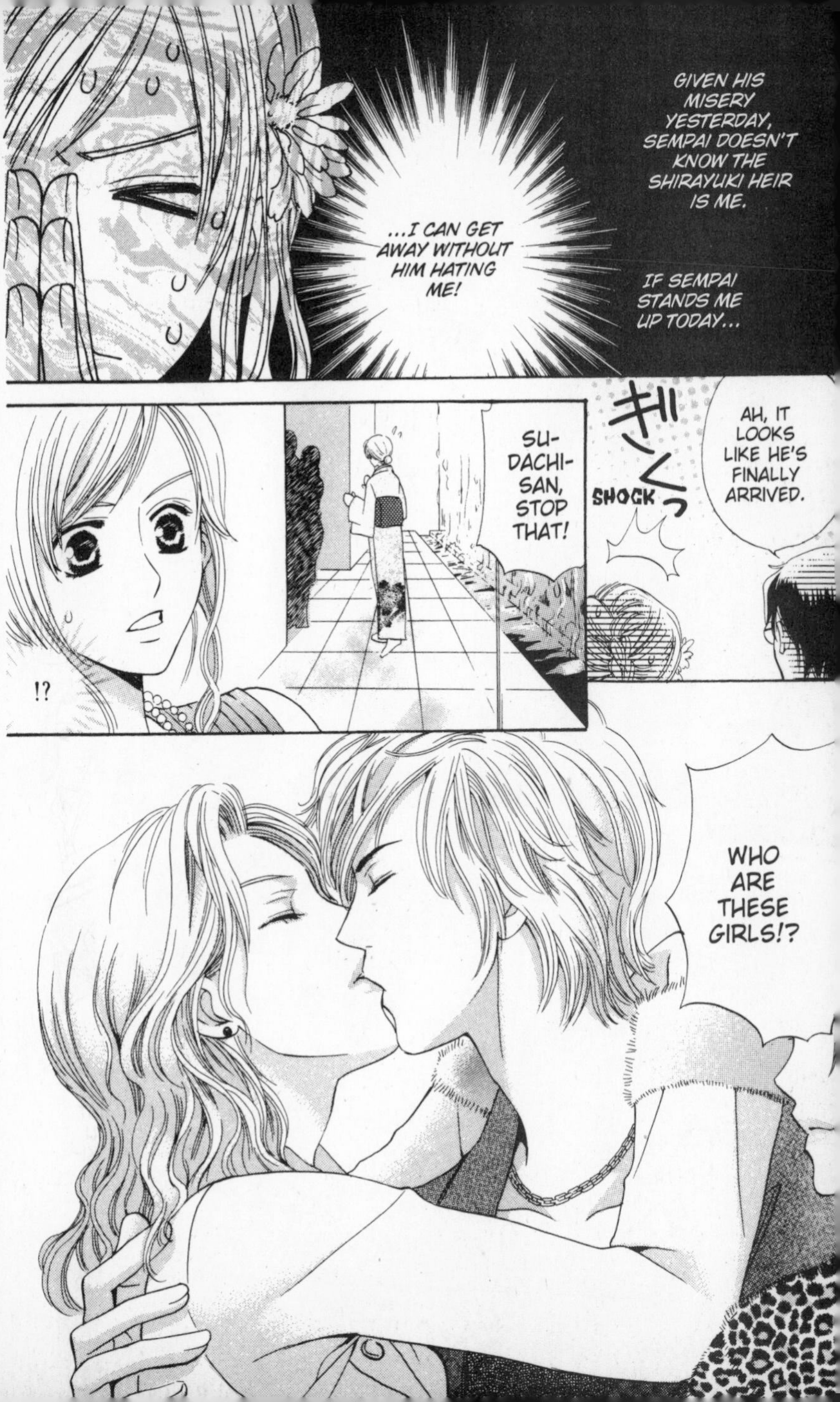
GIVEN HIS MISERY YESTERDAY, SEMPAI DOESN'T KNOW THE SHIRAYUKI HEIR IS ME.
IF SEMPAI STANDS ME UP TODAY...
...I CAN GET AWAY WITHOUT HIM HATING ME!
AH, IT LOOKS LIKE HE'S FINALLY ARRIVED.
ぎくっ
SHOCK
SU-DACHI-SAN, STOP THAT!
!?
WHO ARE THESE GIRLS!?

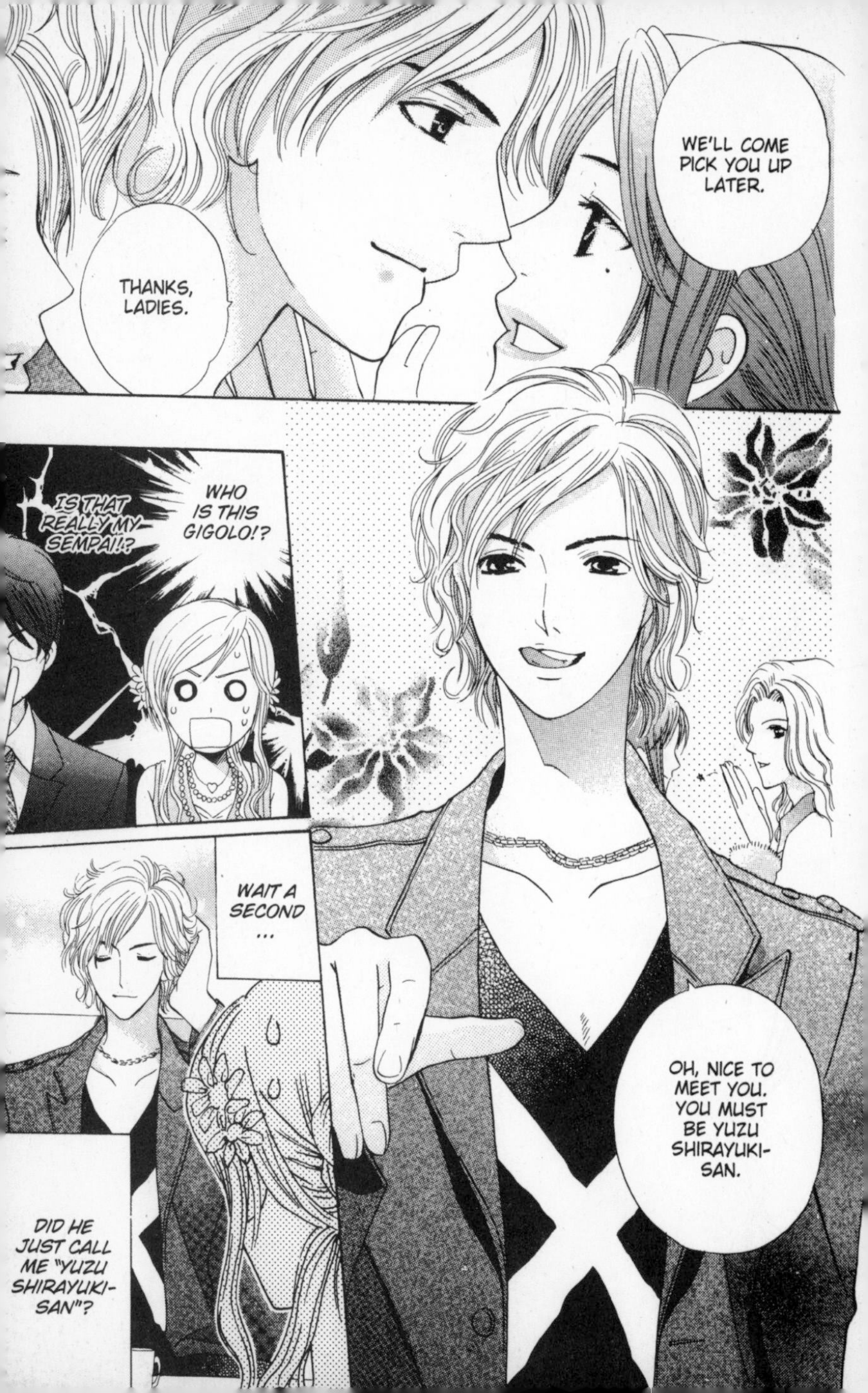
WE'LL COME PICK YOU UP LATER.
THANKS, LADIES.
OH, NICE TO MEET YOU. YOU MUST BE YUZU SHIRAYUKI-SAN.
WHO IS THIS GIGOLO!?
IS THAT REALLY MY SEMPAI!?
WAIT A SECOND ...
DID HE JUST CALL ME "YUZU SHIRAYUKI-SAN"?

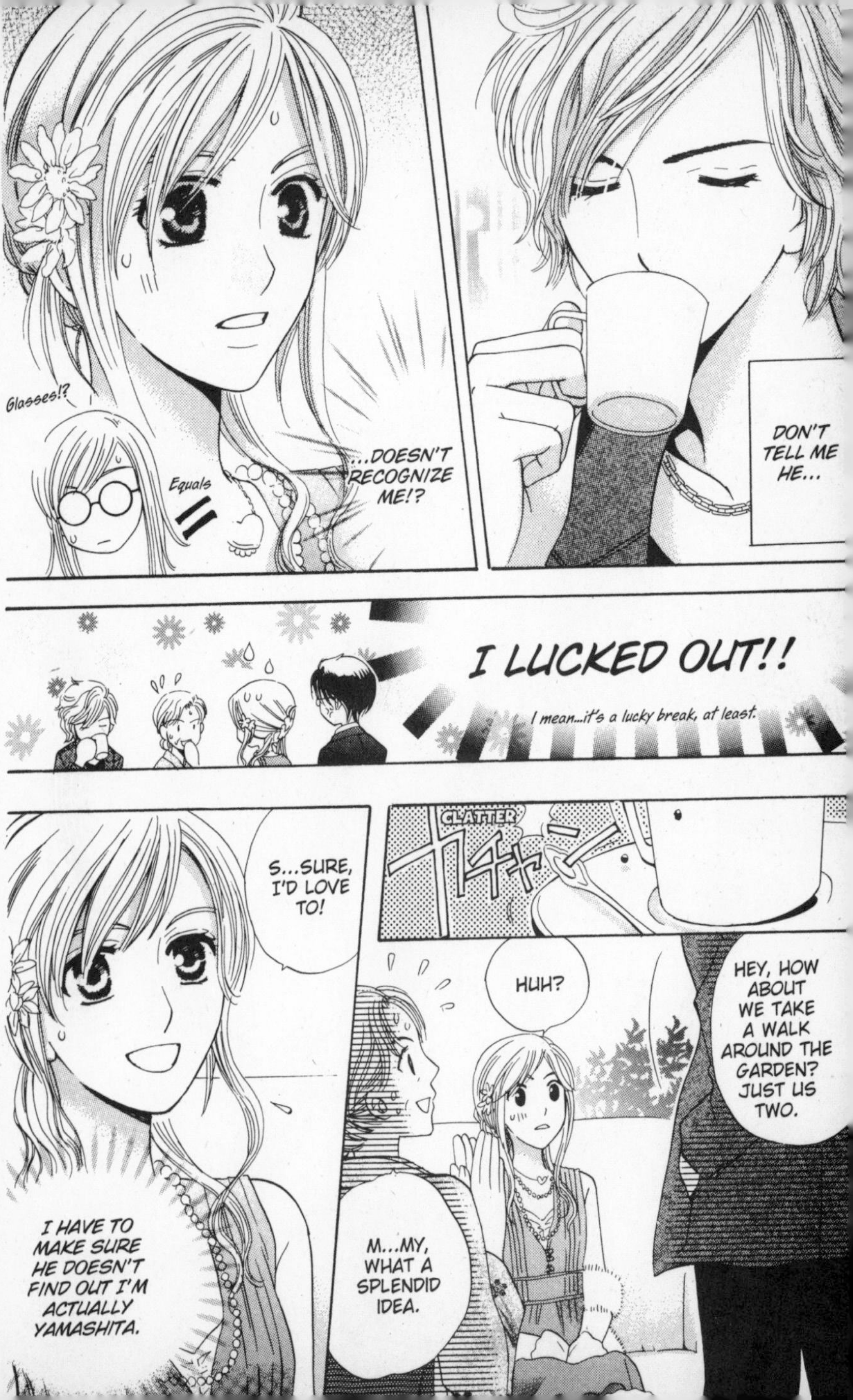
DON'T TELL ME HE...
...DOESN'T RECOGNIZE ME!?
Glasses!?
Equals
I LUCKED OUT!!
I mean...it's a lucky break, at least.
CLATTER
HEY, HOW ABOUT WE TAKE A WALK AROUND THE GARDEN? JUST US TWO.
HUH?
M...MY, WHAT A SPLENDID IDEA.
S...SURE, I'D LOVE TO!
I HAVE TO MAKE SURE HE DOESN'T FIND OUT I'M ACTUALLY YAMASHITA.

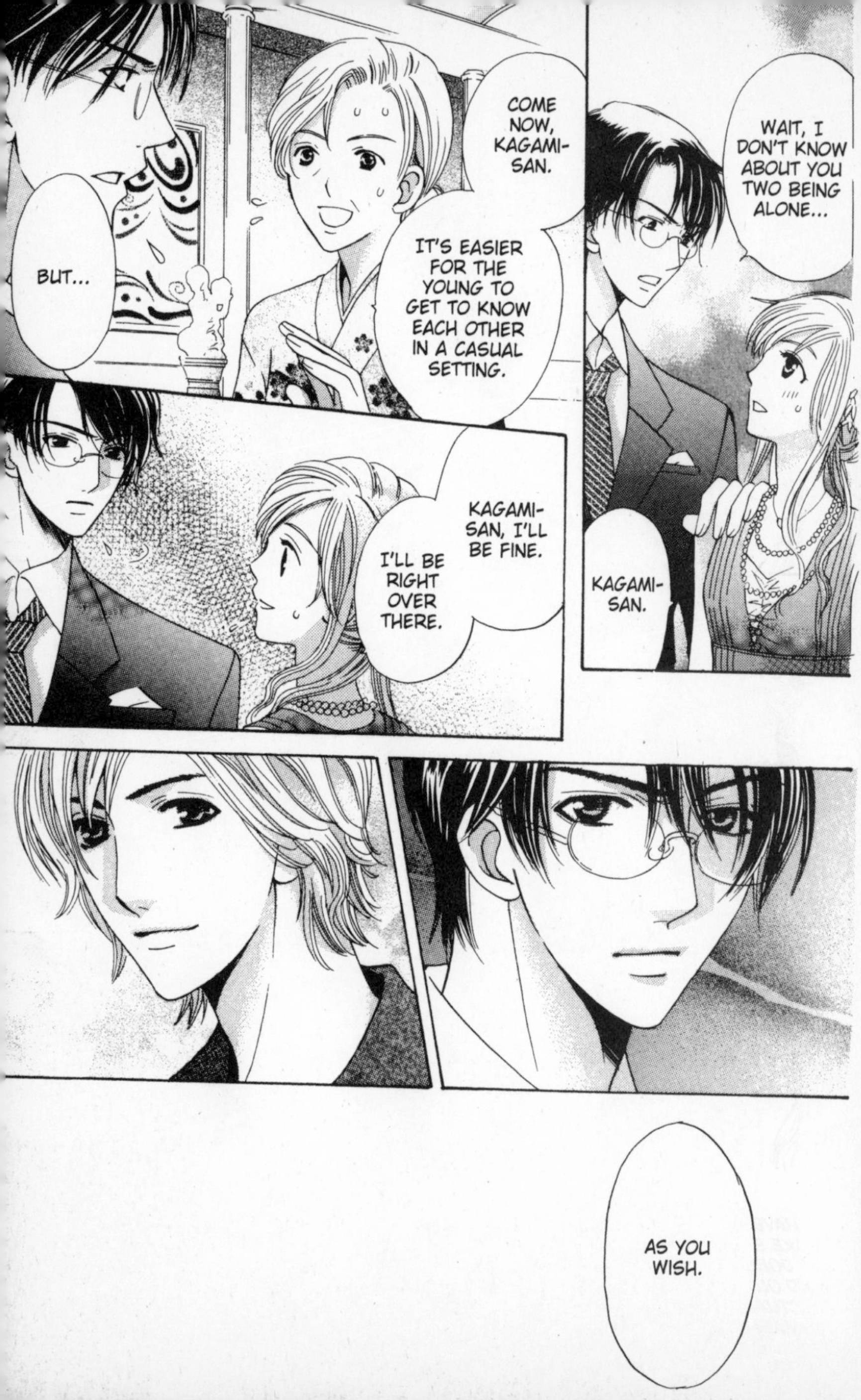
WAIT, I DON'T KNOW ABOUT YOU TWO BEING ALONE...
KAGAMI-SAN.
COME NOW, KAGAMI-SAN.
IT'S EASIER FOR THE YOUNG TO GET TO KNOW EACH OTHER IN A CASUAL SETTING.
BUT...
KAGAMI-SAN, I'LL BE FINE.
I'LL BE RIGHT OVER THERE.
AS YOU WISH.

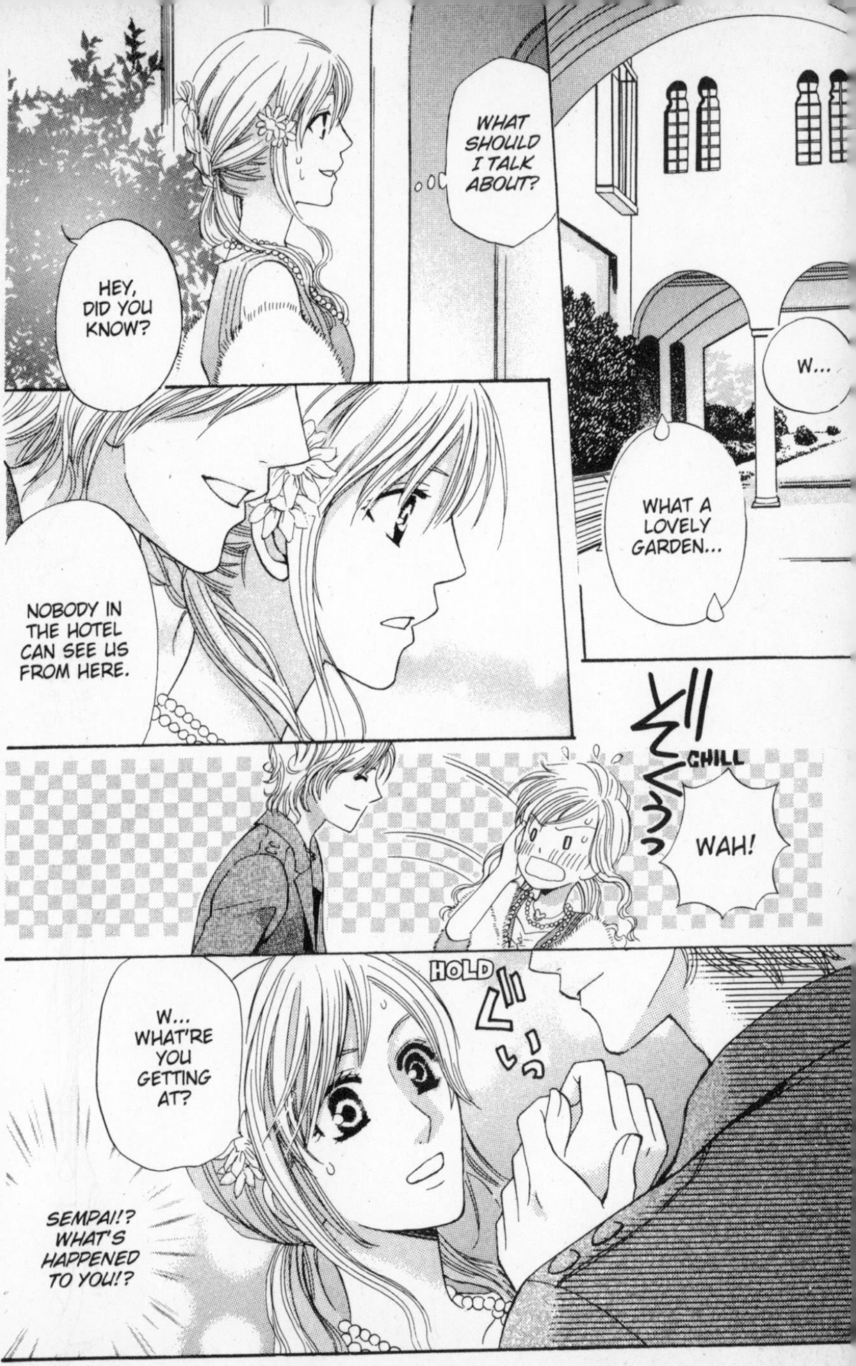
W...
WHAT A LOVELY GARDEN...
WHAT SHOULD I TALK ABOUT?
HEY, DID YOU KNOW?
NOBODY IN THE HOTEL CAN SEE US FROM HERE.
CHILL
WAH!
HOLD
W... WHAT'RE YOU GETTING AT?
SEMPAI!? WHAT'S HAPPENED TO YOU!?

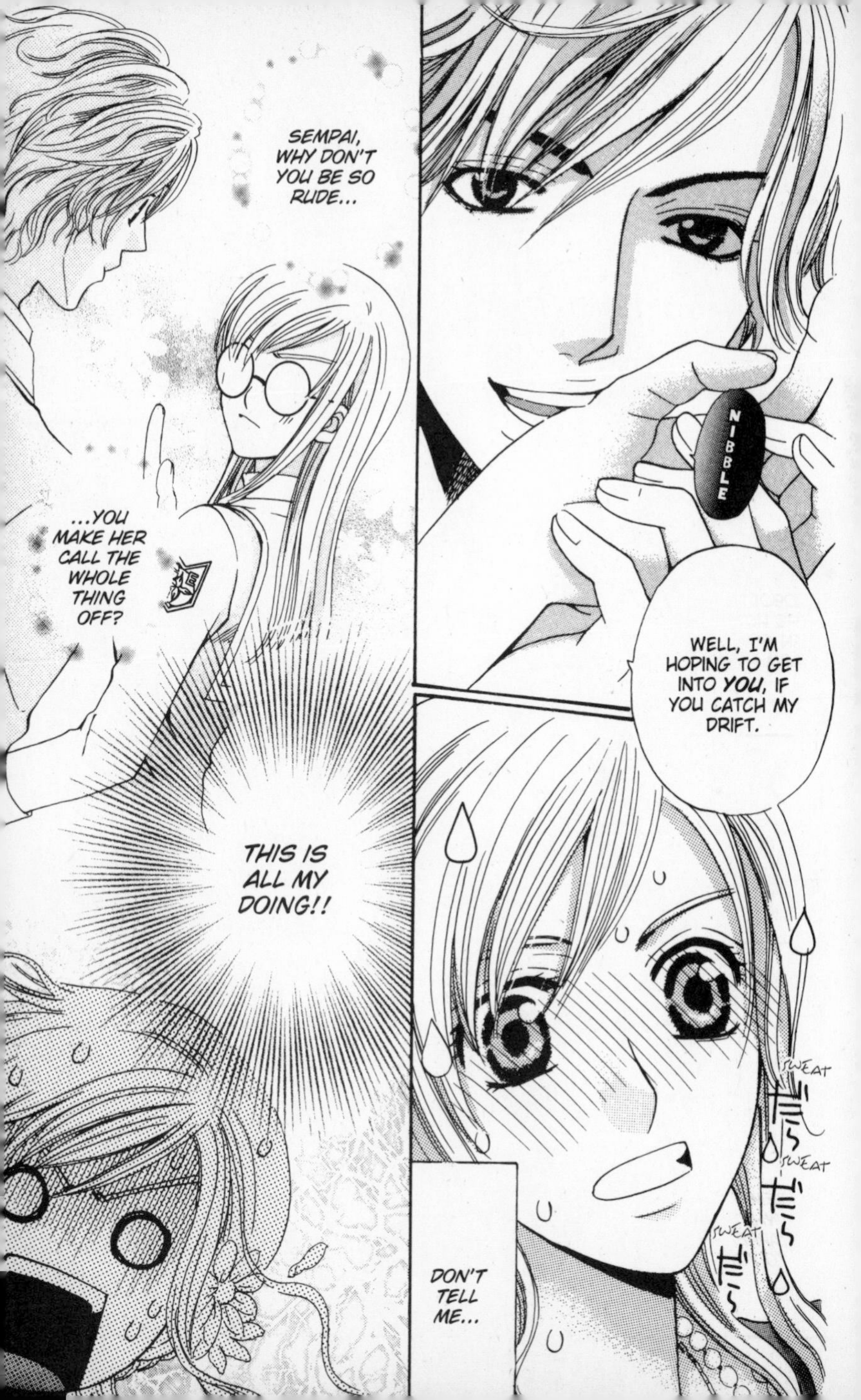
NIBBLE
WELL, I'M HOPING TO GET INTO *YOU*, IF YOU CATCH MY DRIFT.
SWEAT
SWEAT
SWEAT
DON'T TELL ME...
SEMPAI, WHY DON'T YOU BE SO RUDE...
...YOU MAKE HER CALL THE WHOLE THING OFF?
THIS IS ALL MY DOING!!

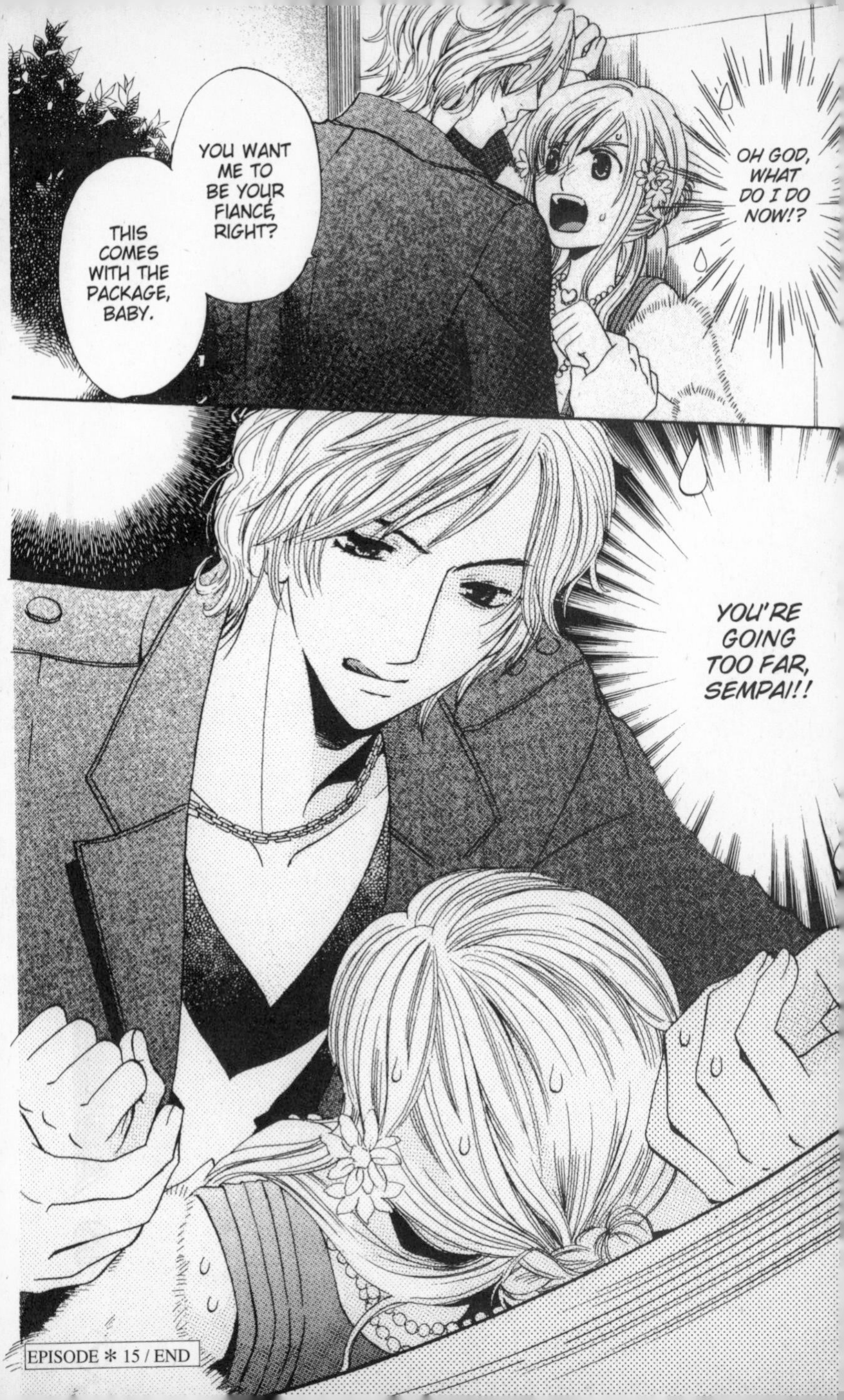
OH GOD, WHAT DO I DO NOW!?
YOU WANT ME TO BE YOUR FIANCÉ, RIGHT?
THIS COMES WITH THE PACKAGE, BABY.
YOU'RE GOING TOO FAR, SEMPAI!!
EPISODE ✻ 15 / END

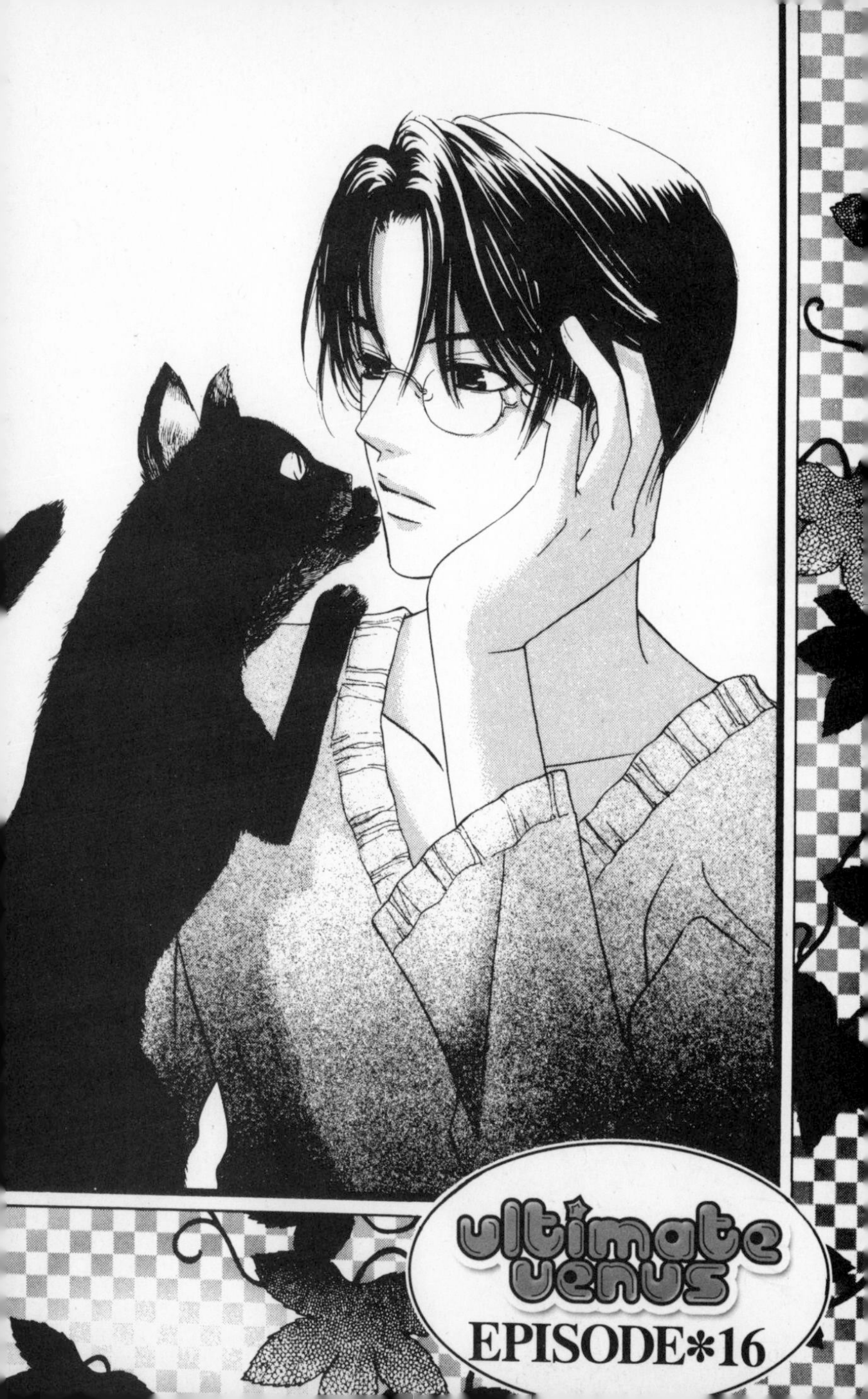
ultimate venus
EPISODE*16

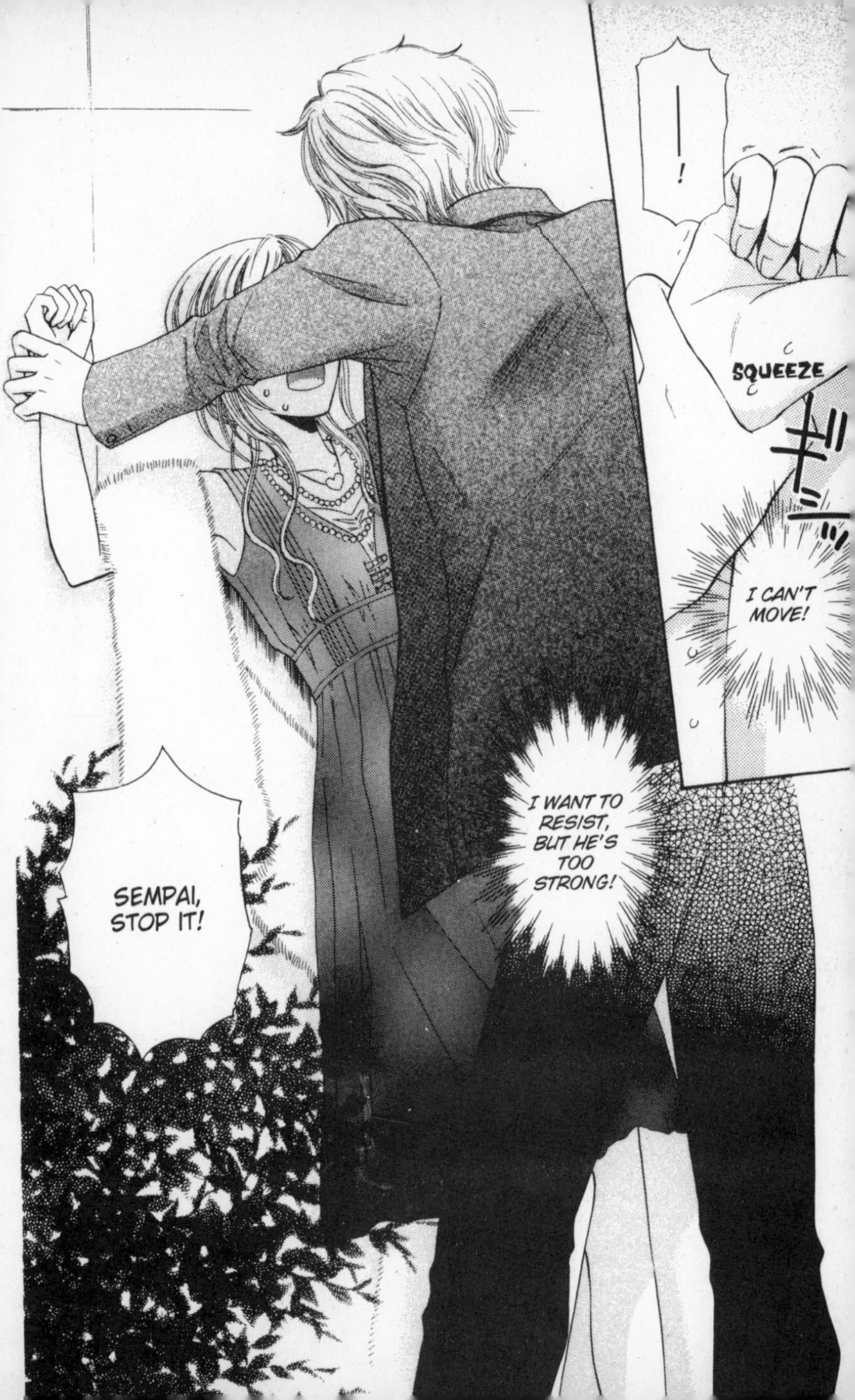
!
SQUEEZE
I CAN'T MOVE!
I WANT TO RESIST, BUT HE'S TOO STRONG!
SEMPAI, STOP IT!

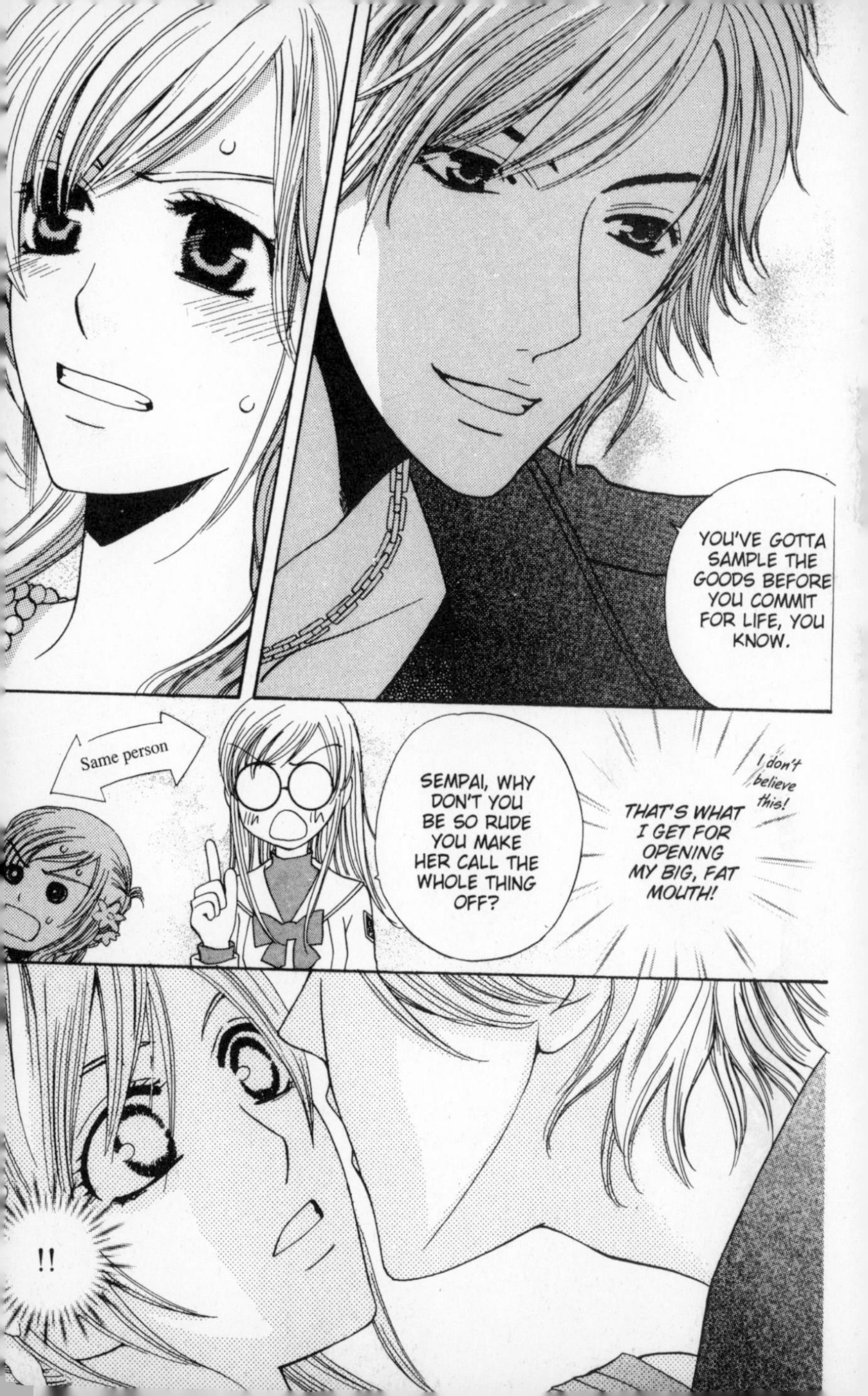
YOU'VE GOTTA SAMPLE THE GOODS BEFORE YOU COMMIT FOR LIFE, YOU KNOW.
I don't believe this!
THAT'S WHAT I GET FOR OPENING MY BIG, FAT MOUTH!
SEMPAI, WHY DON'T YOU BE SO RUDE YOU MAKE HER CALL THE WHOLE THING OFF?
Same person
!!

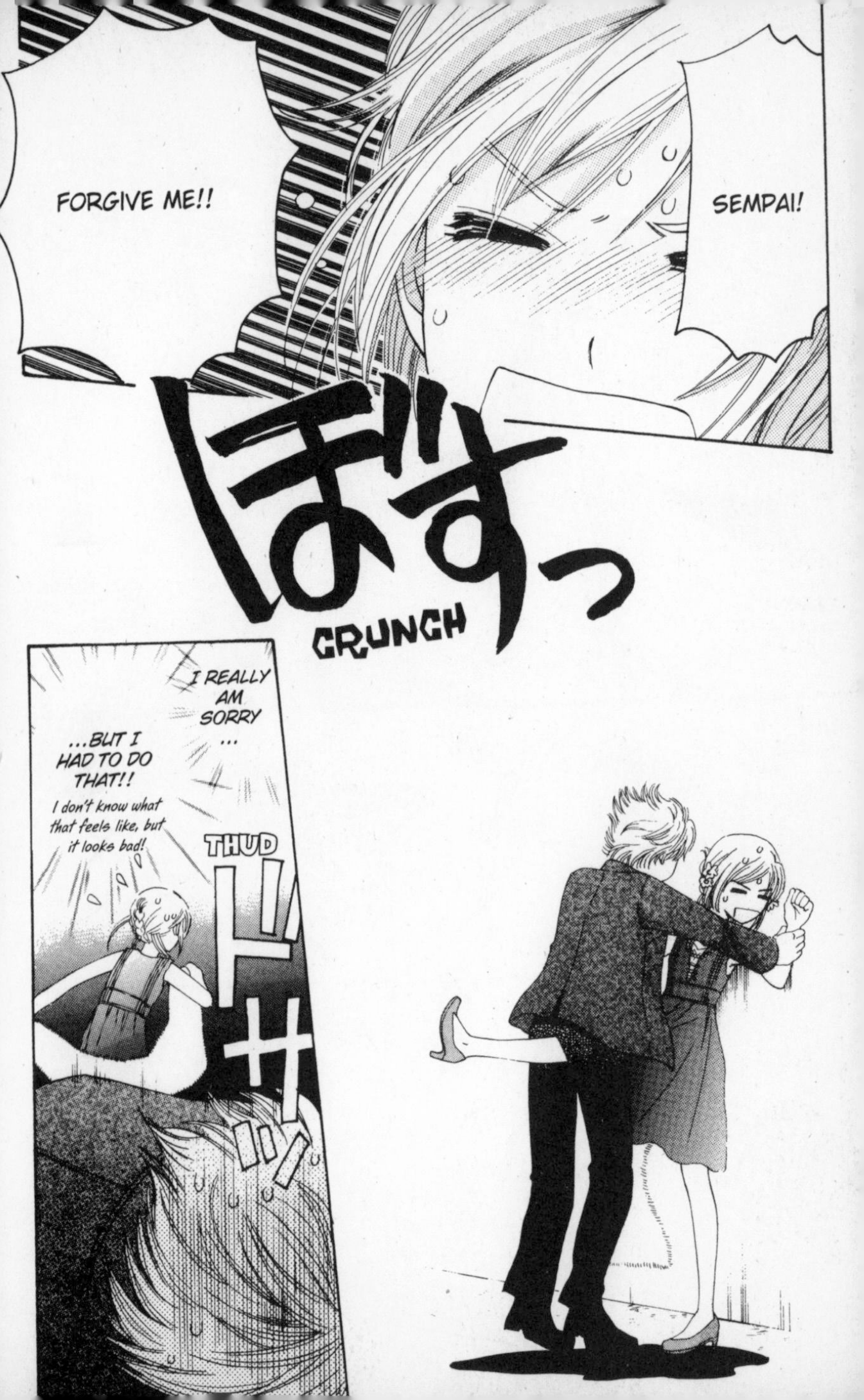
SEMPAI!
FORGIVE ME!!
ぼすっ
CRUNCH
I REALLY AM SORRY ...
...BUT I HAD TO DO THAT!!
I don't know what that feels like, but it looks bad!
THUD
ドサッ

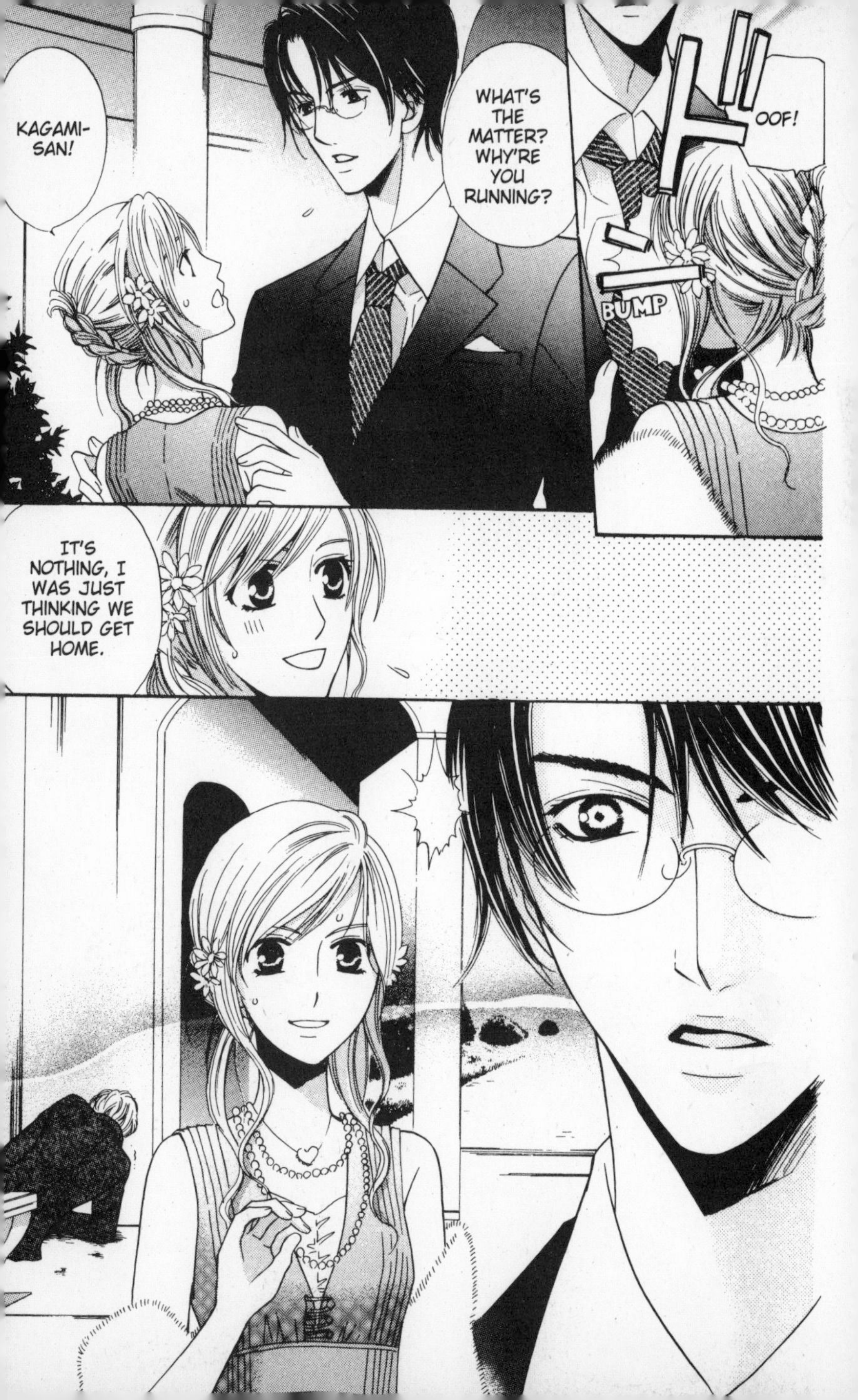
OOF!
BUMP
KAGAMI-SAN!
WHAT'S THE MATTER? WHY'RE YOU RUNNING?
IT'S NOTHING, I WAS JUST THINKING WE SHOULD GET HOME.

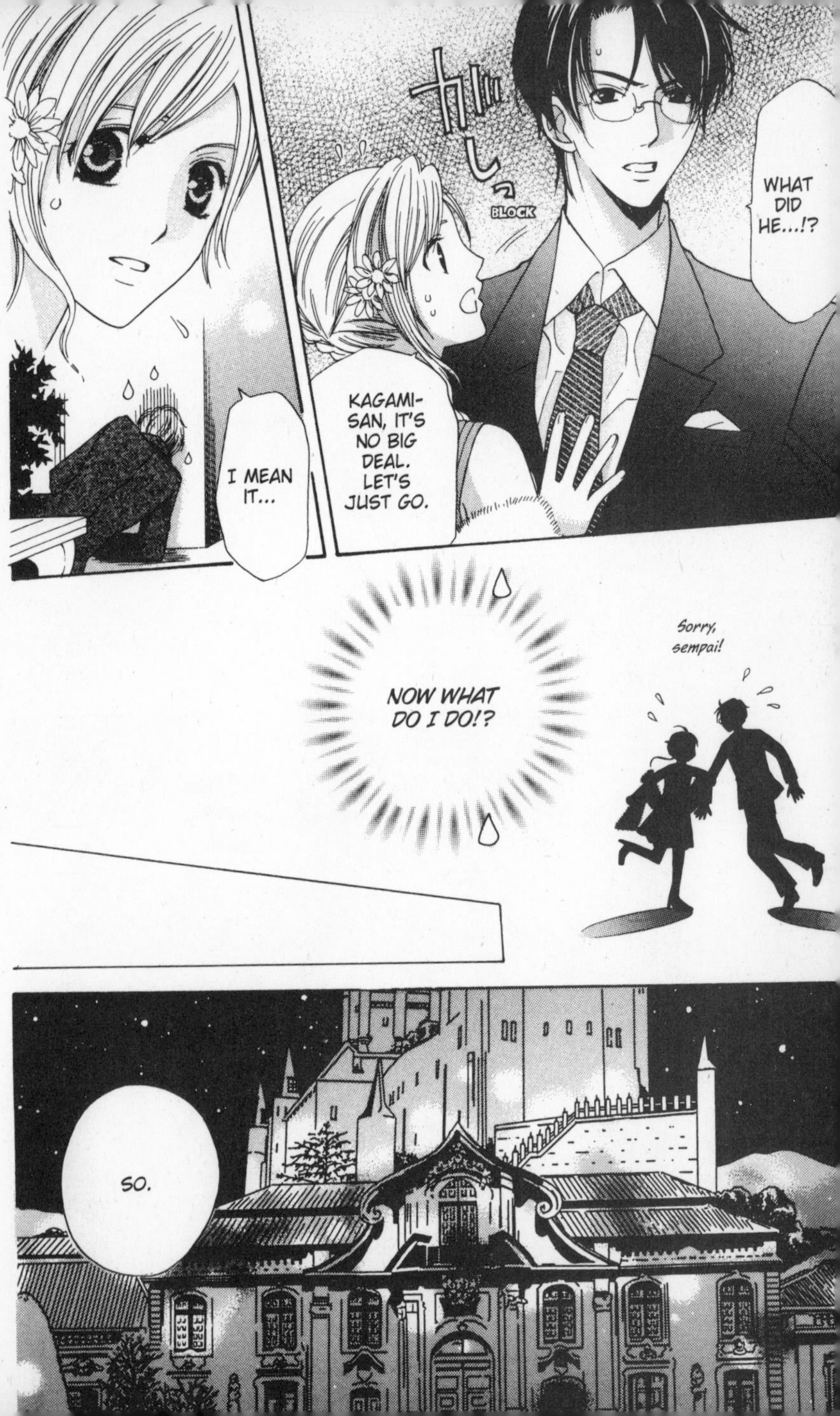
WHAT DID HE...!?
BLOCK
KAGAMI-SAN, IT'S NO BIG DEAL. LET'S JUST GO.
I MEAN IT...
Sorry, sempai!
NOW WHAT DO I DO!?
SO.

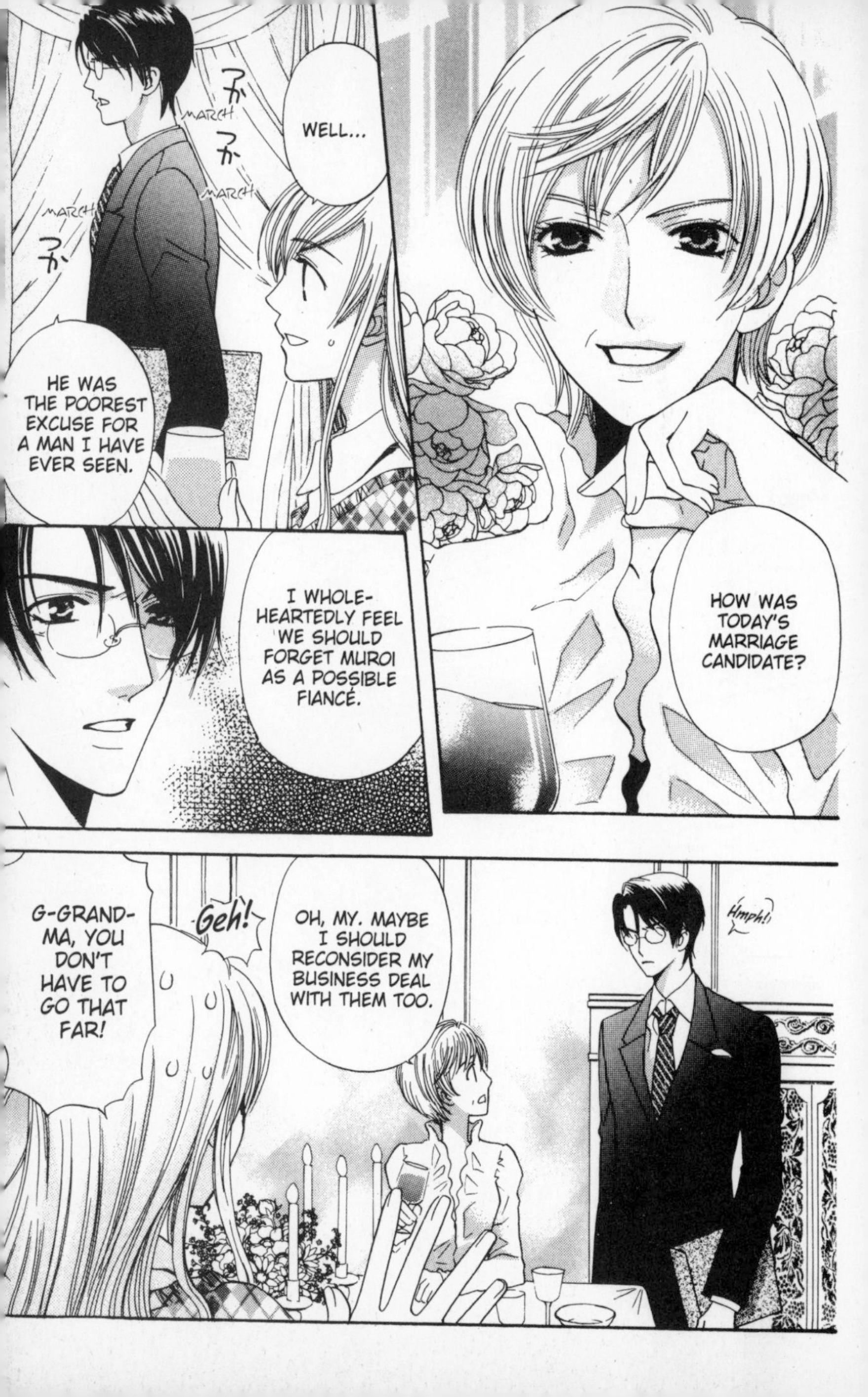
HOW WAS TODAY'S MARRIAGE CANDIDATE?
WELL...
MARCH
MARCH
MARCH
HE WAS THE POOREST EXCUSE FOR A MAN I HAVE EVER SEEN.
I WHOLE-HEARTEDLY FEEL WE SHOULD FORGET MUROI AS A POSSIBLE FIANCÉ.
Hmph!
OH, MY. MAYBE I SHOULD RECONSIDER MY BUSINESS DEAL WITH THEM TOO.
Geh!
G-GRAND-MA, YOU DON'T HAVE TO GO THAT FAR!

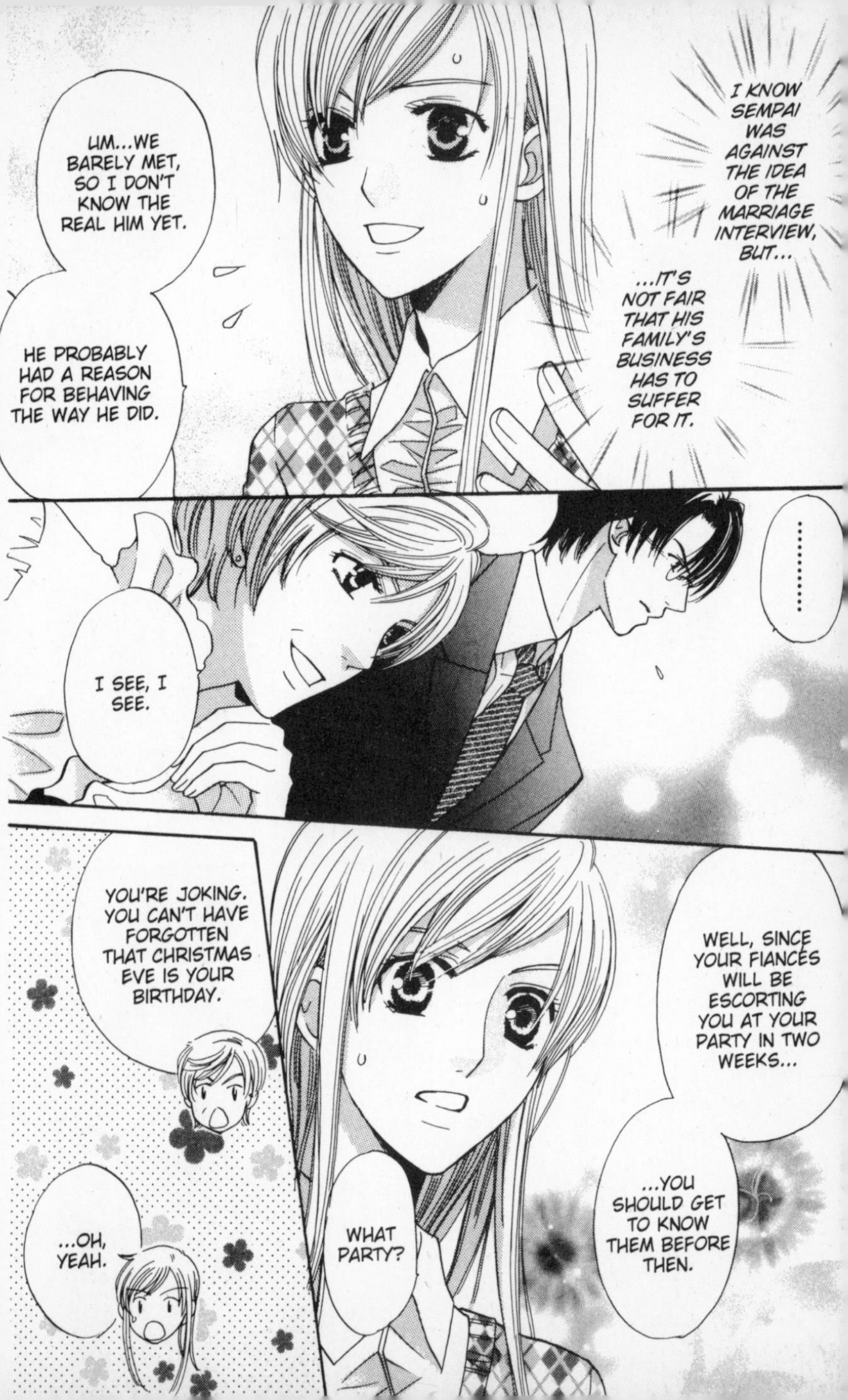
I KNOW SEMPAI WAS AGAINST THE IDEA OF THE MARRIAGE INTERVIEW, BUT...
...IT'S NOT FAIR THAT HIS FAMILY'S BUSINESS HAS TO SUFFER FOR IT.
UM...WE BARELY MET, SO I DON'T KNOW THE REAL HIM YET.
HE PROBABLY HAD A REASON FOR BEHAVING THE WAY HE DID.
....
I SEE, I SEE.
WELL, SINCE YOUR FIANCÉS WILL BE ESCORTING YOU AT YOUR PARTY IN TWO WEEKS...
...YOU SHOULD GET TO KNOW THEM BEFORE THEN.
WHAT PARTY?
YOU'RE JOKING. YOU CAN'T HAVE FORGOTTEN THAT CHRISTMAS EVE IS YOUR BIRTHDAY.
...OH, YEAH.

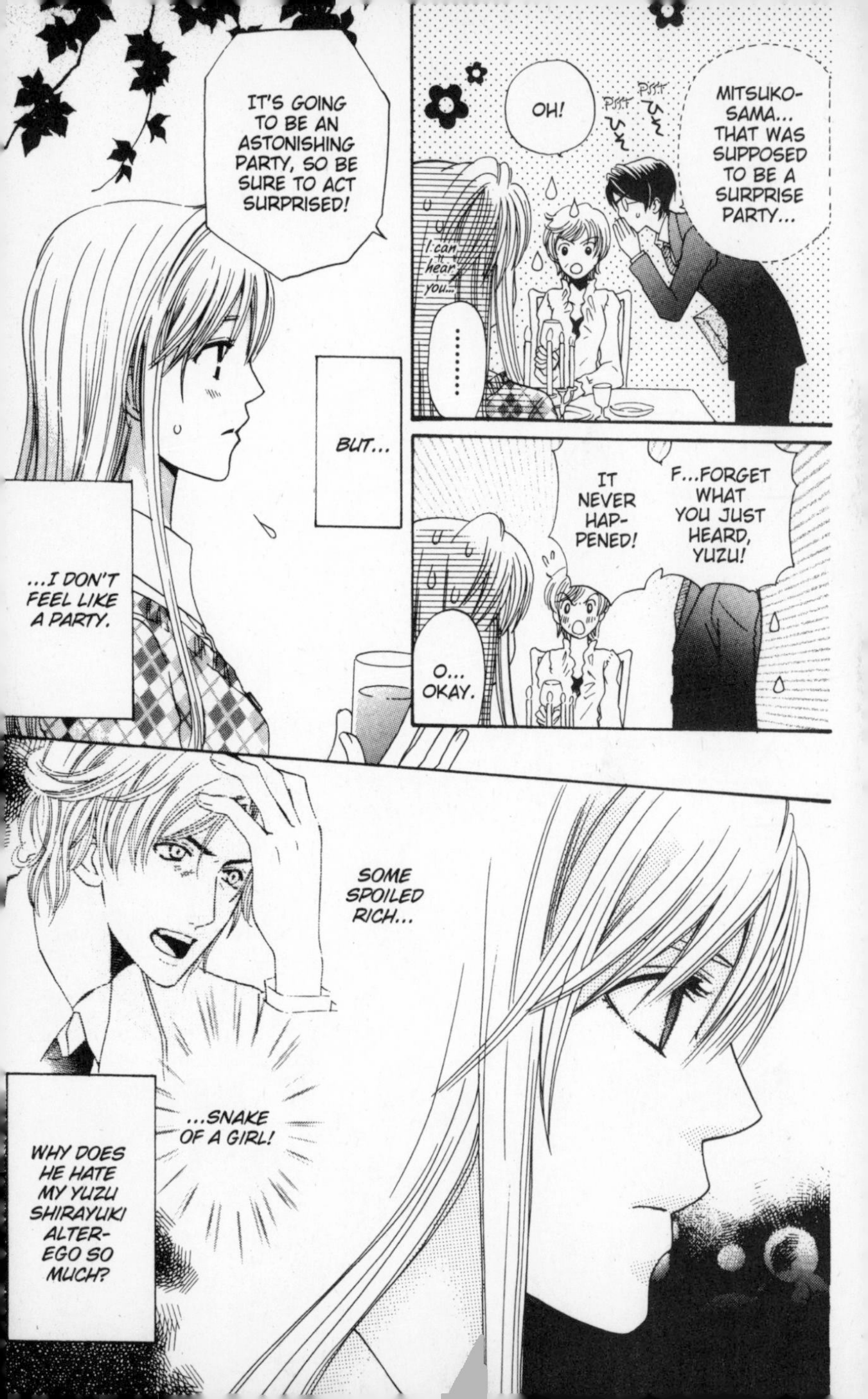
MITSUKO-SAMA... THAT WAS SUPPOSED TO BE A SURPRISE PARTY...
PSST PSST
OH!
I can hear you...
......
F...FORGET WHAT YOU JUST HEARD, YUZU!
IT NEVER HAP-PENED!
O... OKAY.
IT'S GOING TO BE AN ASTONISHING PARTY, SO BE SURE TO ACT SURPRISED!
BUT...
...I DON'T FEEL LIKE A PARTY.
SOME SPOILED RICH...
...SNAKE OF A GIRL!
WHY DOES HE HATE MY YUZU SHIRAYUKI ALTER-EGO SO MUCH?

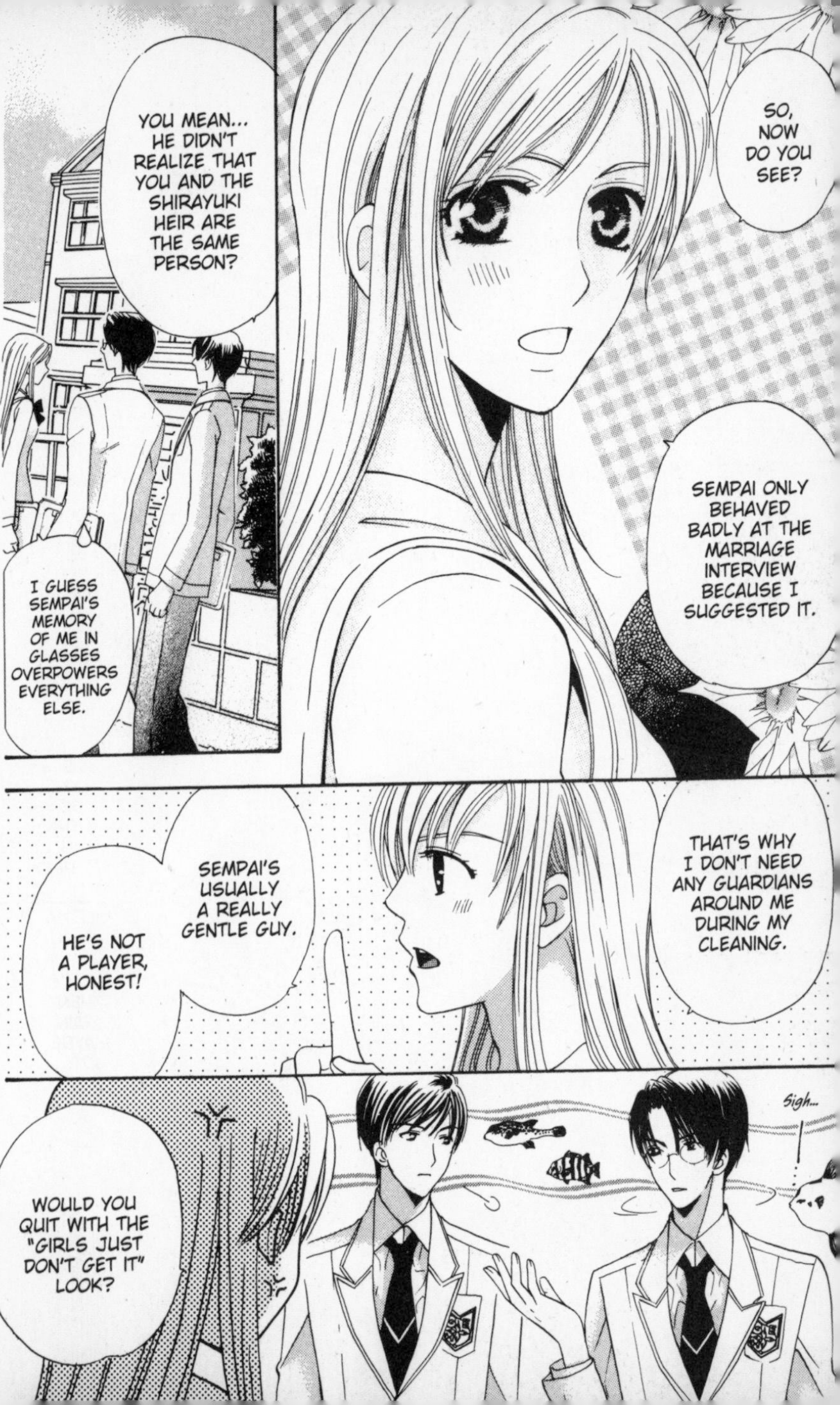
SO, NOW DO YOU SEE?
SEMPAI ONLY BEHAVED BADLY AT THE MARRIAGE INTERVIEW BECAUSE I SUGGESTED IT.
YOU MEAN... HE DIDN'T REALIZE THAT YOU AND THE SHIRAYUKI HEIR ARE THE SAME PERSON?
I GUESS SEMPAI'S MEMORY OF ME IN GLASSES OVERPOWERS EVERYTHING ELSE.
THAT'S WHY I DON'T NEED ANY GUARDIANS AROUND ME DURING MY CLEANING.
SEMPAI'S USUALLY A REALLY GENTLE GUY.
HE'S NOT A PLAYER, HONEST!
Sigh...
WOULD YOU QUIT WITH THE "GIRLS JUST DON'T GET IT" LOOK?

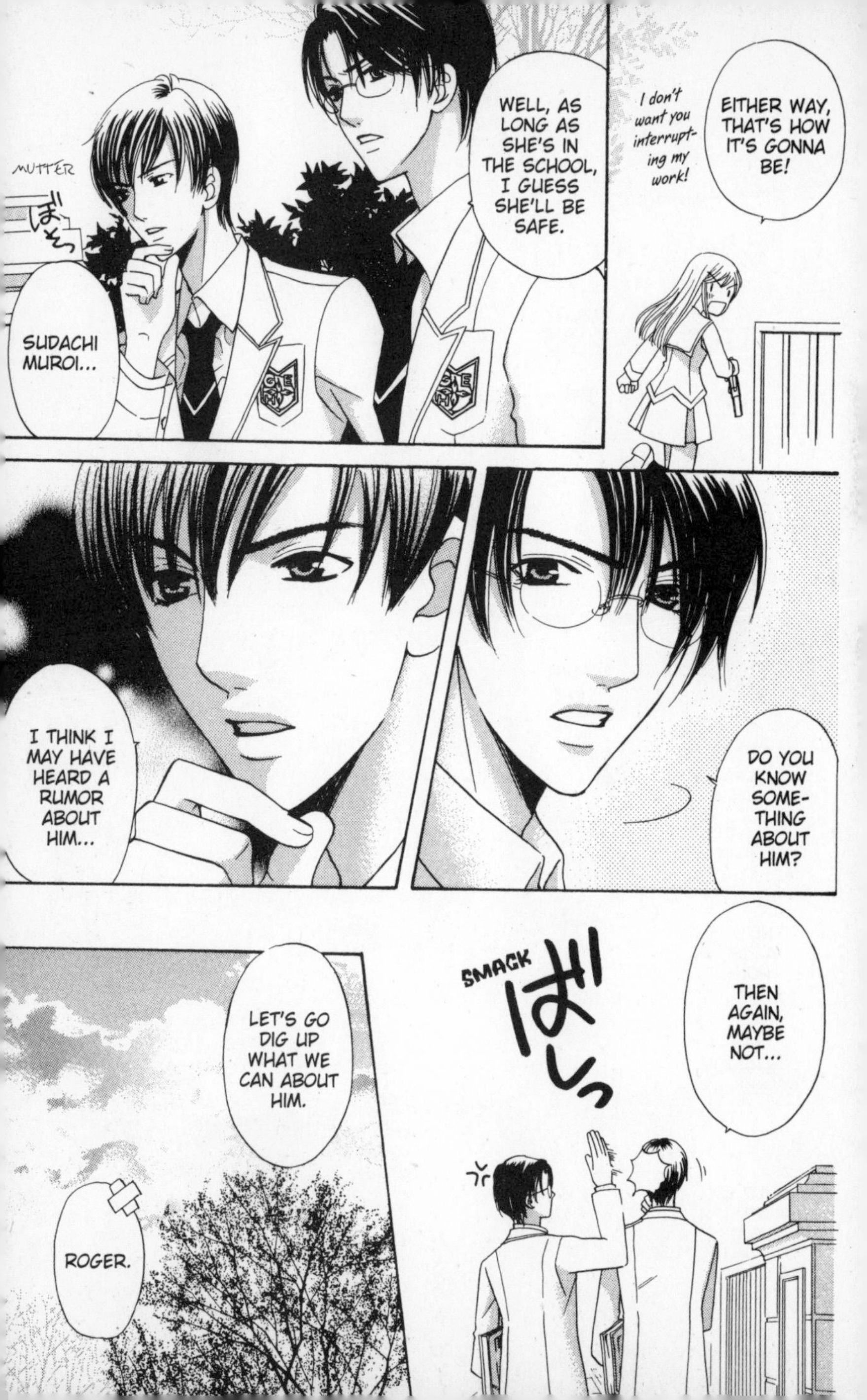
EITHER WAY, THAT'S HOW IT'S GONNA BE!
I don't want you interrupting my work!
WELL, AS LONG AS SHE'S IN THE SCHOOL, I GUESS SHE'LL BE SAFE.
MUTTER
ぼそっ
SUDACHI MUROI...
DO YOU KNOW SOMETHING ABOUT HIM?
I THINK I MAY HAVE HEARD A RUMOR ABOUT HIM...
THEN AGAIN, MAYBE NOT...
SMACK
ぱしっ
LET'S GO DIG UP WHAT WE CAN ABOUT HIM.
ROGER.

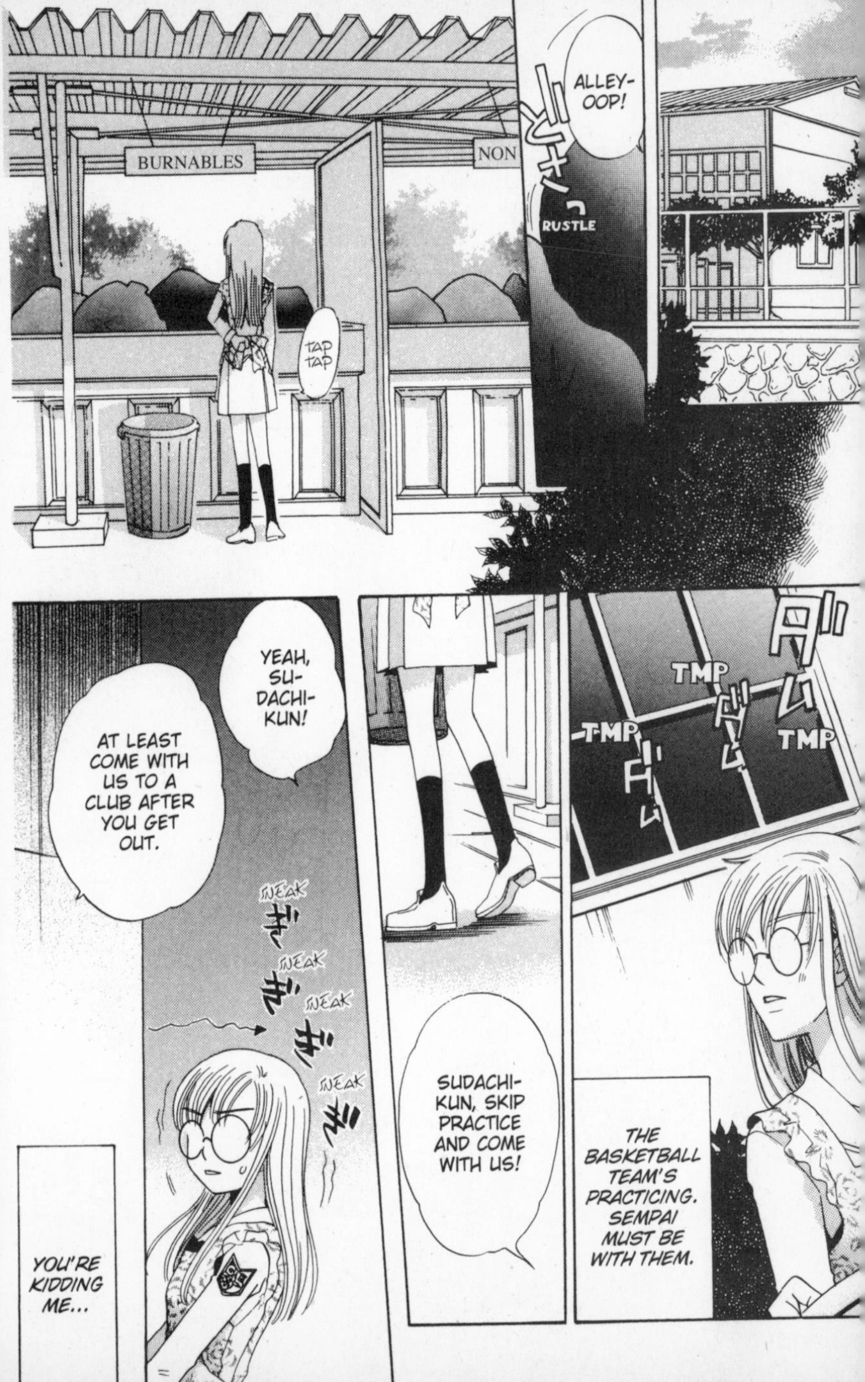

ALLEY-OOP!
RUSTLE
BURNABLES
NON
TAP TAP
TMP
TMP
TMP
THE BASKETBALL TEAM'S PRACTICING. SEMPAI MUST BE WITH THEM.
SUDACHI-KUN, SKIP PRACTICE AND COME WITH US!
YEAH, SU-DACHI-KUN!
AT LEAST COME WITH US TO A CLUB AFTER YOU GET OUT.
SNEAK
SNEAK
SNEAK
SNEAK
YOU'RE KIDDING ME...

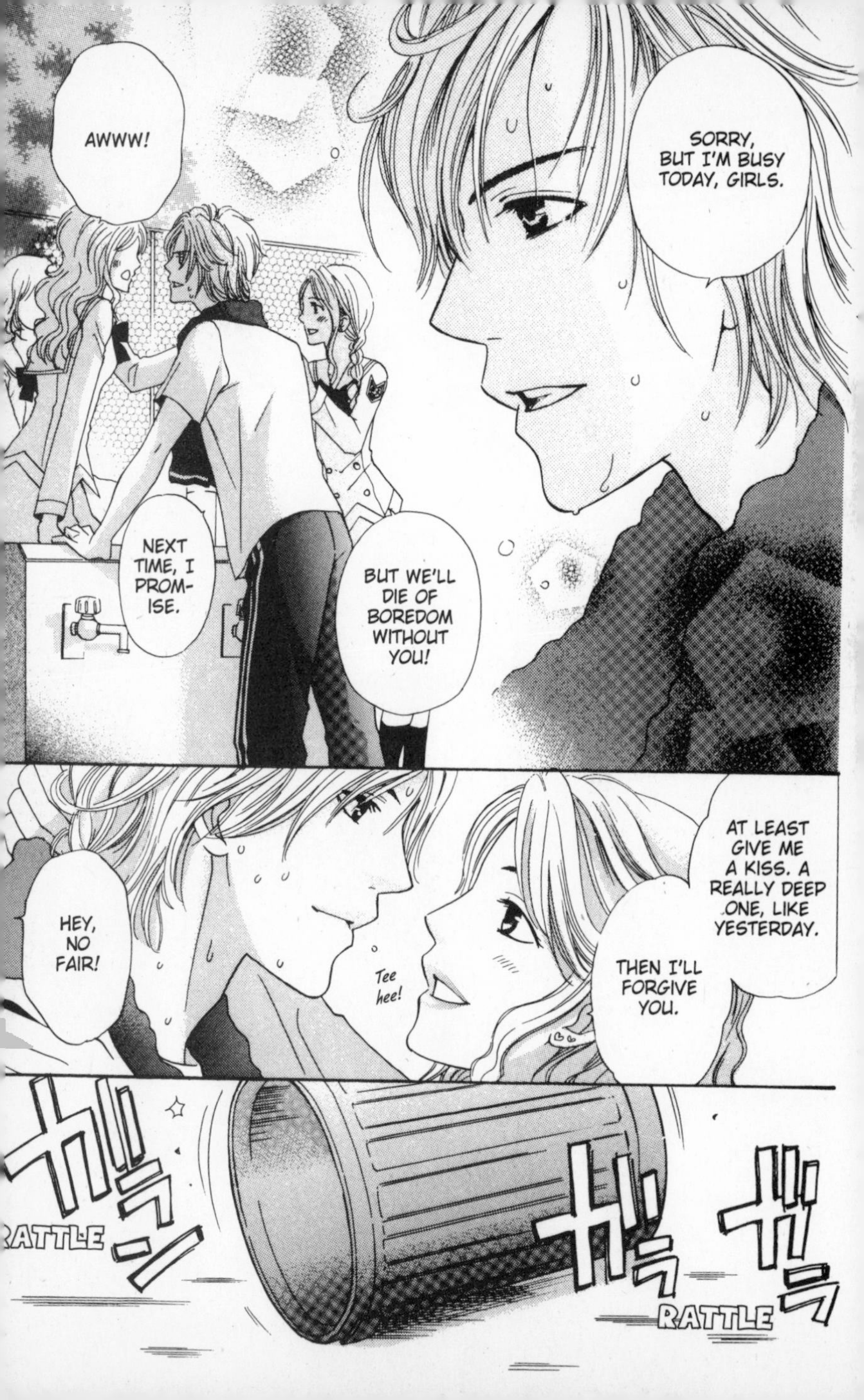
SORRY, BUT I'M BUSY TODAY, GIRLS.
AWWW!
BUT WE'LL DIE OF BOREDOM WITHOUT YOU!
NEXT TIME, I PROMISE.
AT LEAST GIVE ME A KISS. A REALLY DEEP ONE, LIKE YESTERDAY.
THEN I'LL FORGIVE YOU.
Tee hee!
HEY, NO FAIR!
ガラ ガラ
RATTLE
ガラーン
RATTLE

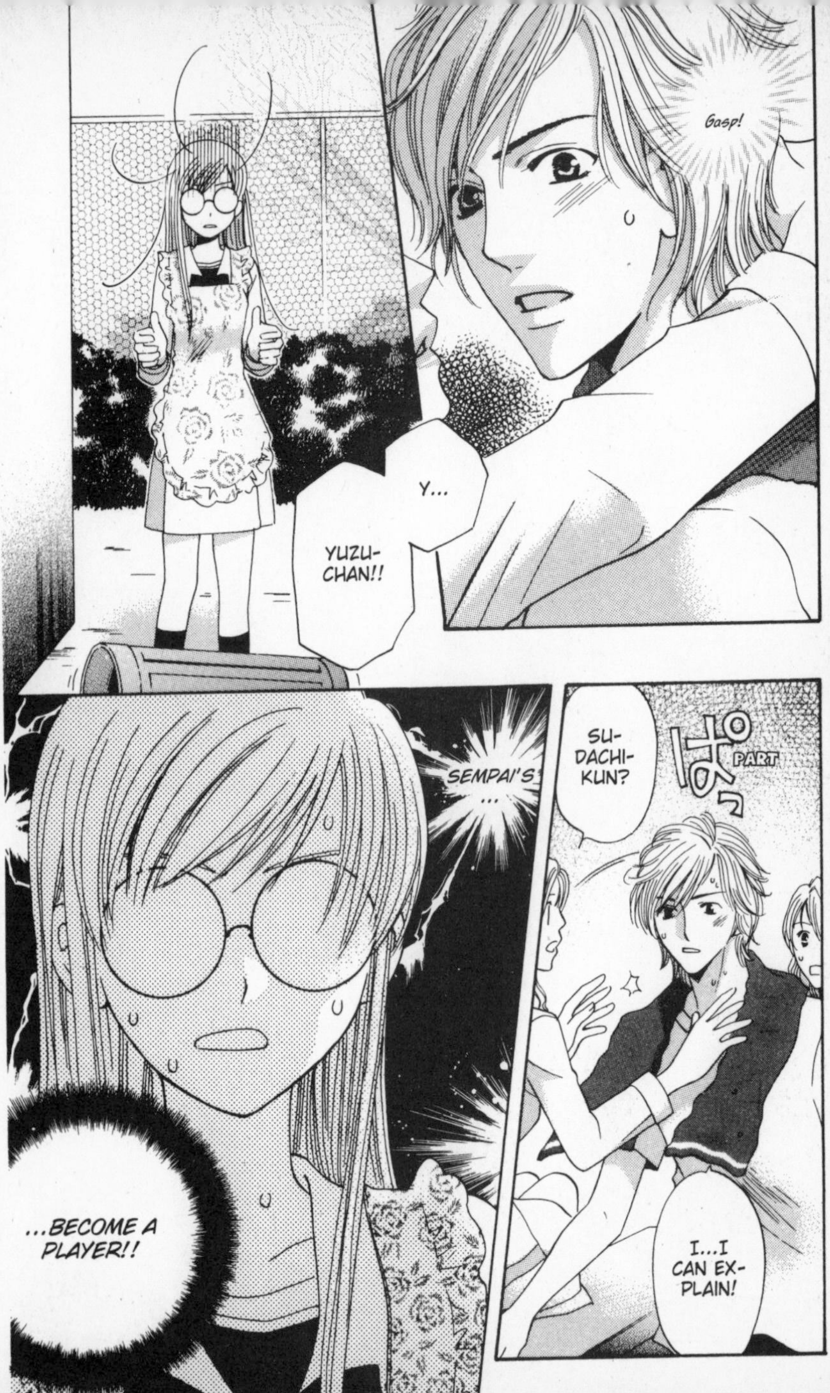
Gasp!
Y...
YUZU-CHAN!!
SU-DACHI-KUN?
ぱっ PART
I...I CAN EX-PLAIN!
SEMPAI'S ...
...BECOME A PLAYER!!

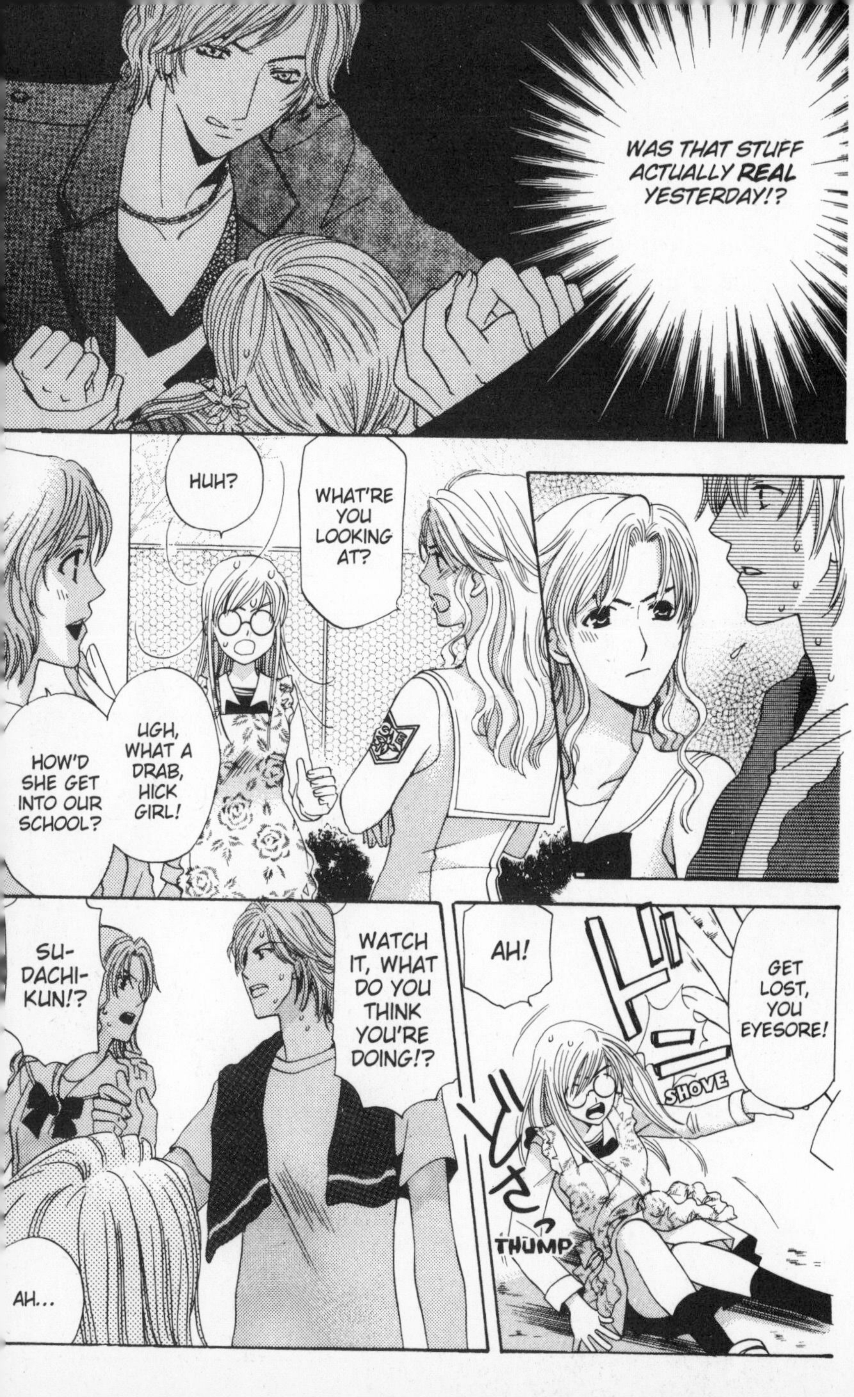
WAS THAT STUFF ACTUALLY REAL YESTERDAY!?
WHAT'RE YOU LOOKING AT?
HUH?
UGH, WHAT A DRAB, HICK GIRL!
HOW'D SHE GET INTO OUR SCHOOL?
GET LOST, YOU EYESORE!
SHOVE
AH!
THUMP
WATCH IT, WHAT DO YOU THINK YOU'RE DOING!?
SU-DACHI-KUN!?
AH...

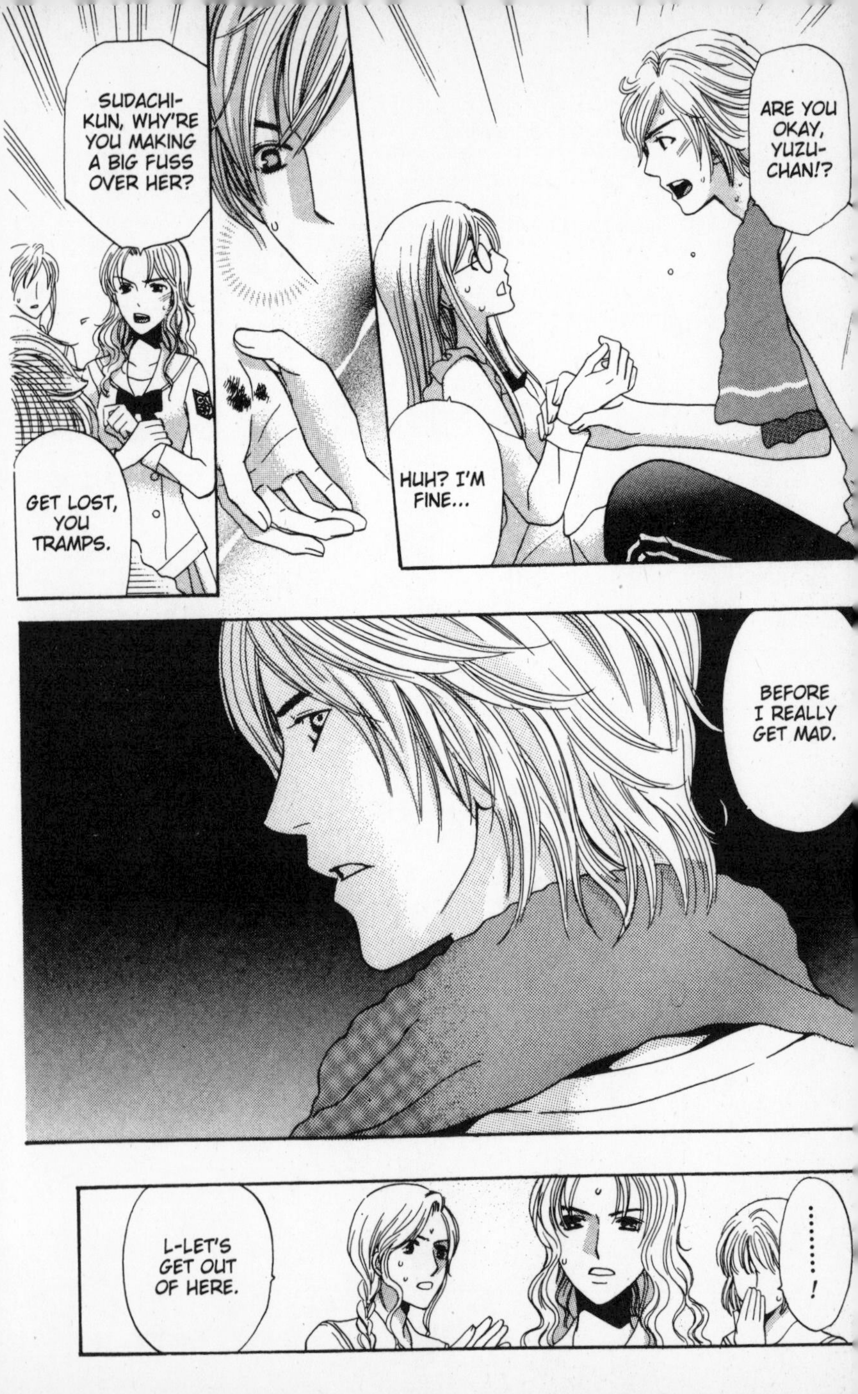
ARE YOU OKAY, YUZU-CHAN!?
HUH? I'M FINE...
SUDACHI-KUN, WHY'RE YOU MAKING A BIG FUSS OVER HER?
GET LOST, YOU TRAMPS.
BEFORE I REALLY GET MAD.
........!
L-LET'S GET OUT OF HERE.

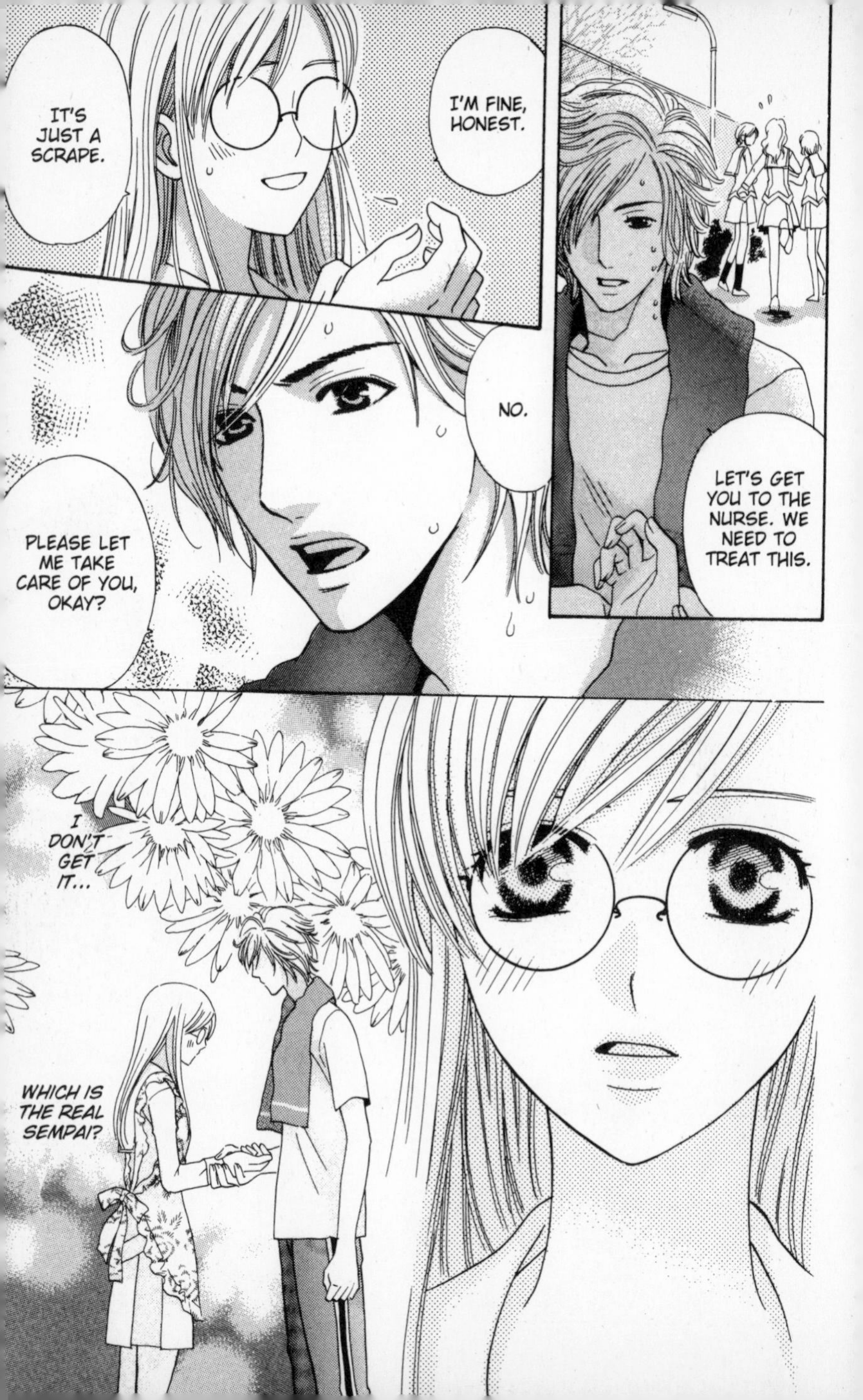
LET'S GET YOU TO THE NURSE. WE NEED TO TREAT THIS.
I'M FINE, HONEST.
IT'S JUST A SCRAPE.
NO.
PLEASE LET ME TAKE CARE OF YOU, OKAY?
I DON'T GET IT...
WHICH IS THE REAL SEMPAI?

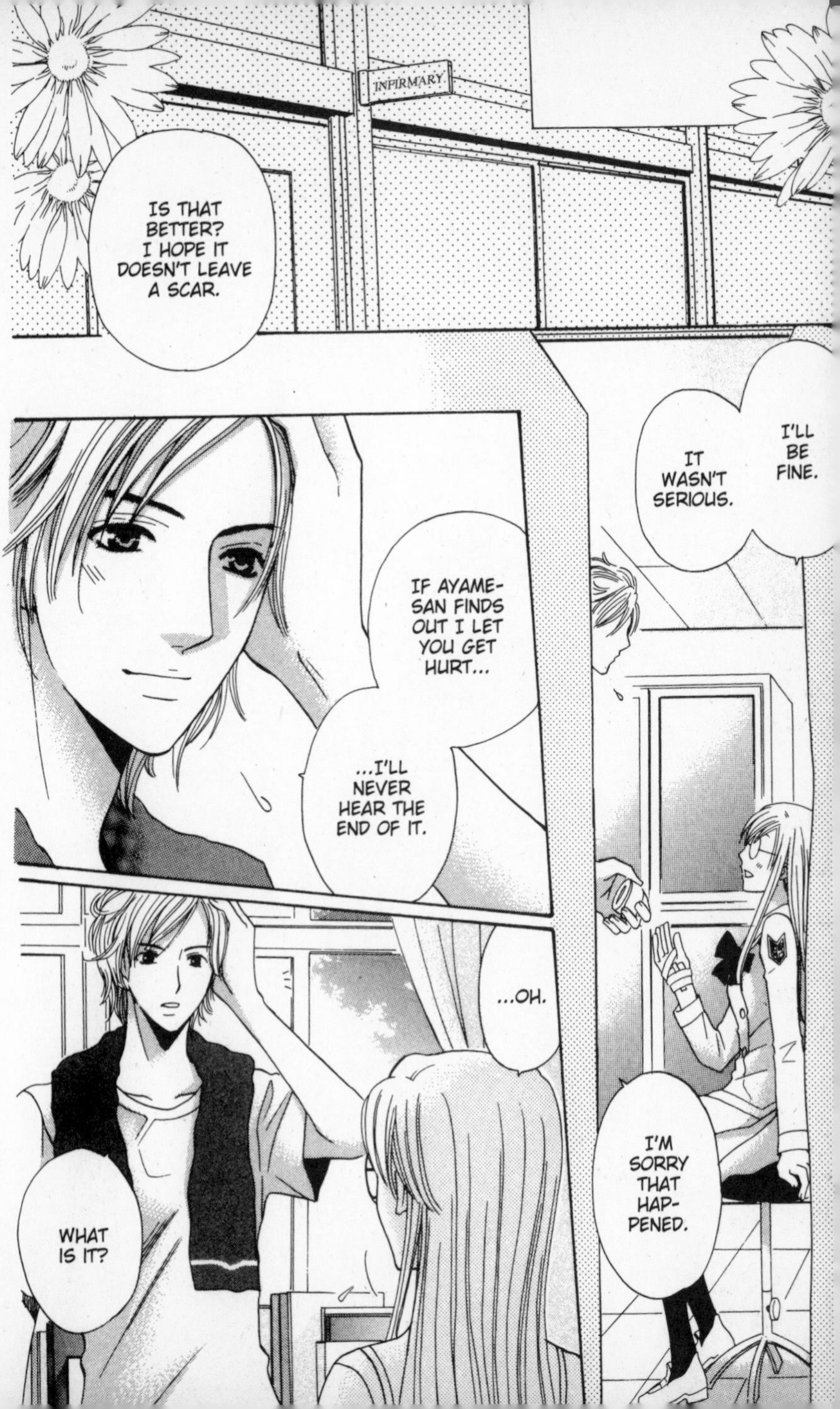
INFIRMARY
IS THAT BETTER? I HOPE IT DOESN'T LEAVE A SCAR.
IT WASN'T SERIOUS. I'LL BE FINE.
I'M SORRY THAT HAPPENED.
IF AYAME-SAN FINDS OUT I LET YOU GET HURT...
...I'LL NEVER HEAR THE END OF IT.
...OH.
WHAT IS IT?

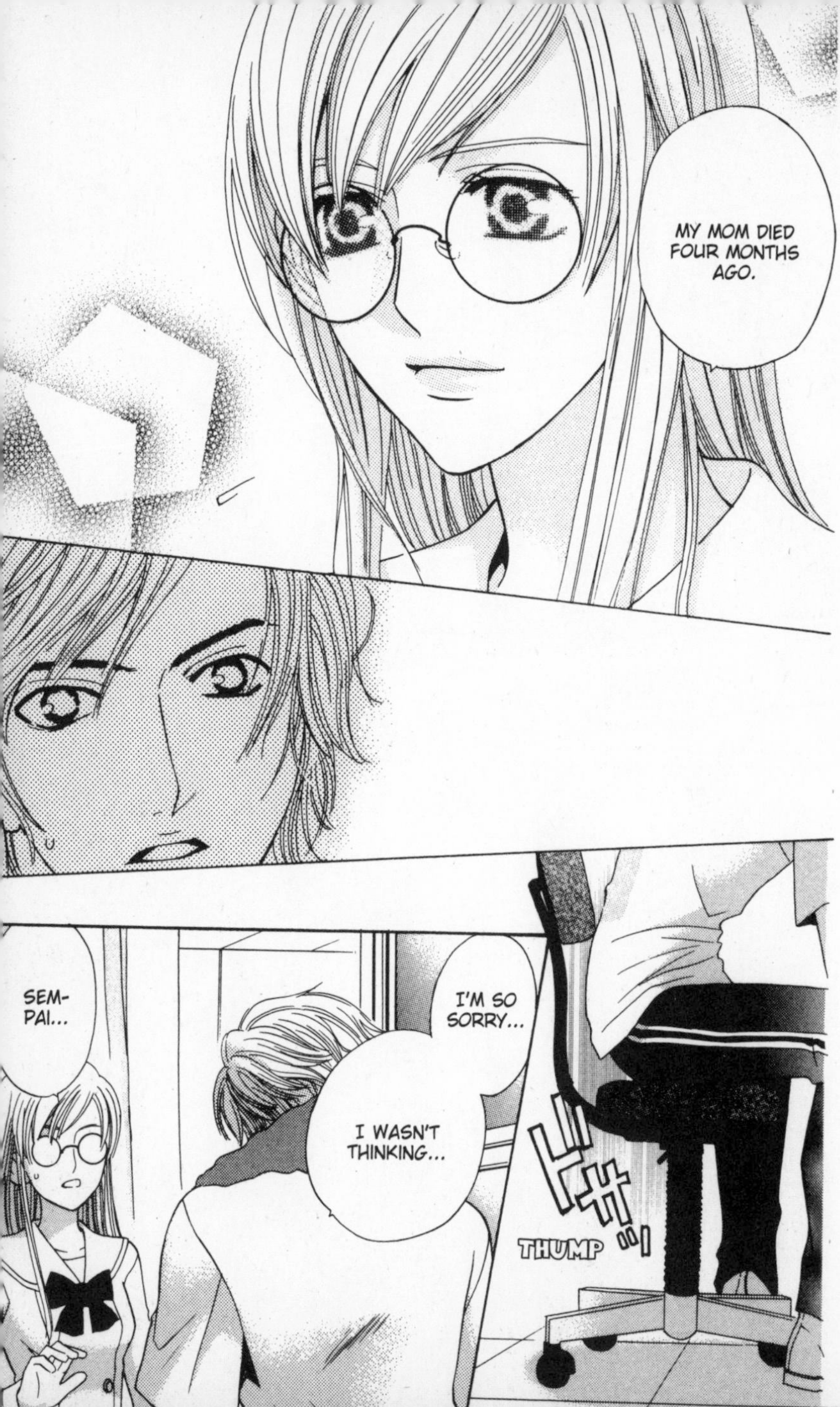
MY MOM DIED FOUR MONTHS AGO.
THUMP
I'M SO SORRY...
I WASN'T THINKING...
SEM-PAI...

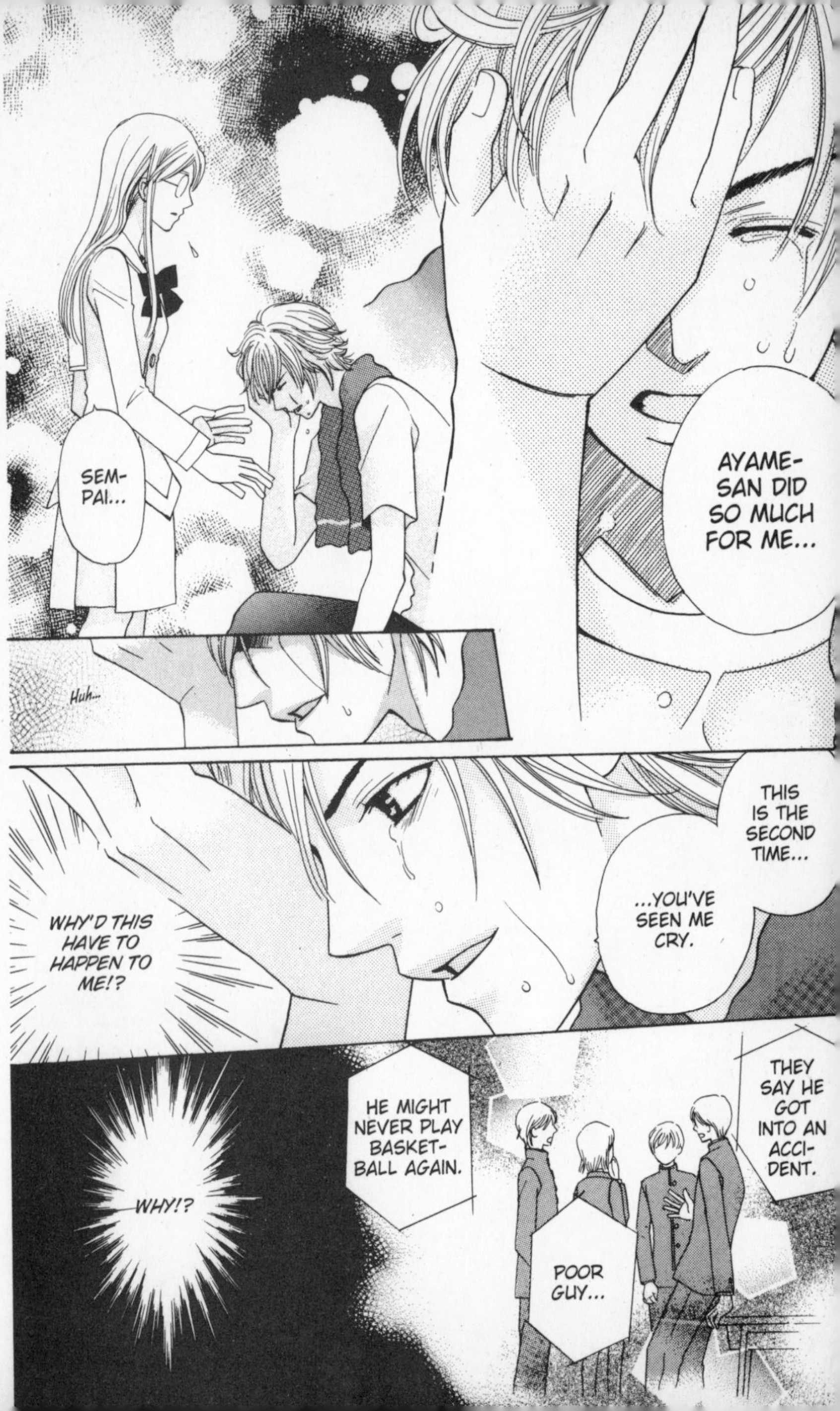
AYAME-SAN DID SO MUCH FOR ME...
SEM-PAI...
Huh...
THIS IS THE SECOND TIME...
...YOU'VE SEEN ME CRY.
WHY'D THIS HAVE TO HAPPEN TO ME!?
THEY SAY HE GOT INTO AN ACCI-DENT.
HE MIGHT NEVER PLAY BASKET-BALL AGAIN.
POOR GUY...
WHY!?

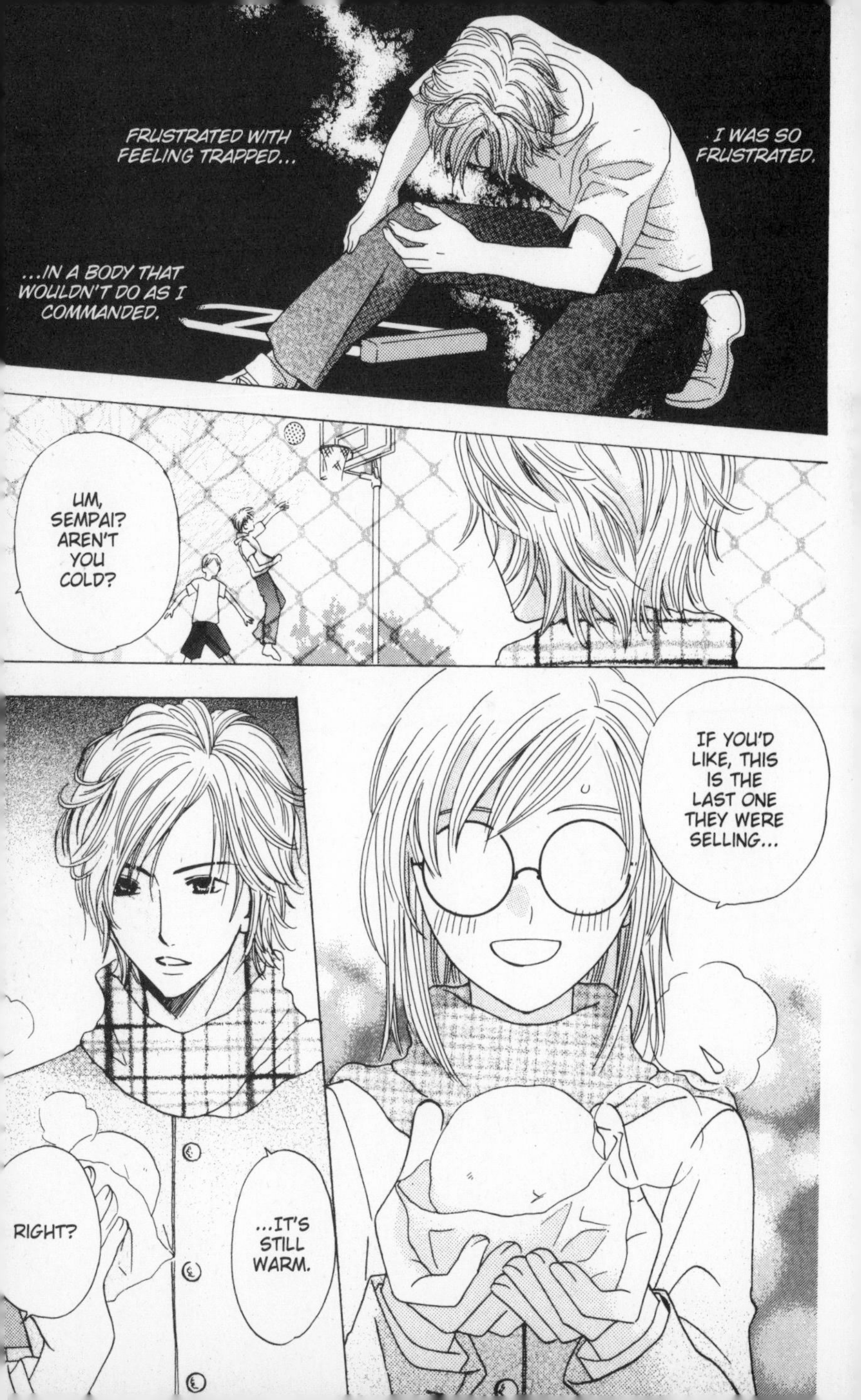
I WAS SO FRUSTRATED.
FRUSTRATED WITH FEELING TRAPPED...
...IN A BODY THAT WOULDN'T DO AS I COMMANDED.
UM, SEMPAI? AREN'T YOU COLD?
IF YOU'D LIKE, THIS IS THE LAST ONE THEY WERE SELLING...
...IT'S STILL WARM.
RIGHT?

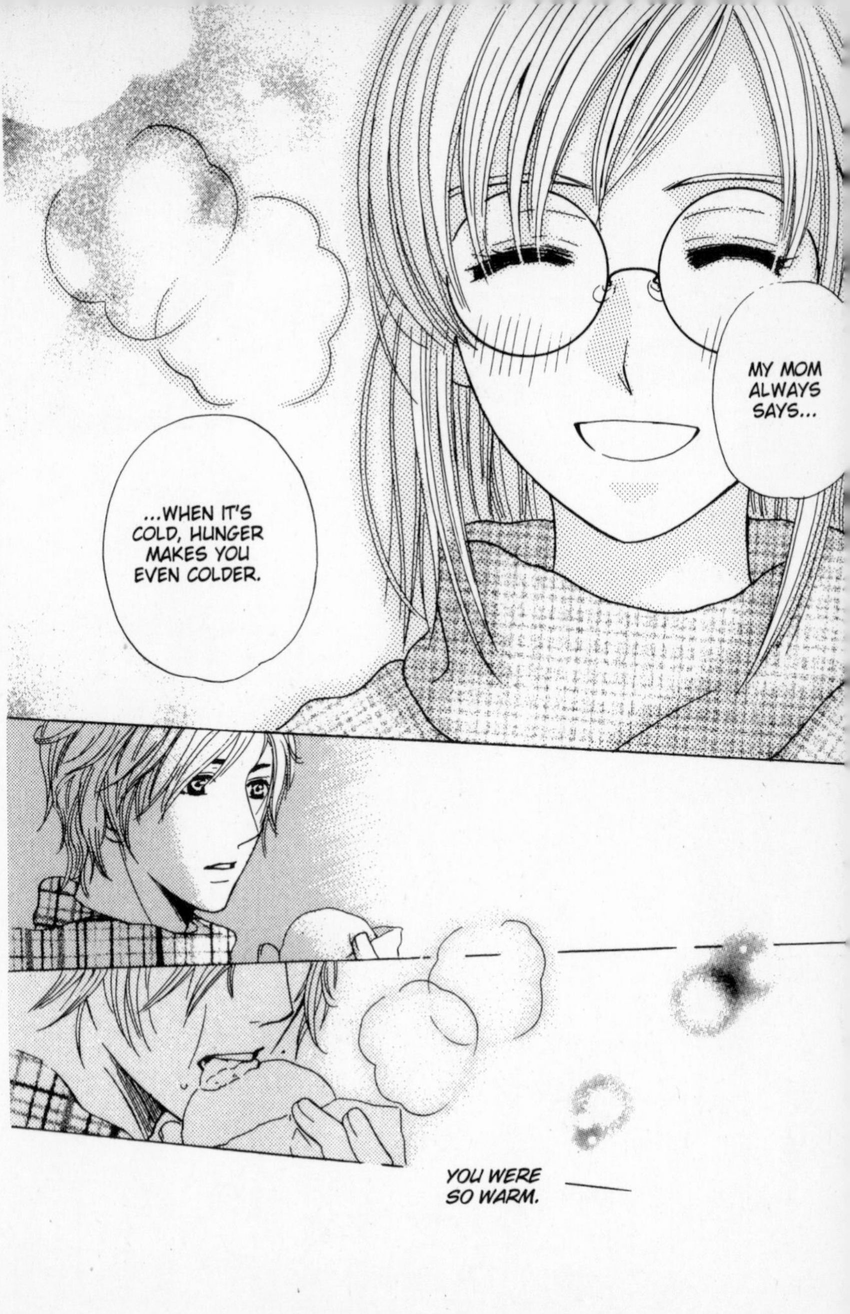
MY MOM ALWAYS SAYS...
...WHEN IT'S COLD, HUNGER MAKES YOU EVEN COLDER.
YOU WERE SO WARM.

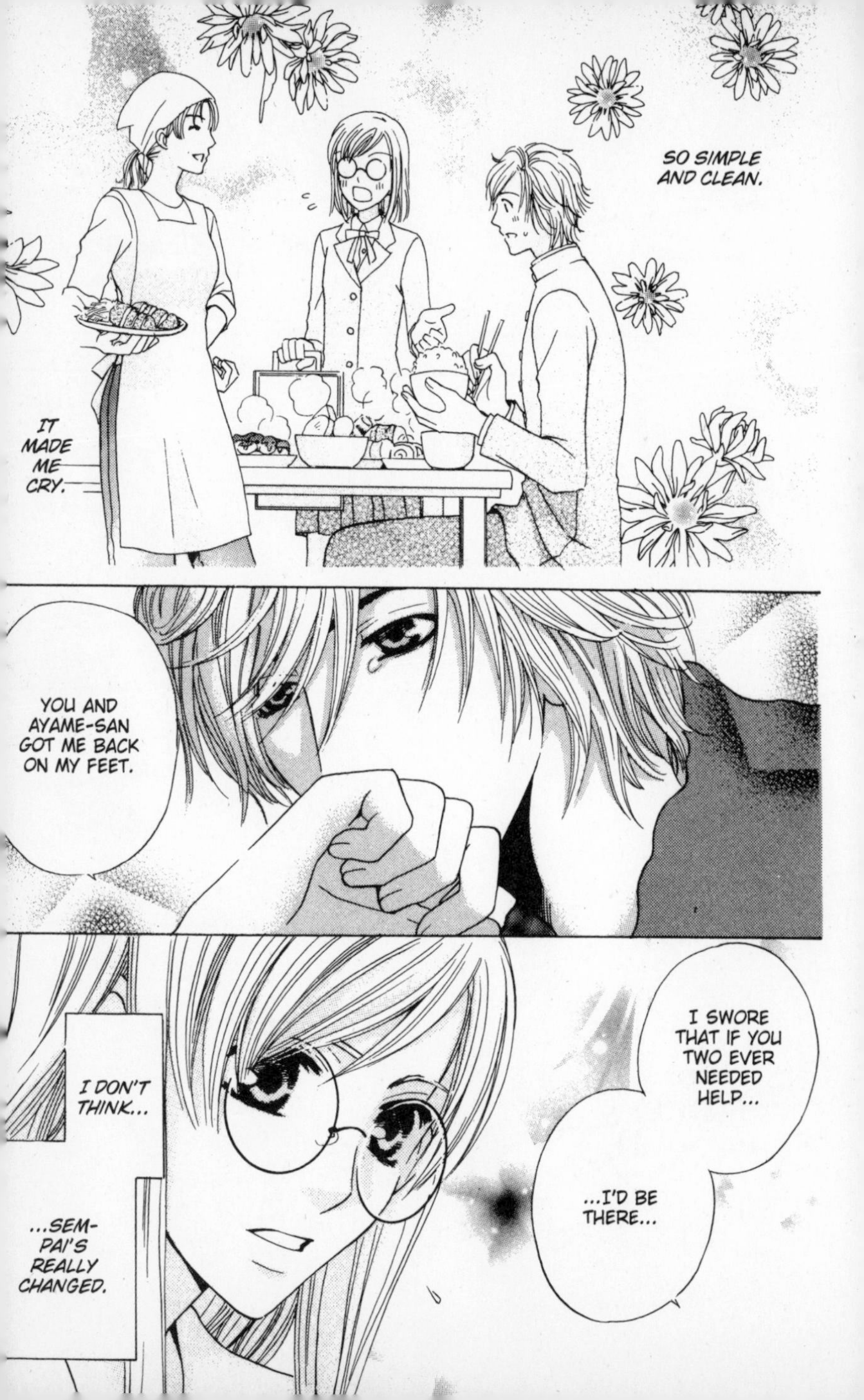
SO SIMPLE AND CLEAN.
IT MADE ME CRY.
YOU AND AYAME-SAN GOT ME BACK ON MY FEET.
I SWORE THAT IF YOU TWO EVER NEEDED HELP...
...I'D BE THERE...
I DON'T THINK...
...SEM-PAI'S REALLY CHANGED.

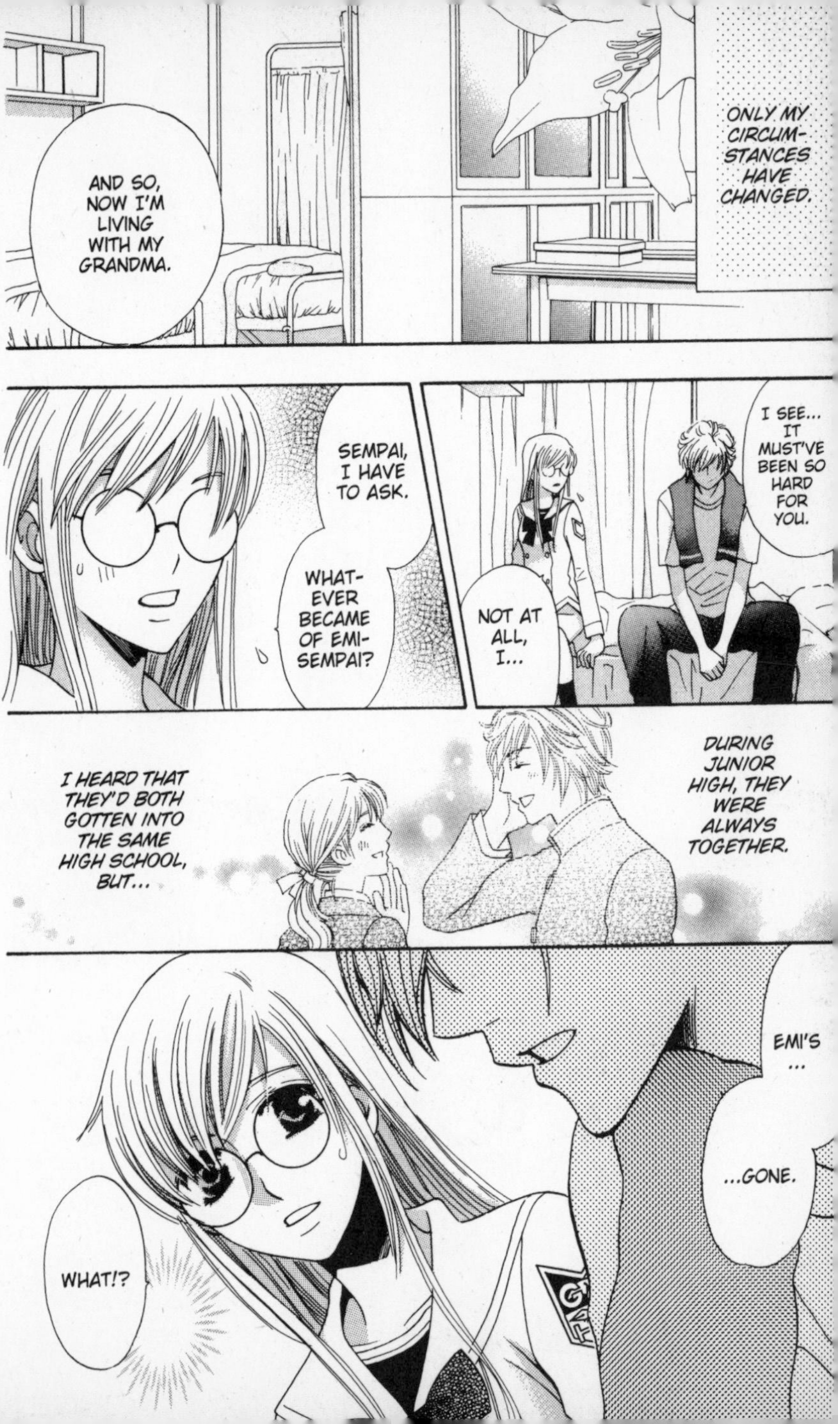
ONLY MY CIRCUM-STANCES HAVE CHANGED.
AND SO, NOW I'M LIVING WITH MY GRANDMA.
I SEE... IT MUST'VE BEEN SO HARD FOR YOU.
NOT AT ALL, I...
SEMPAI, I HAVE TO ASK.
WHAT-EVER BECAME OF EMI-SEMPAI?
DURING JUNIOR HIGH, THEY WERE ALWAYS TOGETHER.
I HEARD THAT THEY'D BOTH GOTTEN INTO THE SAME HIGH SCHOOL, BUT...
EMI'S ...
...GONE.
WHAT!?

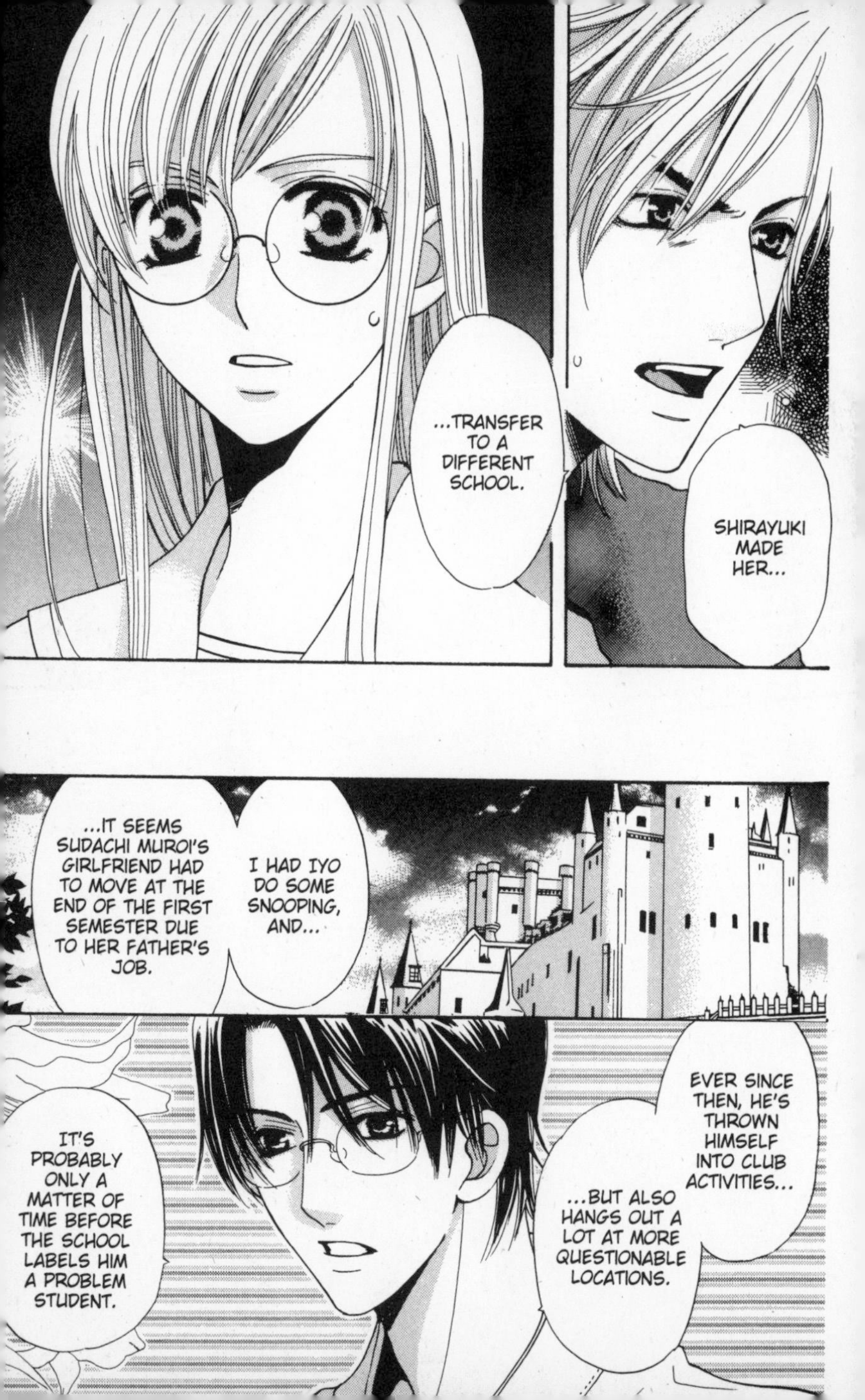
SHIRAYUKI MADE HER...
...TRANSFER TO A DIFFERENT SCHOOL.
I HAD IYO DO SOME SNOOPING, AND...
...IT SEEMS SUDACHI MUROI'S GIRLFRIEND HAD TO MOVE AT THE END OF THE FIRST SEMESTER DUE TO HER FATHER'S JOB.
EVER SINCE THEN, HE'S THROWN HIMSELF INTO CLUB ACTIVITIES...
...BUT ALSO HANGS OUT A LOT AT MORE QUESTIONABLE LOCATIONS.
IT'S PROBABLY ONLY A MATTER OF TIME BEFORE THE SCHOOL LABELS HIM A PROBLEM STUDENT.

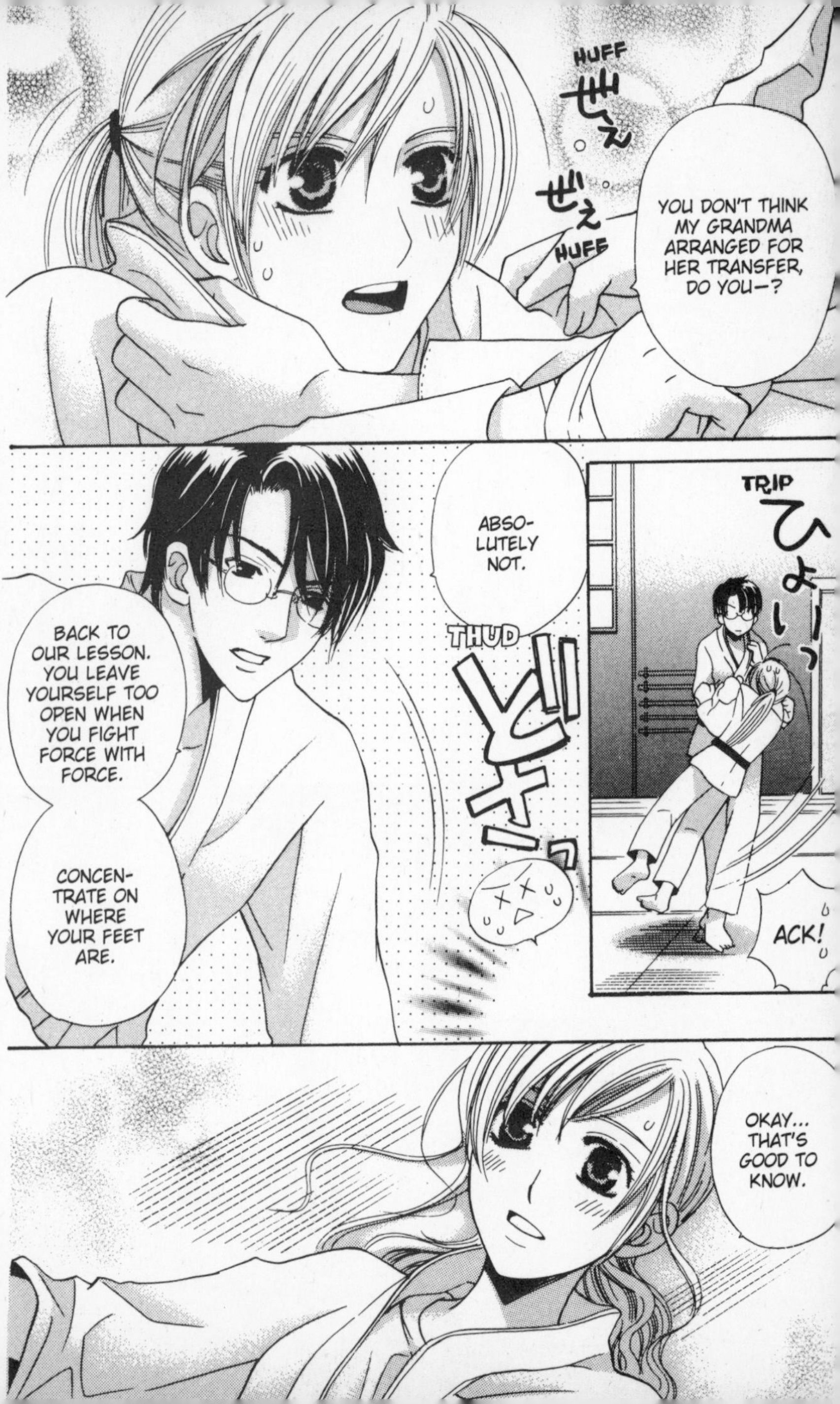

HUFF
ぜぇ
ぜぇ
HUFF
YOU DON'T THINK MY GRANDMA ARRANGED FOR HER TRANSFER, DO YOU—?
TRIP
ひょいっ
ACK!
ABSO-LUTELY NOT.
THUD
どすっ
BACK TO OUR LESSON. YOU LEAVE YOURSELF TOO OPEN WHEN YOU FIGHT FORCE WITH FORCE.
CONCEN-TRATE ON WHERE YOUR FEET ARE.
OKAY... THAT'S GOOD TO KNOW.

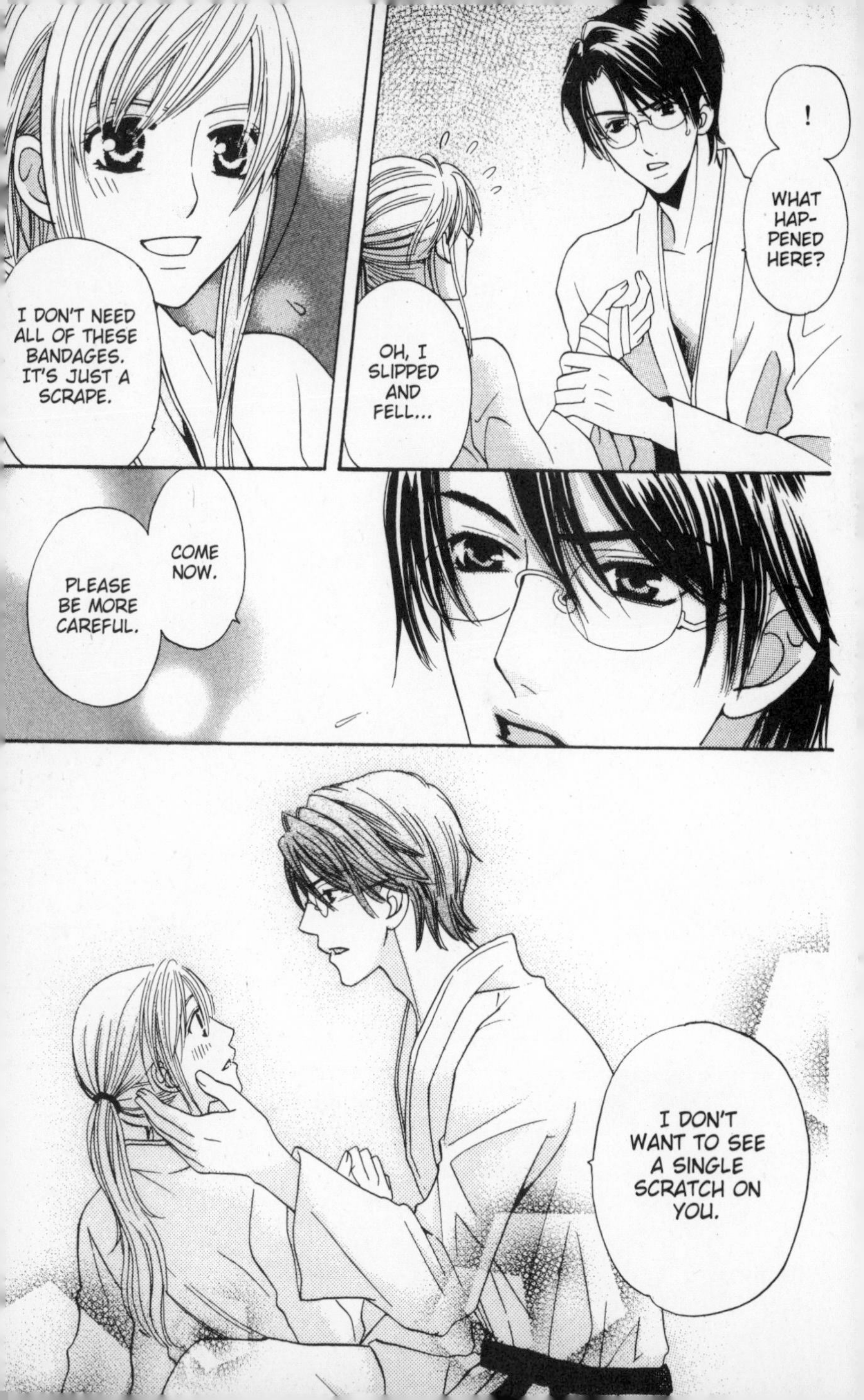
!
WHAT HAP-PENED HERE?
OH, I SLIPPED AND FELL...
I DON'T NEED ALL OF THESE BANDAGES. IT'S JUST A SCRAPE.
COME NOW.
PLEASE BE MORE CAREFUL.
I DON'T WANT TO SEE A SINGLE SCRATCH ON YOU.

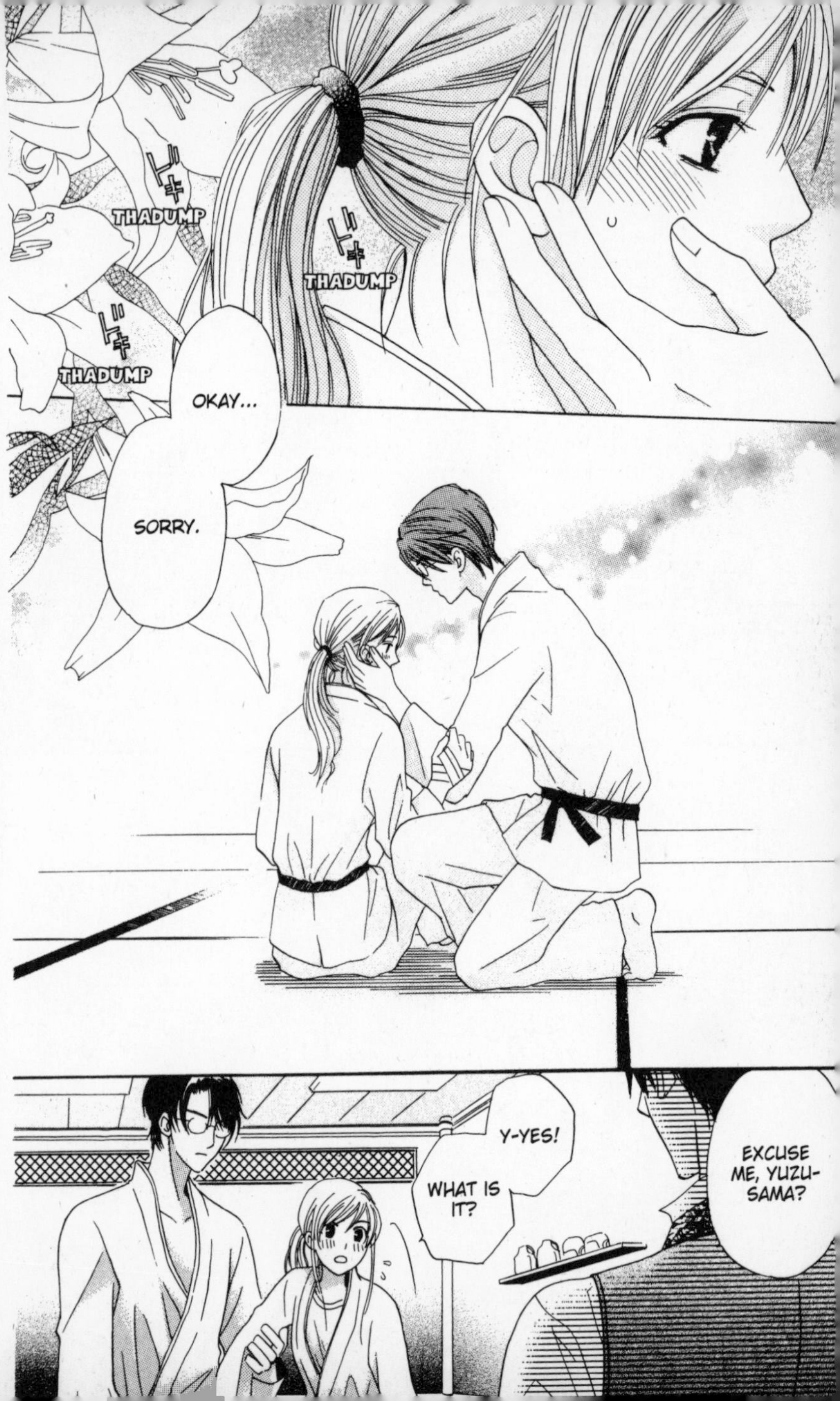
THADUMP
THADUMP
THADUMP
OKAY...
SORRY.
EXCUSE ME, YUZU-SAMA?
Y-YES!
WHAT IS IT?

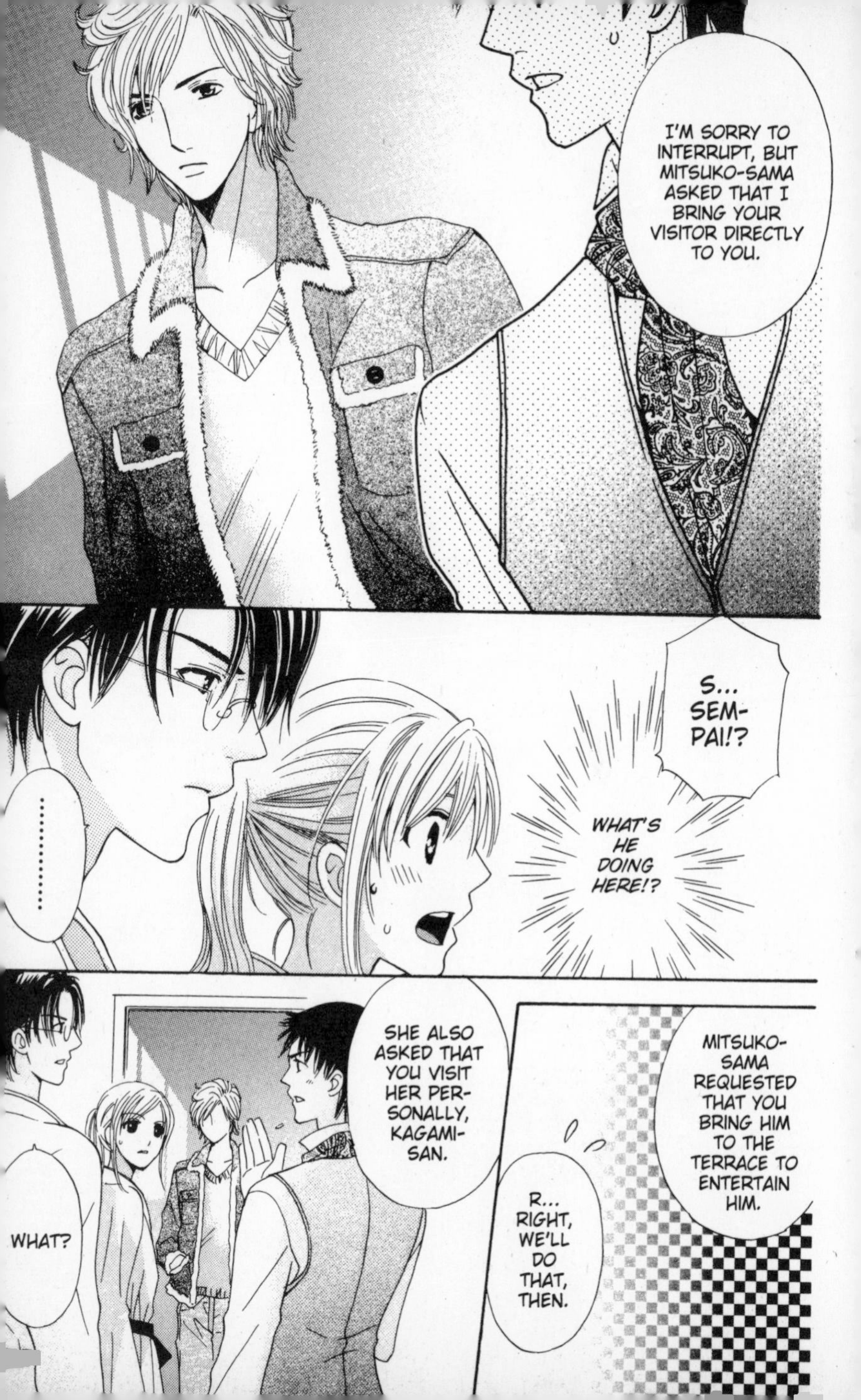
I'M SORRY TO INTERRUPT, BUT MITSUKO-SAMA ASKED THAT I BRING YOUR VISITOR DIRECTLY TO YOU.
S... SEM-PAI!?
WHAT'S HE DOING HERE!?
......
MITSUKO-SAMA REQUESTED THAT YOU BRING HIM TO THE TERRACE TO ENTERTAIN HIM.
R... RIGHT, WE'LL DO THAT, THEN.
SHE ALSO ASKED THAT YOU VISIT HER PERSONALLY, KAGAMI-SAN.
WHAT?

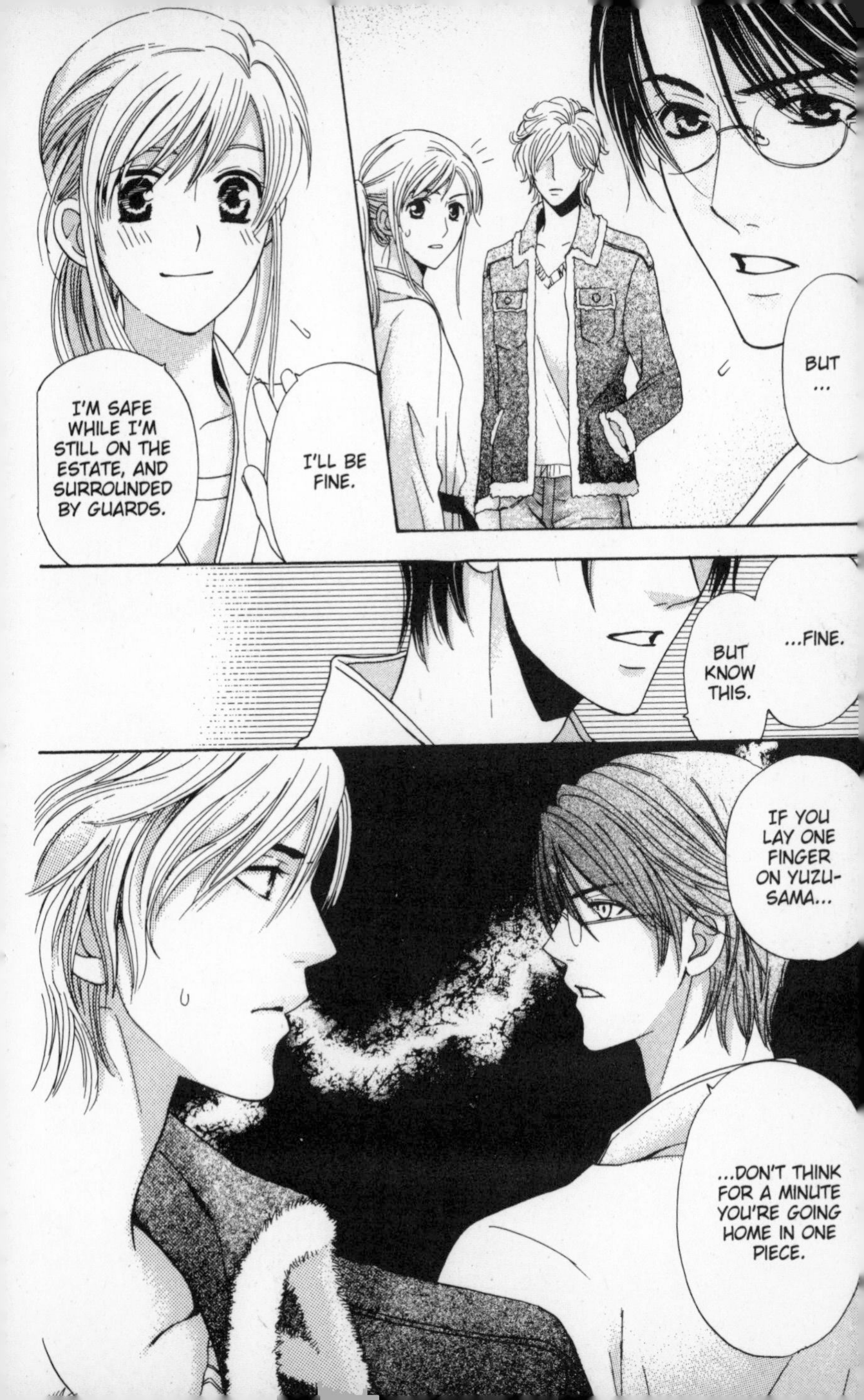
BUT ...
I'LL BE FINE.
I'M SAFE WHILE I'M STILL ON THE ESTATE, AND SURROUNDED BY GUARDS.
...FINE.
BUT KNOW THIS.
IF YOU LAY ONE FINGER ON YUZU-SAMA...
...DON'T THINK FOR A MINUTE YOU'RE GOING HOME IN ONE PIECE.

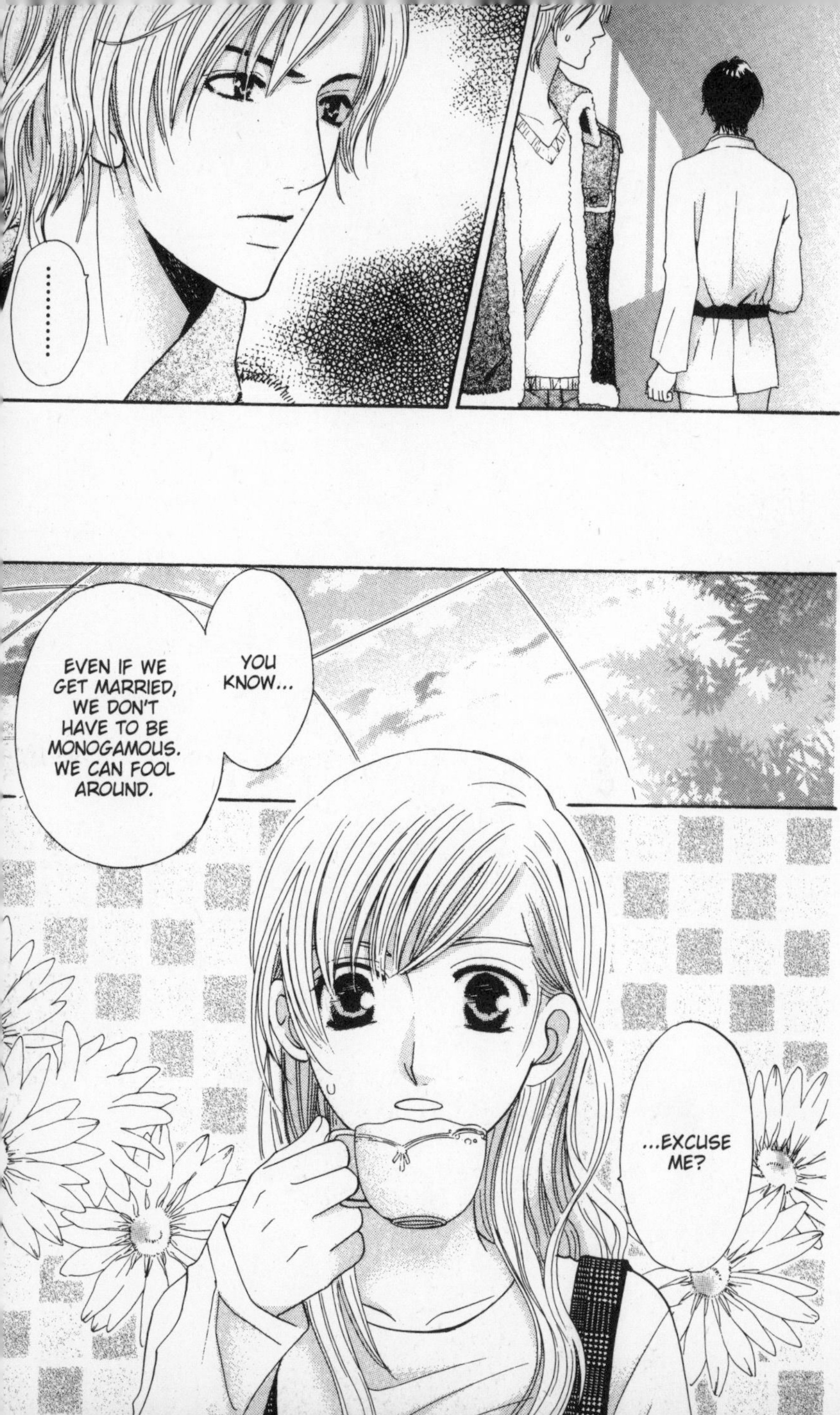
....
YOU KNOW...
EVEN IF WE GET MARRIED, WE DON'T HAVE TO BE MONOGAMOUS. WE CAN FOOL AROUND.
...EXCUSE ME?

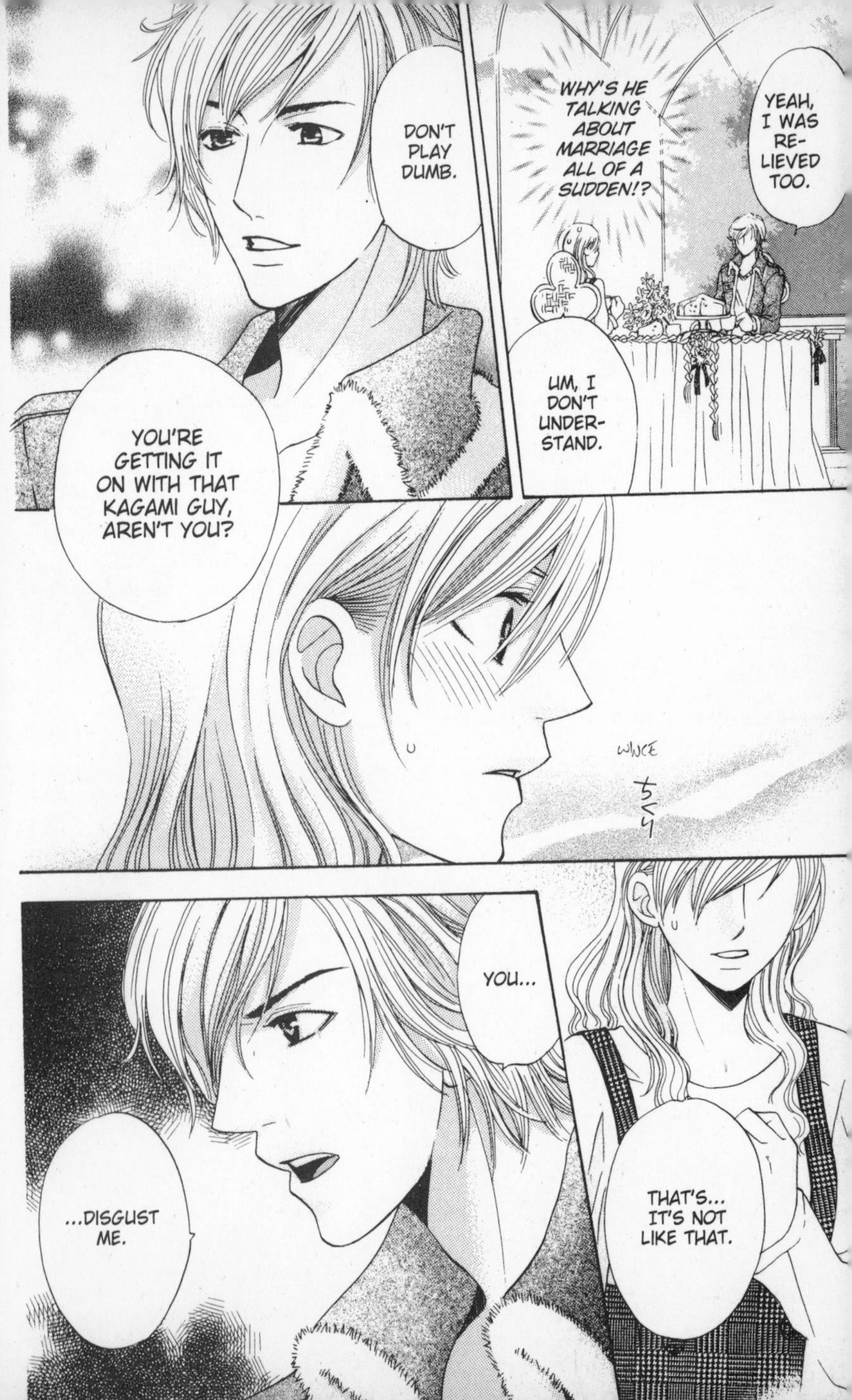
YEAH, I WAS RE-LIEVED TOO.
WHY'S HE TALKING ABOUT MARRIAGE ALL OF A SUDDEN!?
UM, I DON'T UNDER-STAND.
DON'T PLAY DUMB.
YOU'RE GETTING IT ON WITH THAT KAGAMI GUY, AREN'T YOU?
WINCE
ちくり
THAT'S... IT'S NOT LIKE THAT.
YOU...
...DISGUST ME.

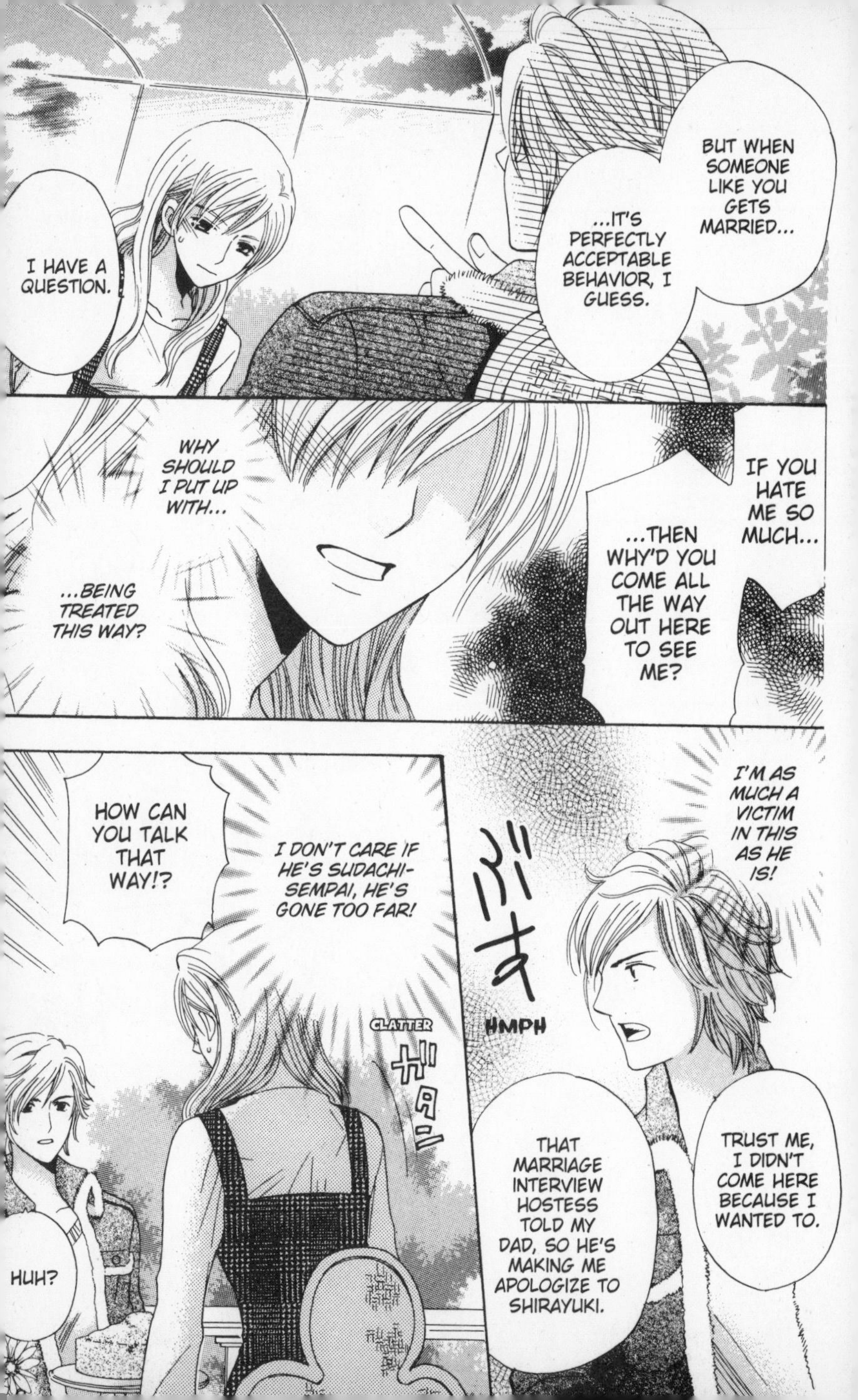
BUT WHEN SOMEONE LIKE YOU GETS MARRIED...
...IT'S PERFECTLY ACCEPTABLE BEHAVIOR, I GUESS.
I HAVE A QUESTION.
IF YOU HATE ME SO MUCH...
...THEN WHY'D YOU COME ALL THE WAY OUT HERE TO SEE ME?
WHY SHOULD I PUT UP WITH...
...BEING TREATED THIS WAY?
I'M AS MUCH A VICTIM IN THIS AS HE IS!
ぶす
HMPH
TRUST ME, I DIDN'T COME HERE BECAUSE I WANTED TO.
THAT MARRIAGE INTERVIEW HOSTESS TOLD MY DAD, SO HE'S MAKING ME APOLOGIZE TO SHIRAYUKI.
HOW CAN YOU TALK THAT WAY!?
I DON'T CARE IF HE'S SUDACHI-SEMPAI, HE'S GONE TOO FAR!
CLATTER
ガタン
HUH?

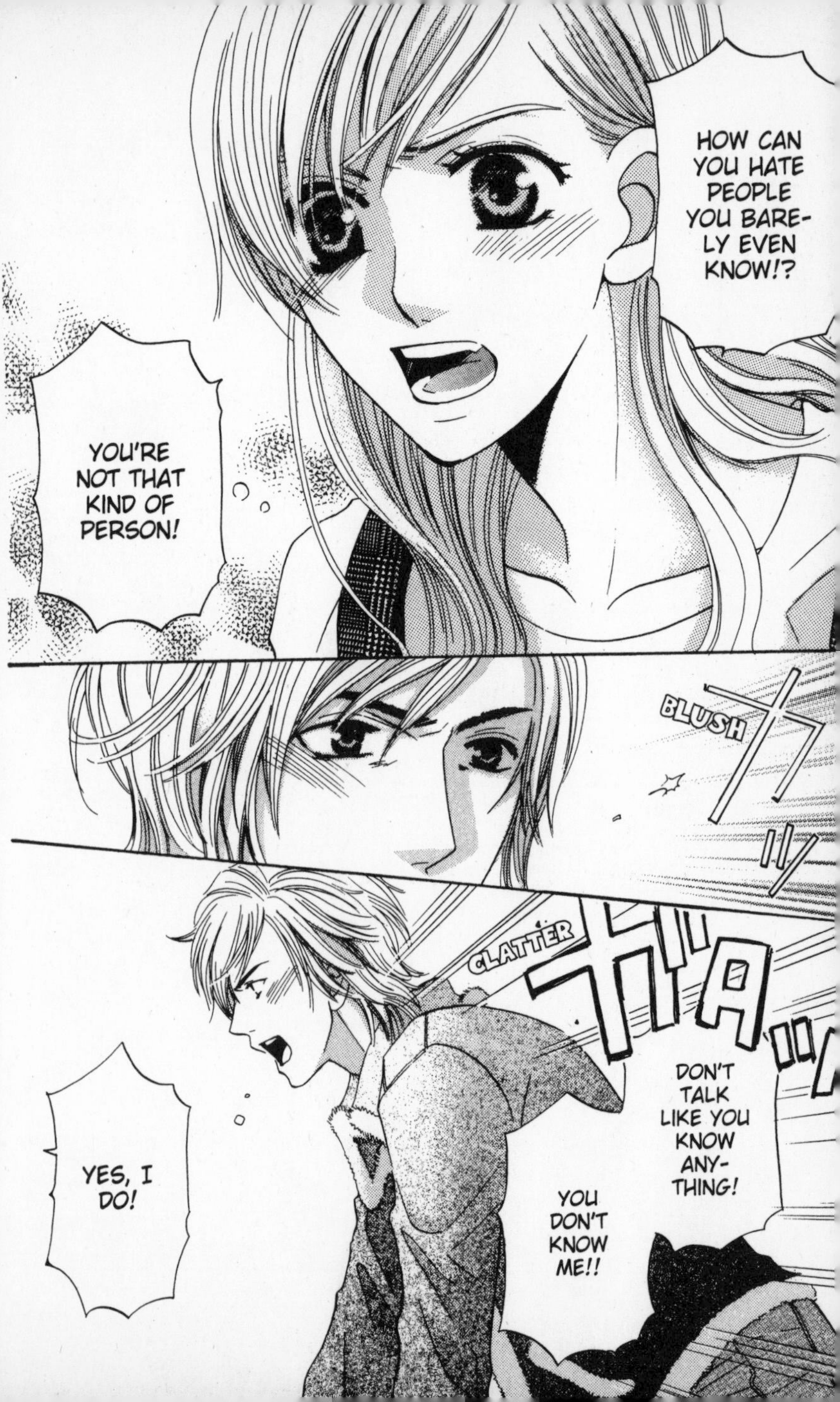
HOW CAN YOU HATE PEOPLE YOU BARELY EVEN KNOW!?
YOU'RE NOT THAT KIND OF PERSON!
BLUSH
CLATTER
DON'T TALK LIKE YOU KNOW ANYTHING!
YOU DON'T KNOW ME!!
YES, I DO!

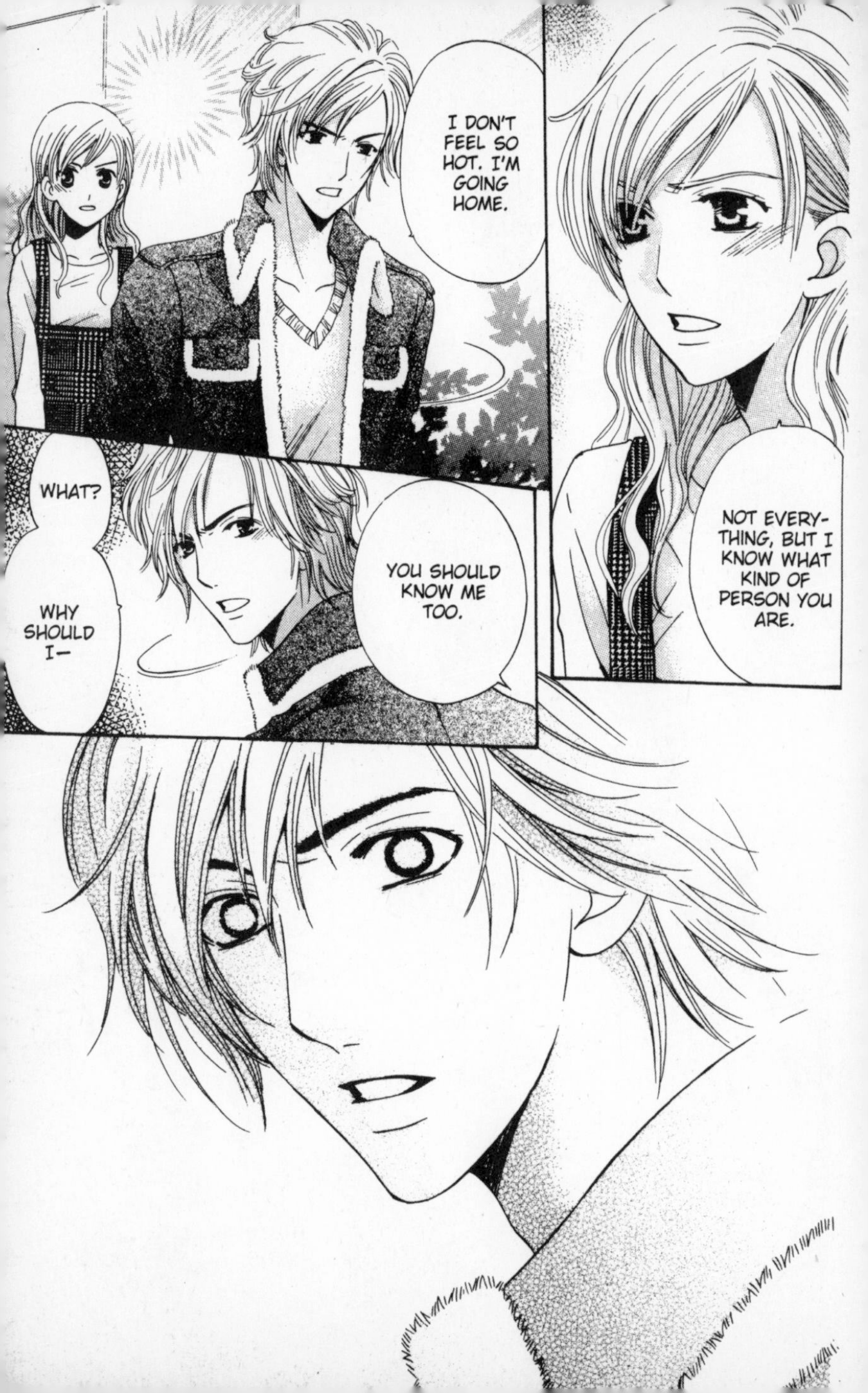
NOT EVERYTHING, BUT I KNOW WHAT KIND OF PERSON YOU ARE.
I DON'T FEEL SO HOT. I'M GOING HOME.
WHAT?
WHY SHOULD I—
YOU SHOULD KNOW ME TOO.

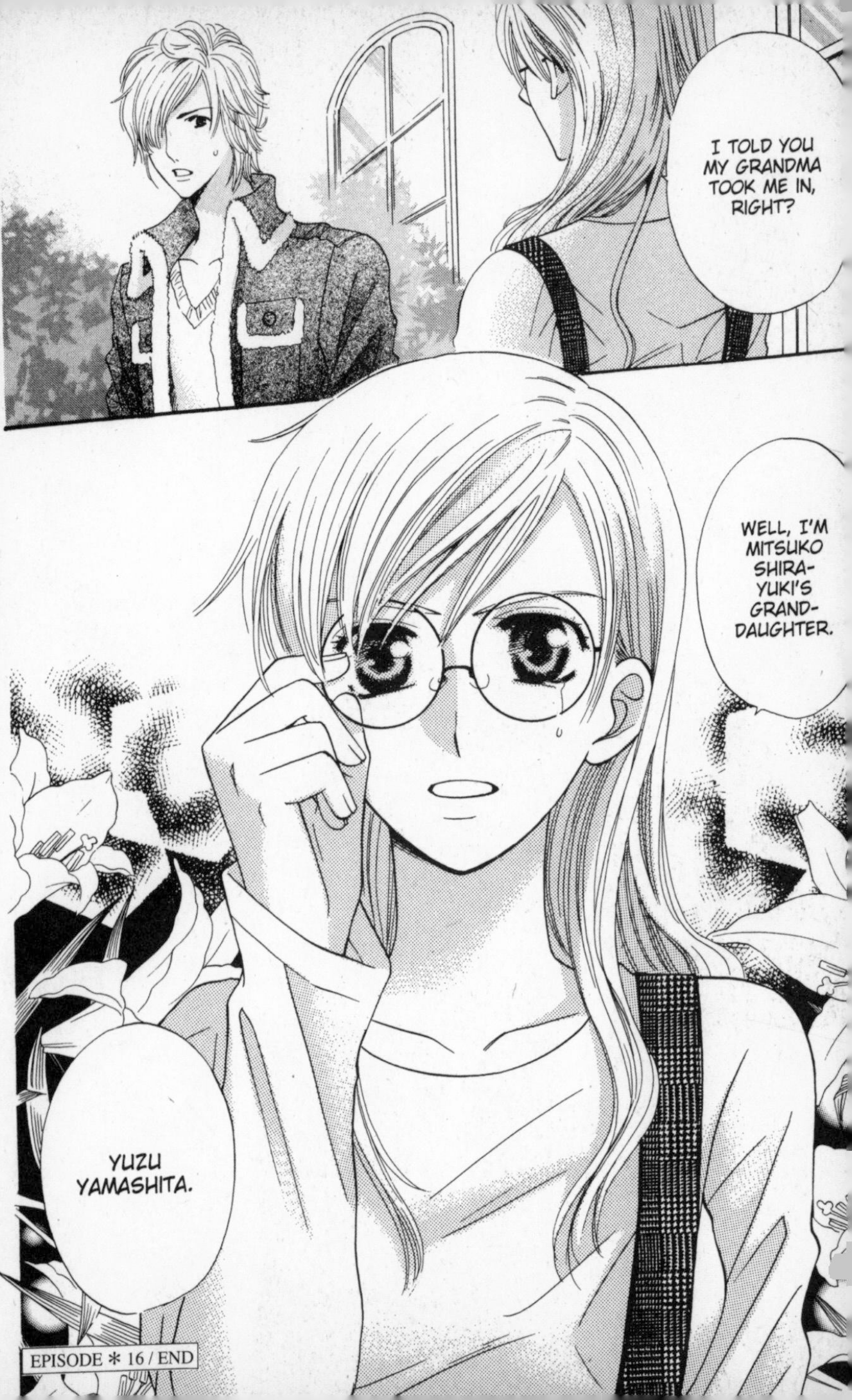
I TOLD YOU MY GRANDMA TOOK ME IN, RIGHT?
WELL, I'M MITSUKO SHIRA-YUKI'S GRAND-DAUGHTER.
YUZU YAMASHITA.
EPISODE * 16 / END

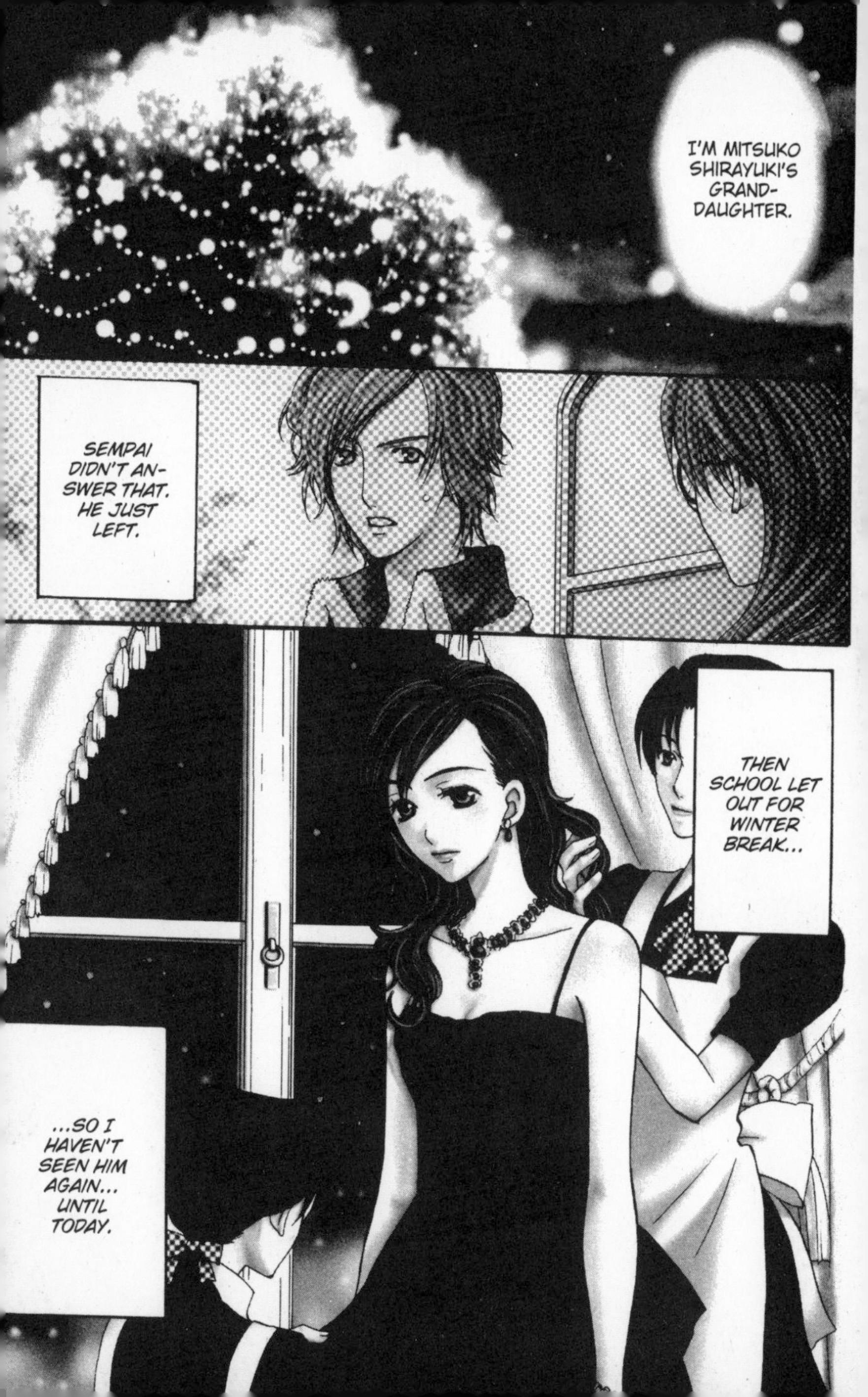
I'M MITSUKO SHIRAYUKI'S GRAND-DAUGHTER.
SEMPAI DIDN'T AN-SWER THAT. HE JUST LEFT.
THEN SCHOOL LET OUT FOR WINTER BREAK...
...SO I HAVEN'T SEEN HIM AGAIN... UNTIL TODAY.

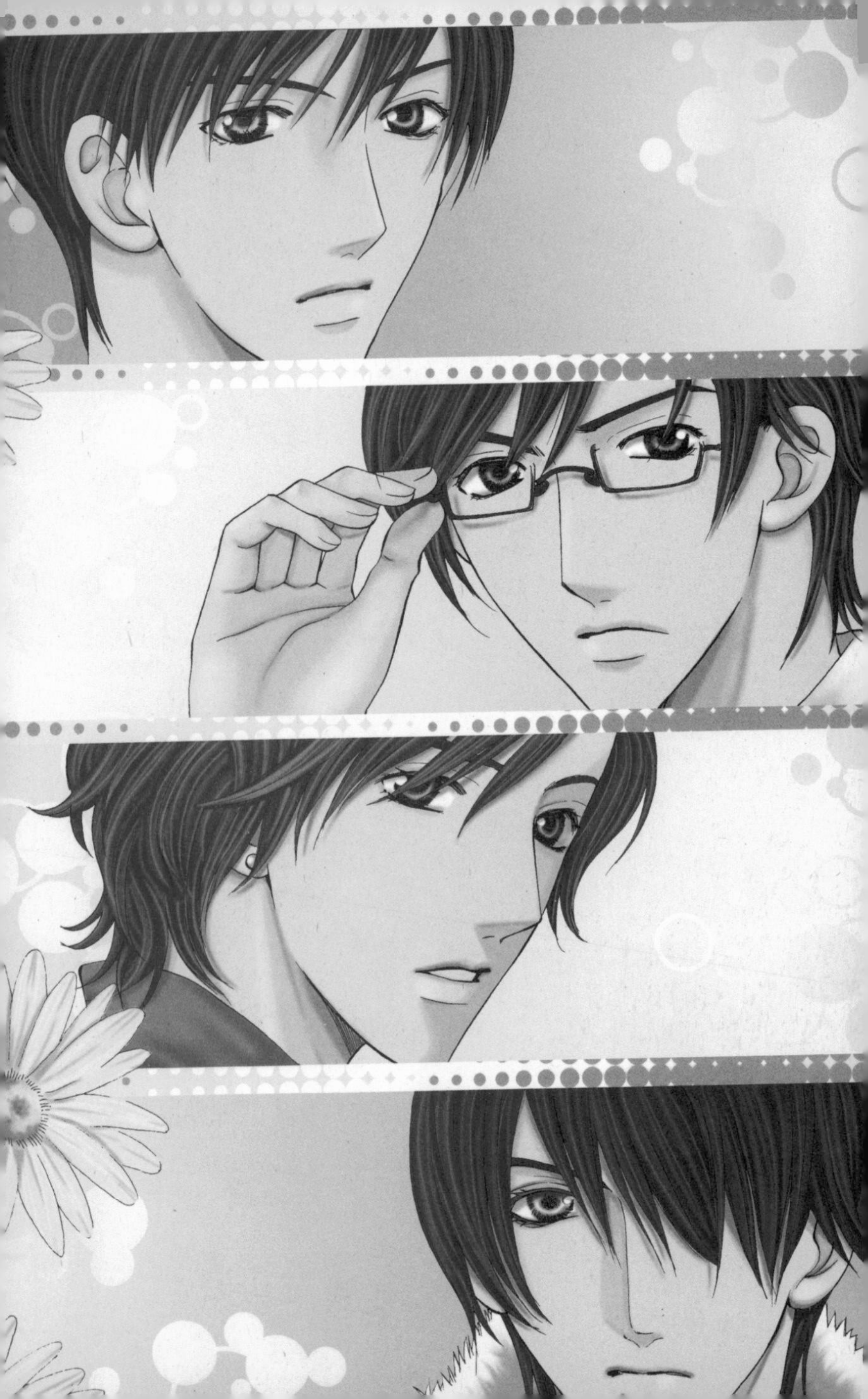

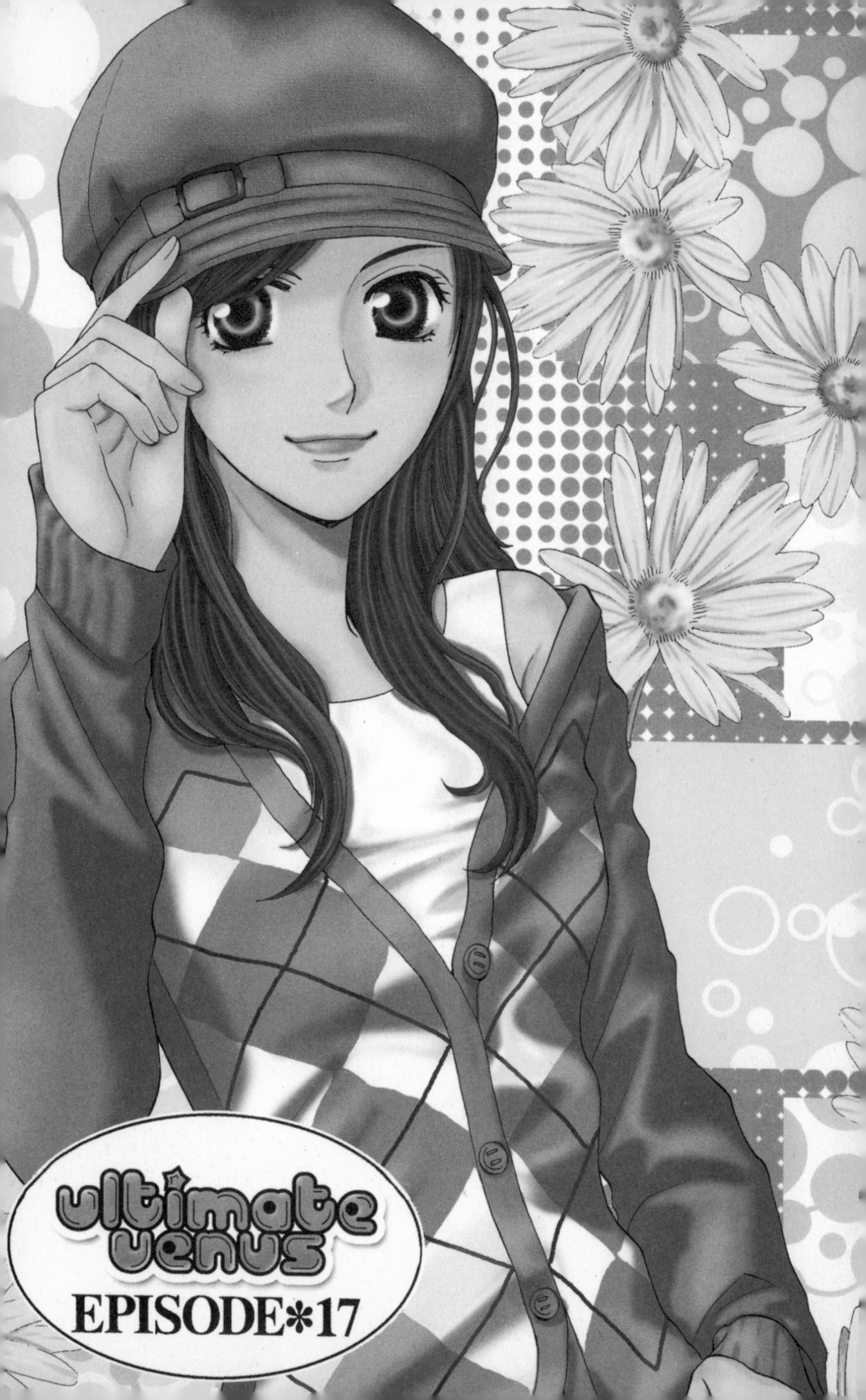
ultimate venus
EPISODE*17

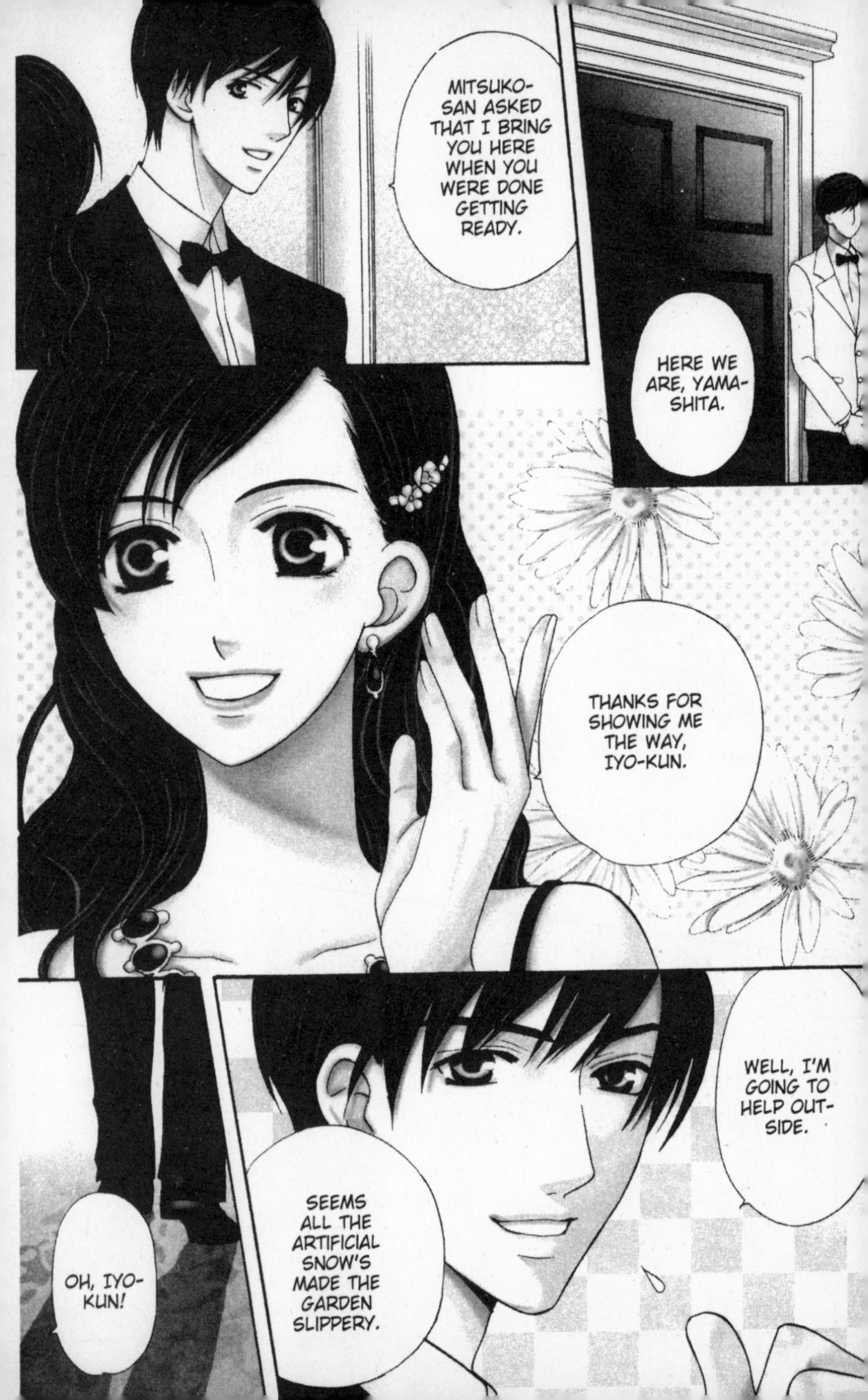
HERE WE ARE, YAMA-SHITA.
MITSUKO-SAN ASKED THAT I BRING YOU HERE WHEN YOU WERE DONE GETTING READY.
THANKS FOR SHOWING ME THE WAY, IYO-KUN.
WELL, I'M GOING TO HELP OUT-SIDE.
SEEMS ALL THE ARTIFICIAL SNOW'S MADE THE GARDEN SLIPPERY.
OH, IYO-KUN!

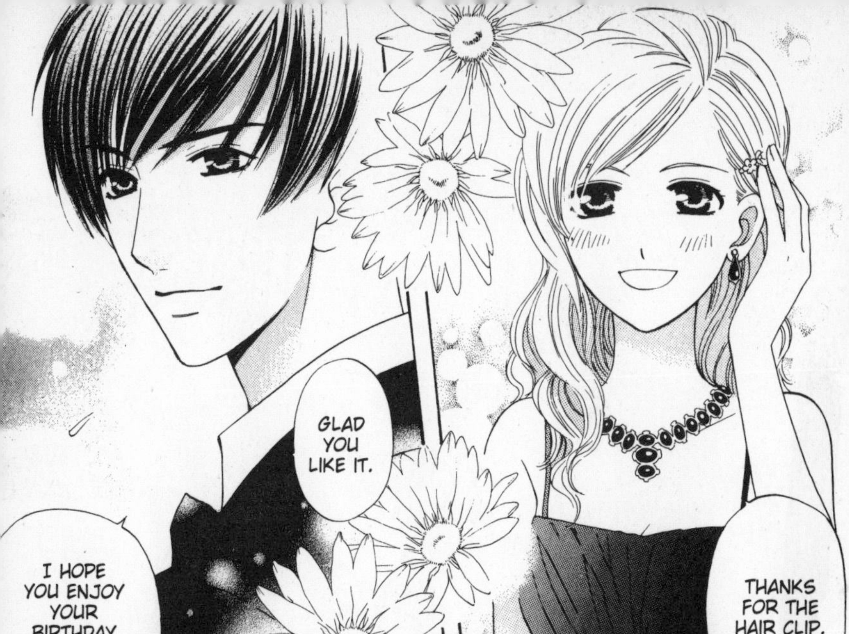
THANKS FOR THE HAIR CLIP.
GLAD YOU LIKE IT.
I HOPE YOU ENJOY YOUR BIRTHDAY PARTY TODAY.
YOU CAN COME IN NOW, YUZU-SAMA.
COM-ING!
I'M NOT THRILLED ABOUT SEEING SEMPAI, BUT...
...I DON'T HAVE MUCH CHOICE.
CREAK

Kanna Kiyomi (age 16)

Birthday: June 29th

Blood Type: AB

Hero: Her brother

Since she has always hidden her claws and played innocent for her brother, she's responsible for his poor judgment when it comes to girls.

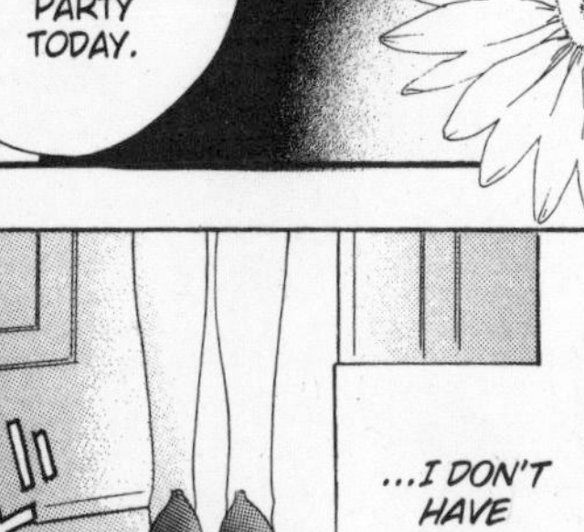

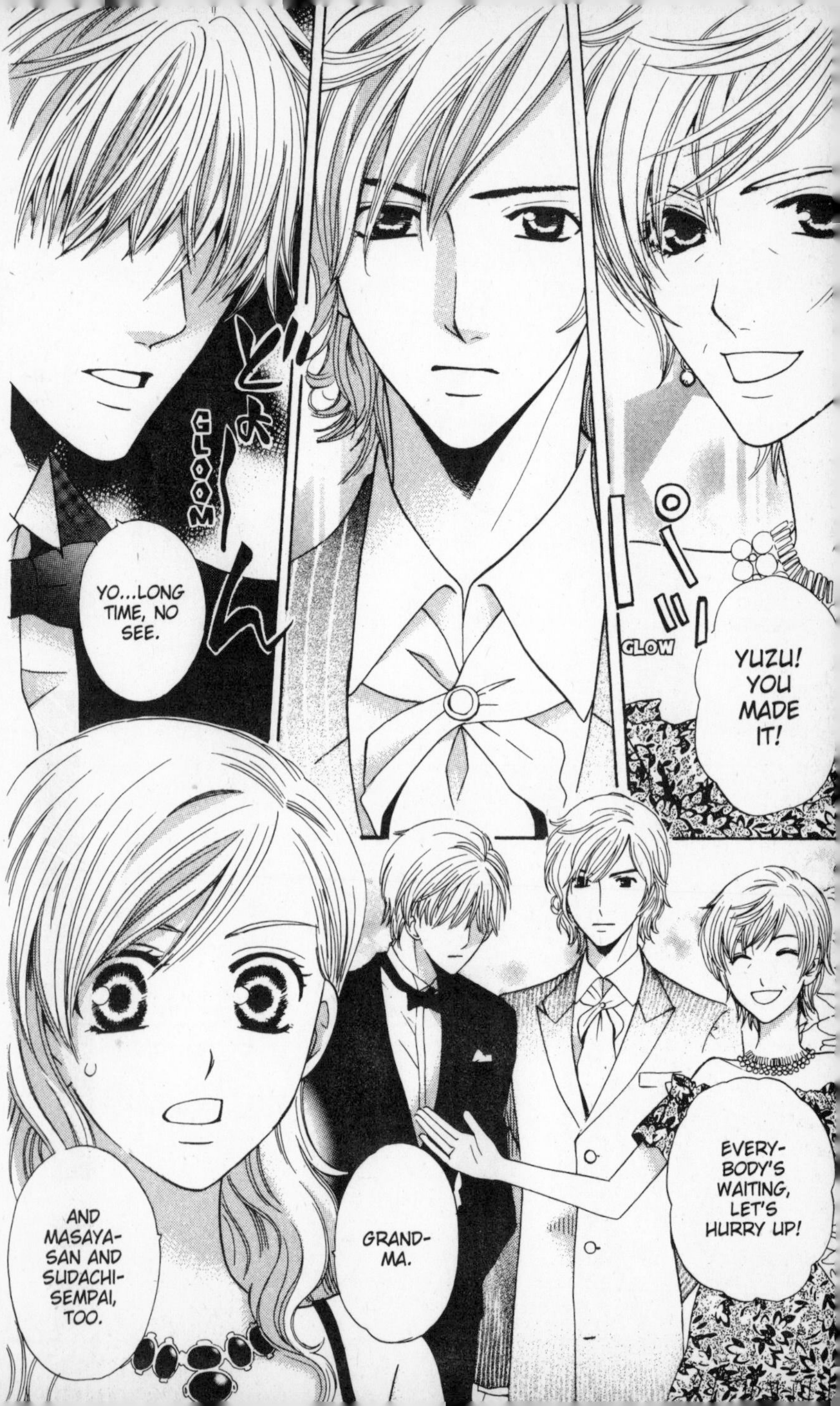

GLOW
YUZU! YOU MADE IT!
GLOOM
YO...LONG TIME, NO SEE.
EVERYBODY'S WAITING, LET'S HURRY UP!
GRANDMA.
AND MASAYA-SAN AND SUDACHI-SEMPAI, TOO.

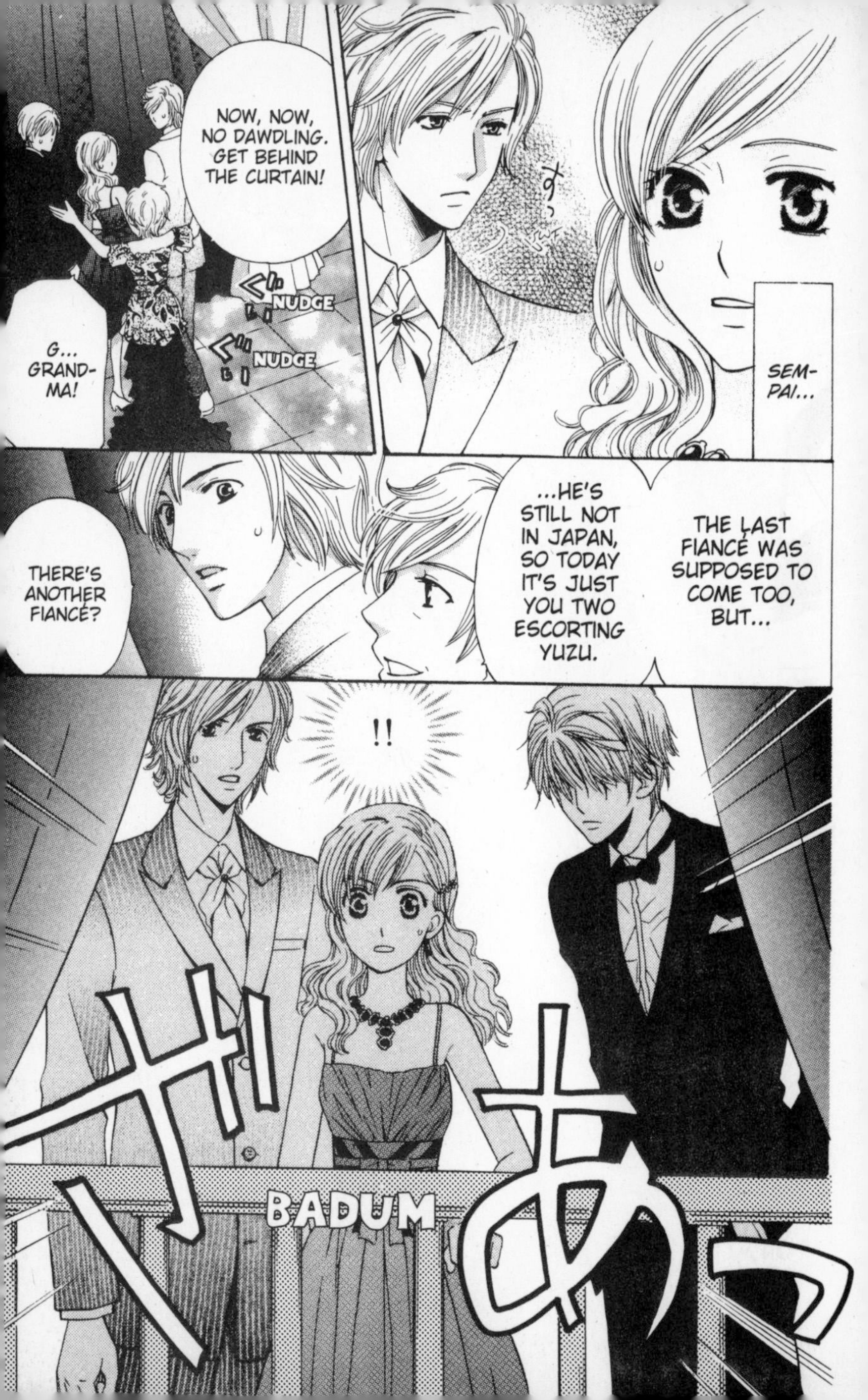
SEMPAI...
NOW, NOW, NO DAWDLING. GET BEHIND THE CURTAIN!
NUDGE
NUDGE
G... GRANDMA!
THE LAST FIANCÉ WAS SUPPOSED TO COME TOO, BUT...
...HE'S STILL NOT IN JAPAN, SO TODAY IT'S JUST YOU TWO ESCORTING YUZU.
THERE'S ANOTHER FIANCÉ?
!!
BADUM

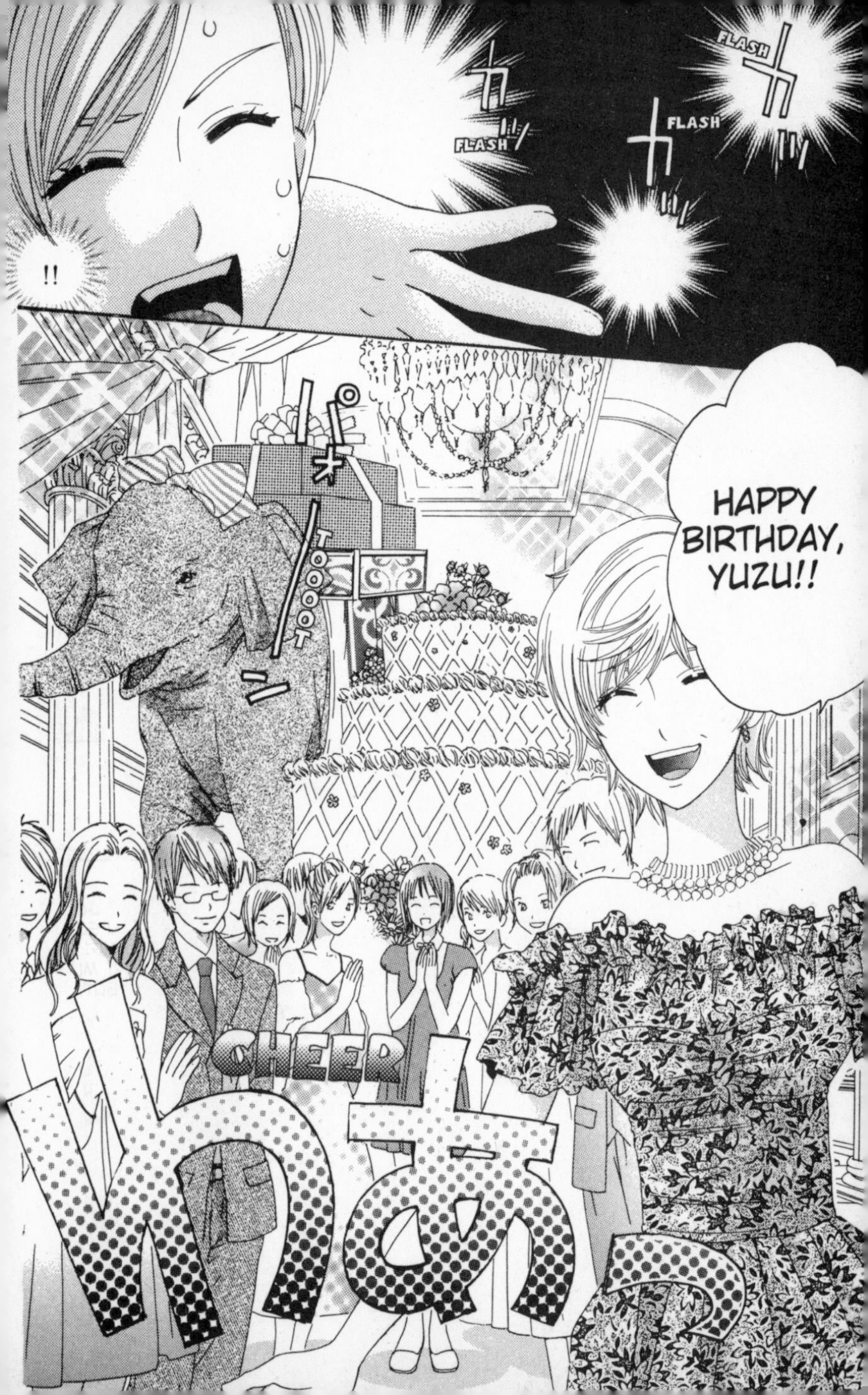
FLASH
FLASH
FLASH
!!
TOOOOOT
HAPPY BIRTHDAY, YUZU!!
CHEER

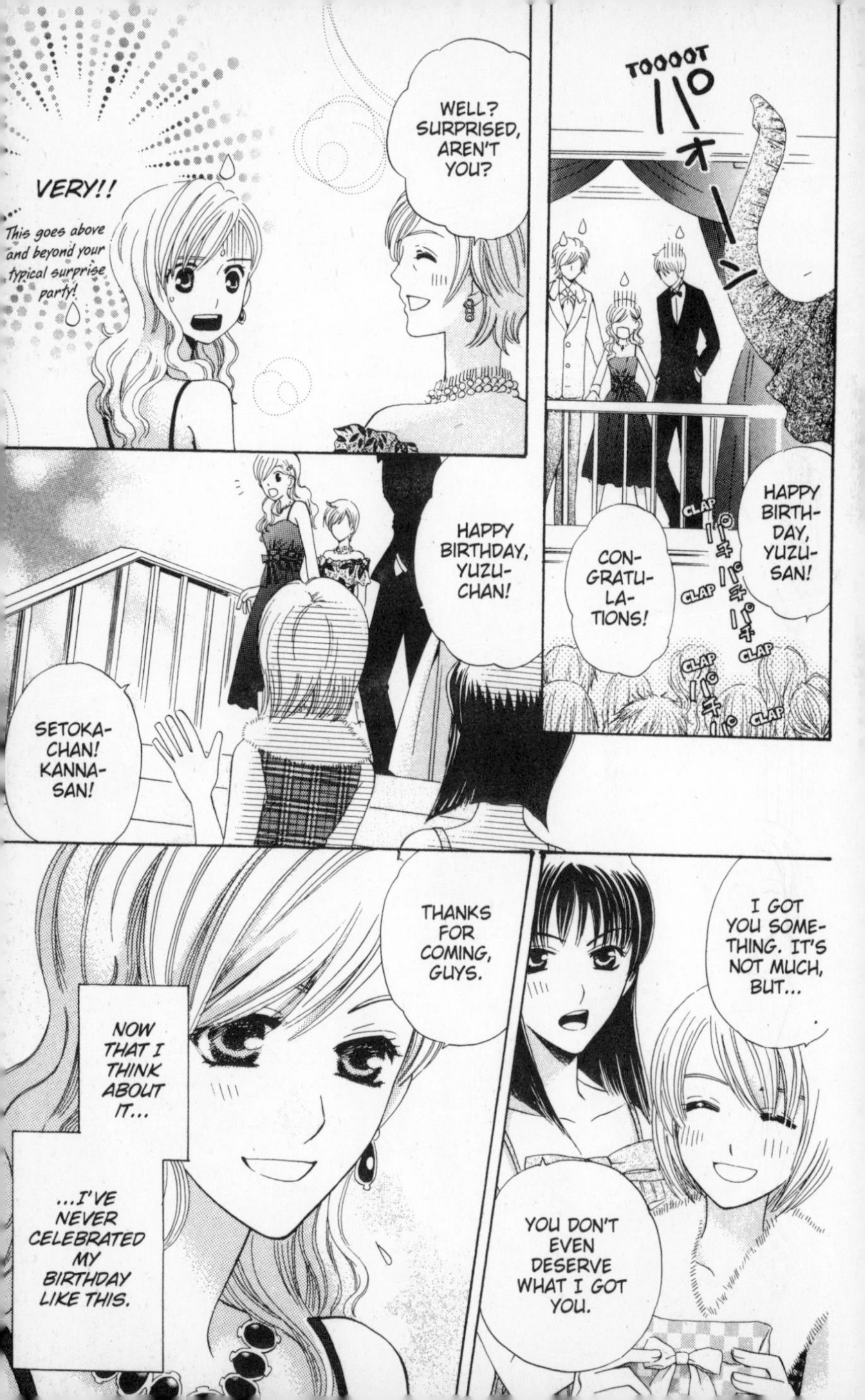
TOOOOT
パオーン
HAPPY BIRTHDAY, YUZU-SAN!
CLAP
パチパチ
CLAP
パチパチ
CONGRATULATIONS!
WELL? SURPRISED, AREN'T YOU?
VERY!!
This goes above and beyond your typical surprise party!
HAPPY BIRTHDAY, YUZU-CHAN!
SETOKA-CHAN! KANNA-SAN!
I GOT YOU SOMETHING. IT'S NOT MUCH, BUT...
YOU DON'T EVEN DESERVE WHAT I GOT YOU.
THANKS FOR COMING, GUYS.
NOW THAT I THINK ABOUT IT...
...I'VE NEVER CELEBRATED MY BIRTHDAY LIKE THIS.

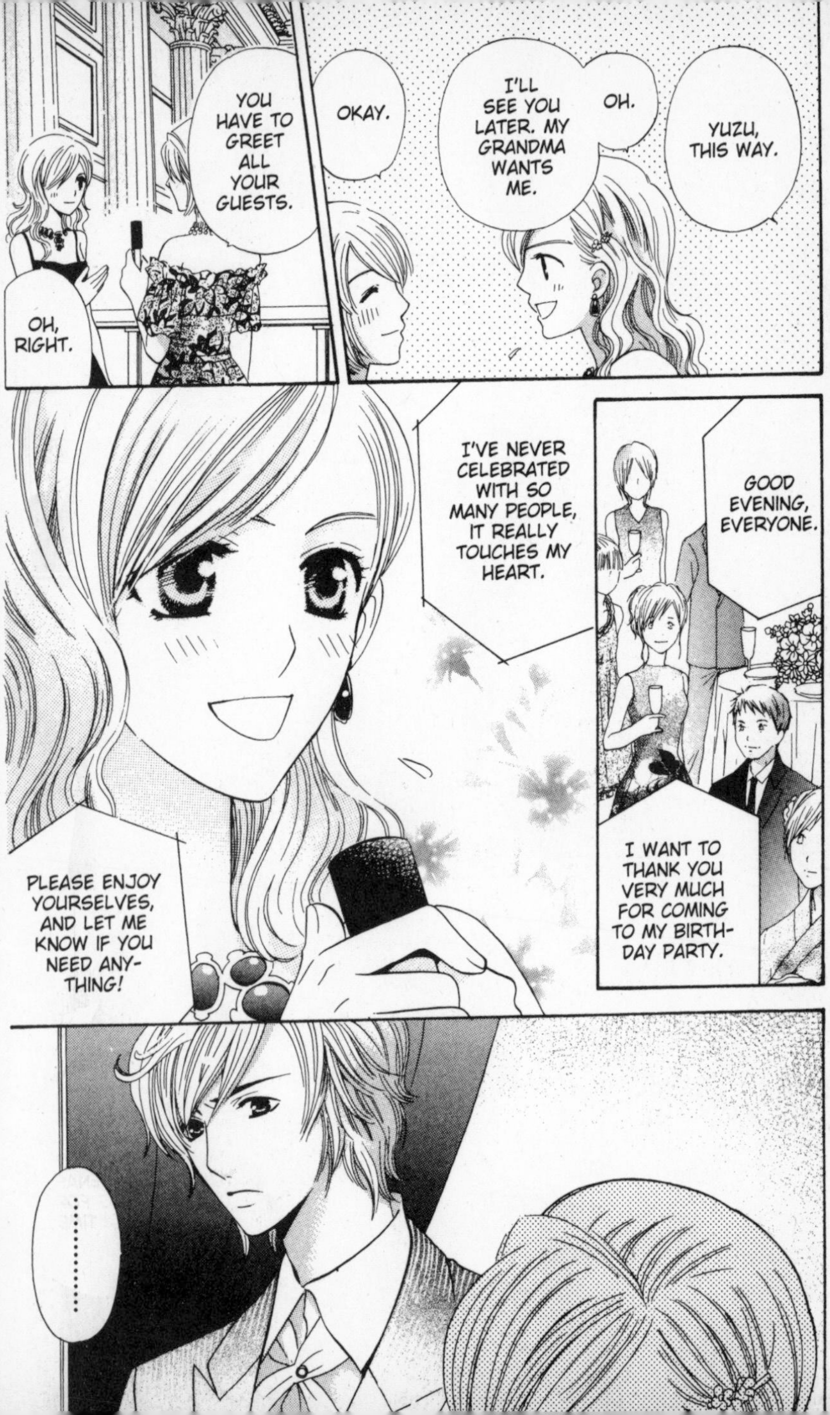
YUZU, THIS WAY.
OH.
I'LL SEE YOU LATER. MY GRANDMA WANTS ME.
OKAY.
YOU HAVE TO GREET ALL YOUR GUESTS.
OH, RIGHT.
GOOD EVENING, EVERYONE.
I WANT TO THANK YOU VERY MUCH FOR COMING TO MY BIRTH-DAY PARTY.
I'VE NEVER CELEBRATED WITH SO MANY PEOPLE, IT REALLY TOUCHES MY HEART.
PLEASE ENJOY YOURSELVES, AND LET ME KNOW IF YOU NEED ANY-THING!
......

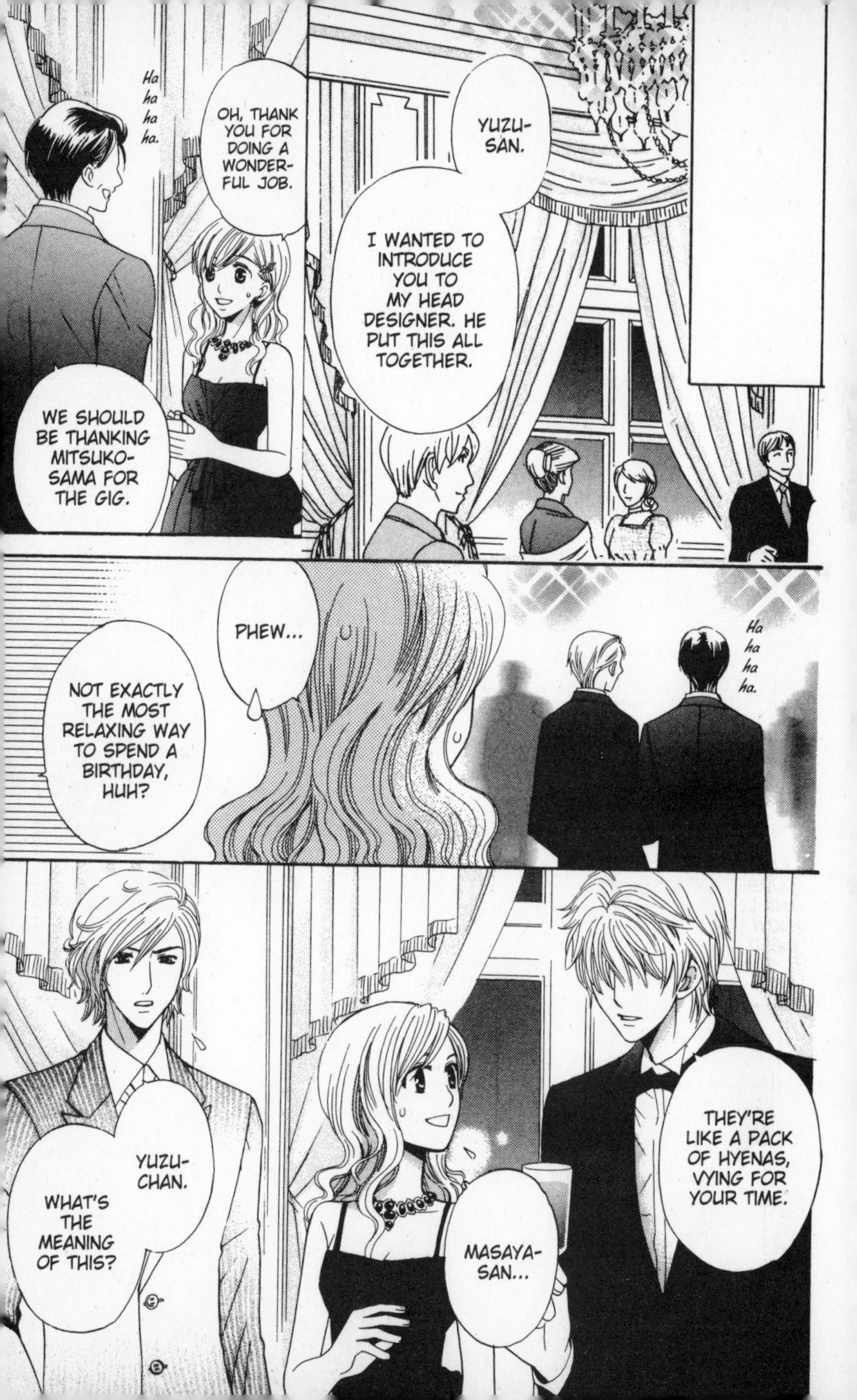
YUZU-SAN.
I WANTED TO INTRODUCE YOU TO MY HEAD DESIGNER. HE PUT THIS ALL TOGETHER.
OH, THANK YOU FOR DOING A WONDERFUL JOB.
Ha ha ha ha.
WE SHOULD BE THANKING MITSUKO-SAMA FOR THE GIG.
Ha ha ha ha.
PHEW...
NOT EXACTLY THE MOST RELAXING WAY TO SPEND A BIRTHDAY, HUH?
THEY'RE LIKE A PACK OF HYENAS, VYING FOR YOUR TIME.
MASAYA-SAN...
YUZU-CHAN.
WHAT'S THE MEANING OF THIS?

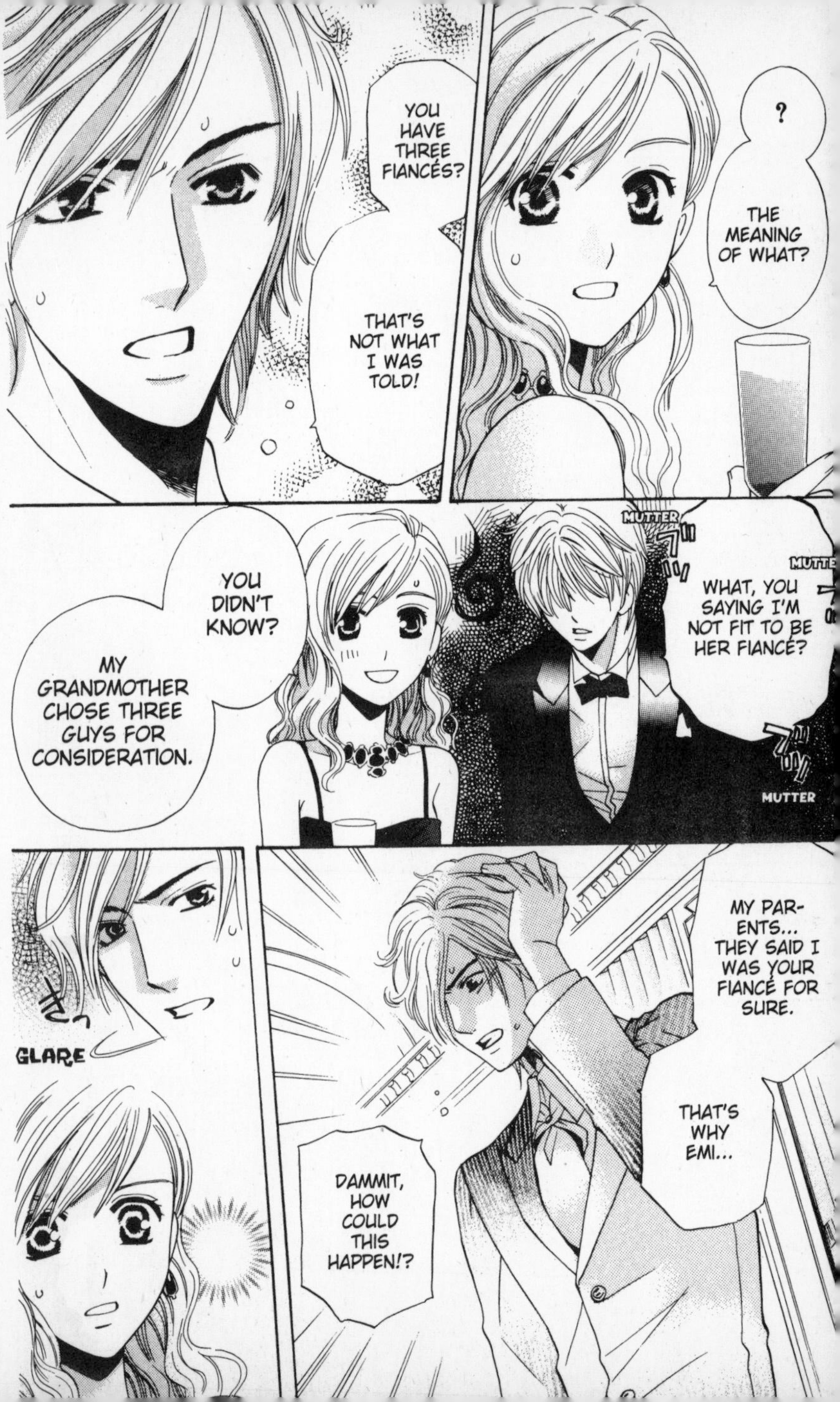
?
THE MEANING OF WHAT?
YOU HAVE THREE FIANCÉS?
THAT'S NOT WHAT I WAS TOLD!
MUTTER
WHAT, YOU SAYING I'M NOT FIT TO BE HER FIANCÉ?
MUTTER
YOU DIDN'T KNOW?
MY GRANDMOTHER CHOSE THREE GUYS FOR CONSIDERATION.
MY PAR-ENTS... THEY SAID I WAS YOUR FIANCÉ FOR SURE.
THAT'S WHY EMI...
DAMMIT, HOW COULD THIS HAPPEN!?
GLARE

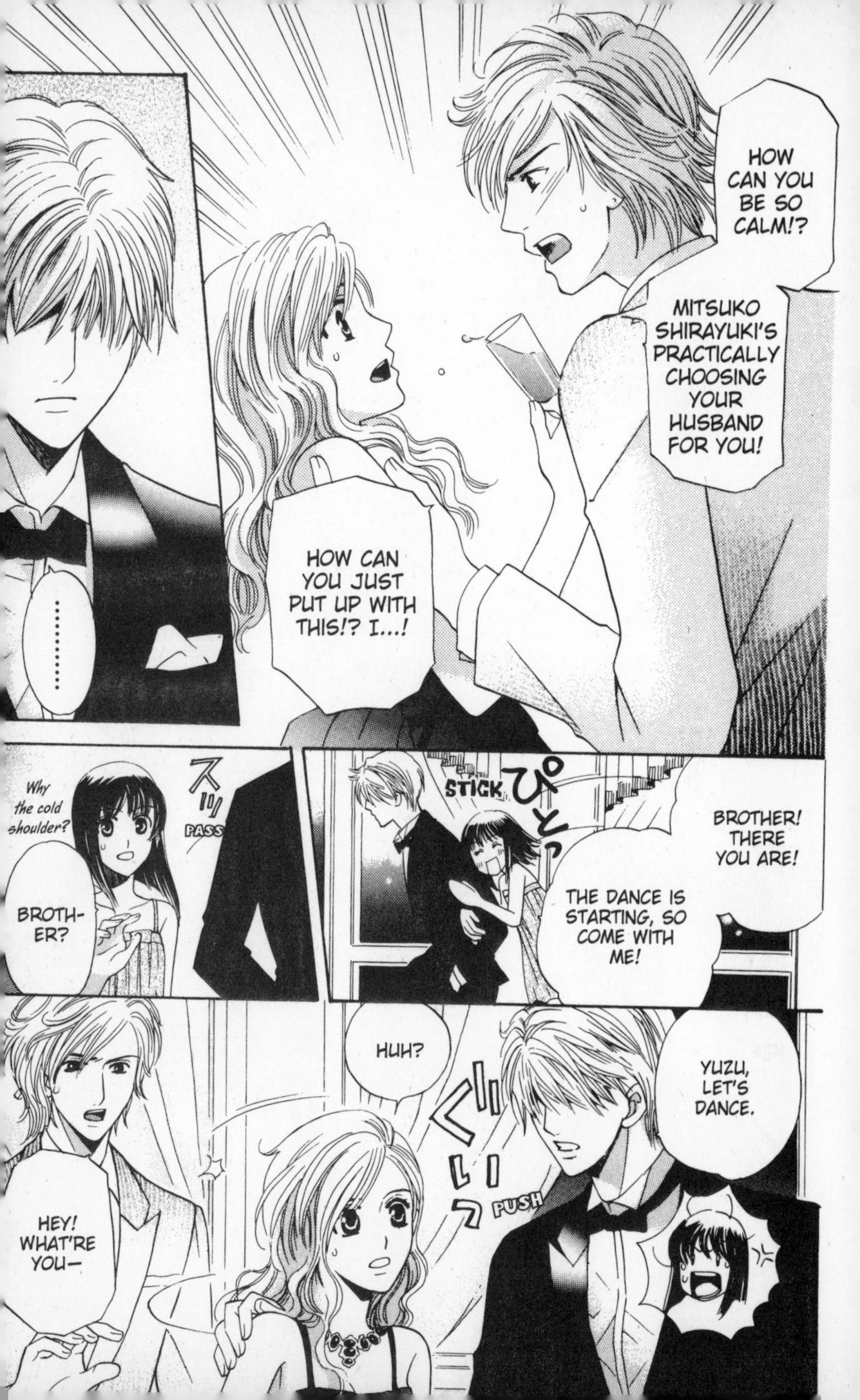
HOW CAN YOU BE SO CALM!?
MITSUKO SHIRAYUKI'S PRACTICALLY CHOOSING YOUR HUSBAND FOR YOU!
HOW CAN YOU JUST PUT UP WITH THIS!? I...!
....
BROTHER! THERE YOU ARE!
THE DANCE IS STARTING, SO COME WITH ME!
STICK
PASS
Why the cold shoulder?
BROTH-ER?
YUZU, LET'S DANCE.
HUH?
PUSH
HEY! WHAT'RE YOU—

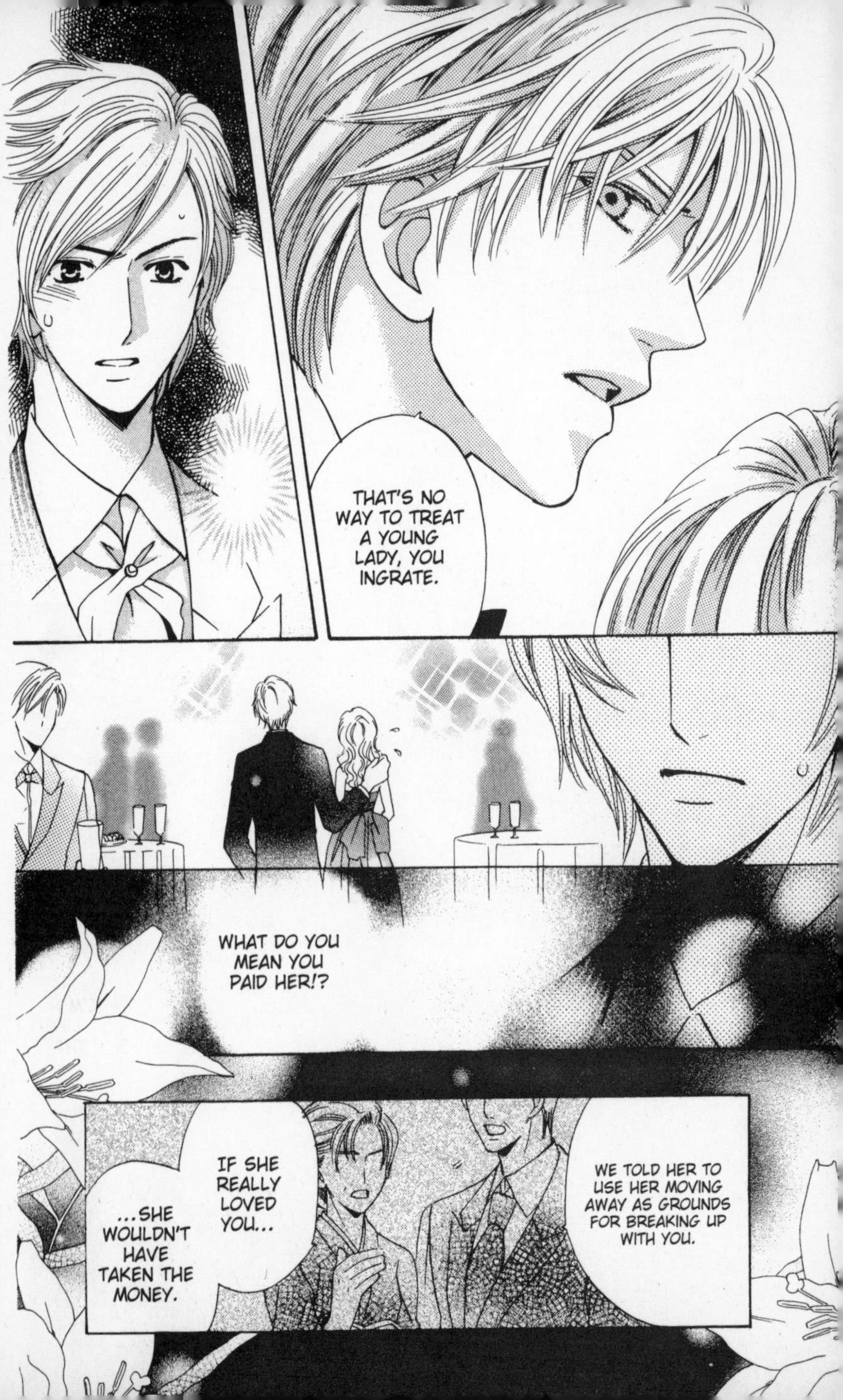
THAT'S NO WAY TO TREAT A YOUNG LADY, YOU INGRATE.
WHAT DO YOU MEAN YOU PAID HER!?
WE TOLD HER TO USE HER MOVING AWAY AS GROUNDS FOR BREAKING UP WITH YOU.
IF SHE REALLY LOVED YOU...
...SHE WOULDN'T HAVE TAKEN THE MONEY.

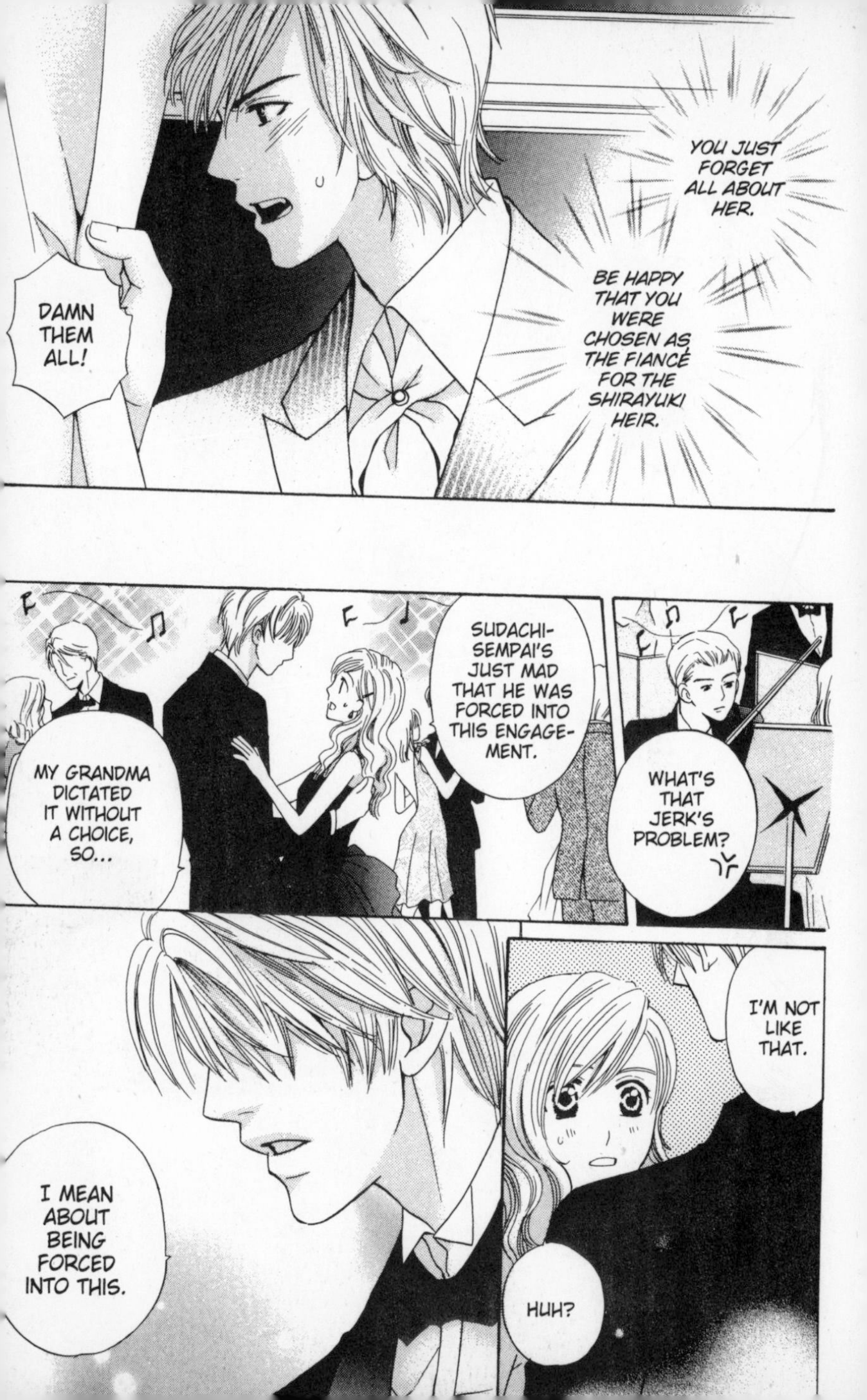
YOU JUST FORGET ALL ABOUT HER.
BE HAPPY THAT YOU WERE CHOSEN AS THE FIANCÉ FOR THE SHIRAYUKI HEIR.
DAMN THEM ALL!
WHAT'S THAT JERK'S PROBLEM?
SUDACHI-SEMPAI'S JUST MAD THAT HE WAS FORCED INTO THIS ENGAGEMENT.
MY GRANDMA DICTATED IT WITHOUT A CHOICE, SO...
I'M NOT LIKE THAT.
HUH?
I MEAN ABOUT BEING FORCED INTO THIS.

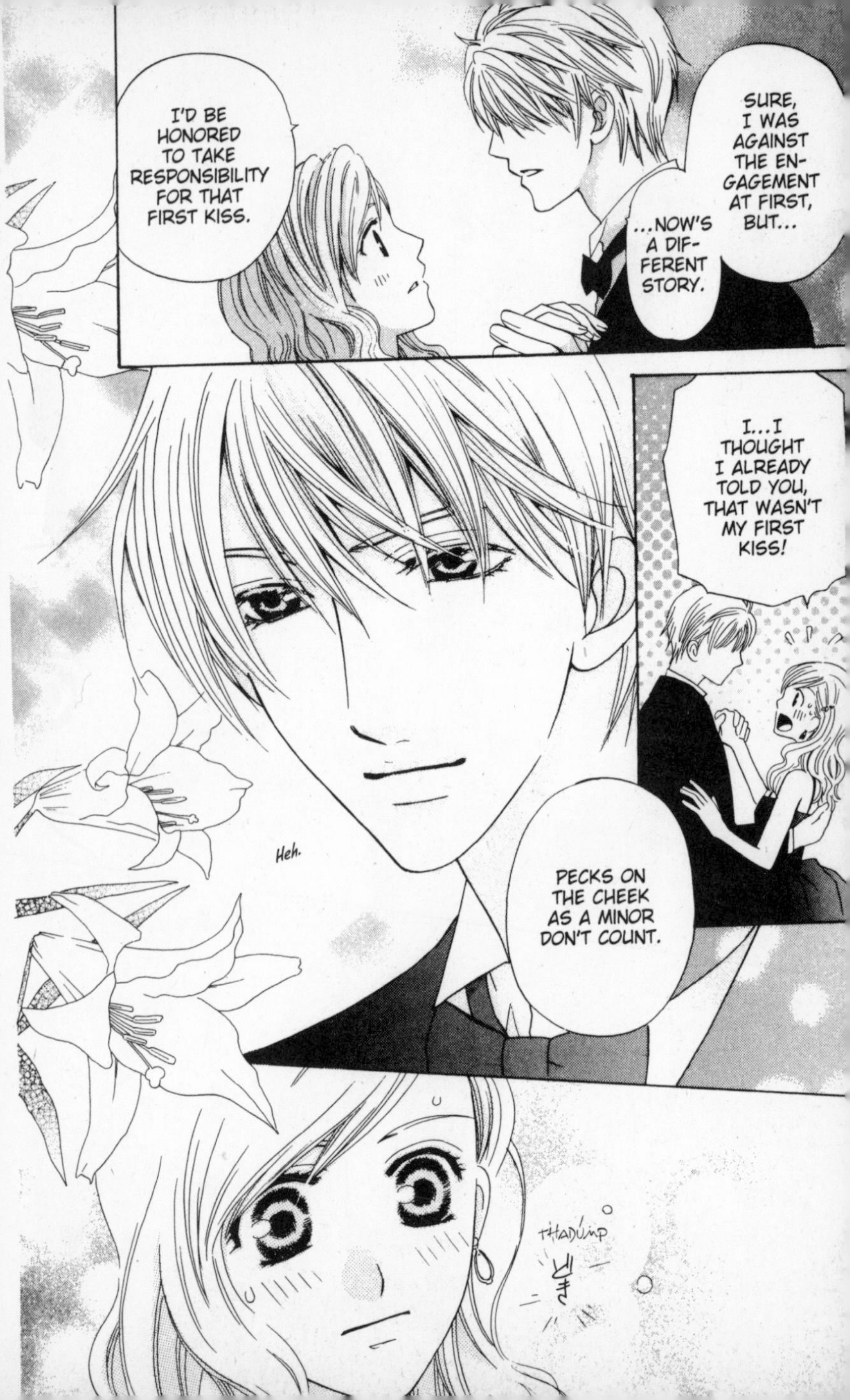
SURE, I WAS AGAINST THE EN-GAGEMENT AT FIRST, BUT...
...NOW'S A DIF-FERENT STORY.
I'D BE HONORED TO TAKE RESPONSIBILITY FOR THAT FIRST KISS.
I...I THOUGHT I ALREADY TOLD YOU, THAT WASN'T MY FIRST KISS!
Heh.
PECKS ON THE CHEEK AS A MINOR DON'T COUNT.
THADUMP
どき

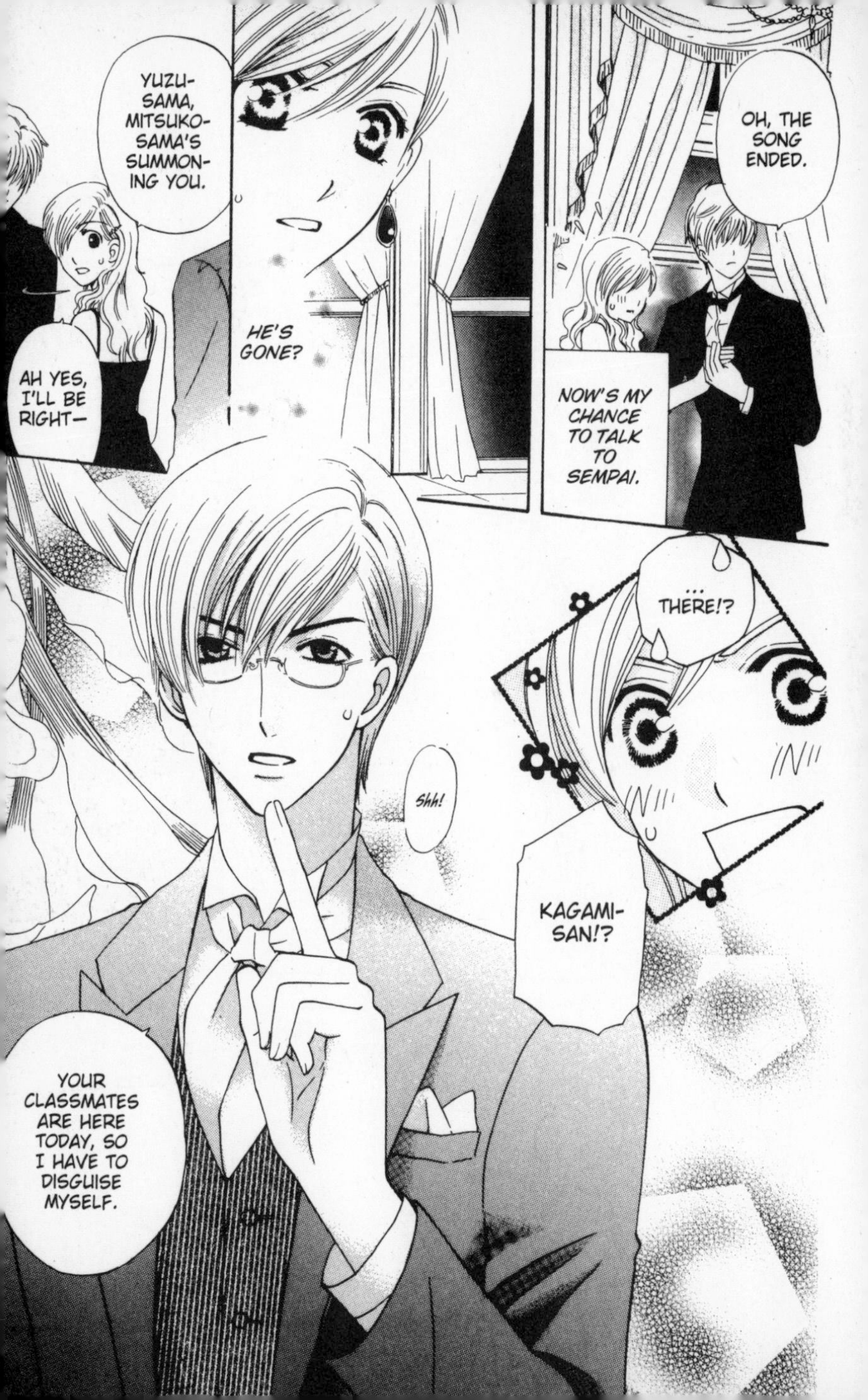

OH, THE SONG ENDED.
NOW'S MY CHANCE TO TALK TO SEMPAI.
HE'S GONE?
YUZU-SAMA, MITSUKO-SAMA'S SUMMONING YOU.
AH YES, I'LL BE RIGHT—
... THERE!?
KAGAMI-SAN!?
Shh!
YOUR CLASSMATES ARE HERE TODAY, SO I HAVE TO DISGUISE MYSELF.

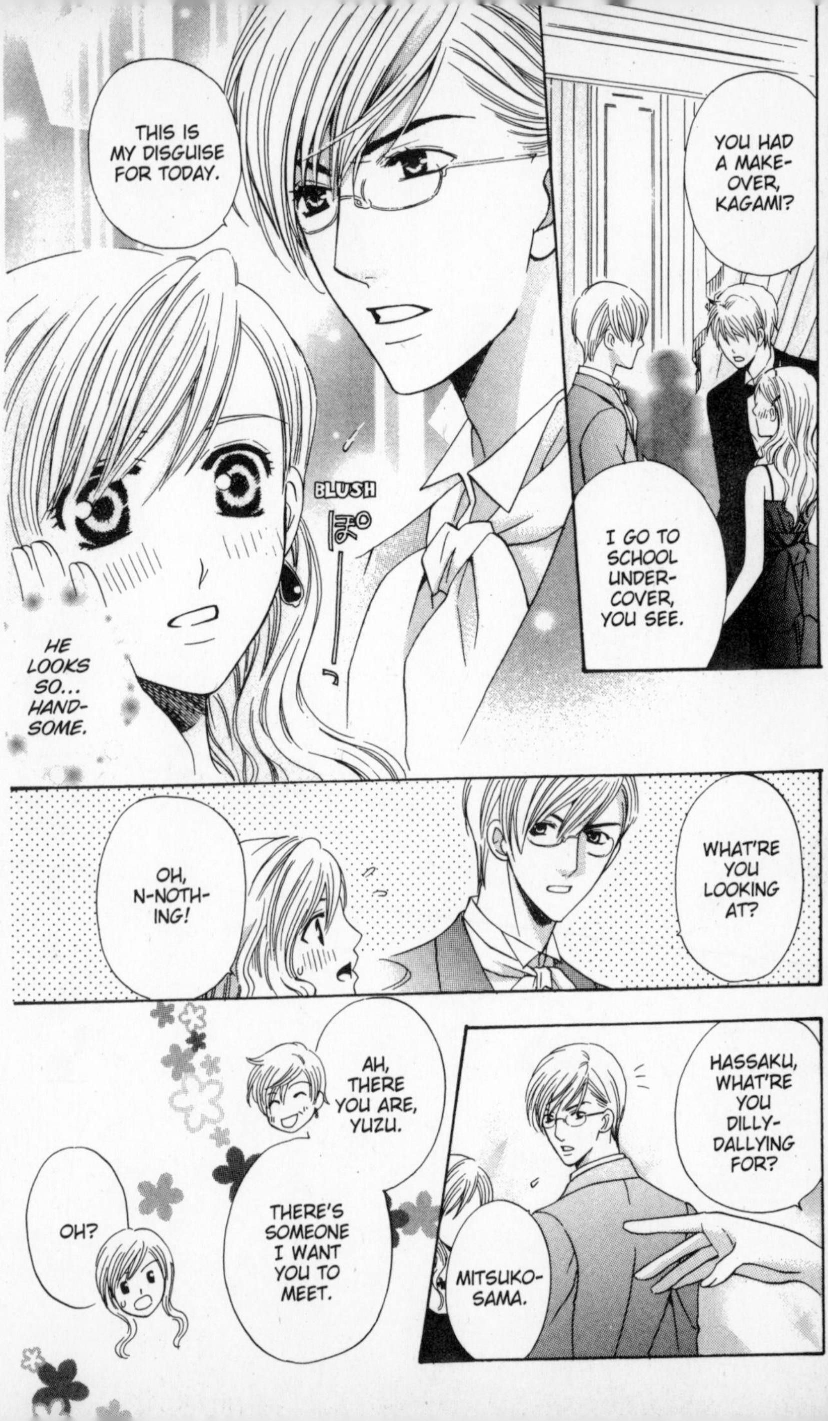
YOU HAD A MAKE-OVER, KAGAMI?
I GO TO SCHOOL UNDER-COVER, YOU SEE.
THIS IS MY DISGUISE FOR TODAY.
BLUSH
HE LOOKS SO... HAND-SOME.
WHAT'RE YOU LOOKING AT?
OH, N-NOTHING!
HASSAKU, WHAT'RE YOU DILLY-DALLYING FOR?
MITSUKO-SAMA.
AH, THERE YOU ARE, YUZU.
THERE'S SOMEONE I WANT YOU TO MEET.
OH?

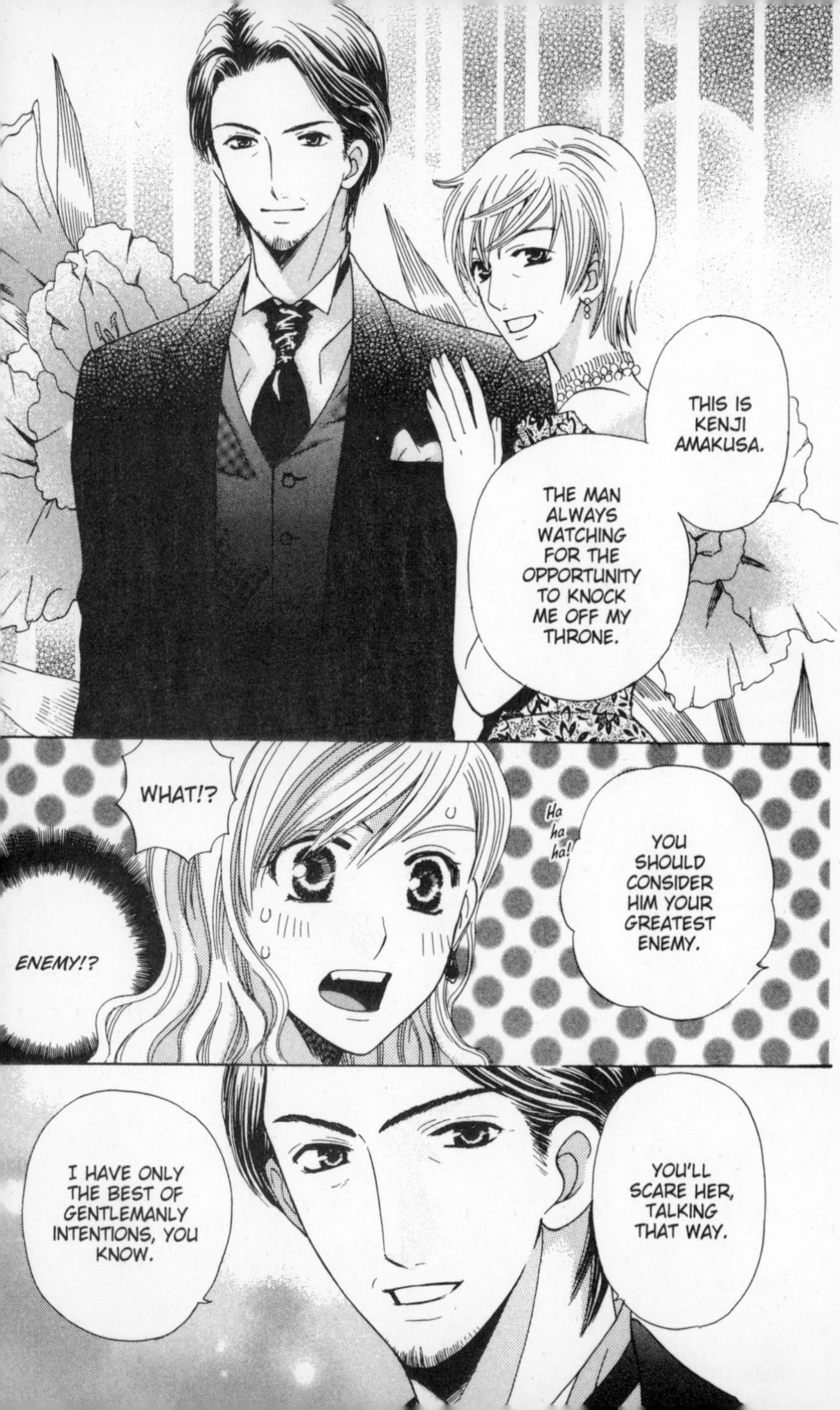
THIS IS KENJI AMAKUSA.
THE MAN ALWAYS WATCHING FOR THE OPPORTUNITY TO KNOCK ME OFF MY THRONE.
YOU SHOULD CONSIDER HIM YOUR GREATEST ENEMY.
Ha ha ha!
WHAT!?
ENEMY!?
YOU'LL SCARE HER, TALKING THAT WAY.
I HAVE ONLY THE BEST OF GENTLEMANLY INTENTIONS, YOU KNOW.

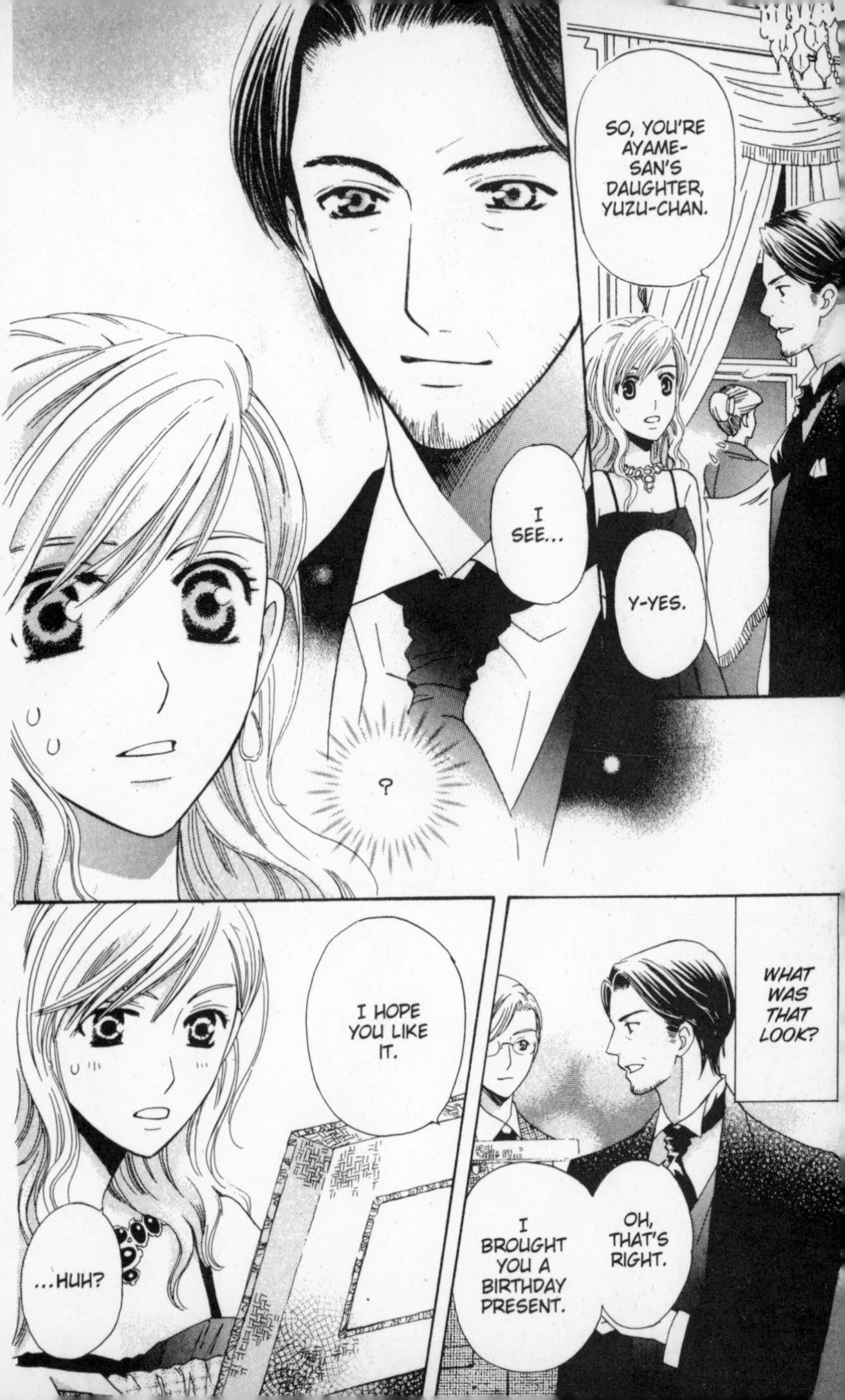
SO, YOU'RE AYAME-SAN'S DAUGHTER, YUZU-CHAN.
Y-YES.
I SEE...
?
WHAT WAS THAT LOOK?
OH, THAT'S RIGHT.
I BROUGHT YOU A BIRTHDAY PRESENT.
I HOPE YOU LIKE IT.
...HUH?

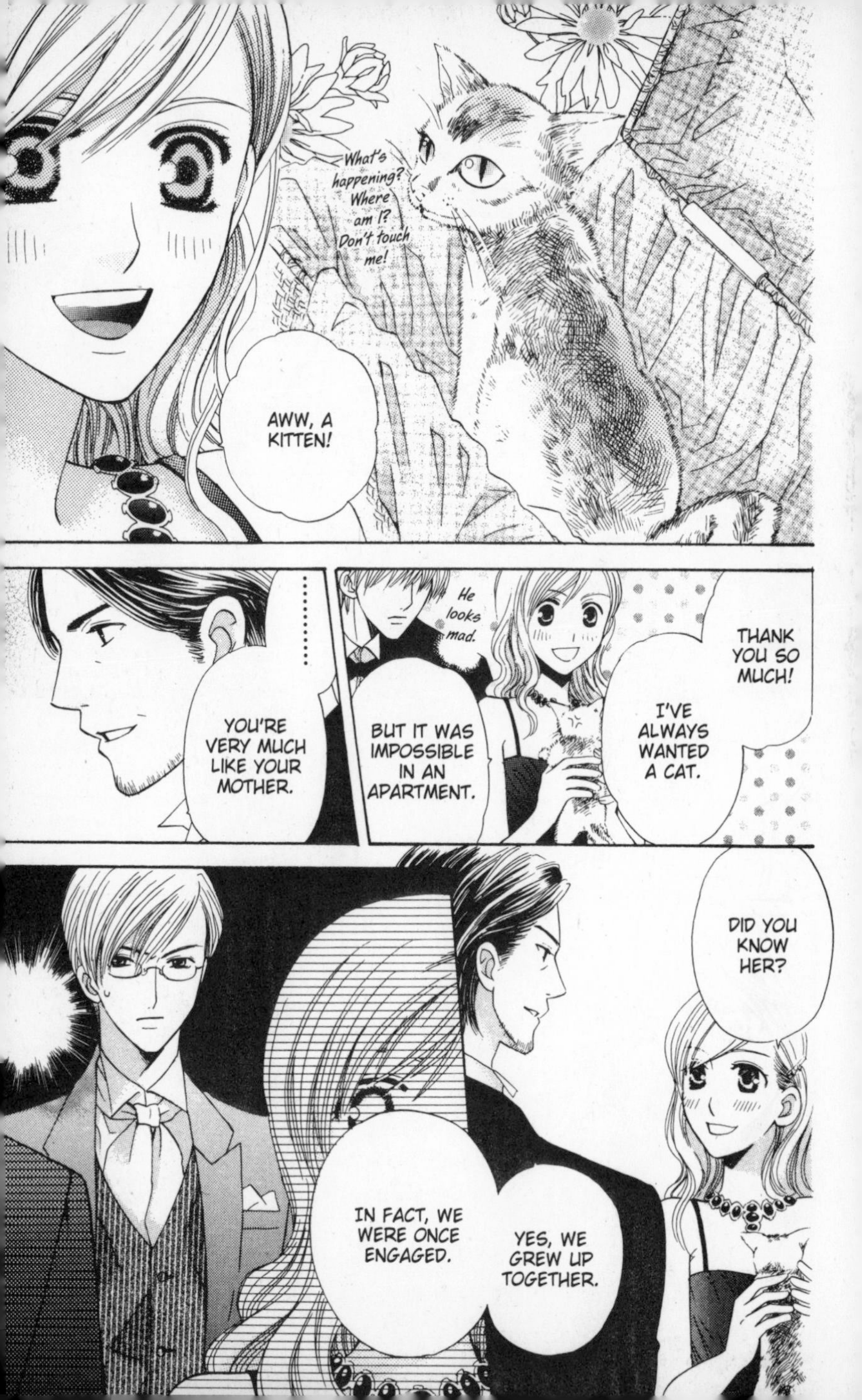
What's happening? Where am I? Don't touch me!
AWW, A KITTEN!
THANK YOU SO MUCH!
I'VE ALWAYS WANTED A CAT.
BUT IT WAS IMPOSSIBLE IN AN APARTMENT.
He looks mad.
......
YOU'RE VERY MUCH LIKE YOUR MOTHER.
DID YOU KNOW HER?
YES, WE GREW UP TOGETHER.
IN FACT, WE WERE ONCE ENGAGED.

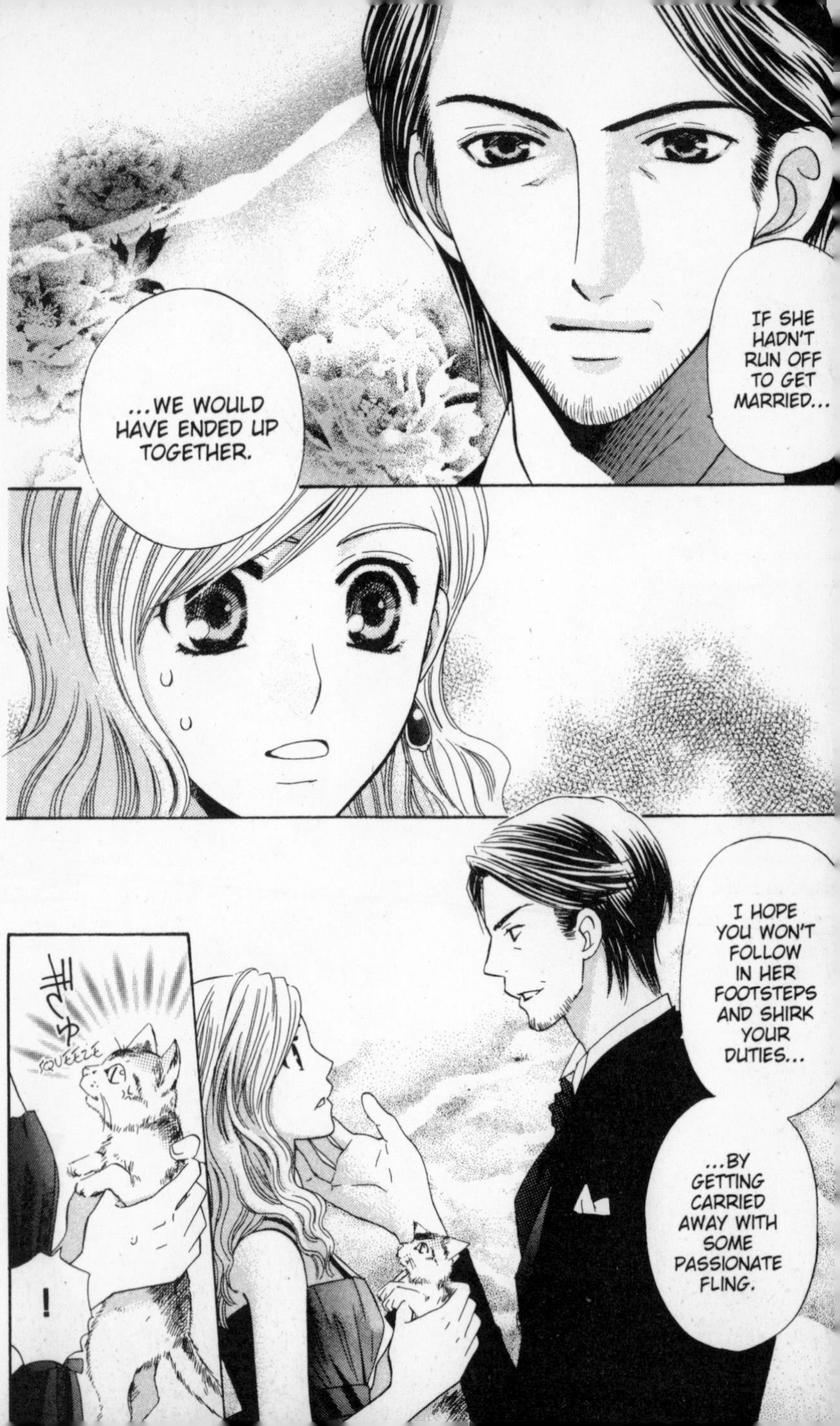
IF SHE HADN'T RUN OFF TO GET MARRIED...
...WE WOULD HAVE ENDED UP TOGETHER.
I HOPE YOU WON'T FOLLOW IN HER FOOTSTEPS AND SHIRK YOUR DUTIES...
...BY GETTING CARRIED AWAY WITH SOME PASSIONATE FLING.
SQUEEZE
!

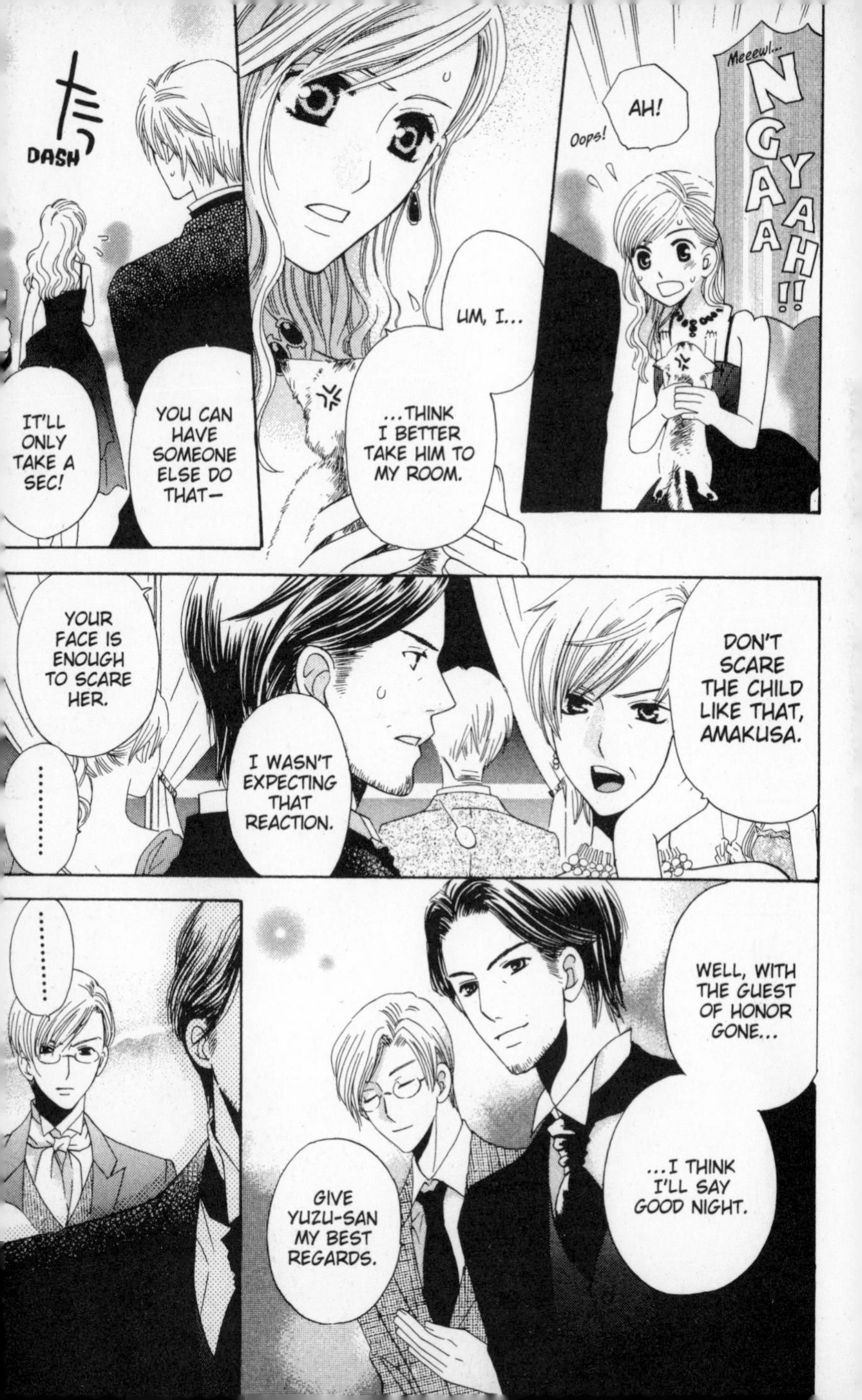
Meeewl...
NGYAAAH!!
AH!
Oops!
UM, I...
...THINK I BETTER TAKE HIM TO MY ROOM.
DASH
YOU CAN HAVE SOMEONE ELSE DO THAT—
IT'LL ONLY TAKE A SEC!
DON'T SCARE THE CHILD LIKE THAT, AMAKUSA.
I WASN'T EXPECTING THAT REACTION.
YOUR FACE IS ENOUGH TO SCARE HER.
......
WELL, WITH THE GUEST OF HONOR GONE...
...I THINK I'LL SAY GOOD NIGHT.
GIVE YUZU-SAN MY BEST REGARDS.
......

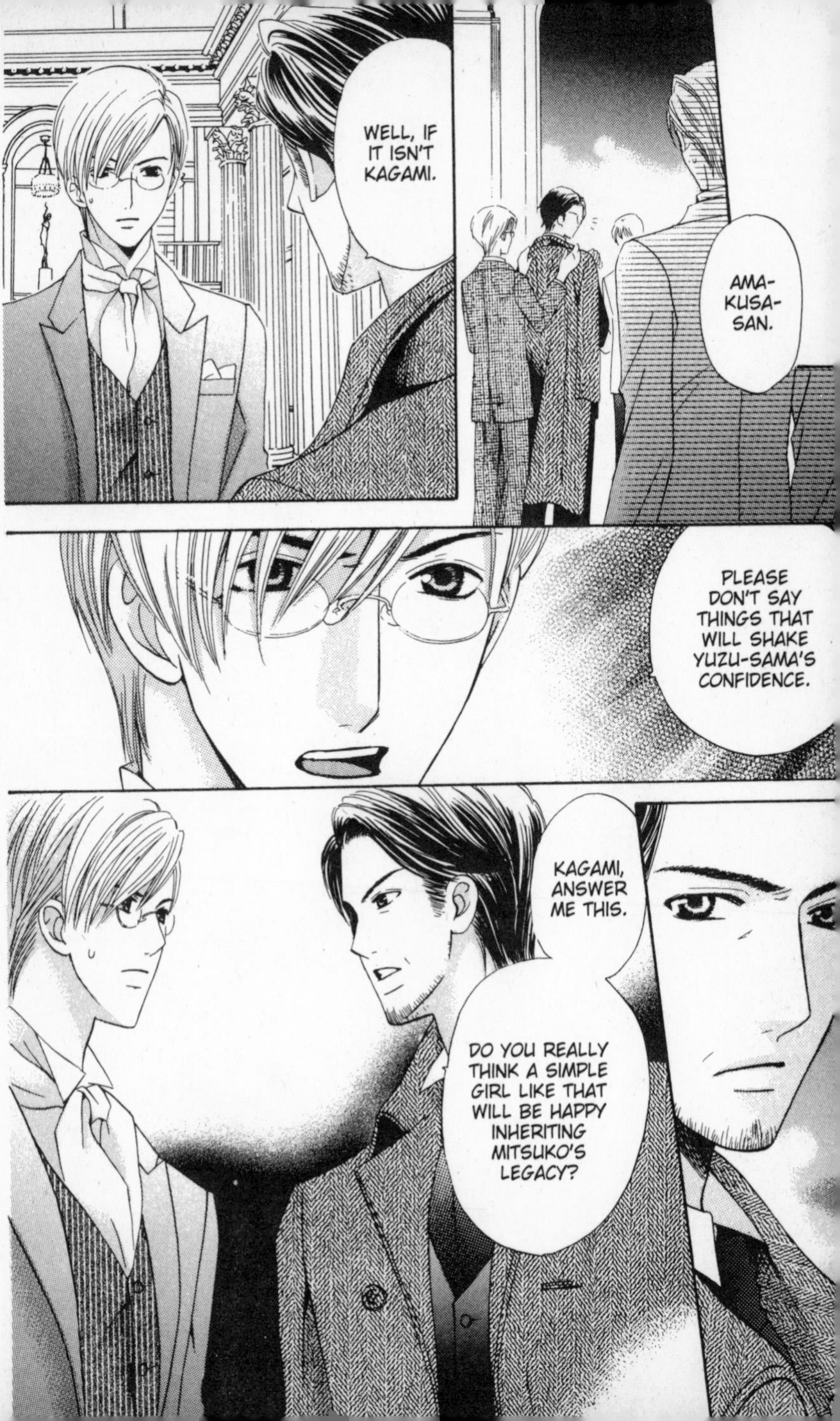
AMA-KUSA-SAN.
WELL, IF IT ISN'T KAGAMI.
PLEASE DON'T SAY THINGS THAT WILL SHAKE YUZU-SAMA'S CONFIDENCE.
KAGAMI, ANSWER ME THIS.
DO YOU REALLY THINK A SIMPLE GIRL LIKE THAT WILL BE HAPPY INHERITING MITSUKO'S LEGACY?

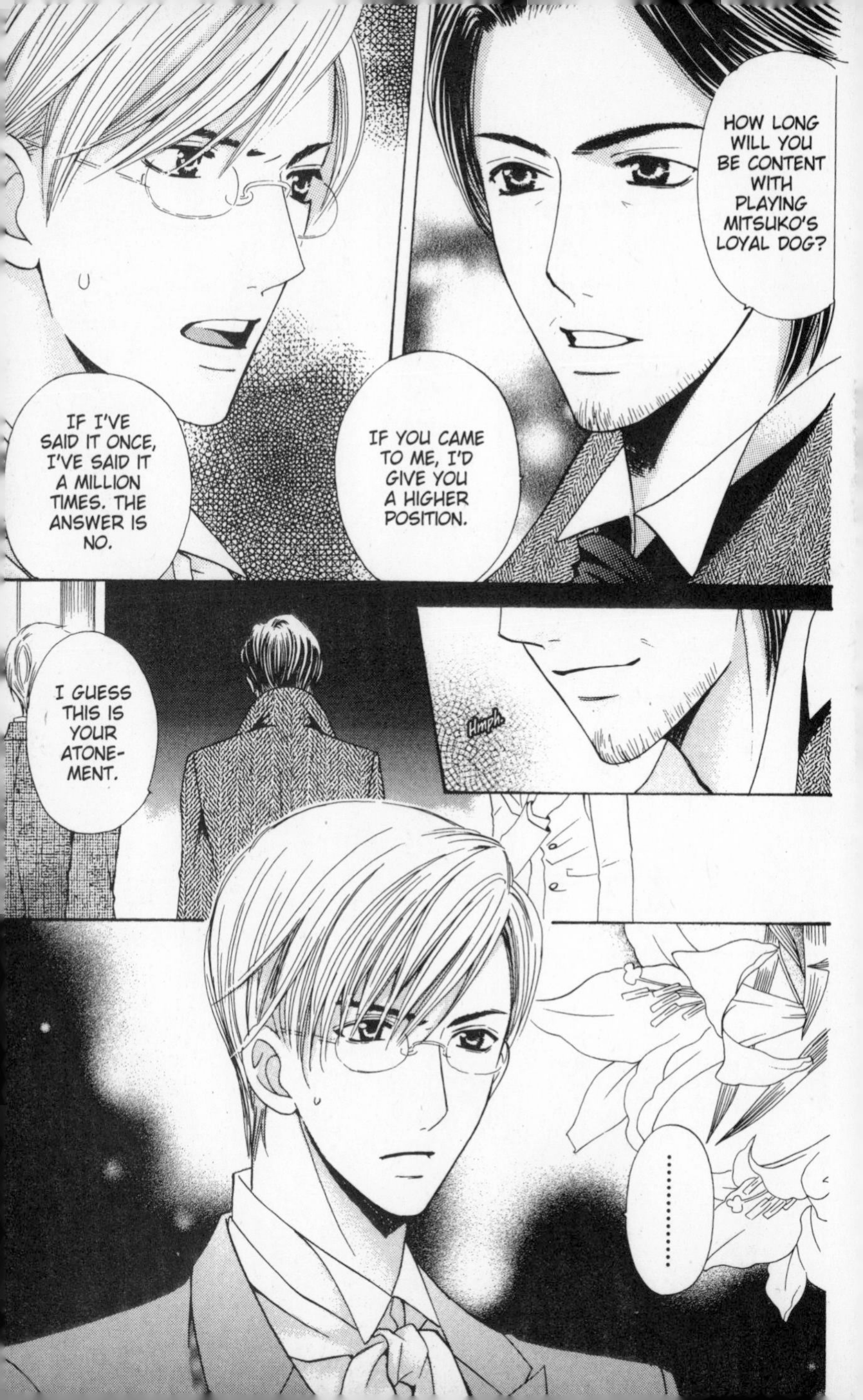
HOW LONG WILL YOU BE CONTENT WITH PLAYING MITSUKO'S LOYAL DOG?
IF YOU CAME TO ME, I'D GIVE YOU A HIGHER POSITION.
IF I'VE SAID IT ONCE, I'VE SAID IT A MILLION TIMES. THE ANSWER IS NO.
Hmph.
I GUESS THIS IS YOUR ATONEMENT.
......

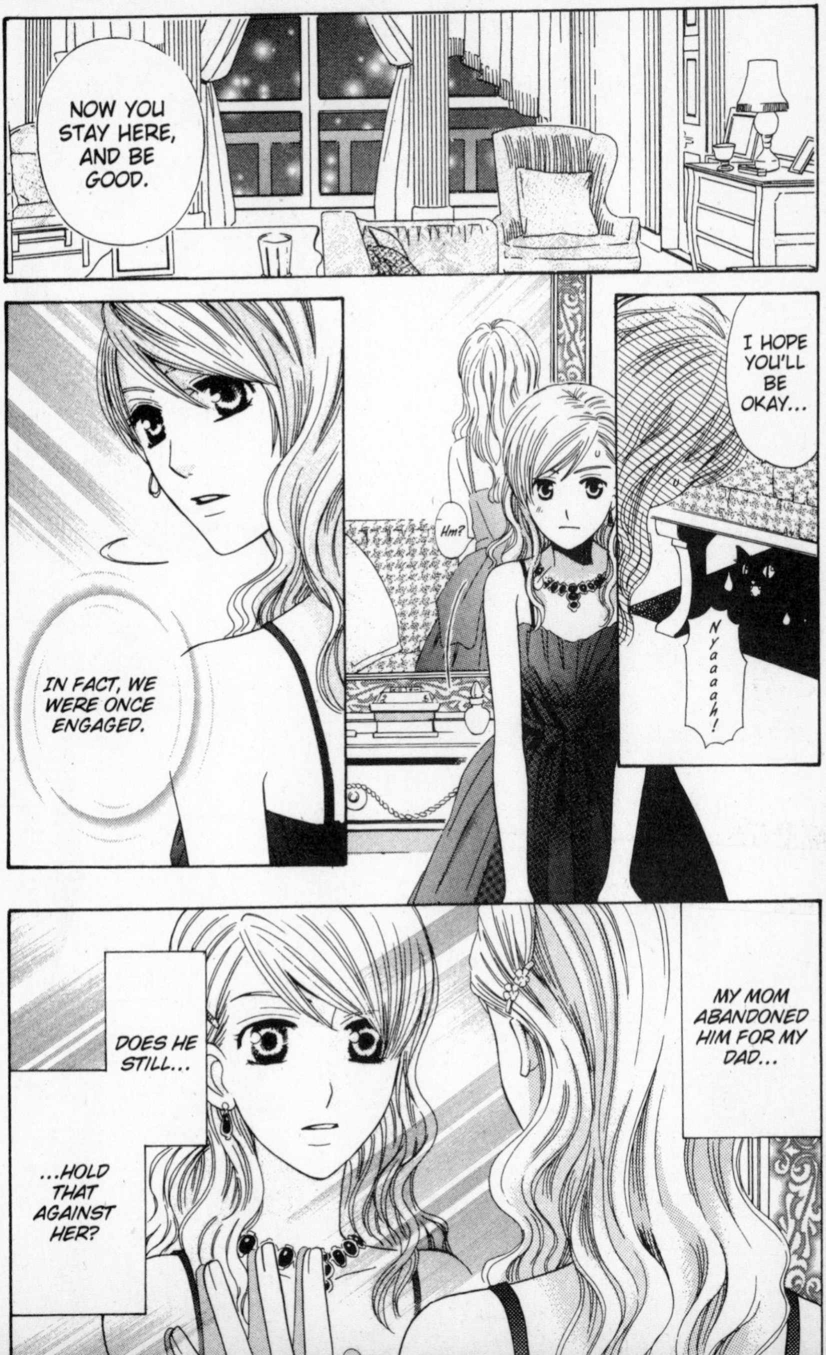
NOW YOU STAY HERE, AND BE GOOD.
I HOPE YOU'LL BE OKAY...
Nyaaaah!
Hm?
IN FACT, WE WERE ONCE ENGAGED.
MY MOM ABANDONED HIM FOR MY DAD...
DOES HE STILL...
...HOLD THAT AGAINST HER?

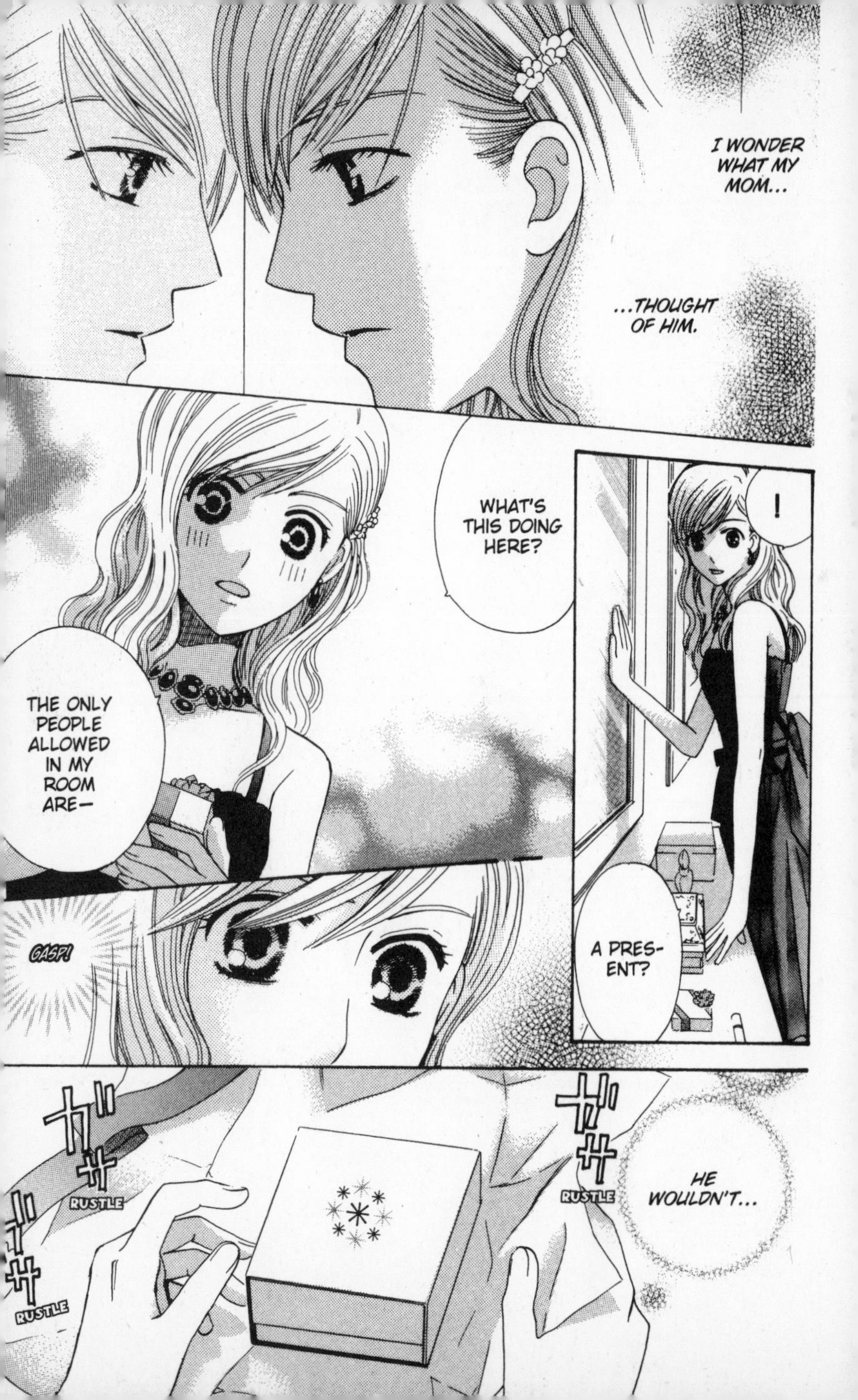
I WONDER WHAT MY MOM...
...THOUGHT OF HIM.
!
A PRES-ENT?
WHAT'S THIS DOING HERE?
THE ONLY PEOPLE ALLOWED IN MY ROOM ARE—
GASP!
RUSTLE
HE WOULDN'T...
RUSTLE
RUSTLE

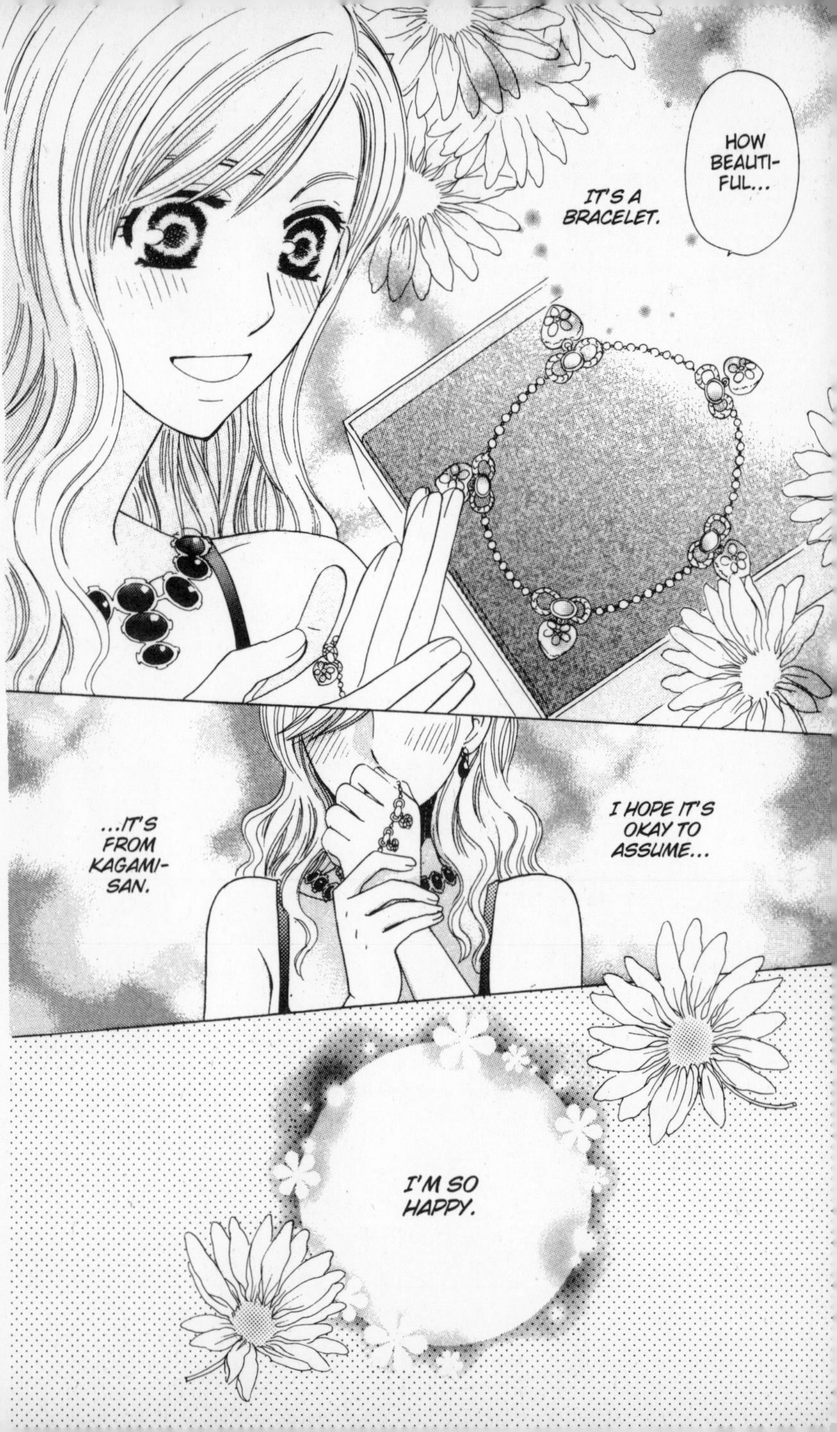
HOW BEAUTI-FUL...
IT'S A BRACELET.
I HOPE IT'S OKAY TO ASSUME...
...IT'S FROM KAGAMI-SAN.
I'M SO HAPPY.

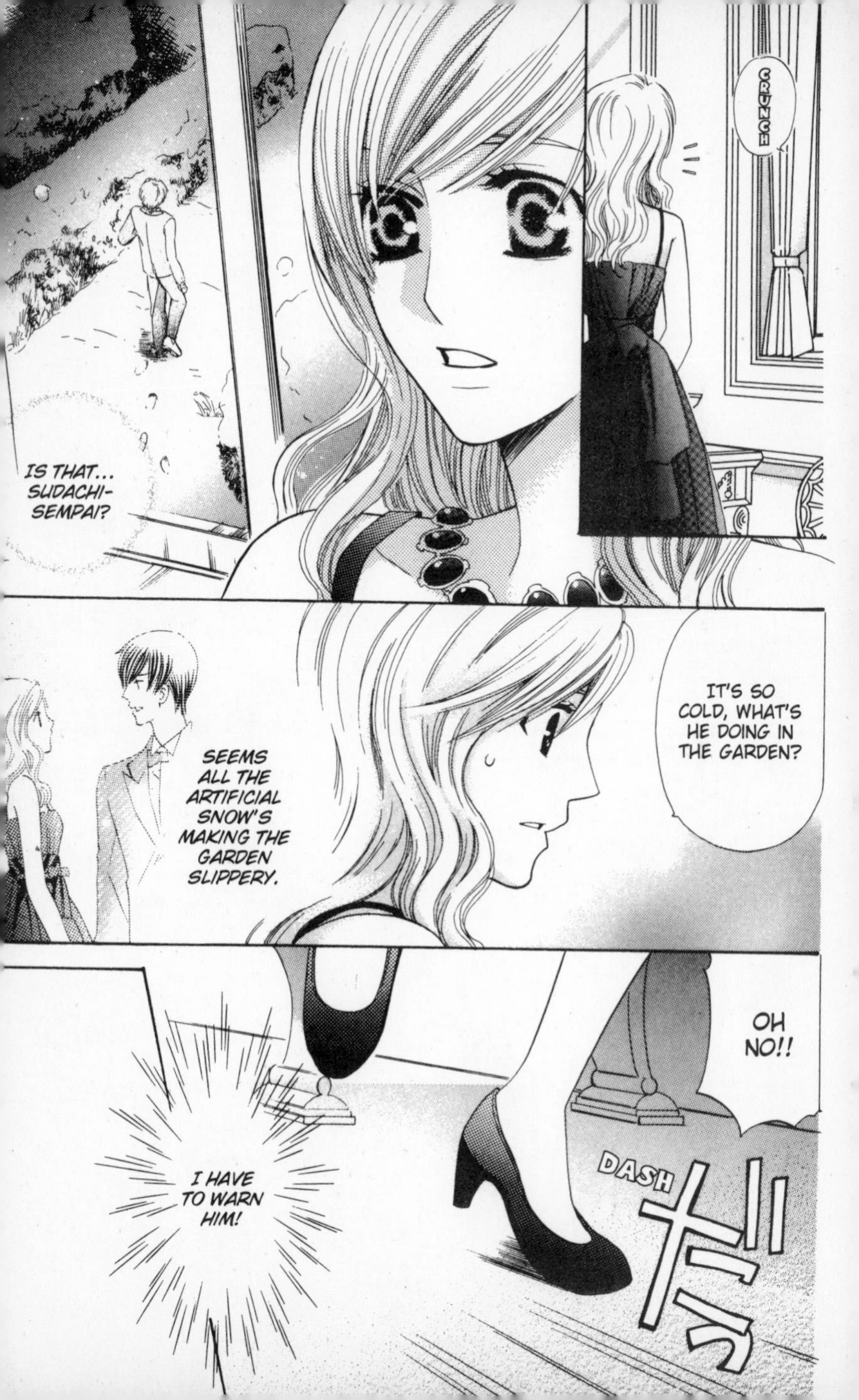
CRUNCH
IS THAT... SUDACHI-SEMPAI?
IT'S SO COLD, WHAT'S HE DOING IN THE GARDEN?
SEEMS ALL THE ARTIFICIAL SNOW'S MAKING THE GARDEN SLIPPERY.
OH NO!!
DASH
I HAVE TO WARN HIM!

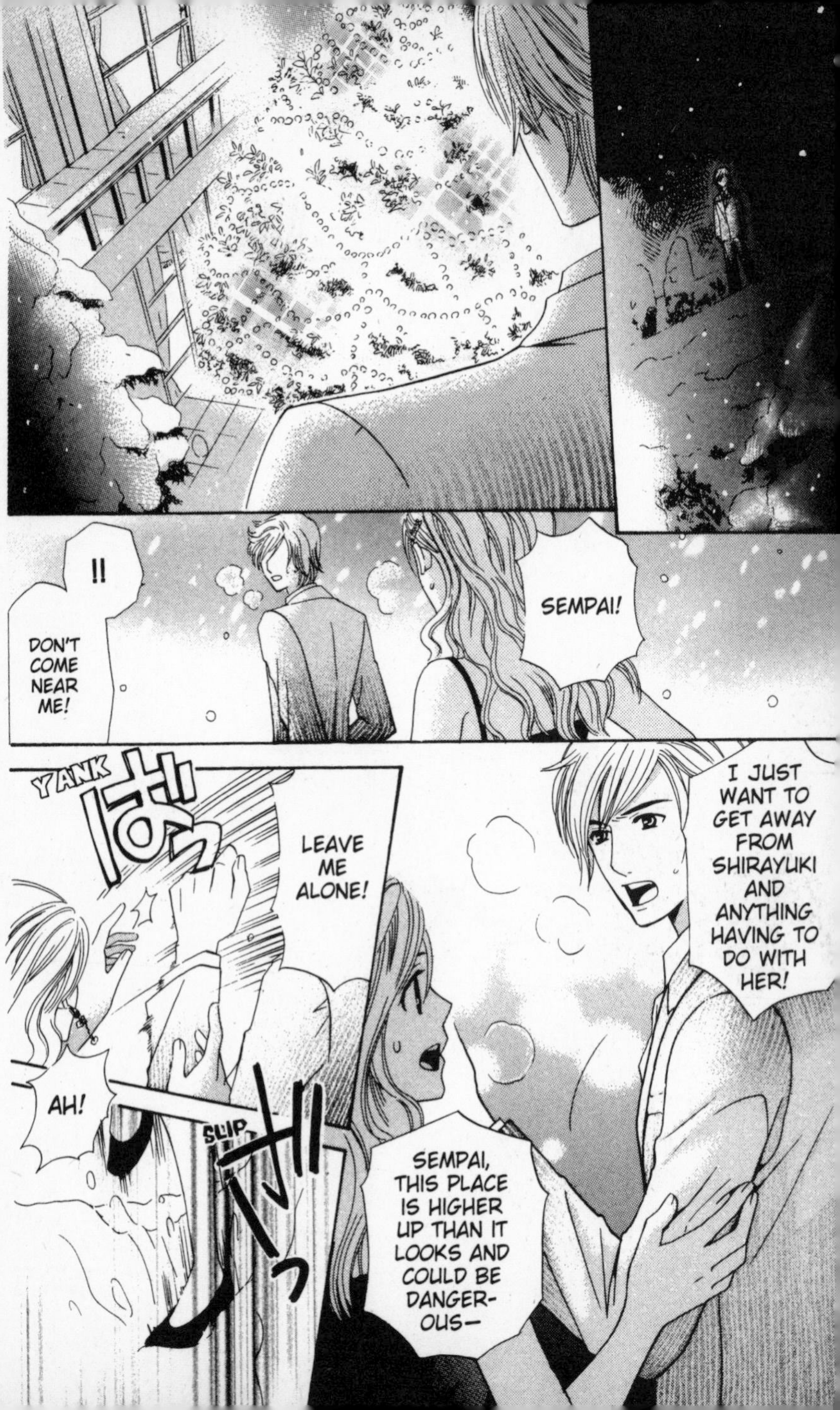
SEMPAI!
!!
DON'T COME NEAR ME!
I JUST WANT TO GET AWAY FROM SHIRAYUKI AND ANYTHING HAVING TO DO WITH HER!
SEMPAI, THIS PLACE IS HIGHER UP THAN IT LOOKS AND COULD BE DANGEROUS—
LEAVE ME ALONE!
YANK
はっ
AH!
SLIP
ずっ

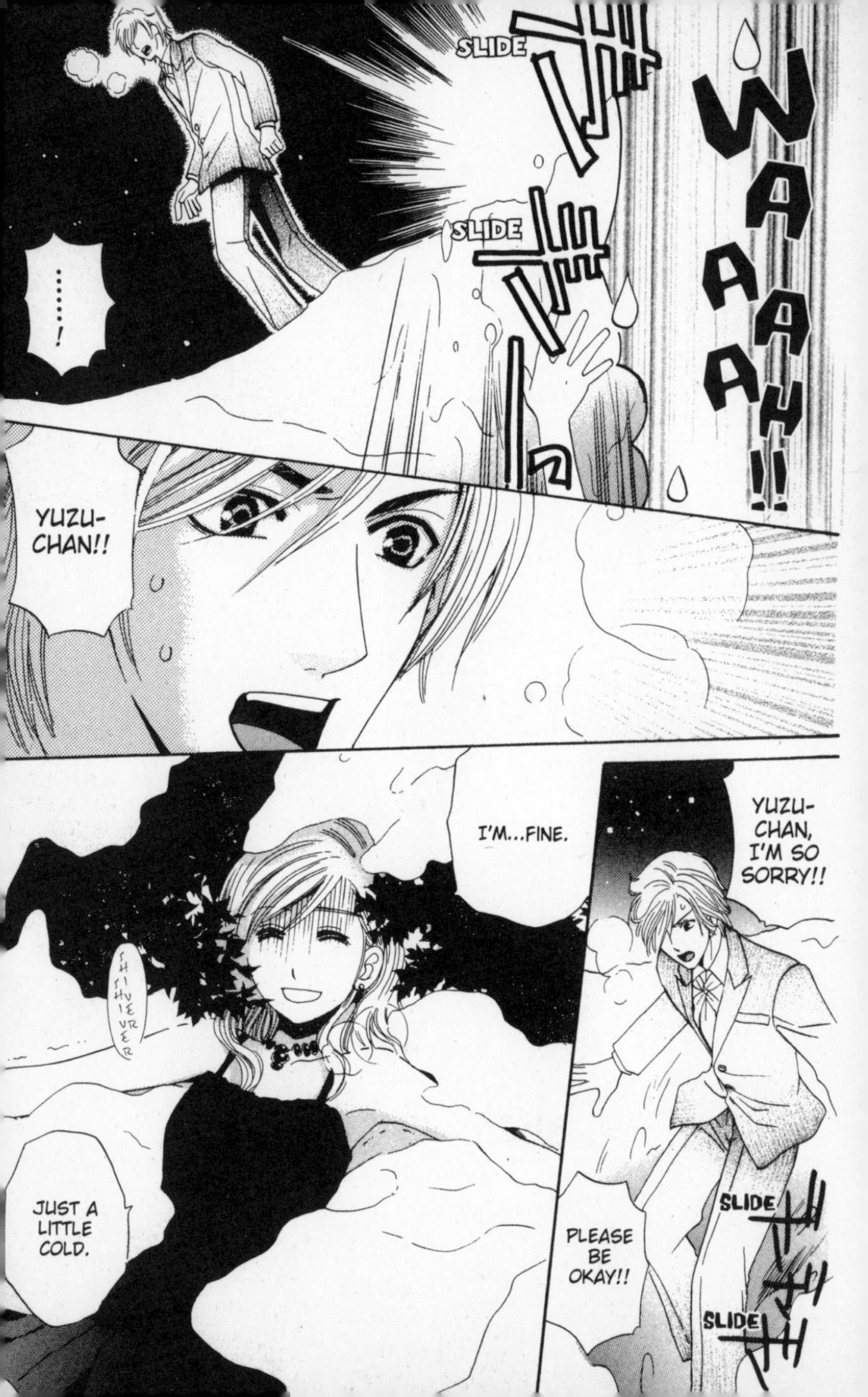
WAAAAAH!!
SLIDE
SLIDE
......!
YUZU-CHAN!!
YUZU-CHAN, I'M SO SORRY!!
PLEASE BE OKAY!!
SLIDE
SLIDE
I'M...FINE.
SHIVER SHIVER
JUST A LITTLE COLD.

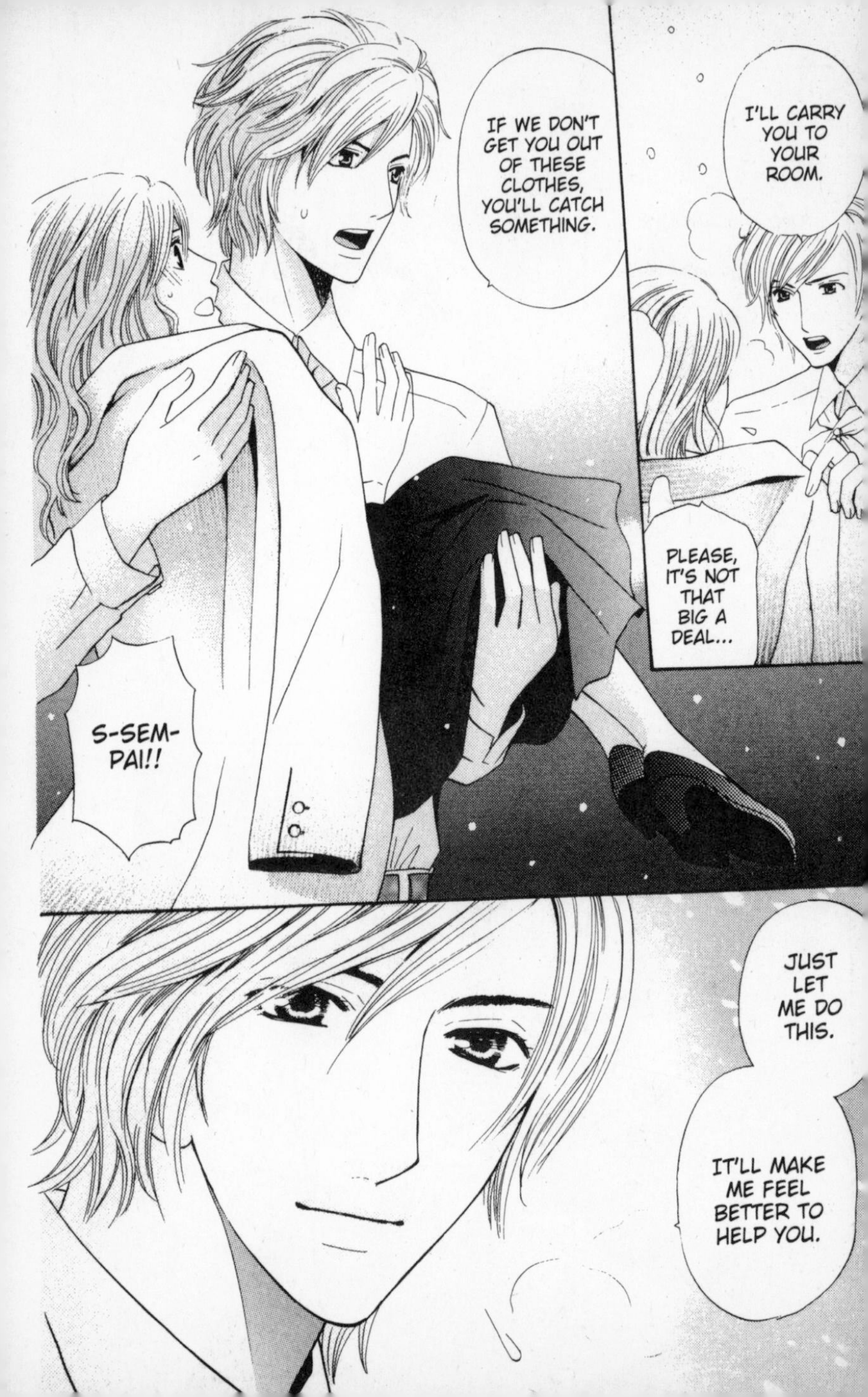
I'LL CARRY YOU TO YOUR ROOM.
PLEASE, IT'S NOT THAT BIG A DEAL...
IF WE DON'T GET YOU OUT OF THESE CLOTHES, YOU'LL CATCH SOMETHING.
S-SEM-PAI!!
JUST LET ME DO THIS.
IT'LL MAKE ME FEEL BETTER TO HELP YOU.

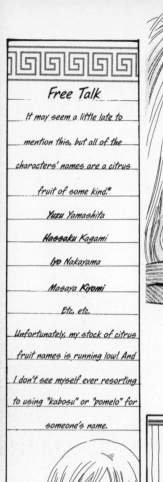

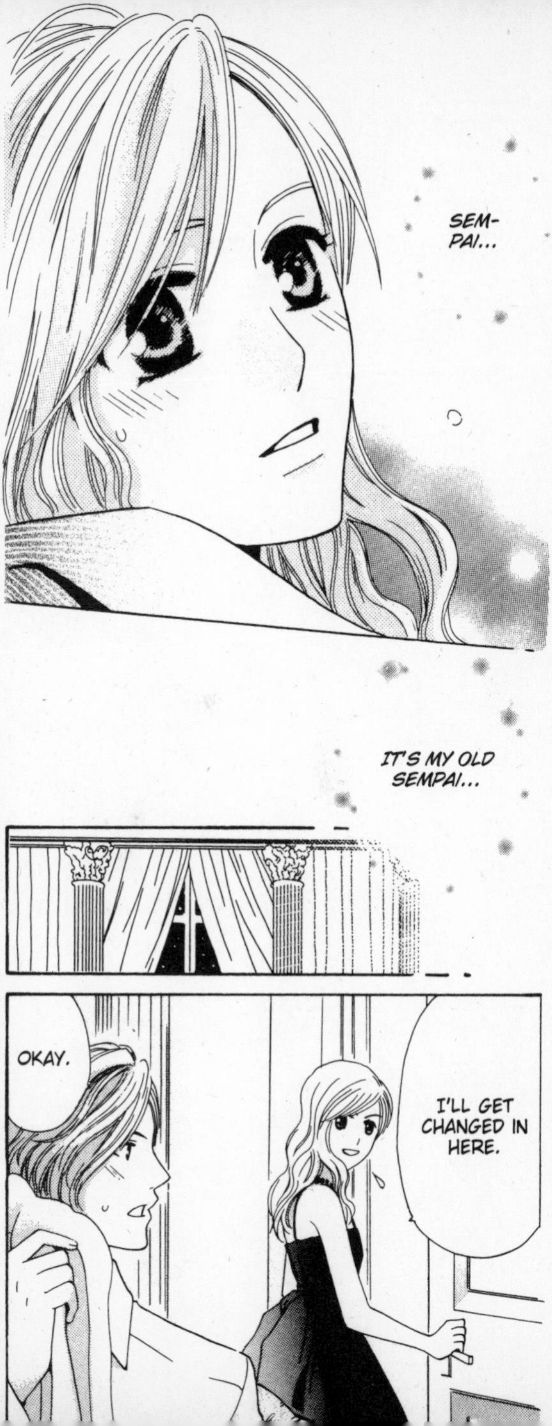
SEM-
PAI...
IT'S MY OLD
SEMPAI...
I'LL GET
CHANGED IN
HERE.
OKAY.

Free Talk

It may seem a little late to mention this, but all of the characters' names are a citrus fruit of some kind.*

Yuzu Yamashita

Hassaku Kagami

Iyo Nakayama

Masaya Kiyomi

Etc, etc.

Unfortunately, my stock of citrus fruit names is running low! And I don't see myself ever resorting to using "kabosu" or "pomelo" for someone's name.

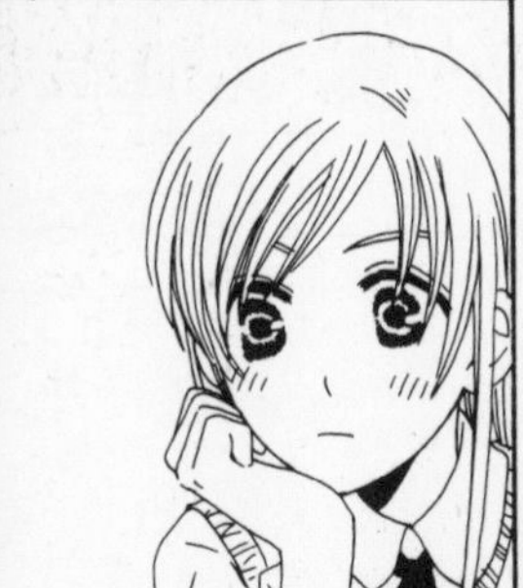

* See translator's notes

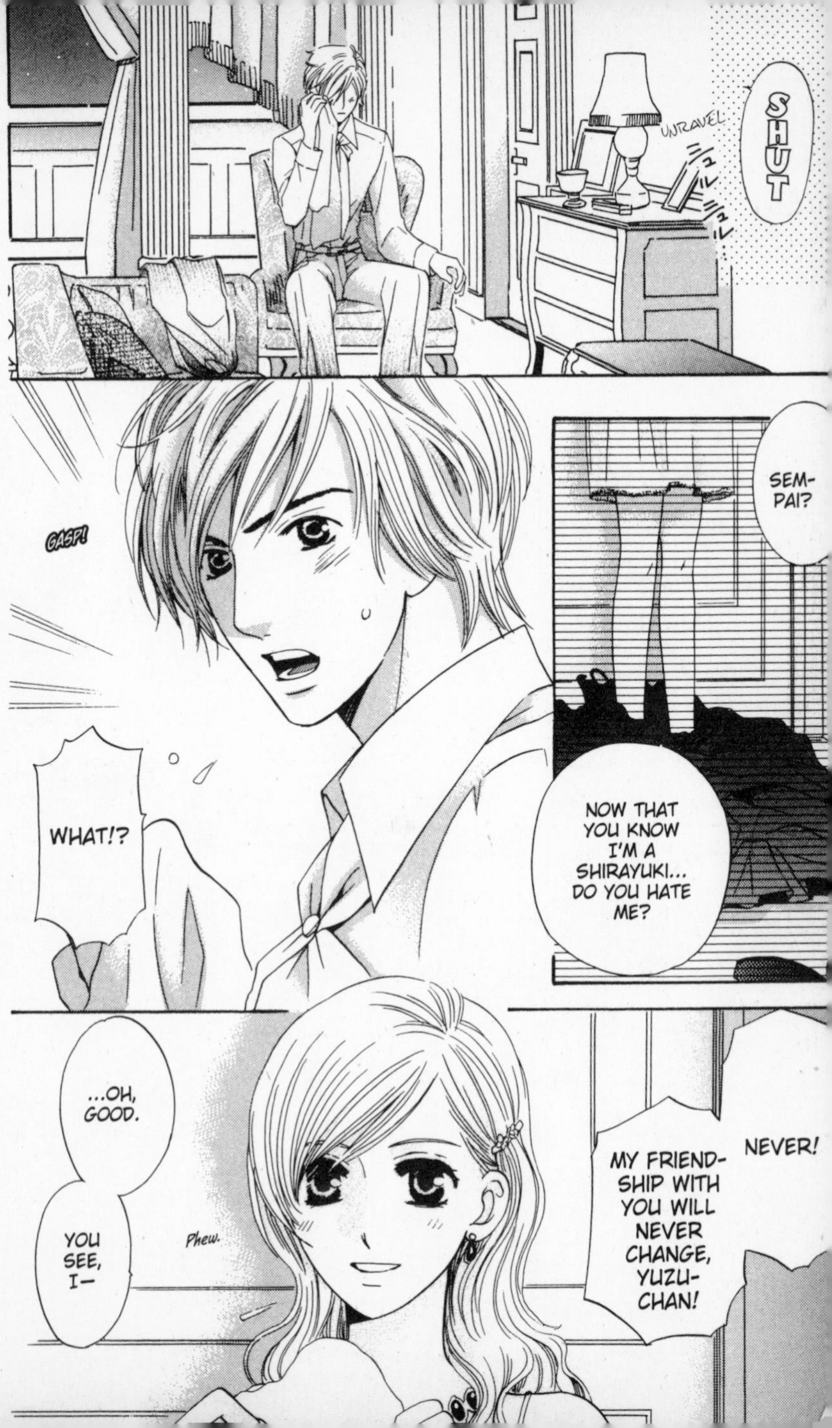
SHUT
UNRAVEL
SEM-PAI?
GASP!
NOW THAT YOU KNOW I'M A SHIRAYUKI... DO YOU HATE ME?
WHAT!?
NEVER!
MY FRIEND-SHIP WITH YOU WILL NEVER CHANGE, YUZU-CHAN!
...OH, GOOD.
Phew.
YOU SEE, I—

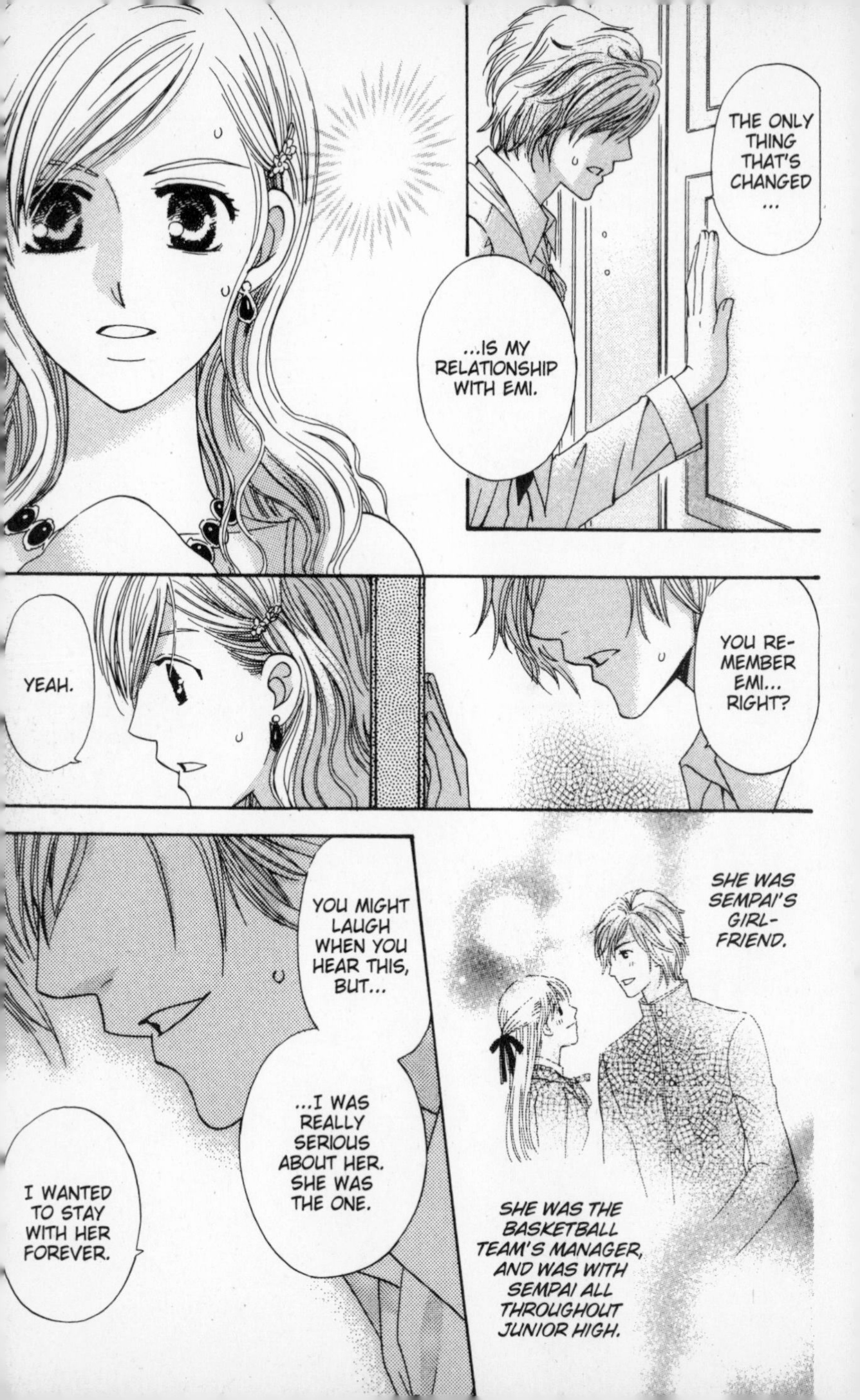
THE ONLY THING THAT'S CHANGED ...
...IS MY RELATIONSHIP WITH EMI.
YOU RE-MEMBER EMI... RIGHT?
YEAH.
SHE WAS SEMPAI'S GIRL-FRIEND.
SHE WAS THE BASKETBALL TEAM'S MANAGER, AND WAS WITH SEMPAI ALL THROUGHOUT JUNIOR HIGH.
YOU MIGHT LAUGH WHEN YOU HEAR THIS, BUT...
...I WAS REALLY SERIOUS ABOUT HER. SHE WAS THE ONE.
I WANTED TO STAY WITH HER FOREVER.

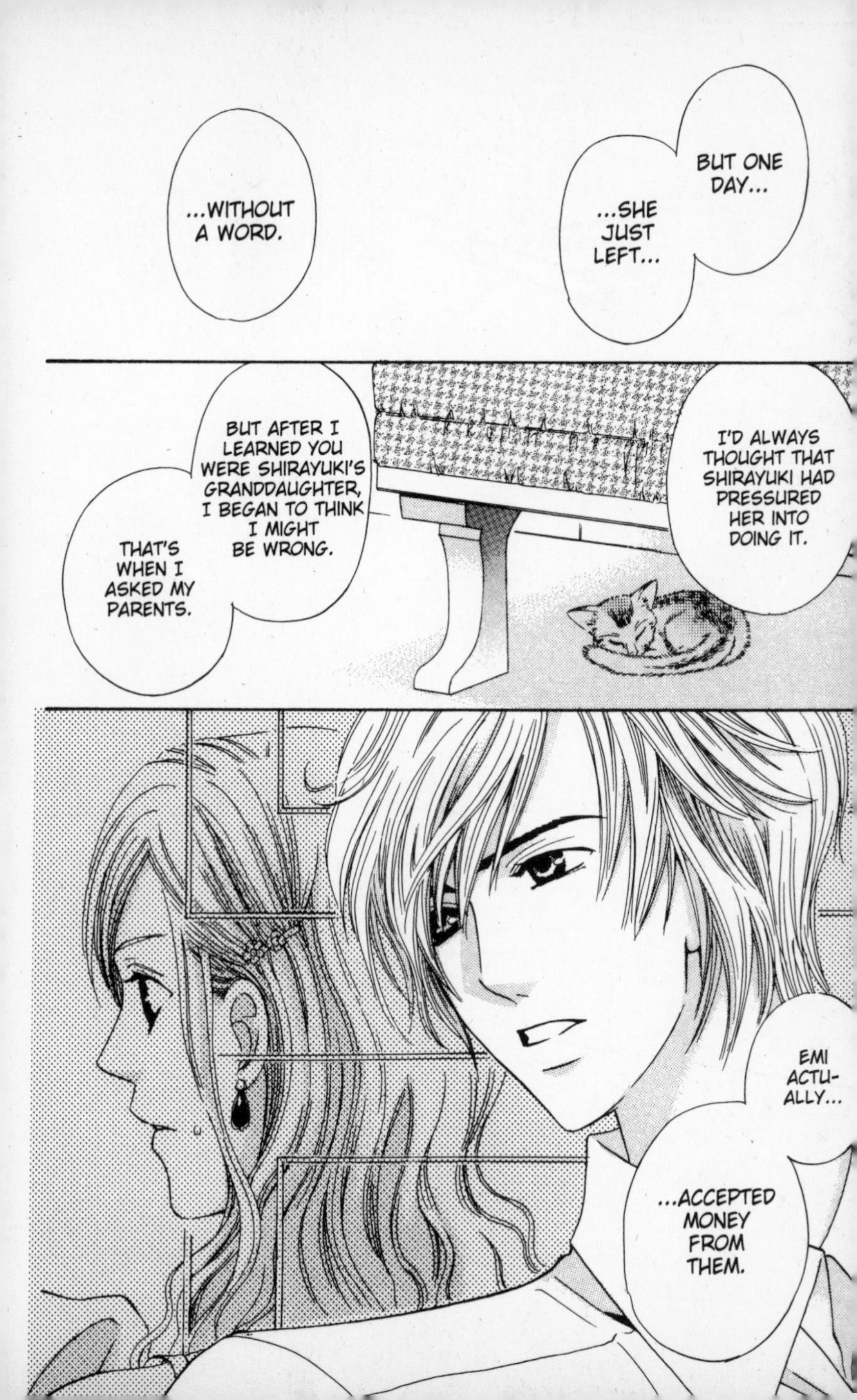
BUT ONE DAY...
...SHE JUST LEFT...
...WITHOUT A WORD.
I'D ALWAYS THOUGHT THAT SHIRAYUKI HAD PRESSURED HER INTO DOING IT.
BUT AFTER I LEARNED YOU WERE SHIRAYUKI'S GRANDDAUGHTER, I BEGAN TO THINK I MIGHT BE WRONG.
THAT'S WHEN I ASKED MY PARENTS.
EMI ACTU-ALLY...
...ACCEPTED MONEY FROM THEM.

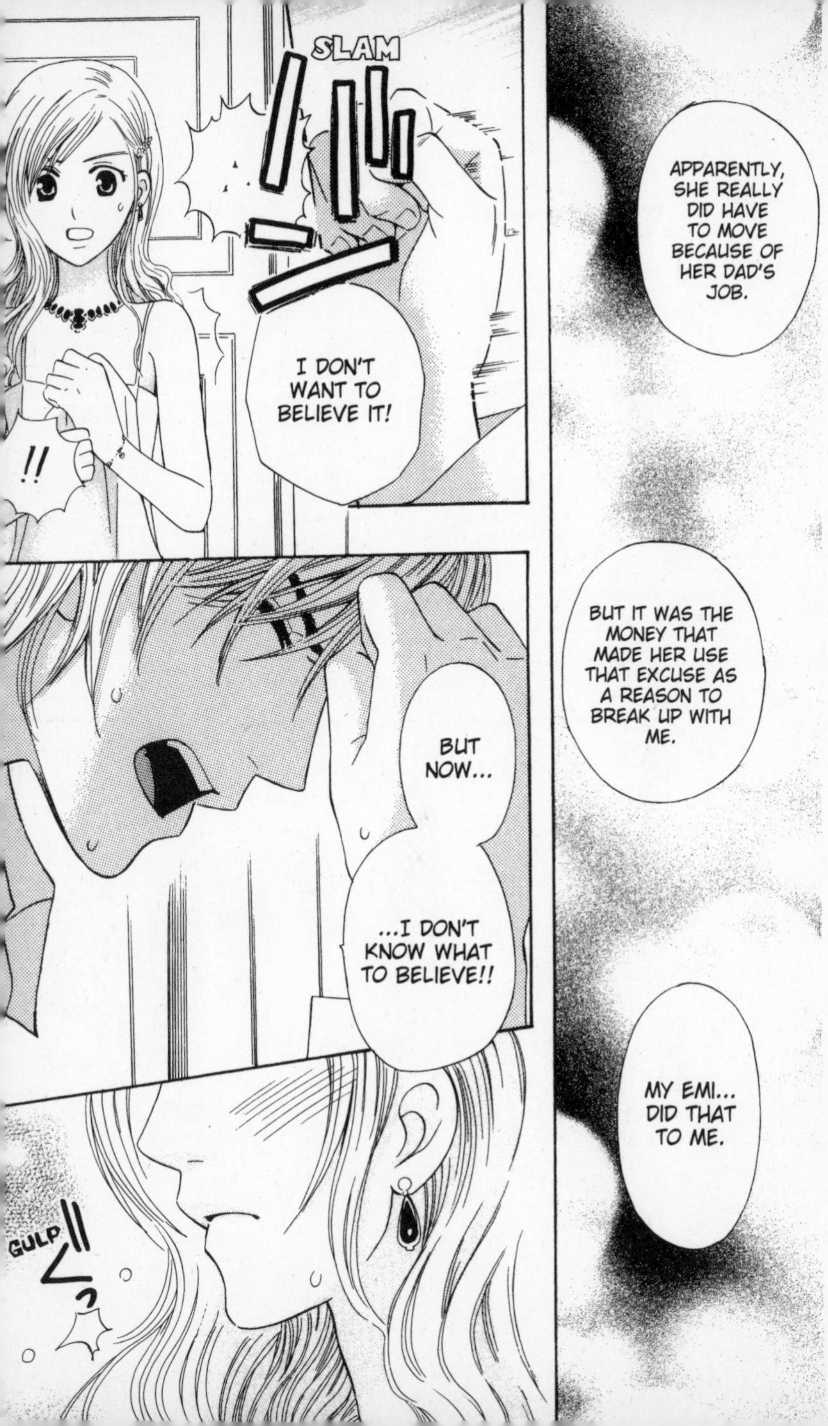
APPARENTLY, SHE REALLY DID HAVE TO MOVE BECAUSE OF HER DAD'S JOB.
BUT IT WAS THE MONEY THAT MADE HER USE THAT EXCUSE AS A REASON TO BREAK UP WITH ME.
MY EMI... DID THAT TO ME.
SLAM
I DON'T WANT TO BELIEVE IT!
!!
BUT NOW...
...I DON'T KNOW WHAT TO BELIEVE!!
GULP

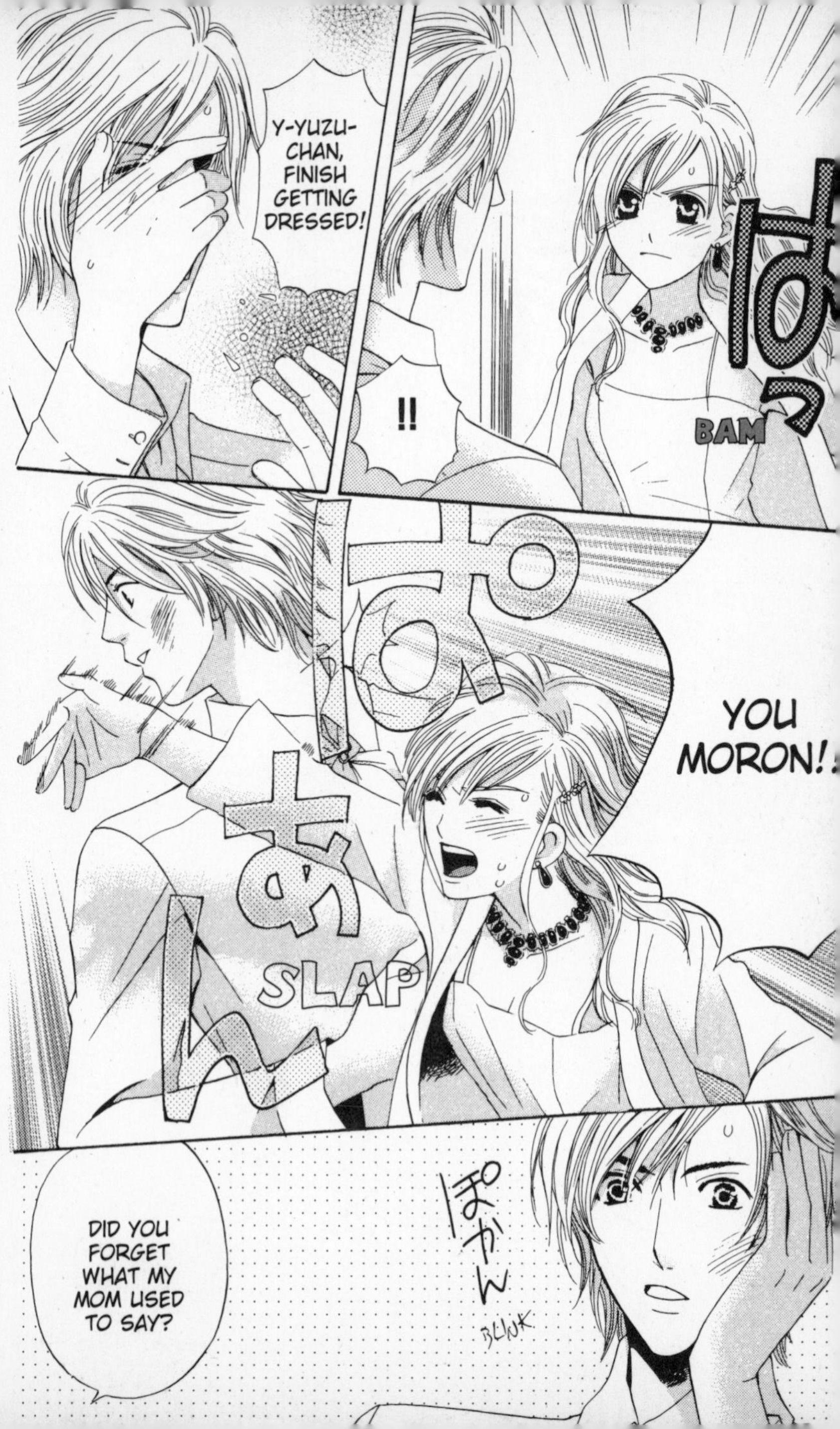

はっ
BAM
!!
Y-YUZU-CHAN, FINISH GETTING DRESSED!
YOU MORON!..
ぱあん
SLAP
ぽかん
BLINK
DID YOU FORGET WHAT MY MOM USED TO SAY?

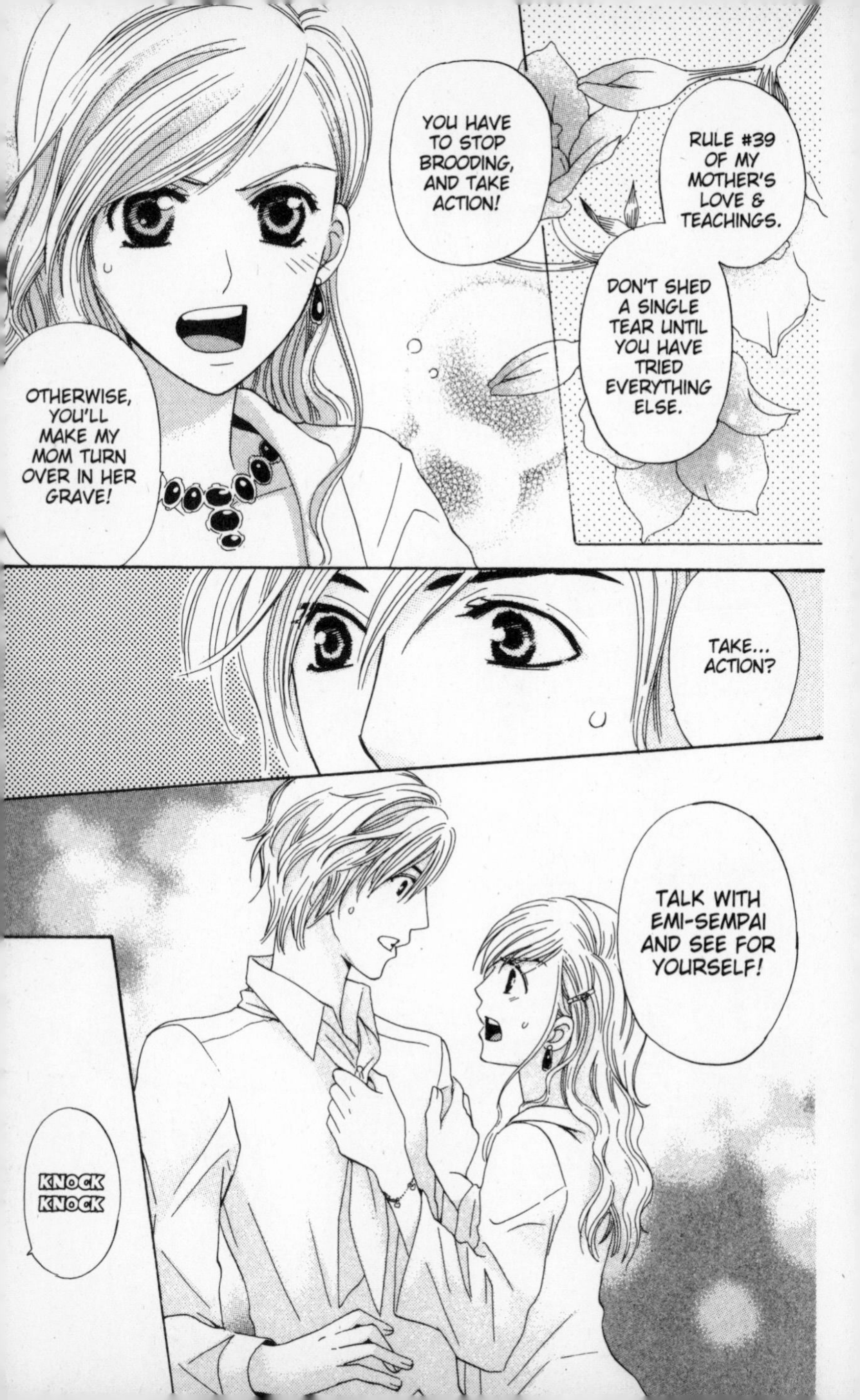
RULE #39 OF MY MOTHER'S LOVE & TEACHINGS.
DON'T SHED A SINGLE TEAR UNTIL YOU HAVE TRIED EVERYTHING ELSE.
YOU HAVE TO STOP BROODING, AND TAKE ACTION!
OTHERWISE, YOU'LL MAKE MY MOM TURN OVER IN HER GRAVE!
TAKE... ACTION?
TALK WITH EMI-SEMPAI AND SEE FOR YOURSELF!
KNOCK KNOCK

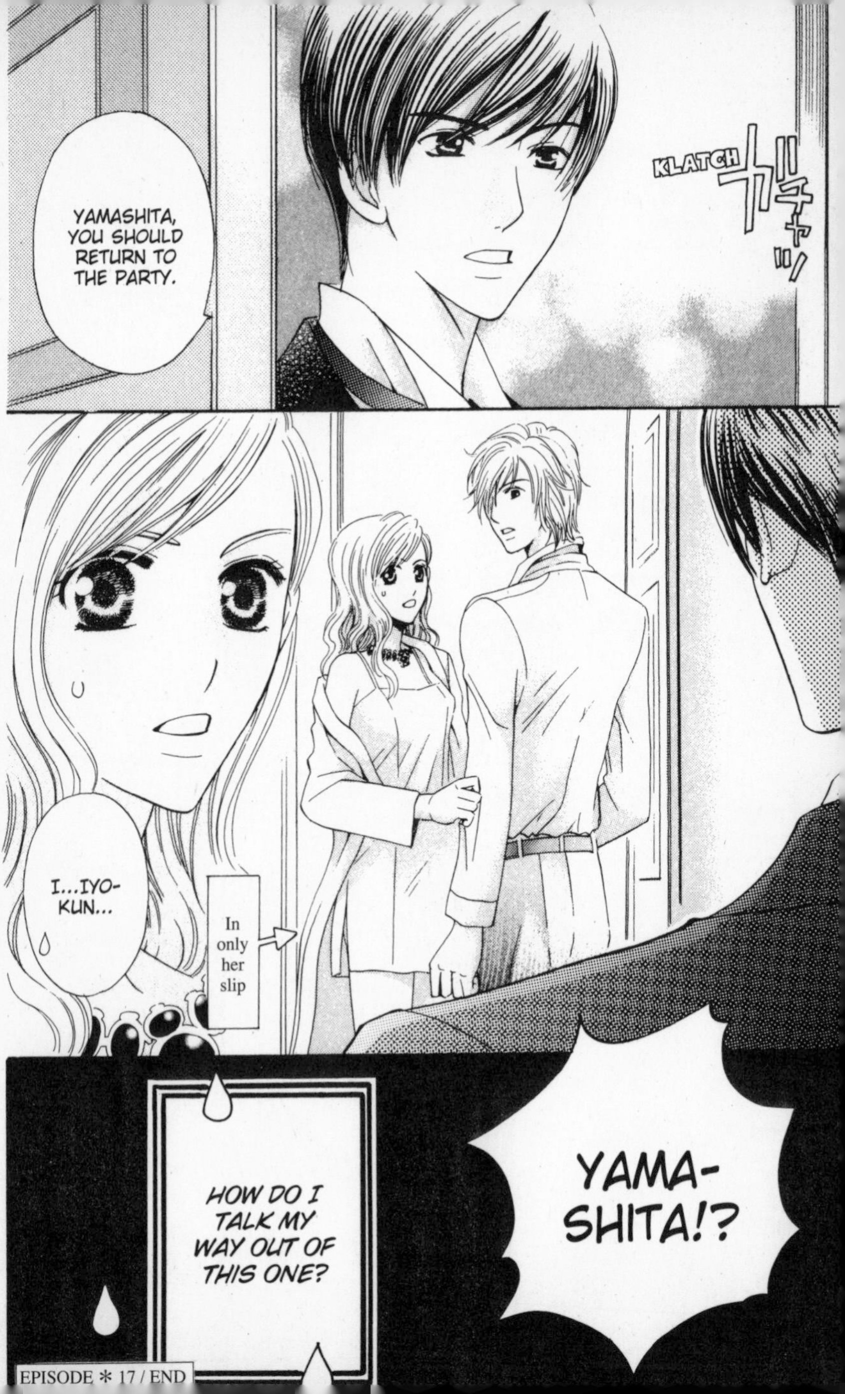
KLATCH
YAMASHITA, YOU SHOULD RETURN TO THE PARTY.
I...IYO-KUN...
In only her slip
YAMA-SHITA!?
HOW DO I TALK MY WAY OUT OF THIS ONE?
EPISODE ✻ 17 / END

AFTERWORD + SPECIAL THANKS

Thank you very much, all of you who picked up this book.

And my deepest gratitude to my editor Kishima-san, as well as Hariguchi-san and Fujiyama-san, who always helped me with my scripts and hurried me along to my deadlines in the kindest of ways.

Well, I hope to see you again in the next volume!

December 12, 2007

Takako Shigematsu

I look forward to your fan letters, too!

Takako Shigematsu

C/O Go! Comi

28047 Dorothy Drive, Suite 200

Agoura Hills, CA 91301

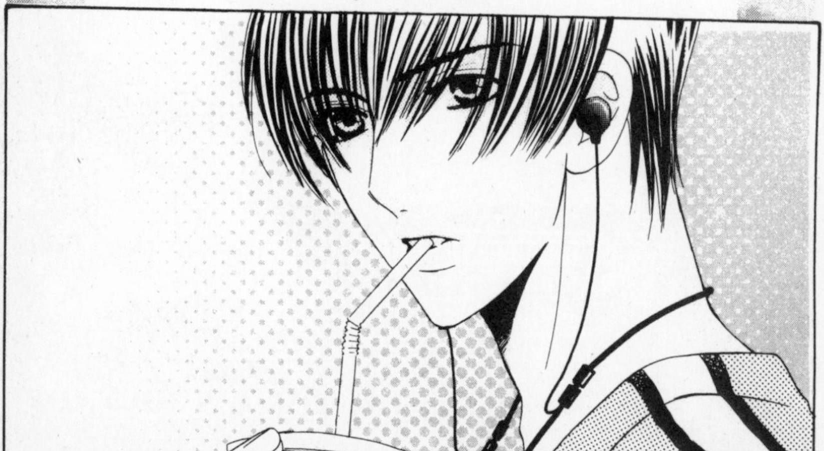

ULTIMATE VENUS VOLUME 4 / END

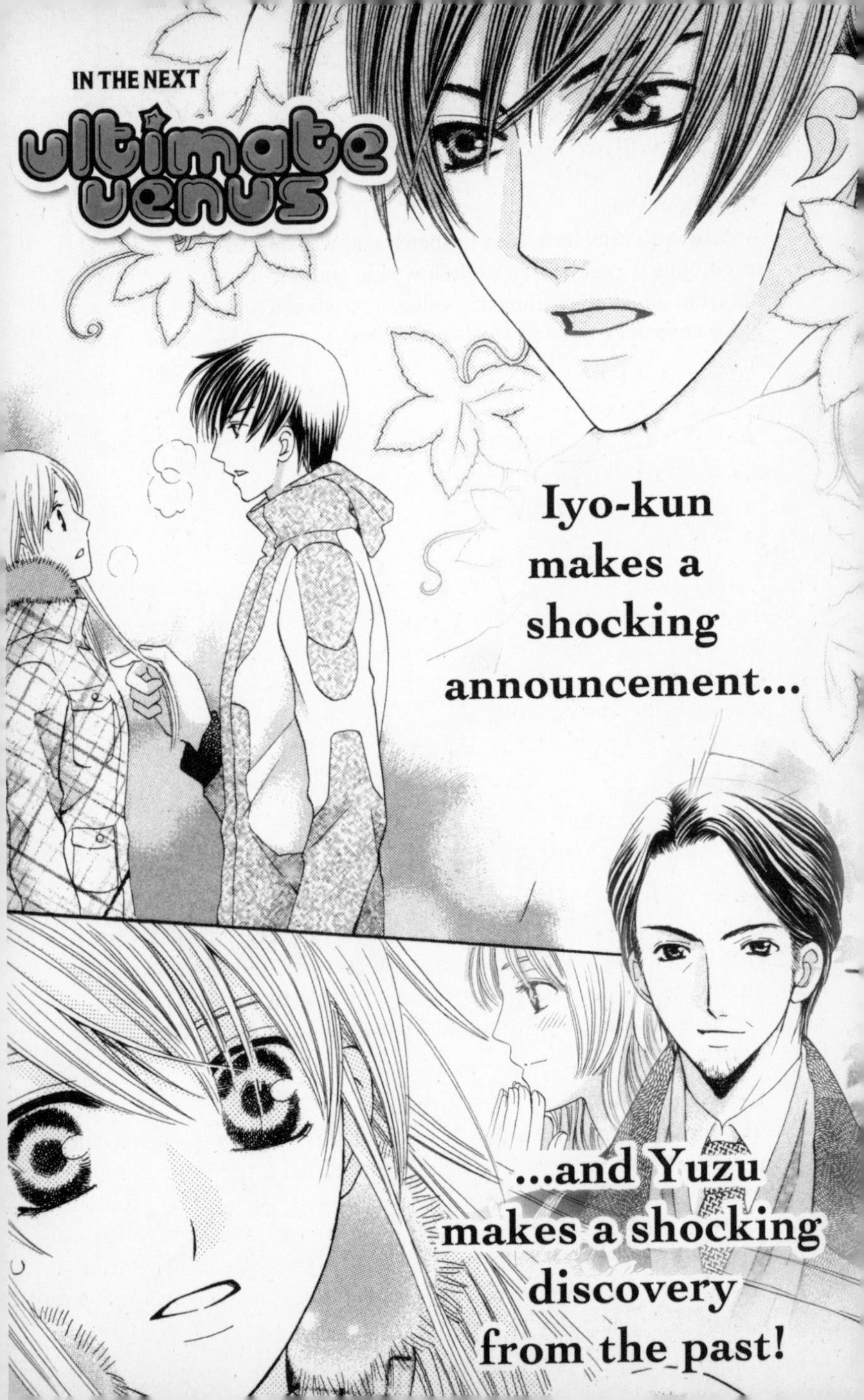
IN THE NEXT
ultimate venus
Iyo-kun makes a shocking announcement...
...and Yuzu makes a shocking discovery from the past!

translator's notes

Citrus Fruit Names

Yuzu Yamashita

A yuzu is a citrus fruit that originated and was cultivated in East Asia, resembling a mandarin in its yellow skin and uneven texture. It stands out from other citrus fruits in its sturdy resistance to the cold and other harsh environmental factors. Our heroine lives up to her name with her robust, never-give-up outlook on life.

Hassaku Kagami

The hassaku is a large orange fruit with a tart, almost sour taste. For that reason, it is typically eaten as one would a grapefruit, with careful picking to avoid the overly sharp tang. Hassaku's cold-shoulder personality is reminiscent of this fruit's flavor.

Iyo Nakayama

The iyo is part of a hybrid family of citrus fruits called "tangors" that was created by cross-breeding tangerines and oranges. Very similar to a grapefruit, they are large with glossy light yellow skin. Their flavor is a balance between sweet and sour...much like our on-again-off-again Iyo-kun.

Masaya *Kiyomi*

The kiyomi was the first "tangor" hybrid to be cultivated in Japan. This fruit is sweet and seedless, with a familiar orange scent.

Sudachi Muroi

Sudachi are small green fruit almost exclusively grown in Japan. Extensive research on this unique fruit has shown evidence of improving overall health when regularly added to one's diet. Sudachi-sempai's athletic personality pays homage to his namesake's health-oriented benefits.

Kenji *Amakusa*

The amakusa is yet another "tangor" hybrid that was invented to achieve the "perfect table fruit". This medium-sized, round fruit is smooth, with deep orange skin and low acidity. Cross-breeding has led to many beneficial traits, including a fairly sturdy resistance to disease, an easy-to-peel skin, and an overall pleasing appearance. This fruit's drive for perfection is reminiscent of our antagonistic Amakusa-san and his high opinion of himself.

ultimate venus hosts a guest!

The last two volumes of **Ultimate Venus** have had a very special guest appearance by a character from another hit series by Takako Shigematsu – **Tenshi Ja Nai!! (I'm No Angel)**. First appearing in an angelic pose inside the wedding chapel in Volume 3 of **Ultimate Venus**, Hikaru Takabayashi expresses her fondest desire to be married to the one she loves. Who is this mysterious young man who sets her heart a-flutter? If you've read **Tenshi Ja Nai!!**, then you're wriggling in your seat right now, shouting the name of a certain someone. If you're thinking who I'm thinking, then the answer is yes!! They're getting *married*!! Yay!!

For Tenshi fans, Hikaru's appearance is a special treat, since what happens in these two volumes is a continuation of where the story left off in Volume 8. One can only hope that Shigematsu-sensei has it in her heart to bring Hikaru back for another visit – and maybe even bring her sexy groom along for the ride!

If you've never read Tenshi before, you can read a preview at gocomi.com. The story begins with Hikaru as a shy young girl who would like nothing more than to be left alone. Unfortunately, her new roommate at an all-girls boarding school is a famous actress – or rather, a famous *actor* who will do anything to force poor Hikaru to keep his secrets! The story takes many romantic twists and turns before reaching its climax. Thanks to **Ultimate Venus**, you already know how it ends – now go find out exactly how shy, awkward Hikaru ended up a gorgeous actress in a beautiful bridal dress!!

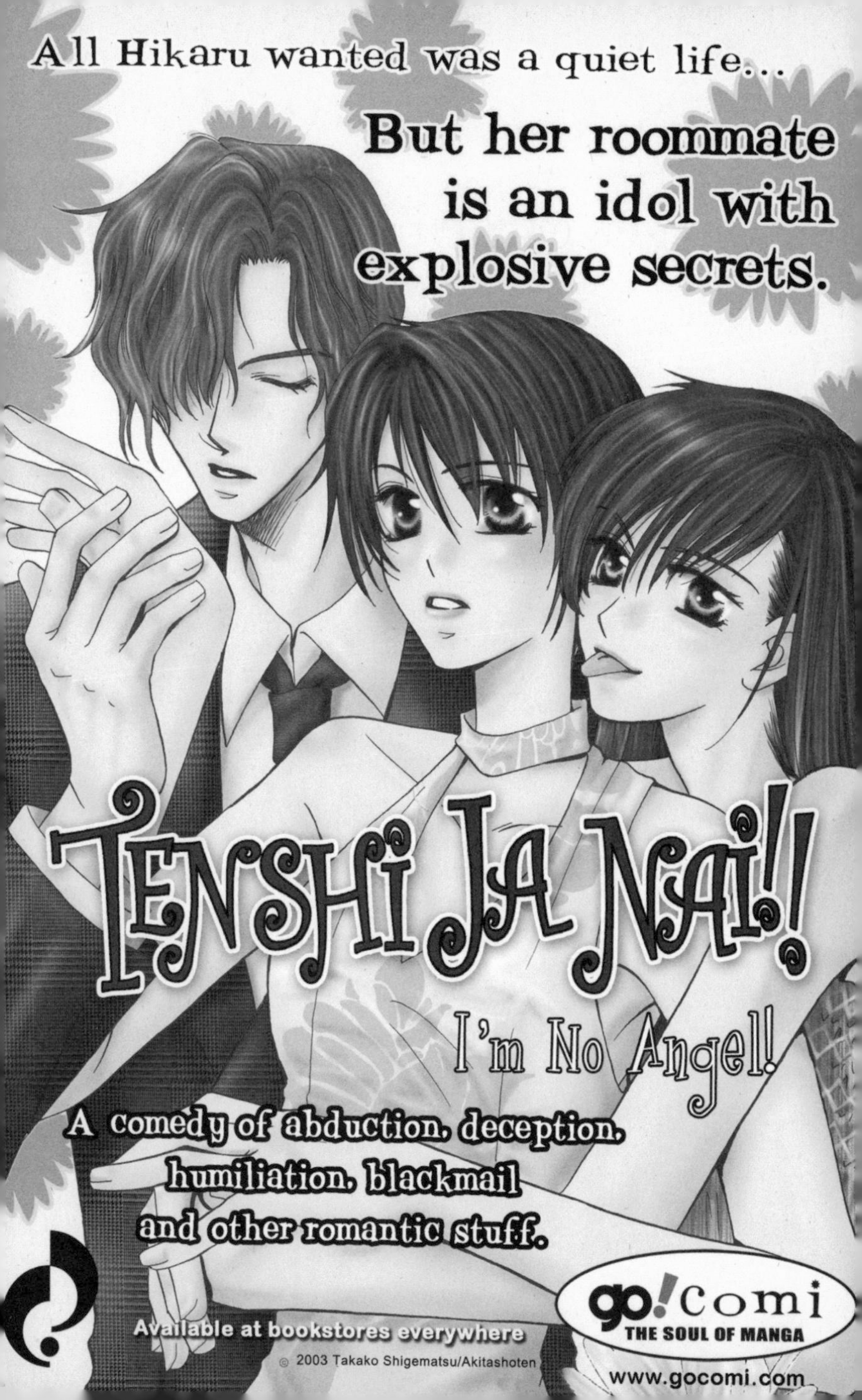

All Hikaru wanted was a quiet life...
But her roommate is an idol with explosive secrets.
TENSHI JA NAI!!
I'm No Angel!
A comedy of abduction, deception, humiliation, blackmail and other romantic stuff.
Available at bookstores everywhere
© 2003 Takako Shigematsu/Akitashoten
go!comi
THE SOUL OF MANGA
www.gocomi.com

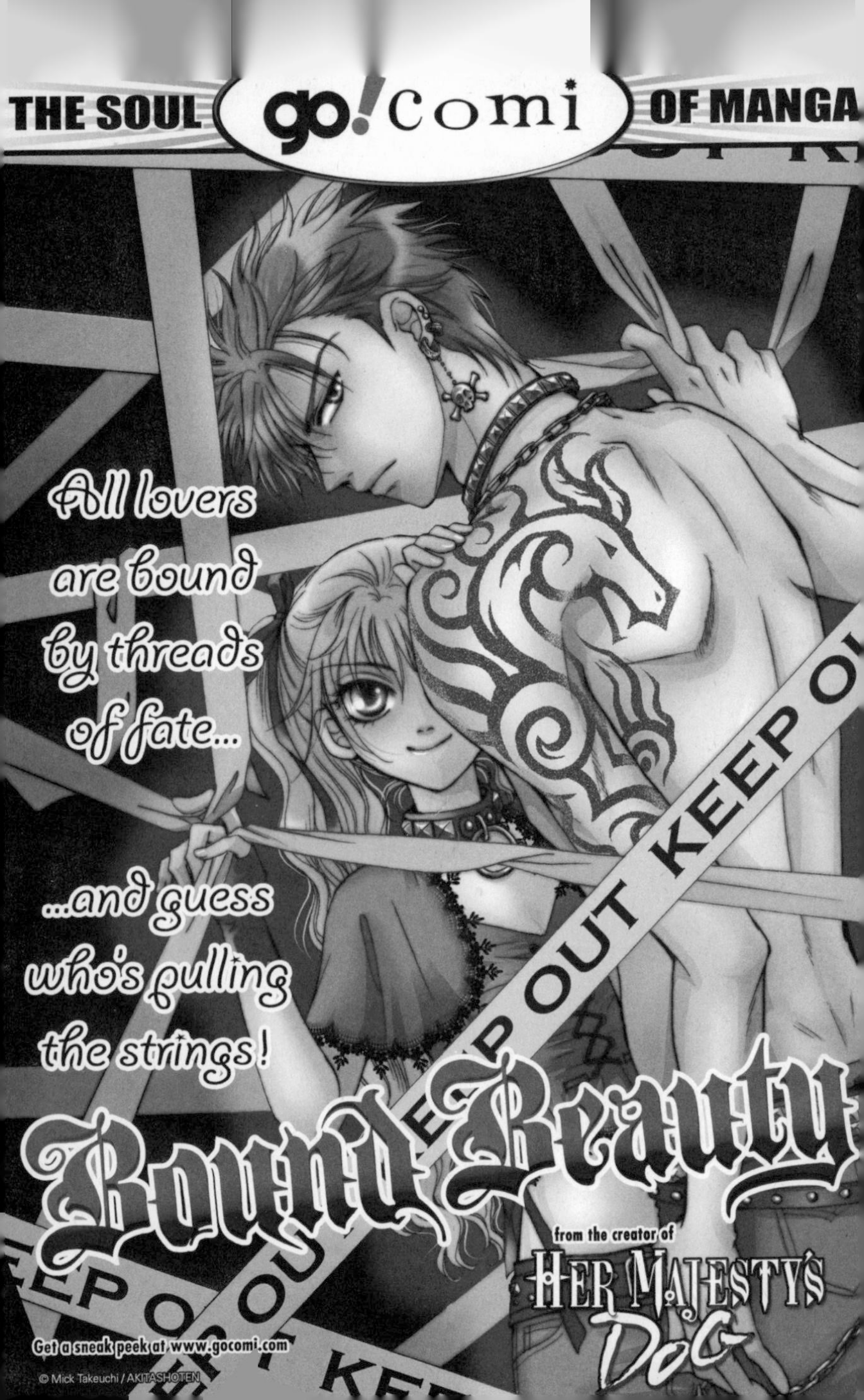
THE SOUL
go!comi
OF MANGA
All lovers are bound by threads of fate...
...and guess who's pulling the strings!
KEEP OUT KEEP O
Bound Beauty
from the creator of
HER MAJESTY'S DOG
Get a sneak peek at www.gocomi.com
© Mick Takeuchi / AKITASHOTEN

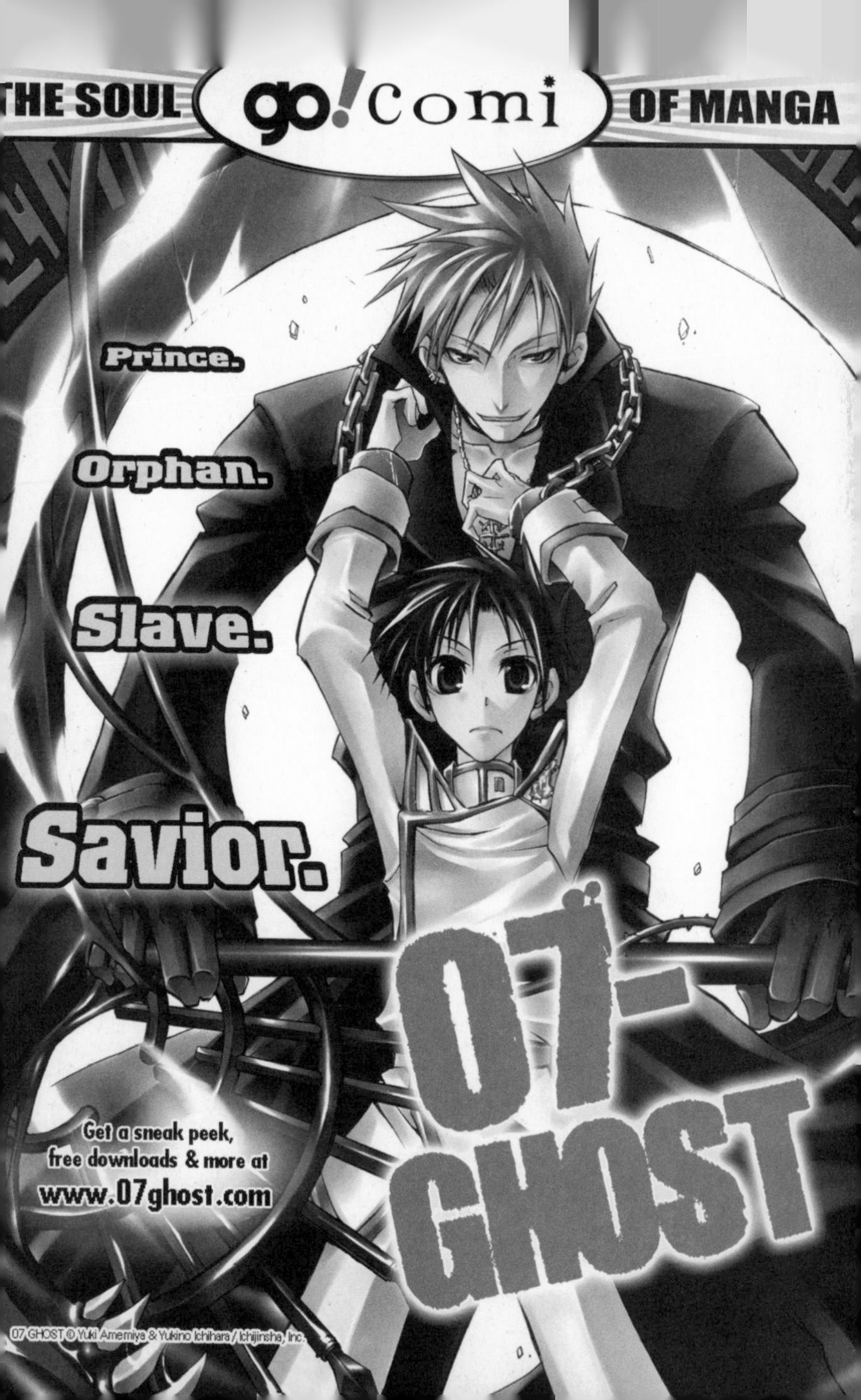

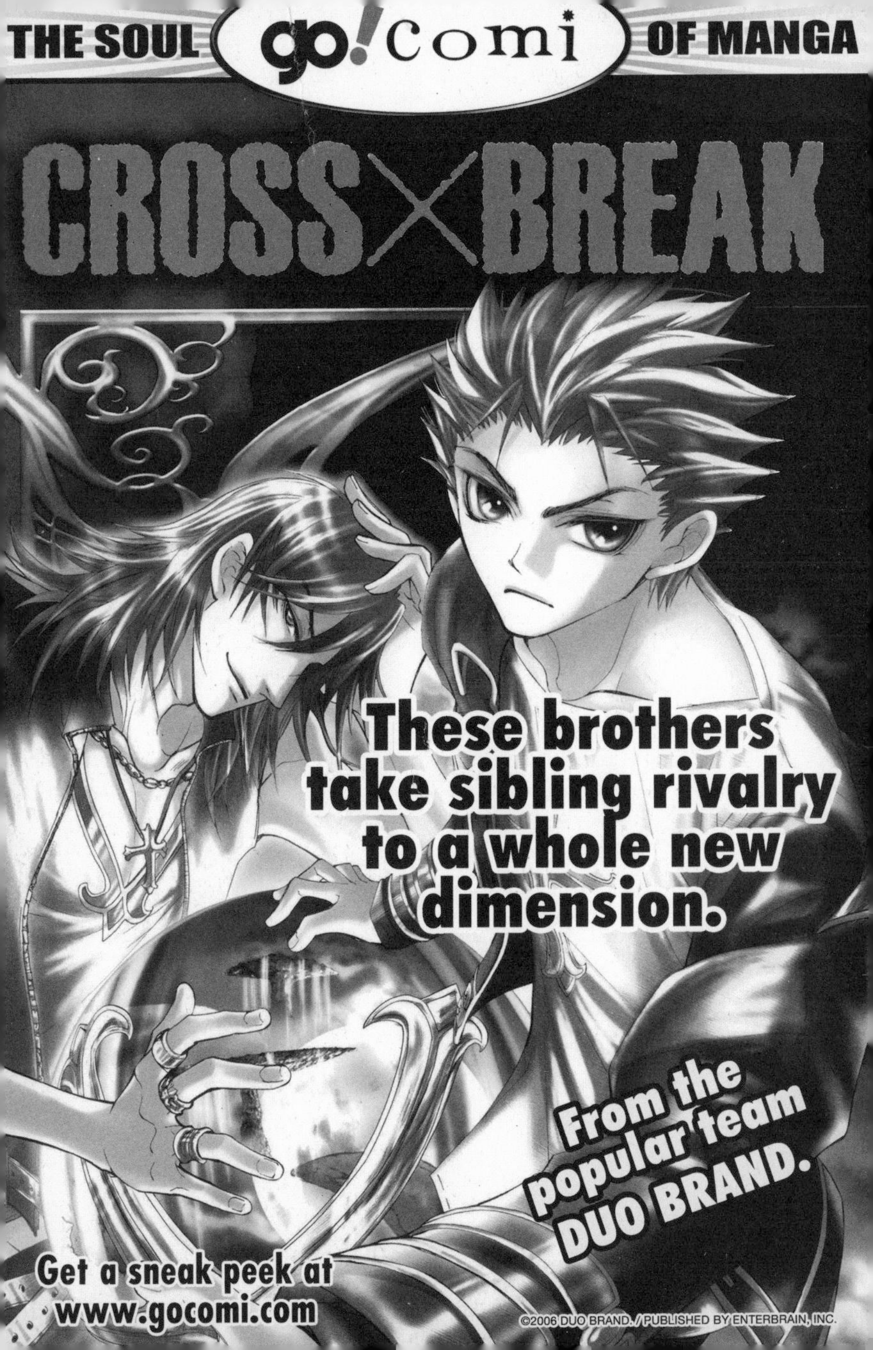
THE SOUL
go!comi
OF MANGA
CROSS×BREAK
These brothers take sibling rivalry to a whole new dimension.
From the popular team DUO BRAND.
Get a sneak peek at www.gocomi.com
©2006 DUO BRAND. / PUBLISHED BY ENTERBRAIN, INC.

Takako Shigematsu

Takako Shigematsu

To the newcomers and
to those coming back for
more, I hope you all enjoy
volume four to the very
last page. The photo above
is of my beloved pet dog.
He's so vigorous when
he eats that he makes it
near impossible to take a
non-blurry picture during
his meals.